Workshop on Natural Language Processing for Internet Freedom (NLP4IF 2019)

Censorship, Disinformation, and Propaganda

Hong Kong, China
4 November 2019

ISBN: 978-1-7138-0086-6

EMNLP-IJCNLP 2019

**Natural Language Processing for Internet Freedom:
Censorship, Disinformation, and Propaganda
NLP4IF 2019**

Proceedings of the Workshop

November 4, 2019
Hong Kong

Preface

Welcome to the second edition of the Workshop on Natural Language Processing for Internet Freedom (NLP4IF 2019). This year, we focused on censorship, disinformation, and propaganda.

We further featured a shared task on the identification of propaganda in news articles. The task included two subtasks with different levels of complexity. Given a news article, the FLC subtask (fragment-level classification) asked for the identification of the propagandistic text fragments and also for the prediction of the specific propaganda technique used in this fragment (18-way classification task). The SLC subtask (sentence-level classification) is a binary classification task, which asked to detect the sentences that contain propaganda. A total of 39 teams submitted runs; 21 teams participated in the FLC subtask and 35 teams took part in the SLC subtask. Fourteen participants submitted a system description paper, which include models based on a wide range of learning models (e.g., neural networks, logistic regression) and representations (e.g., manually-engineered features, distributional representations).

We accepted a total of 24 papers: 10 for the regular track and 14 for the shared task. We are excited that the workshop includes a diverse set of topics: rumor and trolls detection, censorship and controversy, fake news vs. satire, uncovering propaganda and abusive language identification.

We are also thrilled to be able to bring an invited speaker, Elissa Redmiles from Princeton University and Microsoft Research, with a talk on measuring human perception to defend democracy, exploring a specific attack on the freedom of U.S. elections – the IRA Facebook advertisements, which successfully influenced people and avoided detection – and a defense against propaganda, which uses human perceptions to defend against the very propaganda that aims to influence those perceptions.

Last but not least, we would like to thank the program committee and the shared task participants for their help with reviewing the papers, and with advertising the workshop.

The NLP4IF 2019 Organizers:

Anna Feldman
Giovanni Da San Martino
Alberto Barŕon-Cedeño
Chris Brew
Chris Leberknight
Preslav Nakov

Organizers

Anna Feldman, Montclair University (USA)
Giovanni Da San Martino, Qatar Computing Research Institute, HBKU (Qatar)
Alberto Barŕon-Cedeño, Università di Bologna (Italy)
Chris Brew, Facebook (USA)
Chris Leberknight, Monclair University (USA)
Preslav Nakov, Qatar Computing Research Institute, HBKU (Qatar)

Program Committee

Banu Akdenizli, Northwestern University (Qatar)
Dyaa Albakour, Signal Media (UK)
Jisun An, Qatar Computing Research Institute, HBKU (Qatar)
Jed Crandall, University of New Mexico (USA)
Kareem Darwish, Qatar Computing Research Institute, HBKU (Qatar)
Anjalie Field, Carnegie Mellon University (USA)
Gianmarco De Francisci Morales, ISI Foundation (Italy)
Julio Gonzalo, UNED (Spain)
Heng Ji, Rensselaer Polytechnic Institute (USA)
Jeffrey Knockell, The Citizen Lab, University of Toronto (Canada)
Haewoon Kwak, Qatar Computing Research Institute, HBKU (Qatar)
Miguel Martinez, Signal Media, (UK)
Ivan Meza, National Autonomous University of Mexico (Mexico)
Rada Mihalcea, University Michigan, Ann Arbor (USA)
Prateek Mittal, Princeton University (USA)
Alessandro Moschitti, Amazon (USA)
Veronica Perez, University of Michigan (USA)
Hannah Rashkin, University of Washington (USA)
Paolo Rosso, Technical University of Valencia (Spain)
Anna Rumshisky, University of Massachusetts, Lowell (USA)
Mahmood Sharif, Carnegie Mellon University (USA)
Thamar Solorio, University of Houston (USA)
Benno Stein, Bauhaus University Weimar (Germany)
Denis Stukal, New York University (USA)
Yulia Tsvetkov, Carnegie Mellon University (USA)
Svetlana Volkova, Pacific Northwest National Laboratory (USA)
Henning Wachsmuth, University of Padderborn (Germany)
Brook Wu, New Jersey Institute of Technology (USA)

Shared Task Reviewers

Ali Fadel, Jordan University of Science and Technology (Jordan)
André Ferreira Cruz, University of Porto (Portugal)
George-Alexandru Vlad, University Politechnica of Bucharest (Romania)
Gil Rocha, University of Porto (Portugal)
Harish Tayyar Madabushi, University of Birmingham (England)
Henrique Lopes Cardoso, FEUP / LIACC (Portugal)
Ibraheem Tuffaha, Jordan University of Science and Technology (Jordan)

Jinfen Li, Syracuse University, New York (USA)
Kartik Aggarwal, NSIT, New Delhi (India)
Mahmoud Al-Ayyoub, Jordan University of Science and Technology (Jordan)
Malak Abdullah, Jordan University of Science and Technology (Jordan)
Mehdi Ghanimifard, University of Gothenburg (Sweden)
Norman Mapes, Louisiana Tech University, (USA)
Pankaj Gupta, University of Munich (LMU) and Siemens (Germany)
Shehel Yoosuf, Hamad Bin Khalifa University (Qatar)
Tariq Alhindi, Columbia University (USA)
Wenjun Hou, China Agricultural University, Beijing (China)
Yiqing Hua, Cornell University (USA)

Secondary Reviewers

Adam Ek, University of Gothenburg (Sweden)
Usama Yaseen, University of Munich and Siemens (Germany)

Invited Speaker

Elissa Redmiles, Princeton and Microsoft Research (USA)

Table of Contents

Assessing Post Deletion in Sina Weibo: Multi-modal Classification of Hot Topics
Meisam Navaki Arefi, Rajkumar Pandi, Michael Carl Tschantz, Jedidiah R. Crandall, King-wa Fu, Dahlia Qiu Shi and Miao Sha 1

Detecting context abusiveness using hierarchical deep learning
Ju-Hyoung Lee, Jun-U Park, Jeong-Won Cha and Yo-Sub Han 10

How Many Users Are Enough? Exploring Semi-Supervision and Stylometric Features to Uncover a Russian Troll Farm
Nayeema Nasrin, Kim-Kwang Raymond Choo, Myung Ko and Anthony Rios 20

Identifying Nuances in Fake News vs. Satire: Using Semantic and Linguistic Cues
Or Levi, Pedram Hosseini, Mona Diab and David Broniatowski 31

Calls to Action on Social Media: Detection, Social Impact, and Censorship Potential
Anna Rogers, Olga Kovaleva and Anna Rumshisky 36

Mapping (Dis-)Information Flow about the MH17 Plane Crash
Mareike Hartmann, Yevgeniy Golovchenko and Isabelle Augenstein 45

Generating Sentential Arguments from Diverse Perspectives on Controversial Topic
ChaeHun Park, Wonsuk Yang and Jong Park 56

Rumor Detection on Social Media: Datasets, Methods and Opportunities
Quanzhi Li, Qiong Zhang, Luo Si and Yingchi Liu 66

Unraveling the Search Space of Abusive Language in Wikipedia with Dynamic Lexicon Acquisition
Wei-Fan Chen, Khalid Al Khatib, Matthias Hagen, Henning Wachsmuth and Benno Stein 76

CAUnLP at NLP4IF 2019 Shared Task: Context-Dependent BERT for Sentence-Level Propaganda Detection
Wenjun Hou and Ying Chen 83

Fine-Grained Propaganda Detection with Fine-Tuned BERT
Shehel Yoosuf and Yin Yang 87

Neural Architectures for Fine-Grained Propaganda Detection in News
Pankaj Gupta, Khushbu Saxena, Usama Yaseen, Thomas Runkler and Hinrich Schütze 92

Fine-Tuned Neural Models for Propaganda Detection at the Sentence and Fragment levels
Tariq Alhindi, Jonas Pfeiffer and Smaranda Muresan 98

Divisive Language and Propaganda Detection using Multi-head Attention Transformers with Deep Learning BERT-based Language Models for Binary Classification
Norman Mapes, Anna White, Radhika Medury and Sumeet Dua 103

On Sentence Representations for Propaganda Detection: From Handcrafted Features to Word Embeddings
André Ferreira Cruz, Gil Rocha and Henrique Lopes Cardoso 107

JUSTDeep at NLP4IF 2019 Task 1: Propaganda Detection using Ensemble Deep Learning Models
Hani Al-Omari, Malak Abdullah, Ola AlTiti and Samira Shaikh 113

Detection of Propaganda Using Logistic Regression
Jinfen Li, Zhihao Ye and Lu Xiao 119

Cost-Sensitive BERT for Generalisable Sentence Classification on Imbalanced Data
Harish Tayyar Madabushi, Elena Kochkina and Michael Castelle 125

Understanding BERT performance in propaganda analysis
Yiqing Hua 135

Pretrained Ensemble Learning for Fine-Grained Propaganda Detection
Ali Fadel, Ibrahim Tuffaha and Mahmoud Al-Ayyoub 139

NSIT@NLP4IF-2019: Propaganda Detection from News Articles using Transfer Learning
Kartik aggarwal and Anubhav Sadana 143

Sentence-Level Propaganda Detection in News Articles with Transfer Learning and BERT-BiLSTM-Capsule Model
George-Alexandru Vlad, Mircea-Adrian Tanase, Cristian Onose and Dumitru-Clementin Cercel 150

Synthetic Propaganda Embeddings To Train A Linear Projection
Adam Ek and Mehdi Ghanimifard 157

Findings of the NLP4IF-2019 Shared Task On Fine-grained Propaganda Detection
Giovanni Da San Martino, Alberto Barrón-Cedeño and Preslav Nakov 162

Workshop Program

9:00–9:10   Opening

9:10–9:30   *Assessing Post Deletion in Sina Weibo: Multi-modal Classification of Hot Topics*
Meisam Navaki Arefi, Rajkumar Pandi, Michael Carl Tschantz, Jedidiah R. Crandall, King-wa Fu, Dahlia Qiu Shi and Miao Sha

9:30–9:50   *Calls to Action on Social Media: Detection, Social Impact, and Censorship Potential*
Anna Rogers, Olga Kovaleva and Anna Rumshisky

9:50–10:10   *Identifying Nuances in Fake News vs. Satire: Using Semantic and Linguistic Cues*
Or Levi, Pedram Hosseini, Mona Diab and David Broniatowski

10:10–10:30   *Identifying Perspectives in Online News using Weakly Supervised Generative Models*
Srinivasan Iyer and Mike Lewis

10:30–11:00   Coffee Break

11:00–11:20   *Generating Sentential Arguments from Diverse Perspectives on Controversial Topic*
ChaeHun Park, Wonsuk Yang and Jong Park

11:20–11:40   *Unraveling the Search Space of Abusive Language in Wikipedia with Dynamic Lexicon Acquisition*
Wei-Fan Chen, Khalid Al Khatib, Matthias Hagen, Henning Wachsmuth and Benno Stein

11:40–12:00   *Findings of the NLP4IF-2019 Shared Task On Fine-grained Propaganda Detection*
Giovanni Da San Martino, Alberto Barrón-Cedeño and Preslav Nakov

12:00–12:20   *Divisive Language and Propaganda Detection using Multi-head Attention Transformers with Deep Learning BERT-based Language Models for Binary Classification*
Norman Mapes, Anna White, Radhika Medury and Sumeet Dua

12:20–12:40   *Fine-Grained Propaganda Detection with Fine-Tuned BERT*
Shehel Yoosuf and Yin Yang

12:40–14:00   Lunch Break

14:00–15:00   **Invited Talk: Elissa Redmiles (Princeton University/Microsoft),** ***Human Perception to Defend Democracy***

15:00–15:30   Coffee Break

Workshop Program (continued)

15:30-17:00   Poster Presentations:

Detecting context abusiveness using hierarchical deep learning
Ju-Hyoung Lee, Jun-U Park, Jeong-Won Cha and Yo-Sub Han

How Many Users Are Enough? Exploring Semi-Supervision and Stylometric Features to Uncover a Russian Troll Farm
Nayeema Nasrin, Kim-Kwang Raymond Choo, Myung Ko and Anthony Rios

Mapping (Dis-)Information Flow about the MH17 Plane Crash
Mareike Hartmann, Yevgeniy Golovchenko and Isabelle Augenstein

Rumor Detection on Social Media: Datasets, Methods and Opportunities
Quanzhi Li, Qiong Zhang, Luo Si and Yingchi Liu

CAUnLP at NLP4IF 2019 Shared Task: Context-Dependent BERT for Sentence-Level Propaganda Detection
Wenjun Hou and Ying Chen

Neural Architectures for Fine-Grained Propaganda Detection in News
Pankaj Gupta, Khushbu Saxena, Usama Yaseen, Thomas Runkler and Hinrich Schütze

Fine-Tuned Neural Models for Propaganda Detection at the Sentence and Fragment levels
Tariq Alhindi, Jonas Pfeiffer and Smaranda Muresan

On Sentence Representations for Propaganda Detection: From Handcrafted Features to Word Embeddings
André Ferreira Cruz, Gil Rocha and Henrique Lopes Cardoso

JUSTDeep at NLP4IF 2019 Task 1: Propaganda Detection using Ensemble Deep Learning Models
Hani Al-Omari, Malak Abdullah, Ola AlTiti and Samira Shaikh

Detection of Propaganda Using Logistic Regression
Jinfen Li, Zhihao Ye and Lu Xiao

Cost-Sensitive BERT for Generalisable Sentence Classification on Imbalanced Data
Harish Tayyar Madabushi, Elena Kochkina and Michael Castelle

Understanding BERT performance in propaganda analysis
Yiqing Hua

Pretrained Ensemble Learning for Fine-Grained Propaganda Detection
Ali Fadel, Ibrahim Tuffaha and Mahmoud Al-Ayyoub

NSIT@NLP4IF-2019: Propaganda Detection from News Articles using Transfer Learning
Kartik aggarwal and Anubhav Sadana

Sentence-Level Propaganda Detection in News Articles with Transfer Learning and BERT-BiLSTM-Capsule Model
George-Alexandru Vlad, Mircea-Adrian Tanase, Cristian Onose and Dumitru-Clementin Cercel

Synthetic Propaganda Embeddings To Train A Linear Projection
Adam Ek and Mehdi Ghanimifard

Assessing Post Deletion in Sina Weibo: Multi-modal Classification of Hot Topics

Meisam Navaki Arefi and **Rajkumar Pandi** and **Jedidiah R. Crandall**
University of New Mexico, Albuquerque, NM
{mnavaki, rpandi}@unm.edu, crandall@cs.unm.edu

Michael Carl Tschantz
International Computer Science Institute, Berkeley, CA
mct@icsi.berkeley.edu

King-wa Fu and **Dahlia Qiu Shi** and **Miao Sha**
University of Hong Kong, Hong Kong
kwfu@hku.hk, qiushi19.jlu@gmail.com, shamiao@connect.hku.hk

Abstract

Widespread Chinese social media applications such as Weibo are widely known for monitoring and deleting posts to conform to Chinese government requirements. In this paper, we focus on analyzing a dataset of censored and uncensored posts in Weibo. Despite previous work that only considers text content of posts, we take a multi-modal approach that takes into account both text and image content. We categorize this dataset into 14 categories that have the potential to be censored on Weibo, and seek to quantify censorship by topic. Specifically, we investigate how different factors interact to affect censorship. We also investigate how consistently and how quickly different topics are censored. To this end, we have assembled an image dataset with 18,966 images, as well as a text dataset with 994 posts from 14 categories. We then utilized deep learning, CNN localization, and NLP techniques to analyze the target dataset and extract categories, for further analysis to better understand censorship mechanisms in Weibo.

We found that *sentiment* is the only indicator of censorship that is consistent across the variety of topics we identified. Our finding matches with recently leaked logs from Sina Weibo. We also discovered that most categories like those related to anti-government actions (*e.g.* protest) or categories related to politicians (*e.g.* Xi Jinping) are often censored, whereas some categories such as crisis-related categories (*e.g.* rainstorm) are less frequently censored. We also found that censored posts across all categories are deleted in three hours on average.

1 Introduction

Human monitoring of social media posts and the subsequent deletion of posts that are considered sensitive is an important aspect of Internet censorship for academic study. Seeing a post get removed by the censors gives valuable information to researchers, including the content that was censored and the amount of time it was visible before being deleted. This information can provide insights into the censors' policies and priorities. A better understanding of censors' motivations can lead to more effective ways of addressing Internet censorship, be they technical, political, legal, economic, or otherwise.

Censorship of Chinese social media is a complex process that involves many factors. There are multiple stakeholders and many different interests: economic, political, legal, personal, *etc.*, which means that there is not a single strategy dictated by a single government authority (Miller, 2017). Moreover, sometimes Chinese social media do not follow the directives of government, out of concern that they are more strictly censoring than their competitors (Miller, 2017).

Past literature in censorship of Chinese social media has attempted to make general statements about what kinds of features lead to a given post being likely to be censored. Researchers have posited the topic of a post (*e.g.*, what keywords it contains) (Bamman et al., 2012; Zhu et al., 2013), how viral or popular the post is (*e.g.*, how much it is reposted and commented on) (Zhu et al., 2013), the collective action potential (how likely it is to lead to, *e.g.*, protests) (King et al., 2013), and the individual posting the content (Miller and Gallagher, 2019), as major features that determine how high of a priority deleting the post is for the censors. However, no study to date with respect to censorship in China has considered the multimodal nature of social media, and past stud-

Proceedings of the 2nd Workshop on NLP for Internet Freedom: Censorship, Disinformation, and Propaganda, pages 1–9
Hong Kong, China, November 4, 2019 ©2019 Association for Computational Linguistics

ies have relied on relatively narrow datasets (*e.g.*, spanning months rather than years or only following a small set of users).

In this paper, we focus on Sina Weibo and use Weiboscope dataset (Fu et al., 2013), which tracks 120,000 users over 4 years (2015–2018) in Sina Weibo and includes 128,044 posts, of which 64,022 were censored. The WeiboScope dataset has only two categories, censored and uncensored, and does not include the reason for censorship. In particular, this dataset is not labeled by topics and it is very time-consuming to manually categorize them. We identify fourteen topics that both (1) saw a significant amount of censorship in the Weibo-Scope dataset; and, (2) could be identified through both images and text. To analyze the dataset we take a *multi-modal* approach that takes into account both *text* and *images* that appear in posts. We then test the effect of various factors that may affect censorship that were identified by past literature on the lifetime of posts.

Sina Weibo is one of the most popular social media platforms in China ("Weibo" means "microblog" in Chinese). After the Urumqi riots, Chinese authorities shut down all social media platforms including Twitter, Facebook, and local social media platforms. Sina Weibo provides microblogging services similar to Twitter but was designed to block posts with content that does not comply with the Chinese government's requirements. Weibo users can re-post and follow other users, mention other people with @UserName, and add hashtags using #HashName#. More importantly for this study, Weibo also allows embedded photos. As of July 2018, Weibo has over 441 million active users, which surpasses Twitter's 339 million active users (wei, 2017).

To analyze the WeiboScope dataset, we take a semi-automated multi-modal approach and utilize deep learning, CNN localization, and NLP techniques. To train our image and text classifiers, we first assembled our own image and text datasets from 14 interesting categories that are potential topics for censorship on Weibo and any other social media platforms in China. We refer to the image dataset as *CCTI14 (Chinese Censored Topics Images)*, and to the text dataset as *CCTT14 (Chinese Censored Topics Text)*. After training classifiers with CCTI14 and CCTT14, we categorize the WeiboScope dataset into our 14 categories.

These categories are selected based on previous research, domain knowledge, and known censorship events in China. CCTI14 has 18,966 labeled images and CCTT14 has 994 labeled texts from 14 categories as well as an "Other" category. These categories are as follows (in alphabetical order): 1) *Bo Xilai*, 2) *Deng Xiaoping*, 3) *Fire*, 4) *Injury/Dead*, 5) *Liu Xiaobo*, 6) *Mao Zedong*, 7) *People's congress*, 8) *Policeman/Military forces*, 9) *Protest*, 10) *Prurient/Nudity*, 11) *Rainstorm*, 12) *Winnie the Pooh*, 13) *Xi Jinping*, 14) *Zhou Kehua*.

We trained an image classifier over the CCTI14 dataset using the VGG network (Simonyan and Zisserman, 2014) and it achieved a 97% F1-score. We also trained a text classifier over the CCTT14 dataset that achieved a 95% F1-score. We used our classifiers to classify both censored and uncensored posts from the target dataset under study into the above-mentioned 14 categories. Because of a flag in the Weibo API, we can distinguish between deletions by a post's author and by the Weibo system itself, providing ground truth for which posts have been censored.

We found that *sentiment* is the only indicator of censorship that is consistent across the variety of topics we identified. We also found that most of the categories (*e.g.*, protest) are often censored, whereas some categories (*e.g.*, rainstorm) are less frequently censored. This suggests that different topics can be censored with different levels of consistency. We also found that the median lifetime of the posts that were censored in a category is less than three hours on average, which confirms that censors can quickly delete sensitive posts.

To the best of our knowledge, our work is the first to look at both text and image content of posts being censored and not just at the text content. We hope that our datasets, CCTI14 and CCTT14, which are the first datasets labeled by topics assembled for studying China's censorship, can help other researchers to uncover image and text censorship mechanisms in other social media platforms in China, and that our techniques can be applied in other contexts.

In summary, this paper presents the following contributions:

- We introduce CCTI14 and CCTT14, the first image and text datasets labeled by topics assembled specifically for studying image and text censorship in Chinese social media.

- We train a CNN model over CCTI14 that achieves 97% F1-score, and a text classifier over CCTT14 that achieves 95% F1-score, to automatically classify the target dataset under study of this paper, based on both image and text content.

- We use a CNN localization technique to double check that our categories and our trained image model produce an intuitive model.

- For each category, we analyze how quickly and how often it is censored. We also perform survival analysis per category to investigate how different factors interact to affect the lifetime of a post.

- We make CCTI14, CCTT14, our code, and our trained models publicly available to help important efforts such as those to understand image and text censorship or to identify topics that are likely to be censored.

This paper is organized as follows. Section 2 describes the dataset under study of this paper. Section 3 explains our methods. Section 4 presents our analysis and results, and Section 5 presents related work. Finally, Section 6 concludes the paper.

2 WeiboScope Dataset

WeiboScope tracks about 120,000 users from three samples:

1. User accounts with high going-viral potential, measured by the number of followers.

2. A group of accounts whose posts are known to have a high likelihood to be censored, such as individual media, NGOs, human right lawyers, grassroots leaders, or key opinion leaders, etc.

3. A random sample of accounts generated by randomly selecting users' unique identity codes.

By following the tracked users as "friends", the user's recently modified timeline is compared to the previous version, every 20 minutes, to discover if any posts had been deleted. When a post is missing, Weibo returns two possible messages: "weibo does not exist" or "permission denied". The latter is returned when the censors make the post inaccessible to others, and the former message is returned when the user voluntarily deletes the post or the censors remove it entirely. Since there is no feasible way to determine who deleted a post, we only consider posts deleted by a "permission denied" message to be censored.

From January 2015 through April 2018, WeiboScope collected 64,022 censored and more than 40 million uncensored posts by tracking the above-mentioned users. In this paper, to be able to compare censored and uncensored posts, we randomly selected 64,022 uncensored posts from the 40 million uncensored posts. We know that these posts are uncensored since they were not deleted by the censor or the user. Thus the reduced WeiboScope dataset that we study in this paper has 64,022 censored posts and 64,022 uncensored posts from 2015 through 2018.

3 Methods

During the analysis of the target dataset, we encountered a number of challenges that we present here. We also describe CCTI14 and CCTT14 datasets and our image and text classifiers to address these challenges.

3.1 Challenges

Here, we describe the challenges that we encountered over the course of analyzing the target dataset.

The possibility of interactions between multiple factors: To decide whether to censor a post, the censors may use any of the factors recorded in our datasets: images, text, number of reposts, number of comments, or the user account making the post. Furthermore, censors may also use factors not recorded in our datasets, such as number of views or information about the political situation at the time. The last possibility highlights that censorship may change over time. Furthermore, censorship might even depend upon ideally irreverent factors, such as the motivation of a human monitor on a particular day.

Lack of experimental data: Additionally, having access to observational data but not experimental data means that any found patterns may be correlated with censorship but not actually causing it. This issue limits our abilities to draw conclusions about the causes of censorship. While can find patterns predictive of censorship, between this limitation and the multiple possible factors discussed above, we cannot draw firm conclusions about why a post is censored.

Clustering methods do not work here: Lacking pre-defined categories, it may be tempting to automatically categorize the images in the target dataset with clustering algorithms. However, since the target dataset has very diverse images, clustering algorithms do not work well. We tried several clustering algorithms (*e.g.*, hierarchical and K-means), but none of them was able to cluster the images in a way that we could learn something from the categories. The clustering algorithms would either come up with: i) too many categories (where many of them have only a few images), which render the clustering useless, or ii) with a reasonable number of categories each of which contains many diverse images from which, again, nothing could be learned.

There is no image or text dataset available for studying image and text censorship: Furthermore, in order to be able to use ML classification methods to categorize images and texts, annotated image and text datasets are needed that is particularly designed for studying censorship in China, but there is no such datasets publicly available.

To overcome these challenges, we take the very first step in collecting image and text datasets particularly for studying image and text censorship in Chinese social media. We refer to these datasets as *CCTI14 (Chinese Censorsed Topics Images)* and *CCTT14 (Chinese Censorsed Topics Text)*. Then we train classifiers over CCTI14 and CCTT14 to help us in categorizing image and text content of posts in the WeiboScope dataset.

3.2 Image Classifier

In this section, we first describe how we assembled the CCTI14 dataset. Then we present the performance evaluation of our CNN model over CCTI14.

3.2.1 CCTI14 Dataset

To find a list of potentially censored categories in Weibo, we relied on previous research and censorship events in different domains of censorship in China (Zhu et al., 2013; King et al., 2013; Bamman et al., 2012). We ended up with 14 categories spanning diverse domains including collective action (e.g., Protest), Chinese politicians (e.g., Xi Jinping, Deng Xiaoping, and Mao Zedong), crisis and disaster (e.g., rainstorm and fire), political activists (e.g., Liu Xiaobo), and mockery (e.g. Winnie the Pooh). We did not include categories that we were not able to find at least 100 unique images (e.g., Xi Jinping bun) or were too vague

to have them as a separate category (e.g., China anti-corruption). Our categories are not comprehensive, since there is no such comprehensive list of topics that China censors. However, we have tried to pick general categories so that they can be applied for analyzing any other Chinese platforms that practice censorship.

Training Dataset: To assemble a training dataset, we utilized Google Image Search to find images of 200×200 pixels or bigger per category. As has been done by other studies (Bainbridge et al., 2013, 2012), we scraped Google Images and automatically collected images per category. In addition to the 14 categories, we carefully crafted an "Other" class including random images and images that we found could be confused with other categories (e.g., street banner confused with protest and ocean confused with a rainstorm).

As is common practice (Xiao et al., 2010; Bainbridge et al., 2013, 2012), we then manually removed problematic images including those that were too blurry or would fall into more than one category (e.g., an image of both Deng Xiaoping and Mao Zedong). We also manually removed all duplicate images in a category or among several categories. To do so, two trained human annotators verified that images are in the right category, with each annotator spending 5 hours on average on this. In case of a disagreement between annotators about an image, an expert made a decision on the image.

We also used the label preserving image augmentation techniques to add more images to our dataset. Image augmentation is the procedure of taking images and manipulating them in different ways to create many variations of the same image. In this way, not only can we train our classifier on a larger dataset, but also we can make our classifier more robust to image coloring and noise. It has been proven that data augmentation could be very effective in improving the performance of CNNs (Wong et al., 2016; Xu et al., 2016).

We picked six label-preserving data augmentation techniques: i) contrast normalization, ii) affine transformation, iii) perspective transformation, iv) sharpen, v) Gaussian blur, vi) padding. We then applied them to each image in our dataset and added the result images to our dataset.

Testing Dataset: The classifier should be tested against *real-world* censored images from Weibo so that it can be trusted in categorizing the WeiboScope dataset which consists of real censored images. To this end, we assembled a test image dataset from *real-world* censored images. We used two human annotators to manually label a small subset of images from WeiboScope dataset into the 15 categories. Here are the steps that we followed for assembling the testing dataset:

1. We trained two human raters by providing them the definition for each category as well as image samples per category.

2. We randomly selected 1000 censored images from WeiboScope dataset.

3. We asked the raters to categorize these images into the 15 categories.

4. If each category has at least 30 images, go to #5. Otherwise go to #2.

5. In case of a disagreement between raters about an image we asked an expert to categorize the image.

At the end of this process, we measured the inter-rater reliability using Cohen's Kappa coefficient (Cohen, 1960). The inter-rater reliability was 91%, which is satisfactory. Each rater spent 6 hours on average to annotate the dataset.

The final test dataset has 1014 images (which is equal to about 5% of the size of the train dataset), and each category has 30-70 images. Note that since the "Other" category had many more images than other categories, we only kept 70 (randomly selected) images from that category to balance the dataset.

CCTI14's training dataset has 5,038 images before augmentation, and 18,966 images after augmentation from 14 categories and one "Other" class in which each category has 700–1400 images. Also CCTI14's testing dataset has 1014 images from *real-world* censored images from the 15 categories.

3.2.2 CNN Model

In this section, we present our CNN model and evaluate its performance using several metrics. We also explain how we use CNN localization for error analysis.

Classification: We train a CNN classifier using the VGG-16 network (Simonyan and Zisserman, 2014) over the CCTI14's training dataset and then

(a) Protest   (b) Policeman (c) Rainstorm   (d) Fire

Figure 1: Examples of highlighted images.

test it with CCTI14's testing dataset. For the training phase, we split the CCTI14's training dataset, stratified by topic, into primary training set (95% of the data) and development/validation set (5% of the data). The trained classifier achieves **97%** F1-score on the testing dataset.

To reduce the incidence of classifying images that belong to none of our categories as belonging to the most similar category, we used two approaches at the same time: i) *Using an "Other" class:* as described in the previous section, ii) *Using a confidence level threshold:* a confidence level threshold of 80% is used to decide whether to accept the classifier's decision or not, meaning that if the classifier is 80% or more confident about its decision on an image we accept it, otherwise we categorize it as belonging to the "Other" class. We empirically tuned the confidence level threshold on the training data set and achieved the best results with 80%.

We have evaluated the performance of the classifier using several metrics: precision, recall and F1-score.

The F1-score takes into account both precision and recall, making it a more reliable metric for evaluating a classifier. The classifier achieves a precision of 97%, recall of 96% and F1-score of 97% overall.

3.2.3 Performing CNN Localization

To double check our model, we utilized a CNN localization technique introduced by Zhou et al. (Zhou et al., 2016). Using the CNN localization technique, we were able to highlight parts of the images that are considered the most important parts by the CNN to decide to classify an image as a specific category.

We repeatedly used this technique for error analysis and to adjust our model as well as the CCTI14 categories. Figure 1 shows some instances of highlighted images for a few categories. All highlighted parts matched our intuition for each category.

Highlighted examples in Figure 1 confirm that our model is trained to look for the right objects in each category. However, some similar objects still can confuse the classifier. Figure 2 shows some examples of the false positives in our model. Images containing something similar to the main features of each category have been incorrectly categorized as that category.

However, before we do any analysis on the categorized images we manually remove false positives from the 14 categories. Since removing false positives from image categories is fairly easy and it's not very time-consuming, we opt to do so to make our categorized data even cleaner.

3.3 Text Classifier

To be able to categorize text content of posts into our 14 categories, we built a text classifier. To train our classifier we assembled our own text dataset from *real-world* Weibo posts that we refer to as *CCTT14*. In below we explain how we assembled CCTT14 and then we describe the performance of our text classifier.

3.3.1 CCTT14 Dataset

We assembled a text dataset from *real-world* Weibo posts from the same 14 categories as CCTT14 as well as an "Other" category, that we refer to as *CCTT14*. Here are the steps we took to assemble this dataset:

1. We first trained two human annotators that were native Chinese speakers by providing them the definition of each category as well as examples of each category.

2. We then partitioned all posts in the Weibo-Scope dataset using keywords related to each category. We used the keywords extracted by Knockel et al. (Knockel et al., 2015) from four Chinese applications as well as the keywords provided by other online resources. The goal of this step was to make the manual annotation process more efficient and less time consuming.

3. We randomly selected 1000 posts from the output of the previous step.

4. We asked the two trained annotators to annotate the selected 1000 posts.

5. We only kept posts that both annotators agreed on their category and if each category

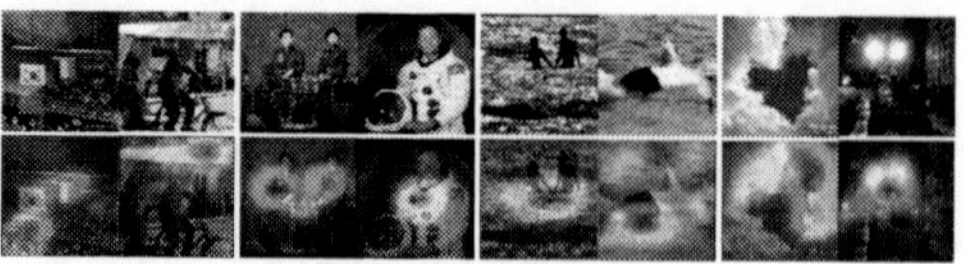

(a) Protest   (b) Policeman (c) Rainstorm   (d) Fire

Figure 2: Examples of false positives.

had at least 50 posts, we stopped. Otherwise, go to (3).

The final dataset has 994 labelled posts in which each category has 50-90 posts. Each annotator spent about 12 hours on the whole process, and the inter-reliability of raters was 76%, which was satisfactory.

3.3.2 Classifier performance

We tried different text classifiers (*e.g.*, naive bayes, random forest, neural networks) over CCTT14 and achieved the highest F1-score with multinomial logistic regression. We leveraged unigrams, bigrams, and trigrams as the feature vectors. We also used CoreNLP (Manning et al., 2014) tool for word segmentation and tokenization. The classifier achieves a precision of 96%, recall of 94%, and F1-score of 95% overall when we tested our classifier using 10-fold cross validation.

4 Analysis and Results

In this section, we present our results on the WeiboScope dataset. We used our classifiers to categorize censored and uncensored posts into our 14 categories and then performed our analysis on the result.

4.1 Censorship Rate

To discover how often a category is censored and what percent of posts in each category is censored, we compared the number of posts found in that category within the censored posts with that of those within the uncensored posts. Table 1 shows the number of posts found in each category as well as the percentage of posts in each category that was censored. A post ends up in a category if it has either an image or text in the category. As one can see in this table, most categories (*e.g.*, protest) are often censored, whereas some categories (*e.g.*, rainstorm) are less frequently censored. This confirms that the consistency of censorship varies by topic/category. For example, more sensitive categories may experience a higher deletion rate.

Category	#Cens. posts	#Uncens. posts	Cens. Rate
Bo Xilai	665	336	64%
Deng Xiaoping	281	125	70%
Fire	431	530	45%
Injury/Dead Body	1799	1029	51%
Liu Xiaobo	184	123	60%
Mao Zedong	1093	486	70%
People's Congress	145	113	56%
Policeman	1311	927	59%
Protest	536	220	71%
Prurient/Nudity	2664	2551	51%
Rainstorm	153	207	43%
Winnie the Pooh	160	177	48%
Xi Jinping	1745	1029	63%
Zhou Kehua	102	134	43%

Table 1: Percentage of censored posts per category.

4.2 Life Time

To reveal how quickly posts in a category are censored, we plotted the lifetime distribution of censored posts in that category in minutes. Lifetime is measured as the difference between the time a post is created and the time it is deleted. Figure 3 presents the lifetime distribution per category. As one can see, the median lifetime for all categories is less than 180 minutes, meaning that most of the posts are censored in less than three hours.

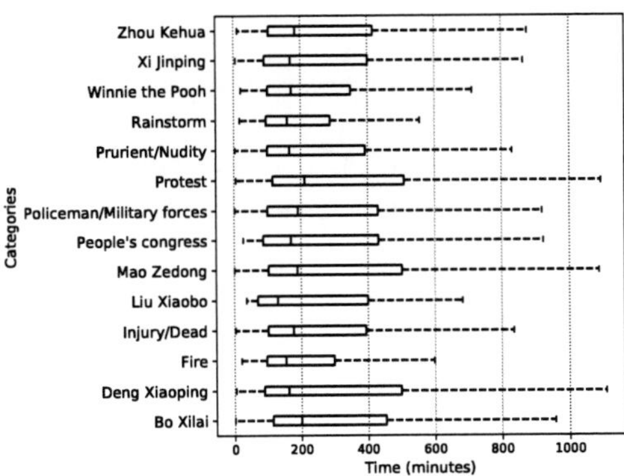

Figure 3: Categories vs. life time

4.3 Survival Analysis

Survival analysis is used for analyzing data where the outcome variable is the time until an event of interest happens. For example, if the event of interest is death, then the survival time is the time in years, weeks or minutes, etc. until a person dies. In our case, the event of interest is being censored, then the survival time for a post is the time until it is censored. In addition, in survival analysis there are two types of observations: i) those that the event of interest happens during the time of observation (censored posts in our case), ii) those that the event of interest does not happen during the time of observation (uncensored posts in our case). That enables us to take into account both censored and uncensored posts into consideration, despite other researchers that have only considered the censored posts (Zhu et al., 2013).

To analyze how different factors interact to affect censorship, we performed a survival analysis per category over the following measured factors: i) whether the image matches this category, ii) whether the text matches this category, iii) number of reposts, iv) number of comments, and v) text sentiment. To compute the sentiment score we utilized CoreNLP (Manning et al., 2014) tool that supports Chinese.

Table 2 shows the results of survival analysis per category. Coefficients in survival analysis relate to hazard (risk of dying or risk of being censored in our case). A positive coefficient for Image, Text, #Repost, and #Comment variables means more risk of getting censored and thus shorter lifetime. For example, almost all of the "Image" variables have positive coefficient which means having an image that matches that category increases the risk of being censored and therefore shorter lifetime. On the other hand, sentiment is a score between 0-4 (0 being very negative and 4 being very positive). A negative coefficient for sentiment means as we increase the sentiment score (*i.e.* being more positive), it decreases the risk of being censored and therefore longer lifetime.

As shown in Table 2, sentiment always has a negative sign and it is always statistically significant at 5%. That suggests that **sentiment is the strongest indicator of censorship across all categories**. Our finding matches with recently leaked logs from Weibo that they were asked by the government to remove all posts about an specific incident, but Weibo advised its censorship department to only deal with the negative content (Miller and Gallagher, 2019).

It is also interesting that image category almost always has a positive sign which suggests that having an image that matches that category increases

Category	Image		Text		#Repost		#Comment		Sentiment	
	Coef.	P	Coef.	P	Coef.	P	Coef.	P	Coef.	P
Bo Xilai	0.19	<0.005	0.14	0.41	0.00	0.01	0.00	0.28	**-0.20**	0.04
Deng Xiaoping	0.62	0.01	0.04	0.87	0.00	0.41	0.00	0.52	**-0.23**	<0.005
Fire	0.73	<0.005	0.13	0.59	0.00	0.01	0.00	<0.005	**-0.11**	0.02
Injury/Dead Body	0.63	0.02	-0.02	0.94	0.00	0.12	0.00	0.54	**-0.24**	<0.005
Liu Xiaobo	0.25	0.19	-0.07	0.12	0.00	0.13	0.00	0.24	**-0.27**	0.04
Mao Zedong	0.31	0.09	0.05	0.85	0.00	0.40	0.00	0.04	**-0.28**	0.01
People's Congress	0.16	0.07	-0.21	0.18	0.00	0.03	0.00	0.34	**-0.47**	<0.005
Policeman	0.19	0.24	0.09	0.62	0.00	<0.005	0.00	0.36	**-0.15**	0.05
Protest	0.78	<0.005	-0.25	0.28	0.00	0.27	0.00	0.29	**-0.06**	0.05
Prurient	0.74	<0.005	0.09	0.68	0.00	<0.005	0.00	0.19	**-0.20**	<0.005
Rainstorm	-0.50	0.48	-0.87	0.25	0.00	0.19	0.00	0.01	**-0.31**	0.02
Winnie the Pooh	0.44	0.09	-0.16	0.14	0.00	0.03	0.00	0.16	**-0.35**	<0.005
Xi Jinping	0.49	<0.005	-0.51	<0.005	0.00	0.74	0.00	0.07	**-0.09**	0.01
Zhou Kehua	0.22	<0.005	-0.08	0.11	0.00	0.04	0.00	0.23	**-0.17**	<0.005

Table 2: Survival regression per category.

the risk of censorship, but sometimes it is not statistically significant and thus we can not draw firm conclusions about the image category.

5   Related Work

The Weibo platform is popular and previous researchers have attempted to study its censorship mechanism. King *et al.* (King et al., 2013) collected a dataset of censored posts, by checking for the deleted posts *every 24 hours*, over *six months* in 2011. Using that dataset, they identified the collective action potential of posts as a major indicator of censorship. Bamman *et al.* (Bamman et al., 2012) used a dataset collected over *three months* in 2011, and performed a statistical analysis of deleted posts and showed that posts with some sensitive words are more likely to be deleted. Zhu *et al.* (Zhu et al., 2013) collected a dataset of censored posts by tracking *3,567 users* over *three months* in 2012. They investigated how quickly, on a scale of minutes, posts in Weibo are removed. They also performed a logistic regression over *censored data only* to analyze the interaction of different factors, *by ignoring sentiment and topics*, and showed that whether a post contains an image has the highest impact on censorship.

Ng *et al.* (Ng et al., 2018a) built a Naive Bayes classifier over *344* censored and uncensored posts related to Bo Xilai scandal to predict censorship. They indicated that posts with subjective content, *e.g.* expressions of mood and feeling, are likely to be censored. Ng *et al.* (Ng et al., 2018b) collected *2,171* censored and uncensored posts from 7 categories and built a text classifier based on linguistic features (*e.g.*, sentiment) to predict censorship. They indicated that the strongest linguistic feature in censored posts is readability.

6   Conclusion

In this paper, we analyzed a dataset of censored and uncensored posts from Weibo using deep learning, NLP techniques, and manual effort. We first introduced the CCTI14 and CCTT14 datasets with 14 categories designed particularly for studying image and text censorship in China. Then we trained classifiers on CCTI14 and CCTT14 and used the classifiers to classify the target dataset so that we can analyze censorship mechanisms in Weibo.

Using our classifiers, we found that *sentiment* is the only indicator of censorship that is consistent across the variety of topics we identified. Our finding matches with recently leaked logs from Weibo. We also found that some categories (*e.g.*, protest) are often censored, while some categories (*e.g.*, rainstorm) are less frequently censored. Our analysis suggests that all the posts from our 14 categories are deleted in less than three hours on average, which confirms that censors can delete sensitive content very quickly. Taken as a whole and within the body of other related research, our results call into question the idea that censorship are binary decisions devoid of timing or context. The "there are a set of sensitive topics and any content within that set are censored" view of censorship needs to be reevaluated.

Acknowledgments

We would like to thank the NLP4IF 2019 anonymous reviewers for valuable feedback. This research has been supported by the U.S. National Science Foundation (Grant Nos. #1518918, #1518523).

References

2017. Most popular social networks worldwide as of july 2018, ranked by number of active users. *Online:https://www.statista.com/statistics/272014/ global-social-networks-ranked-by-number-of-users/*.

Wilma Bainbridge, Phillip Isola, Idan Blank, and Aude Oliva. 2012. Establishing a database for studying human face photograph memory. In *Proceedings of the Annual Meeting of the Cognitive Science Society*, volume 34.

Wilma A Bainbridge, Phillip Isola, and Aude Oliva. 2013. The intrinsic memorability of face photographs. *Journal of Experimental Psychology: General*, 142(4):1323.

David Bamman, Brendan O'Connor, and Noah Smith. 2012. Censorship and deletion practices in chinese social media. *First Monday*, 17(3).

Jacob Cohen. 1960. A coefficient of agreement for nominal scales. *Educational and psychological measurement*, 20(1):37–46.

King-wa Fu, Chung-hong Chan, and Michael Chau. 2013. Assessing censorship on microblogs in china: Discriminatory keyword analysis and the real-name registration policy. *IEEE Internet Computing*, 17(3):42–50.

Gary King, Jennifer Pan, and Margaret E Roberts. 2013. How censorship in china allows government criticism but silences collective expression. *American Political Science Review*, 107(2):326–343.

Jeffrey Knockel, Masashi Crete-Nishihata, Jason Q Ng, Adam Senft, and Jedidiah R Crandall. 2015. Every rose has its thorn: Censorship and surveillance on social video platforms in china. In *5th USENIX Workshop on Free and Open Communications on the Internet (FOCI 15)*.

Christopher Manning, Mihai Surdeanu, John Bauer, Jenny Finkel, Steven Bethard, and David McClosky. 2014. The stanford corenlp natural language processing toolkit. In *Proceedings of 52nd annual meeting of the association for computational linguistics: system demonstrations*, pages 55–60.

Blake Miller. 2017. The limits of commercialized censorship in china.

Blake Miller and Mary Gallagher. 2019. Who not what: The logic of chinas information control strategy. *RR, China Quarterly*.

Kei Yin Ng, Anna Feldman, and Chris Leberknight. 2018a. Detecting censorable content on sina weibo: A pilot study. In *Proceedings of the 10th Hellenic Conference on Artificial Intelligence*, page 41. ACM.

Kei Yin Ng, Anna Feldman, Jing Peng, and Chris Leberknight. 2018b. Linguistic characteristics of censorable language on sinaweibo. *arXiv preprint arXiv:1807.03654*.

Karen Simonyan and Andrew Zisserman. 2014. Very deep convolutional networks for large-scale image recognition. *arXiv preprint arXiv:1409.1556*.

Sebastien C Wong, Adam Gatt, Victor Stamatescu, and Mark D McDonnell. 2016. Understanding data augmentation for classification: when to warp? *arXiv preprint arXiv:1609.08764*.

Jianxiong Xiao, James Hays, Krista A Ehinger, Aude Oliva, and Antonio Torralba. 2010. Sun database: Large-scale scene recognition from abbey to zoo. In *Computer vision and pattern recognition (CVPR), 2010 IEEE conference on*, pages 3485–3492. IEEE.

Yan Xu, Ran Jia, Lili Mou, Ge Li, Yunchuan Chen, Yangyang Lu, and Zhi Jin. 2016. Improved relation classification by deep recurrent neural networks with data augmentation. *arXiv preprint arXiv:1601.03651*.

Bolei Zhou, Aditya Khosla, Agata Lapedriza, Aude Oliva, and Antonio Torralba. 2016. Learning deep features for discriminative localization. In *Computer Vision and Pattern Recognition (CVPR), 2016 IEEE Conference on*, pages 2921–2929. IEEE.

Tao Zhu, David Phipps, Adam Pridgen, Jedidiah R Crandall, and Dan S Wallach. 2013. The velocity of censorship: High-fidelity detection of microblog post deletions. In *USENIX Security Symposium*, pages 227–240.

Detecting context abusiveness using hierarchical deep learning

Ju-Hyoung Lee
Yonsei University
Seoul, Republic of Korea
juhyounglee@yonsei.ac.kr

Jun-U Park
Yonsei University
Seoul, Republic of Korea
junupark@yonsei.ac.kr

Jeong-Won Cha
Changwon National University
Changwon, Republic of Korea
jcha@changwon.ac.kr

Yo-Sub Han
Yonsei University
Seoul, Republic of Korea
emmous@yonsei.ac.kr

Abstract

Abusive text is a serious problem in social media and causes many issues among users as the number of users and the content volume increase. There are several attempts for detecting or preventing abusive text effectively. One simple yet effective approach is to use an abusive lexicon and determine the existence of an abusive word in text. This approach works well even when an abusive word is obfuscated. On the other hand, it is still a challenging problem to determine abusiveness in a text having no explicit abusive words. Especially, it is hard to identify sarcasm or offensiveness in context without any abusive words. We tackle this problem using an ensemble deep learning model. Our model consists of two parts of extracting local features and global features, which are crucial for identifying implicit abusiveness in context level. We evaluate our model using three benchmark data. Our model outperforms all the previous models for detecting abusiveness in a text data without abusive words. Furthermore, we combine our model and an abusive lexicon method. The experimental results show that our model has at least 4% better performance compared with the previous approaches for identifying text abusiveness in case of with/without abusive words.

1 Introduction

As the number of social media data increases, abusive text such as online harassment, stalking, trolling and cyber-bullying becomes an important social issue. According to a Pew Research Center study[1] published in 2017, 66% of Internet users have observed someone being harassed and 41% have personally experienced harassment by themselves in online. There have been various attempts to detect or prevent abusive text and, in practice, the abusive word dictionary is the most efficient tool to identify abusive text even if an abusive word is obfuscated. However, if a text does not contain any abusive words explictly yet the abusiveness is clear in context, then it becomes a very challenging problem. For instance, E1) is an abusive comment that explicitly contains abusive words, and E2) is an abusive comment without abusive words.

- E1: Go you cocker cockuser <u>motherfuck</u> uncle <u>suckefing</u> you go <u>fuck</u> your mom you dirty little <u>ass fuck bitch</u> i will kill you i know where you live i will rape you yoru <u>fucking ass</u>.

- E2: I know how having the templates on their talk page helps you assert dominance over them. I know I would bow down to the almighty administrators. But then again, I'm going to <u>go play outside. . . with your mon. . .</u>

There are several approaches for detecting abusiveness using an abusive lexicon (Chen et al., 2012; Lee et al., 2018; Wiegand et al., 2018). These approaches work well when there is an abusive word in text. However, there is no explicit abusive words in text yet the text is abusive in context, the problem of identifying its abusiveness is challenging. We tackle this problem using an ensemble deep learning model.

---

[1] https://www.pewinternet.org/2017/10/10

Proceedings of the 2nd Workshop on NLP for Internet Freedom: Censorship, Disinformation, and Propaganda, pages 10–19
Hong Kong, China, November 4, 2019 ©2019 Association for Computational Linguistics

Our model consists of two detection models. One is a Convolutional Neural Network (CNN) with bidirectional Long Short-Term Memory model (LSTM), and the other is the hierarchical C-LSTM model to understand the hierarchical structures in text. Each model specializes in understanding of long and short sentences. We evaluate our model using three popular benchmark social media datasets, Wikipedia, Facebook and Twitter. The experimental results show that our model outperforms the other baselines as well as the state of the art. We also run an additional experiment and evaluate the performance with respect to a sentence length for understanding context. The experimental results show that the hierarchical model is effective to solve the long dependency problem. Our contributions are summarized as follows:

- We design a hierarchical deep learning model that understands the hierarchical structure in long sentences with implicit abusiveness.

- We propose an ensemble model that combines two classifiers for understanding both of short and long sentences.

- We present an efficient abusive detection system using both our model and an abusive word dictionary.

We discuss the related work on abusiveness detection in Section 2 and propose our model in Section 3. We explain our datasets in Section 4. Then we evaluate our model by running several experiments in Section 5, and analyze the experimental results in Section 6. We suggest a few future directions and conclude the paper in Section 7.

2 Related Work

2.1 Text classification

Over the years, neural network models showed a great improvement in text classification. The emergence of Recurrent Neural Network (RNN) (Liu et al., 2016), which preserves the information continuity over time, and CNN (Kim, 2014), which preserves the local information of data, opened up a new indicator of text classification. Schwenk et al. (2017) presented Very-Deep CNN (VD-CNN) that uses only small convolutions and pooling operations for text processing. Zhou et al. (2015) proposed a C-LSTM model that combines CNN and LSTM to reflect the local information and the time continuity. Zhou et al. (2015) also introduced Attention-Based Bidirectional Long Short-Term Memory Networks (Attn-BLSTM) that can capture the semantic information among sentences using the attention mechanism (Bahdanau et al.). Researchers also added the structural characteristics of data into the learning model design. For example, Yang et al. (2016) proposed a hierarchical attention mechanism that mirrors the hierarchical structure of documents and solves the long-term dependency problem.

2.2 Lexicon-based abusive detection

As abusive text increases, there are several attempts to detect or prevent abusive text effectively. The most classical method is to determine the presence of abusive words. Chen et al. (2012) proposed the Lexical Syntactic Feature (LSF) architecture to detect offensive content and identify potential offensive users in social media together with user's writing style and cyberbullying content. Wiegand et al. (2018) proposed lexicons of abusive words that take advantage of a base lexicon by taking negative polar expressions. Lee et al. (2018) proposed a detection method by enhancing the abusive lexicon from the existing abusive words using Word2vec and deciding abusiveness together with n-grams and edit-distance for obfuscated abusive words.

2.3 Learning-based abusive detection

Djuric et al. (2015) proposed to learn the distributed low dimensional representation of comments using neural language models. Their model solves the high dimensionality and sparsity issues. Xiang et al. (2012) proposed a novel semi-supervised approach for detecting profanity content. It exploits linguistic regularities in profane language via statistical topic modeling. Zhang et al. (2016) noticed that lots of noise and errors in social media data made the abusive detection challenging. They proposed a Pronunciation-based Convolutional Neural Network (PCNN) and solved the error problem of data via phoneme codes of text as the features for a CNN. Zhang and Luo (2018) combined the convolutional and gated recurrent unit networks to detect hate speech on Twitter. They show that their method is able to capture both word sequence and order information in short texts compared to all the previous deep learning models. Srivastava et al. (2019) presented an approach that automatically classifies a toxic comment using a Multi Dimension Capsule Network. They also provide an analysis of their model's interpretation.

2.4 Ensemble model

Malmasi and Zampieri (2018) tackled the problem of identifying hate speech in social media using ensemble classifiers that consist of linear Support Vector Machine (SVM). Fauzi and Yuniarti (2018) suggested another ensemble method for an effective hate speech detection in Indonesian language and improved the detection performance. Cheng et al. (2019) utilized the time interval characteristic in social media for designing a detection model. In particular, they proposed a Hierarchical Attention Networks for Cyber-bullying Detection (ANCD) together with an ensemble technique applied to the deep learning model by separating users and messages from social media. It predicts the interval of time between two adjacent comments and shows that these tasks can improve the performance of cyber-bullying detection. van Aken et al. (2018) proposed an ensemble method that consists of Bidirectional LSTM (Bi-LSTM) and attention-based networks. They also conducted an in-depth error analysis of the toxic comment classification.

3 Methods and Ensemble

The proposed system consists of two parts as depicted in Figure 1. First, an abusive lexicon detects explicit abusiveness when there exists an (obfuscated) abusive word in text. Second, the ensemble deep learning model detects implicit abusiveness that does not contain any abusive words.

3.1 Lexicon of abusive words

We use an abusive lexicon (Wiegand et al., 2018) that takes advantage of the corpora and lexical resources. We also apply several efficient gadgets (Lee et al., 2018) based on blacklist, n-grams, punctuation and words with special characters to detect intentionally obfuscated words.

3.2 C-LSTM

Zhou et al. (2015) proposed C-LSTM that combines CNN and LSTM for text classification, and has advantages of both architectures. The CNN extracts a sequence of local information of sentences and LSTM obtains the representation of a sentence.

CNN: The CNN (Kim, 2014) extracts local information by preserving the word order and contextual information. We use the word embedding matrix W_e with 300 dimensions and convolution, which involves the 3 window vectors and 100 filters to obtain multiple features. We apply a non-linear function using a Rectified Linear Unit (ReLU) and the 1D max-pooling operation with pool size of 4 over the feature map to take the down-sampled maximum value. Let α_i denote d-dimensional word vectors through an embedding matrix W_e for the ith word x_i in a sentence. We have a window vector w_i with k consecutive word vectors. A filter m convolves with the window vectors at each position in a valid way to generate a feature map c_i. For n filters with the same length, the generated n feature maps can be rearranged as feature representation for each window w_i as follow:

$$\alpha_i = W_e x_i,$$
$$w_i = [\alpha_i, \alpha_{i+1}, \ldots, \alpha_{i+k-1}],$$
$$c_i = f(w_i \circ m + b),$$
$$c_i = ReLU(c_i),$$
$$\hat{c}_i = max_4(c_i),$$
$$W = [c_1, c_2, \ldots, c_n].$$

Bidirectional LSTM: The LSTM extracts orderly information (Zhang and Luo, 2018) by preserving a sequence of words or character n-grams. We use bidirectional LSTM, which has two LSTM layers instead of the standard LSTM to have information from backward and forward simultaneously. We use 100 features in the hidden state, followed by a dropout layer with a rate of 0.5. Afterward, we apply the 1D max-pooling operation to reduce the dimensionality of the LSTM output features $\overrightarrow{O}_j$ and $\overleftarrow{O}_j$. Finally, a linear-layer with the sigmoid function predicts the binary label classification and the softmax function predicts the multi-label classification.

$$\overrightarrow{O}_j = \overrightarrow{LSTM}(c_j),$$
$$\overleftarrow{O}_j = \overleftarrow{LSTM}(c_j),$$
$$v = max\{O\},$$
$$p = \{sigmoid, softmax\}(W_c v + b_c).$$

3.3 Hierarchical C-LSTM Networks

Yang et al. (2016) introduced hierarchical attention network for document classification that has

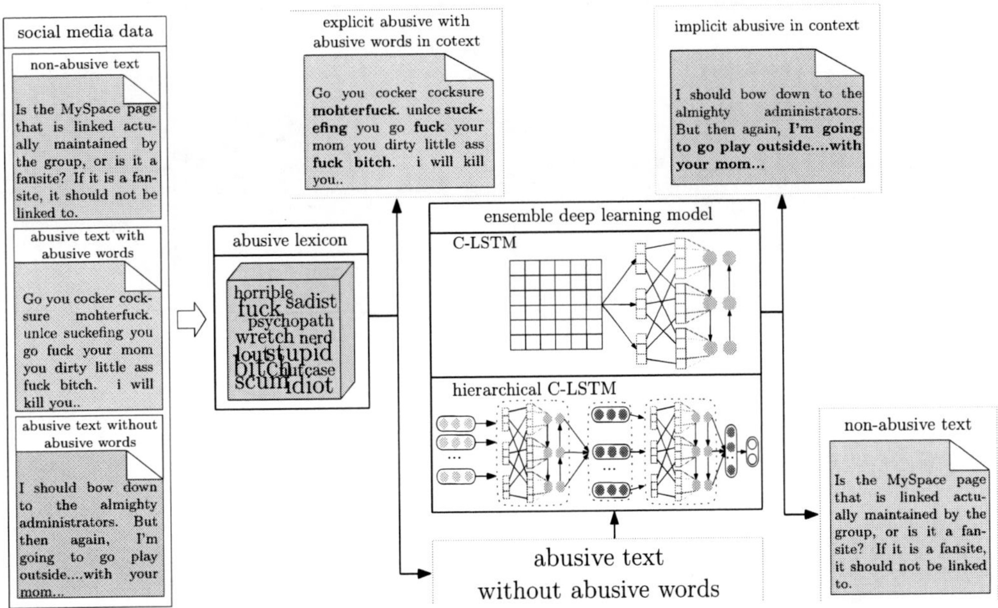

Figure 1: A proposed abusiveness detection mechanism by combining deep learning and an abusive lexicon

word attention and sentence attention. They suggested two distinctive characteristics: 1) it has a hierarchical structure that mirrors document has a hierarchical structure, and 2) it has two attention mechanism to prevent the loss of information in case of a long sentence. Since the abusiveness in context is preserved in a hierarchical structure, we propose a hierarchical C-LSTM network that is able to understand the hierarchical structure and uses a C-LSTM model instead of RNN attention model to extract the local information of a sentence. Let x_{it} be the tth word vector in the ith sentence s, and W_e be an embedding matrix.

$$X_{it} = W_e x_{it},$$
$$S_i = C_{LSTM}(X_{it}),$$
$$v = C_{LSTM}(S),$$
$$v = ReLU(v),$$
$$p = \{sigmoid, softmax\}(W_c v + b_c).$$

Hierarchical structure: A text often consists of several sentences and the structure of these multi-sentences is crucial to understand its context. We obtain the multi-sentence structure features using C-LSTM. Because online sentences often have punctuation errors including repeated occurrences, we split each sentence into fixed length in the data preprocessing described in Section 4.

3.4 Word Embedding

Word embedding provides a dense representation of words and their relative meanings. We use a pre-trained language model because there are many out of vocabulary words due to misspelling or newly created word. We use a fastText embedding (Bojanowski et al., 2017) of 300 dimensions trained with sub-word information on common crawl. For out-of-vocabulary words, we initialize the embedding with random weights.

3.5 Ensemble Learning

Each detection model has its own predictive power and scope. In the case of C-LSTM network, when a sentence is short, it can capture both word sequence and order information well. However, when a sentence is long, it cannot avoid the long-term dependency problem, which causes information loss. Hierarchical C-LSTM network can solve this problem to some extent by obtaining the local feature in each sentence. Therefore, we design an abusive detection model that is an ensemble of C-LSTM and hierarchical C-LSTM network as depicted in Figure 2. The proposed system also incorporates additional features associated with implicit abusiveness of text in local and global context level. For the ensemble, we concatenate the output of v_1 and v_2 through a C-LSTM and the output of u through a hierarchical C-LSTM. Then,

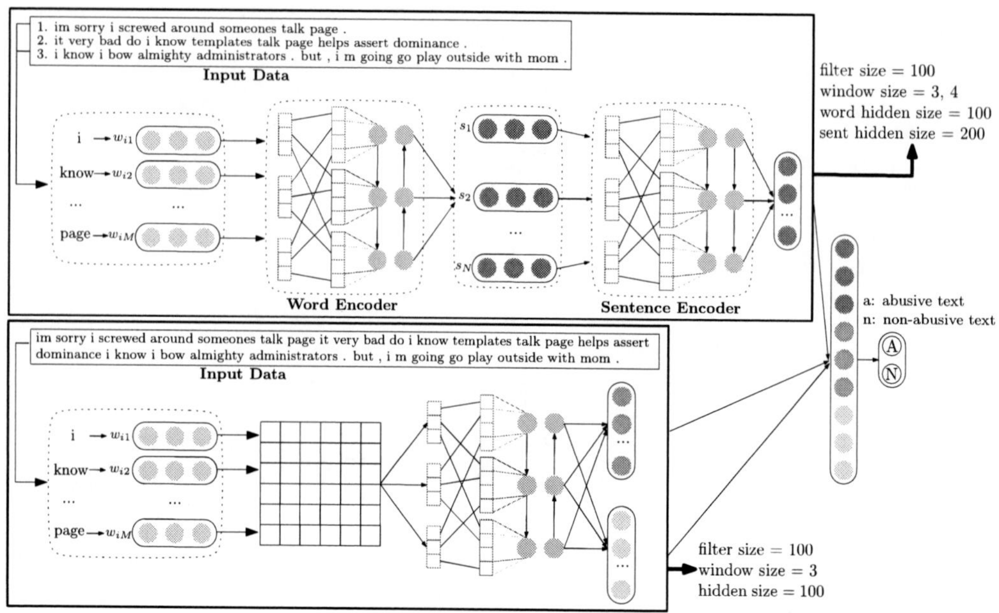

Figure 2: Ensemble of C-LSTM and hierarchical C-LSTM network

we apply a non-linear function using ReLU and feed this vector p to a fully-connected layer in order to predict the output.

$$v_1, v_2 = C_{LSTM(input)},$$
$$u = Hierarchical_{C_{LSTM(input)}},$$
$$p = concatenate(v_1, v_2, u),$$
$$p = ReLU(p),$$
$$p = linear_{layer(p)}.$$

4 Datasets

class	# of occurrences
Clean (Train)	80977 (96%)
Implicit Toxic (Train)	2948 (4%)
Clean (dev)	9019 (96%)
Implicit Toxic (dev)	307 (4%)
Clean (Test)	33541 (83%)
Explicit Toxic (Test)	5085 (13%)
Implicit Toxic (Test)	1158 (4%)

Table 1: Class distribution of Wikipedia dataset.

4.1 Kaggle Toxic Comment

Kaggle dataset is published by Google's Jigsaw for the toxic comment classification challenge. This dataset consists of comments from

class	# of occurrences
NAG (Train)	4159 (46%)
Implicit CAG (Train)	3223 (36%)
Implicit OAG (Train)	1651 (18%)
NAG (Dev)	1029 (46%)
Implicit CAG (Dev)	806 (36%)
Implicit OAG (Dev)	420 (18%)
NAG (F)	491 (65%)
Explicit CAG (F)	35 (5%)
Explicit OAG (F)	56 (7%)
Implicit CAG (F)	95 (13%)
Implicit OAG (F)	73 (10%)
NAG (T)	431 (38%)
Explicit CAG (T)	85 (7%)
Explicit OAG (T)	103 (9%)
Implicit CAG (T)	328 (29%)
Implicit OAG (T)	188 (17%)

Table 2: Class distribution of Facebook (F) and Twitter (T) datasets.

Wikipedia's talk page edits. Each comment categorized as one of the following six classes toxic, severe toxic, obscene, threat, insult and identity hate. We turn multi-class into binary-class to evaluate the performance of the abusive lexicon with ensemble deep learning model. We consider a toxic dataset if any of the six classes are applicable. Then, we split the dataset of 93,251 sentences into 90% training and 10% validation. We also use 39,784 test sentences provided by Kaggle as summarized in Table 1.

4.2 TRAC-1

TRAC-1 is a dataset shared by cyberbullying workshop. This dataset consists of 15,000 aggression annotated Facebook posts and comments. It makes a 3-way classification among Overtly Aggressive (OVG), Covertly Aggressive (CAG), and Non-Aggressive (NAG). We split the dataset into 80% training and 20% validation. Then, we use two test datasets from Facebook and Twitter provided by TRAC-1 to evaluate the performance as summarized in Table 2.

4.3 Data preprocessing

before preprocessing
I salute . . Neel Patel,, U r just amazing. Each & every comment of urs is true & correct...India n world need people like U...Love u my brother. God bless U...& pls don't stop here. Keep ur comments on every required post...
after preprocessing
i salute . ( )(.) neel patel (,,) u r just amazing. Each (&) every comment of urs is true (&) correct.(..)india n world need people like u.(..) love u my brother.god bless u. (..)(&) pls don(')t stop here. keep ur comments on every required post.(..)

Table 3: Data preprocessing example.

In the data preprocessing, we convert all characters to be lowercase, and remove whitespace, punctuations, non-English characters, URLs and Twitter and Facebook mentions. Table 3 is an example of this data preprocessing. We use a Natural Language Toolkit (NLTK) and regular expressions for data preprocessing.

5 Experiments

We run the following two experiments to verify the effectiveness of the deep learning module for implicit abusiveness and the abusive lexicon for explicit abusiveness:

1. Both training and testing datasets consist of implicit abusive text only.

2. The training dataset consists of implicit abusive text only, and the testing dataset consists of both explicit and implicit abusive text.

We use several baseline models and a few variants of our proposed ensemble model to evaluate the detection performance. We train all the models using cross-entropy as the loss function and Adam Optimizer (Kingma and Ba, 2015). For the evaluation metric, we choose the micro-average F1 measure because of the class strong imbalance in the dataset. In addition, we use Area under the Receiver Operating Characteristic curve (ROC AUC) to evaluate whether it can distinguish the difference between classes. All results are an average score of 5 evaluations.

5.1 Results

Deep learning performance: Table 4 compares our hierarchical model against the baselines as well as state-of-the-arts. Our model shows the best performance for the on Wikipedia dataset, however, there are no improvements from its baseline model C-LSTM and CNN for the Facebook and Twitter datasets. This is because the three datasets have different sentence lengths and sizes. The Wikipedia dataset has relatively large long sentences whereas the Facebook and Twitter datasets have rather short sentences. As mentioned in Section 3, since hierarchical C-LSTM applies hierarchical structure and often longer sentences preserve much more structural information, we have better performance on Wikipedia.

Ensemble performance: We use an ensemble of C-LSTM as a scalable approach to extract for small and short sentence features. Table 4 shows our ensemble with only one C-LSTM outperforms. Ensemble with two C-LSTM shows the better performance than individual models on three datasets. However, it has poor performance on Wikipedia compared to ensemble with only one C-LSTM. These show that the ensemble of additional models does not improve the performance.

Lexicon with deep learning performance: Our method combining an abusive lexicon and a deep learning model has the best performance. HAN improves performance of F1 measure 5.28% and AUC 7.06% on Wikipedia and our hierarchical model (HCL) improves performance of F1 measure 9.79% and ensemble model improves 12.74% on Facebook and Twitter. The result shows that the combined approach is more effective than any individual approach.

Comparison of F1 measure and AUC on three datasets consisting of **implicit abusive sentences**				
model	Wikipedia		Facebook	Twitter
	F1	AUC	F1	F1
LSTM (Wang et al., 2015)	94.24	91.95	50.08	50.17
Bi-LSTM (Zhou et al., 2016)	95.55	91.91	50.93	50.50
CNN (Kim, 2014)	95.46	90.95	53.83	60.50
C-LSTM (Zhang et al., 2018)	95.70	91.66	52.88	59.60
HAN (Yang et al., 2016)	96.32	89.21	50.25	54.09
HCL	**96.36**	92.91	53.15	58.43
HCL+C-LSTM	96.08	**93.03**	**54.77**	60.55
HCL+C-LSTM+C-LSTM	95.61	93.00	54.12	**62.51**
Comparison of F1 measure and AUC on three datasets consisting of **explicit and implicit abusive sentences**				
model	Wikipedia		Facebook	Twitter
	F1	AUC	F1	F1
LSTM	90.35	92.02	53.88	53.71
Bi-LSTM	91.65	91.94	54.74	52.80
CNN	91.45	92.06	53.54	56.33
C-LSTM	91.67	92.13	53.74	57.23
HAN	91.53	90.93	51.97	55.99
HCL	91.89	92.31	51.13	53.22
HCL+C-LSTM	91.54	92.55	53.91	52.62
HCL+C-LSTM+C-LSTM	**91.97**	**92.71**	**55.11**	**57.50**
Comparison of F1 measure and AUC on three datasets consisting of **explicit and implicit abusive using both an abusive lexicon and a deep learning model**				
model	Wikipedia		Facebook	Twitter
	F1	AUC	F1	F1
LSTM	94.97	98.50	58.36	56.26
Bi-LSTM	96.12	98.32	59.07	56.54
CNN	96.04	98.31	61.48	65.53
C-LSTM	96.25	98.45	60.69	64.54
HAN	96.81	97.99	58.37	59.57
HCL	**96.82**	98.68	60.92	63.51
HCL+C-LSTM	96.58	**98.73**	60.74	65.36
HCL+C-LSTM+C-LSTM	96.17	98.70	**62.51**	**67.09**

Table 4: Results of different models on Wikipedia, Facebook and Twitter datasets, HAN: Hierarchical Attention Neural Net, HCL: Hierarchical C-LSTM. Explicit abusive is when there is an (obfuscated) abusive word, and implicit abusive is no abusive word yet abusive in context.

model	data length ($|T|$)	F1	AUC
C-LSTM		**87.61**	94.36
HCL	$0 < |T| < 100$	84.57	93.88
HCL+C-LSTM+C-LSTM		87.41	**94.62**
C-LSTM		87.45	94.22
HCL	$100 < |T| < 200$	86.35	93.90
HCL+C-LSTM+C-LSTM		**87.87**	**94.61**
C-LSTM		87.33	95.34
HCL	$200 < |T|$	90.52	**96.56**
HCL+C-LSTM+C-LSTM		**90.69**	96.55

Table 5: Comparisons of F1 measure and AUC using Wikipedia dataset which has under 100 words, over 100 and under 200 words and over 200 words.

type	data		example	predicted label	true label
type-1	W	52%	black people deserve to die	0	1
	F	37%	shutdownjnu do it	NAG	CAG
	T	39%	families as well lol	NAG	CAG
type-2	W	13%	actually help us u dont help at all so help dick heads from ur unexpected guest	0	1
	F	3%	what to say about shutdownjnu just shut up	NAG	OAG
	T	2%	sensex in maternity ward .good morning cnbc tv	NAG	CAG
type-3	W	35%	poo poo poo poo poo poo poo poo poo poo poo poo poo poo poo poo poo poo poo poo poo poo poo poo poo poo	1	0
	F	60%	send umar khalid to afzal before its too late . do n t let him become another afzal guru in real ! shutdownjnu madarsajnu	NAG	OAG
	T	59%	kinner to vo h jo bar bar pakistan dwara hamare uper hamle hone par bhi apna much chhipa k baitha h kinner vo h jo bar bar bina bulaye pakistan ja raha h	CAG	NAG

Table 6: Example of error caused by the proposed model for the Wikipedia (W), Facebook (F) and Twitter (T) dataset. 0: abusive, 1: non-abusive.

5.2 Experiment with short/long sentences

Previously, we have claimed that C-LSTM is specialized in short sentences and Hierarchical C-LSTM is specialized in long sentences. We verify this claim using different sentence lengths. Because the Wikipedia dataset contains a lot of punctuation errors, we use the number of words instead of sentences for this experiment. We categorize the dataset into three parts (<100, 100~200, 200<) by counting the number of words in sentences. Note that Founta et al. (2019) suggests a sentence of under 100 words to be a short sentence. We use the micro-average F1 measure and AUC for evaluation metric. As presented in Table 5, C-LSTM has better performance of F1 measure 3.04%, 1.1% and AUC 0.48%, 0.32% com-

pared to HCL in sentences with under 100 words, and over 100 and under 200 words. HCL has better performance of F1 measure 3.19% and AUC 1.22% compared to C-LSTM in sentences which have over 200 words. This experiment verifies that each model is specialized in relation to the size of sentences. Finally, our ensemble model shows the best performance except for a slight difference of 0.2% compared to C-LSTM.

6 Error analysis

We manually categorize the resulting errors into three types: short sentences of less than five words (type-1), sentences with new explicit words (type-2), and sentences having misspelled words, which cause wrong decisions (type-3). Table 6 shows examples of these types of errors.

From the type-1, we can see that our model is confused in understanding the meaning of short sentences of less than five words. It is hard for our model to understand the context of short sentences, since these are few words that does not contain abusive words. The type-2 is an error caused by obfuscated and new abusive words that are not in the current abusive lexicon, such as "esss", "a**hole", "betches", and "b1tch". In order to solve these issues, we need to improve and modify the abusive lexicon furthermore. The type-3 is an error caused by the presence of repetitive and misspelled words. Because online comments often do not basically follow formal language conventions, there are many unstructured, informal and often misspelled and abbreviations. These make the abusive detection very difficult. One can handle these problems in two ways: preprocessing the data with grammar checker or improving the performance with pre-trained embedding model.

7 Conclusion and Future work

We have tackled the problem of detecting abusiveness when there are no abusive words in text using deep learning. We have designed a hierarchical deep learning model that extracts global features for long sentences. We have also proposed an ensemble models that combine two classifiers extracting local and global features. Finally, we have combined our model for context abusiveness and an abusive lexicon method. We have evaluated the proposed system on Wikipedia, Facebook and Twitter datasets. The experimental results confirm that our hierarchical model outperforms in implicit abusive sentences of more than 100 words. Ensemble model outperforms baselines as well as the state of the art in most cases. The combination of an abusive lexicon and a deep learning model shows the best performance in comparison to the individual method.

We plan to develop methods to detect implicit abusiveness in short sentences. Furthermore, we aim to build a new abusive detection method using additional language models.

Acknowledgments

This work was supported by the Institute of Information & Communications Technology Planning & Evaluation (IITP) grant funded by the Korea government (MSIT) (No. 2018-0-00247).

References

Betty van Aken, Julian Risch, Ralf Krestel, and Alexander Löser. 2018. Challenges for toxic comment classification: An in-depth error analysis. In *Proceedings of the 2nd Workshop on Abusive Language Online*, pages 33–42.

Dzmitry Bahdanau, Kyunghyun Cho, and Yoshua Bengio. Neural machine translation by jointly learning to align and translate. In *Proceedings of the 3rd International Conference on Learning Representations*.

Piotr Bojanowski, Edouard Grave, Armand Joulin, and Tomas Mikolov. 2017. Enriching word vectors with subword information. *Transactions of the Association for Computational Linguistics*, 5:135–146.

Ying Chen, Yilu Zhou, Sencun Zhu, and Heng Xu. 2012. Detecting offensive language in social media to protect adolescent online safety. In *Proceedings of the International Conference on Privacy, Security, Risk and Trust, and International Confernece on Social Computing*, pages 71–80.

Lu Cheng, Ruocheng Guo, Yasin Silva, Deborah Hall, and Huan Liu. 2019. Hierarchical attention networks for cyberbullying detection on the instagram social network. In *Proceedings of the Society for Industrial and Applied Mathematics International Conference on Data Mining*, pages 235–243.

Nemanja Djuric, Jing Zhou, Robin Morris, Mihajlo Grbovic, Vladan Radosavljevic, and Narayan Bhamidipati. 2015. Hate speech detection with comment embeddings. In *Proceedings of the 24th International Conference on World Wide Web Companion*, pages 29–30.

Mochammed Ali Fauzi and Anny Yuniarti. 2018. Ensemble method for indonesian twitter hate speech detection. *Electrical Enginerring and Computer Science*, 11:294–299.

Antigoni-Maria Founta, Despoina Chatzakou, Nicolas Kourtellis, Jeremy Blackburn, Athena Vakali, and Ilias Leontiadis. 2019. A unified deep learning architecture for abuse detection. In *Proceedings of the 11th Conference on Web Science*, pages 105–114.

Yoon Kim. 2014. Convolutional neural networks for sentence classification. In *Proceedings of the Conference on Empirical Methods in Natural Language Processing*, pages 1746–1751.

Diederik P. Kingma and Jimmy Ba. 2015. Adam: A method for stochastic optimization. In *Proceedings of the 3rd International Conference on Learning Representations*.

Ho-Suk Lee, Hong-Rae Lee, Jun-U. Park, and Yo-Sub Han. 2018. An abusive text detection system based on enhanced abusive and non-abusive word lists. *Decision Support Systems*, 113:22–31.

Pengfei Liu, Xipeng Qiu, and Xuanjing Huang. 2016. Recurrent neural network for text classification with multi-task learning. In *Proceedings of the 25th International Joint Conference on Artificial Intelligence*, pages 2873–2879.

Shervin Malmasi and Marcos Zampieri. 2018. Challenges in discriminating profanity from hate speech. *Experimental and Theoretical Artificial Intelligence*, 30(2):187–202.

Holger Schwenk, Loïc Barrault, Alexis Conneau, and Yann LeCun. 2017. Very deep convolutional networks for text classification. In *Proceedings of the 15th Conference of the European Chapter of the Association for Computational Linguistics*, pages 1107–1116.

Saurabh Srivastava, Prerna Khurana, and Vartika Tewari. 2019. Detecting aggression and toxicity in comments using capsule network. In *Proceedings of the Third Workshop on Abusive Language Online*, pages 157–162.

Xin Wang, Yuanchao Liu, Chengjie Sun, Baoxun Wang, and Xiaolong Wang. 2015. Predicting polarities of tweets by composing word embeddings with long short-term memory. In *Proceedings of the 53rd Annual Meeting of the Association for Computational Linguistics and the 7th International Joint Conference on Natural Language Processing*, pages 1343–1353.

Michael Wiegand, Josef Ruppenhofer, Anna Schmidt, and Clayton Greenberg. 2018. Inducing a lexicon of abusive words – a feature-based approach. In *Proceedings of the Conference of the North American Chapter of the Association for Computational Linguistics: Human Language Technologies*, pages 1046–1056.

Guang Xiang, Bin Fan, Ling Wang, Jason I. Hong, and Carolyn Penstein Rosé. 2012. Detecting offensive tweets via topical feature discovery over a large scale twitter corpus. In *Proceedings of the 21st International Conference on Information and Knowledge Management*, pages 1980–1984.

Zichao Yang, Diyi Yang, Chris Dyer, Xiaodong He, Alexander J. Smola, and Eduard H. Hovy. 2016. Hierarchical attention networks for document classification. In *Proceedings of the Conference of the North American Chapter of the Association for Computational Linguistics: Human Language Technologies*, pages 1480–1489.

Xiang Zhang, Jonathan Tong, Nishant Vishwamitra, Elizabeth Whittaker, Joseph P. Mazer, Robin Kowalski, Hongxin Hu, Feng Luo, Jamie Macbeth, and Edward Dillon. 2016. Cyberbullying detection with a pronunciation based convolutional neural network. In *Proceedings of the 15th International Conference on Machine Learning and Applications*, pages 740–745.

Ziqi Zhang and Lei Luo. 2018. Hate speech detection: A solved problem? the challenging case of long tail on twitter. *The Computing Research Repository, CoRR*, abs/1803.03662.

Ziqi Zhang, David Robinson, and Jonathan A. Tepper. 2018. Detecting hate speech on twitter using a convolution-gru based deep neural network. In *Proceedings of the Semantic Web – 15th International Conference*, pages 745–760.

Chunting Zhou, Chonglin Sun, Zhiyuan Liu, and Francis C. M. Lau. 2015. A C-LSTM neural network for text classification. *The Computing Research Repository, CoRR*, abs/1511.08630.

Peng Zhou, Zhenyu Qi, Suncong Zheng, Jiaming Xu, Hongyun Bao, and Bo Xu. 2016. Text classification improved by integrating bidirectional LSTM with two-dimensional max pooling. In *Proceedings the 26th International Conference on Computational Linguistics: Technical Papers*, pages 3485–3495.

How Many Users Are Enough? Exploring Semi-Supervision and Stylometric Features to Uncover a Russian Troll Farm

Nayeema Nasrin[1,2]**, Kim-Kwang Raymond Choo**[1,3]**, Myung Ko**[1,2]**,** and **Anthony Rios**[1,2]

[1]Department of Information Systems and Cyber Security
University of Texas at San Antonio
San Antonio, TX 78249, USA

[2]{nayeema.nasrin, myung.ko, anthony.rios}@utsa.edu
[3]raymond.choo@fulbrightmail.org

Abstract

Social media has reportedly been (ab)used by Russian troll farms to promote political agendas. Specifically, state-affiliated actors disguise themselves as native citizens of the United States to promote discord and promote their political motives. Therefore, developing methods to automatically detect Russian trolls can ensure fair elections and possibly reduce political extremism by stopping trolls that produce discord. While data exists for some troll organizations (e.g., Internet Research Agency), it is challenging to collect ground-truth accounts for new troll farms in a timely fashion. In this paper, we study the impact the number of labeled troll accounts has on detection performance. We analyze the use of self-supervision with less than 100 troll accounts as training data. We improve classification performance by nearly 4% F1. Furthermore, in combination with self-supervision, we also explore novel features for troll detection grounded in stylometry. Intuitively, we assume that the writing style is consistent across troll accounts because a single troll organization employee may control multiple user accounts. Overall, we improve on models based on words features by ~9% F1.

1 Introduction

Social media platforms, such as Twitter, can be helpful in monitoring events, particular for ongoing emergency events (i.e. time-critical situations) (Yin et al., 2015). For example, Twitter has been used to create earthquake monitoring systems by monitoring tweets in real-time (Sakaki et al., 2010). However, Twitter has also become the subject of public scrutiny regarding unwanted actors who are exploiting the social media platform to steer public opinion for their political gain.[1] Twitter, like many other social net-

[1]https://nyti.ms/2Uwr36y

working services, has both positive and negative sides of its rendered services. However, when it is used unfairly, malicious actors can manipulate Twitter to influence a potentially large audience by using fake accounts, or worse, by hiring troll farms (Zhang et al., 2016), organizations that employ people to provoke conflict via the use of inflammatory or provocative comments. In general, for this paper, we study models for classifying users as being part of a troll farm.

There has been many inquiries concerning the interference into the 2016 presidential election by the Russian government (Badawy et al., 2018). The Internet Research Agency (IRA)—a troll farm that positioned fraudulent accounts on major social accounts such as Facebook, YouTube and Twitter (Mueller, 2019)—engaged in an online campaign for Russian business and political interests. The IRA's accounts have been created in such a way that they are portrayed as real American accounts. Masking the sponsor of a message such that it appears to originate, and be supported by, grassroots participants is also known as astroturfing (Peng et al., 2017). Based on a 2018 Pew Report, 53% of the Americans participate in some form of civic or political activities on social media during the year (Anderson et al., 2018). Therefore, the magnitude of exploitation by troll farms in influencing opinion on social media is significant. With this growing concern, it is critical that the troll accounts are detected.

Given ground-truth troll farm accounts, researchers have studied if they can develop classifiers to find other members of the troll farm organizations (Im et al., 2019). Even though all the accounts in their dataset are no longer active on Twitter (i.e., they have been banned), based on their classifier, they find that accounts with similar characteristics are still active. However, while social media is swarming with troll accounts (Metaxas

Proceedings of the 2nd Workshop on NLP for Internet Freedom: Censorship, Disinformation, and Propaganda, pages 20–30
Hong Kong, China, November 4, 2019 ©2019 Association for Computational Linguistics

and Mustafaraj, 2012), building large datasets of real troll accounts is challenging, especially as new troll farms are formed with different political agendas. It is hard to annotate new troll accounts because they masquerade as citizens, news media outlets, or individual journalists on social media (Paul and Matthews, 2016). Without extensive domain expertise, and external knowledge regarding specific troll organizations, it is challenging for the research community to gather newly annotated users to train more predictive models.

In this paper, we study two specific issues related to troll farm classification. First, we analyze how three different sets of features impacts our classifier's performance. Specifically, we look at *content*, *behavioral*, and *stylistic* features. Based on the political agenda a troll farm is pushing, it is intuitive that there will be common tokens associated with the organization (e.g., #fakenews). However, it is possible that writing style can improve predictive performance. Intuitively, if we assume that certain employees at a troll organization control multiple accounts, then even if the topical information (i.e., content) varies across the accounts, the writing style should be similar. Thus, we hypothesize that features that are predictive for authorship attribution (Sari et al., 2018), can be applied to the troll farm domain.

Second, we study how the number of annotated trolls impacts the classifier's performance. While more data is generally better, there are still many interesting questions that need to be addressed. For example, how many annotated trolls do we need to build a classifier? Would adding more data significantly improve the performance? Can we achieve similar performance using few annotated accounts? What types of errors does the classifier make if we have limited ground-truth troll data? Manually verifying an account as a Russian troll at scale is not feasible. As a result, this leads to an open challenge in text classification i.e., how can we effectively leverage unannotated tweets to improve the classifier's performance. This necessitates the design of a novel/effective machine learning method to detect anonymous fake accounts. Moreover, detecting the bad actors on Twitter/social media that are trying to influence opinion of unaware users will be critical in the future to ensure unbiased elections, and to minimize the impact of information warfare.

Overall, our work is the most similar to Im et al.

(2019). In contrast to Im et al. (2019), our work differs in two substantial ways. First, while they explored one set of stylistic features (e.g., stopwords), we ground our work by exploring state-of-the-art stylometric features originally developed for authorship attribution (Sari et al., 2018). Second, their work was focused on showing that troll accounts are likely still out there. Yet, in this manuscript, we are more interested in understanding classifier performance and behavior, not analyzing possible unseen troll accounts still active on Twitter. Moreover, via a detailed error analysis, we study possible biases the classifier has with regards to both false positives and false negatives. For example, the classifier trained using recent IRA data is biased against politically active conservatives, resulting in more false positives.

The contributions of the paper are listed below:

- Based on the hypothesis that a single troll organization employee can control multiple social media accounts, we introduce state-of-the-art stylometric and behavioral features, in combination with standard ngrams, to develop a novel troll detection method. Moreover, we compare content-based features against stylometric/behavioral features, analyzing which group has the biggest impact on classifier accuracy.

- We study how the number of annotated troll accounts affects classifier performance. We also show that simple methods that only use content-based features do not effectively make use of large quantities of training data as well as methods with stylistic and behavioral features. Furthermore, we use a simple, yet effective, semi-supervised method to improve performance in the presence of severe data scarcity.

- Finally, we perform a detailed error analysis across different training set sizes. From the error analysis, we investigate how to improve the model further, as well as analyzing the types of biases the models make, and whether the biases are reduced, or enhanced, by adding more training data.

2   Related Work

Overall, our work is related to three major research areas: Russian troll analysis, text classification, and semi-supervised learning.

Russian Trolls. Researchers have studied Russian propaganda on social media across various domains, including, but not limited to, politics and healthcare. The spread of propaganda is a form of information warfare (Denning, 1999). Broniatowski et al. (2018), for example, explained how Russian trolls discussed vaccine-relevant messages to promote discord. Specifically, they created divisive messages that legitimized the debate by polarization. Their work sought to understand the role played by trolls in the promotion of content related to vaccination. Stewart et al. (2018) studied how Russian trolls polarized topics using retweet network and community detection algorithms. Specifically, they showed that trolls aggravated the context of a domestic conversation surrounding gun violence and race relations. Badawy et al. (2018) explored the manipulation effects by analyzing users that re-shared tweets generated from Russian trolls during 2016 U.S. election campaign. Using bot detection techniques and text-analysis, they identified the percentages of liberal and conservative, showing that most of the tweets were conservative-leaning tweets in an attempt to help the presidential campaign.

Surprisingly, IRA linked accounts, which have been identified by Twitter as evidence and later on submitted to United States Senate Judiciary Subcommittee on Crime and Terrorism, have also been found to be associated with Brexit (Llewellyn et al., 2018). These accounts attempted to promote discord for various topics regarding the European Union and migration. Similarly, the IRA had also participated in the #BlackLivesMatter in accounts identified by Arif et al. (2018). Their work elaborated on how these bad actors impersonated real users to manipulate audiences in accordance to their political agenda.

Text Classification. There are several types of machine learning-based text classification methods available such as generative, discriminative, linear, kernel-based, and deep learning methods. In machine learning, generally text classification is a task of automatically assigning set of predefined categories to unstructured texts. Kim (2014) introduced convolutional neural network for text classification. Yang et al. (2016) introduced a hierarchical attention mechanism that simultaneously weights sentences and words based on their predictive importance. While neural networks have produced state-of-the-art results for a wide variety of tasks, the focus of this paper is on interpretable models with features grounded in stylometry combined with easy-to-understand behavior information.

With regards to interpretable models, Joulin et al. (2016) showed that in many cases linear classifiers still create strong baselines, and are faster than neural networks. Generally, linear classifiers are often faster and more efficient than neural network on large datasets. As we will discuss in Section 3, we use a dataset consisting of 700,000 Twitter users, with more than 17 million tweets. Therefore, for our task, efficiency is important. Moreover, given the recent concern of the carbon footprint of natural language processing models, linear models should continue to be studied (Strubell et al., 2019; Schwartz et al., 2019).

Recently, stylometry-grounded features have been used for authorship attribution, including in malware code authorship attribution (Kalgutkar et al., 2019). For example, Sari et al. (2018) explored the connection between topical (content) features combined with various stylistic features, including, but not limited to, capitalization and punctuation usage. Similarly, Abbasi and Chen (2008) introduced "writeprints", method of identifying authorship across the internet. They combined traditional features such as lexical, syntactic, structural, content-specific, with idiosyncratic attributes (e.g., spelling mistakes). They utilized a transform-based technique that uses a pattern disruption algorithm to capture feature variations.

Semi-Supervised Text Classification. Finding training data to train a troll classifier is challenging in practice, and results in a needle-in-a-haystack situation. One of the aims of this paper is to study whether large quantities of unlabeled data can be automatically annotated to augment small amounts of training data to more accurately detect Russian trolls.

There has been a lot of work regarding semi-supervision, for both image, video, and text classification (Li et al., 2019; Mallinar et al., 2019). Wang et al. (2009), for example, applied semi-supervised learning algorithms for video annotation. They presented a technique that was developed based on the classical kernel density estimation approach using both labeled and unlabeled data to estimate class conditional probability densities. Habernal and Gurevych (2015) created a clustering-based semi-supervised method to annotate unlabeled text. The aim was to make the model better at identifying scene text with the semi-supervised learning from the unannotated dataset. Rajendran et al. (2016) proposed a semi-supervised algorithm for argument detection. In this work, we primary focus on methods previously developed for other tasks Rajendran et al. (2016, 2018). Specifically, we focus on self-supervision, a model agnostic method of automatically annotating unlabeled data.

3 Data

To be consistent with prior work, our data collection is similar to Im et al. (2019). We provide the basic statistics for our dataset in Table 1. In 2018, federal agents released 3,841 accounts found to be associated with the IRA. We focus on the 2,284 accounts that have selected English as the main language in their profile. Intuitively, we are interested in classifying bad actors that masquerade themselves as a normal user from the United States (US). Note that while most of the tweets are in English, there are occasional tweets in other languages. Furthermore, we collect each user's last 200 tweets, assuming that each user has that many available tweets. We limit to the last 200 tweets because this is the number of tweets we can collect for an active user with a single Twitter API call.

While we have ground-truth troll accounts, we do not have a standardized non-troll dataset. Therefore, we gathered a 701,614 random Twitter accounts constrained to the continental US. Tweets were collected from August 2018 to January 2019. Furthermore, for each account, we retrieved their last 200 tweets, as available. It is important to note that some users posted fewer than 200 times. The collected user's tweets represent our control, or not-troll accounts. Overall, the data is unbalanced, where the control makes up 99.676% of the total accounts, and the Russian troll accounts represent only 0.324% of the entire dataset. The imbalance matches the real-world assumption that troll accounts are rare (Im et al., 2019).

We split the dataset into four groups: Train, Validation, Test, and Unlabeled. Each group contains both troll and control accounts. The unlabeled set is used for training our model using a semi-supervised technique.

	Train	Val	Test	Unlab.	Total
Troll	924	206	229	925	2,284
Control	284,153	63,146	70,162	284,153	701,614

Table 1: Dataset statistics.

4 Method

Based on previous studies (Sari et al., 2018; Abbasi and Chen, 2008; Stamatatos, 2009; Im et al., 2019), in Section 4.1, we discuss the three groups of features we used in our model: stylistic, content and behavioral. Intuitively, we identify trolls by what they say (content) and how they say it (stylistic and behavioral). Furthermore, in Section 4.2 we explain the semi-supervised method (self-supervision) we used to analyze whether unlabeled data can be automatically annotated to improve our model performance.

4.1 Features

We use three groups of features: Content, Stylistic, and Behavioral. In this section, we describe each feature group in details.

Content Features (C). The content features represent the topics that people discuss on Twitter (Sari et al., 2018). To represent content, we use bag-of-words (BoW). This group of features was also used for troll detection in Im et al. (2019). Specifically, we use unigram word counts. Moreover, we limit the vocabulary to the 5000 most common unigrams. The reason we limit the vocabulary is to avoid overfitting. For instance, slight shifts in content may occur over time. However, the broad political agenda that trolls are perpetuating may stay relatively stable. For example, in the IRA dataset, there are many tweets regarding the #BlackLivesMatter movement to promote discord because it was a popular topic on the news at the time (Arif et al., 2018). Ideally, we want to detect when trolls promote discord, not simply remember a few specific topics discussed during a certain time period.

Stylistic Features (S). We adopt the following stylistic features from Sari et al. (2018): average word length, number of short words, percentage of digits, percentage of upper-case letters, frequency of alphabetic characters, frequency of each unique digit, richness of vocabulary, frequency of stop words and frequency of punctuation. These features are both of lexical and syntactic in nature. The number of short words is determined by counting tokens that contain no more than four characters. Richness of vocabulary was calculated by counting the number of hapax and dis legomena, i.e., the number of words that appear only once or twice in the corpus. We also count the frequency of stop words. We use the 179 stop words provided in the Natural Language Toolkit (BIRD and LOPER, 2004). The rest of the features are explained in Sari et al. (2018).

Behavioral Features (B). In a study on political communication on Twitter, it was shown that emotionally charged tweets are retweeted repeatedly and quicker than average neutral tweets (Stieglitz and Dang-Xuan, 2013). Earlier work has shown that hashtags, shared links, and user mention patterns are predictive of Russian trolls (Broniatowski et al., 2018; Im et al., 2019; Zannettou et al., 2019). For our model, we use three behavioral features. Specifically, we calculate the number of times a user adds hashtags, mentions, and links/URLs to their tweets. Intuitively, tweets that repeatedly share links, or use a large number of hashtags, could indicate bot activity, or someone promoting a specific agenda.

4.2 Self-Supervision (Self)

To address the question "How can we automatically annotate unlabeled data?", we use a technique called self-supervision. Intuitively, self-supervision is an iterative method that slowly adds unlabeled instances to the training data. First, the model is trained on the original annotated training dataset. Next, it is applied to the unlabeled dataset. The most confident Russian trolls, based on the classifier score, are added to the training dataset as new troll instances. The process is repeated for a fixed number of iterations. Furthermore, only a fixed number of unlabeled instances k are only added to the training dataset at each iteration. Only unlabeled examples with a score greater than t are added to the training dataset.

4.3 Implementation Details

As our base classifier, we use a linear support vector machine with L2 regularization. We gridsearch over the C values 0.0001, 0.001, 0.01, 0.1, 1, and 10. The best C value is chosen using the validation dataset. We repeat the self-supervision process for 25 iterations. Moreover, k is set to 10. Therefore, no more than 10 examples are added during each iteration with a threshold t of 0.

	Precision	Recall	F1
C	0.635	0.738	0.683
CBS	0.745	0.764	0.754
CBS+Self	0.815	0.729	0.770

Table 2: Overall results on the test dataset. The results are generated from models trained on all of the Russian troll users in the training dataset.

	Precision	Recall	F1
Best Model (CBS)	0.761	0.772	0.766
- CB (without S)	0.668	0.723	0.695
- CS (without B)	0.785	0.602	0.681
- BS (without C)	0.595	0.578	0.586

Table 3: Ablation results using the validation dataset for the three major feature groups: Stylistic (S), Behavioral (B), and Content (C). The results are generated from the model trained on all of the Russian troll users in the training dataset.

The self-supervision hyperparameters were chosen based on the validation dataset.

5 Results

In this section, we evaluate two of the major contributions of this paper: the stylometric features and self-supervision.

Stylometric Features. In Table 2, we compare our model (CBS+Self) trained using the entire troll dataset. We compare it to (CBS), our model without self-supervision, and to simply using content (C), without stylometric features. Overall, we find that the model CBS+Self outperforms the other two baselines, with an improvement of nearly 2% over CBS and 9% over C. While not directly comparable, we find that C performs comparably to the bag-of-words model presented in Im et al. (2019). Thus, implying that the control dataset may have similar data distributions. Moreover, compared to Im et al. (2019), we do not use any profile features nor do we extract information about the language, unless a language specific token was one of the 5,000 most common words when combined with the control group. Overall, we only rely on linguistic style, simple behavior information, and general topical content to make predictions.

Feature Ablation. We perform an ablation study across the three feature groups on the validation dataset in Table 3. Specifically, we analyze the

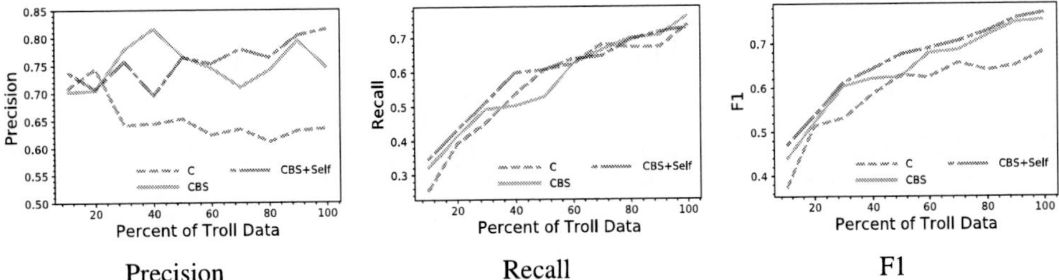

Precision Recall F1

Figure 2: Precision, recall, and F1 test results are plotted using different percentages of troll data during training.

loss in precision, recall, and F1 scores by excluding a feature set from the CBS model and recording its performance. Excluded features are indicated by the minus (-) symbol. Overall, we find that removing content features results in the largest drop in performance, with a 20% drop. This is expected given content features were also the most predictive in Im et al. (2019). The next largest drop is from removing behavioral features, followed by stylistic. However, removing stylistic features results in the second largest drop in precision, while behavioral features have the second largest drop in recall.

Self-Supervision. In Figure 2, we plot the precision, recall, and F1 for the three major models using different percentages of the troll training dataset. We observe that CBS outperforms C across all percentages of troll data with regards to F1. Similarly, CBS+Self consistently results in around a 2% F1 improvement over CBS. Interestingly, precision has a near linear improvement as more trolls are used for training. Yet, recall stays relatively consistent, or for C, slightly decreases. From the plots, we can make two important conclusions. First, adding more troll data improves overall prediction, at least based on F1. It seems that because of the diversity of topics discussed across troll accounts, it is not easy to detect a significant amount of trolls. Moreover, we find that adding more troll data results in a nearly linear increase in recall. Yet, precision is erratic, resulting in neither large improvements nor decreases. Second, while CBS results in consistent improvements over C, showing the positive impact of behavioral and stylistic features, more data does not necessarily help precision. This suggests that new information must be incorporated for further improvement. We examine the false positive and false negative errors in more detail in Section 6.1.

6 Discussion and Limitations

To address two questions, "What type of errors are reduced by adding behavioral and stylistic features?" and "What errors are reduced as more data is collected?". Specifically, we perform a manual error analysis and discuss our study's limitations.

6.1 Error Analysis

In order to assess the quality of our classifier, we analyze the false positive and false negative errors made by the models. Particularly, we study error differences between C and CBS. Moreover, we analyze the different errors made by classifiers trained on different percentages of troll accounts. For error analysis, one of the authors manually analyzed the errors and grouped them into semantic categories. Specifically, we selected a total of 100 false positives and negatives if available. Otherwise, if there were fewer than 100 errors, we annotated all of them. The aim of the analysis is twofold. First, we want to provide insights into what the models are unable to learn (i.e., weaknesses). Second, we want to provide insight for future avenues of work.

6.1.1 False Positives

The false semantic groups and counts of false positive errors are displayed in Table 4a. Overall, we grouped errors into four semantic classes: Bots, Political, Unknown Character, and Misc. None of the models had more than 100 false positives in the validation dataset.

Bots. A common source of false positives appear to fall into the "bot" category. We find that the number of bot-related false positives increases from 5 to 9. Intuitively, the C model fails to distinguish the repetitive nature of the troll accounts from Bots. Example of bot accounts includes users that repeatedly share links in every tweet.

	C		CBS	
	10%	100%	10%	100%
Bot	5	9	5	5
Political	10	20	10	13
Unknown Character	4	7	3	3
Misc.	11	27	11	29
Total Error	30	63	29	50

False Positives

	C		CBS	
	10%	100%	10%	100%
Support	14	6	14	6
Discord	14	10	13	7
Political Concealment	12	10	12	9
Unknown Character	19	13	19	5
Misc.	41	23	42	20
Total Error	100	62	100	47

False Negatives

Table 5: Manual analysis of false positives and false negatives for the Content (C) and Content+Behavioral+Style (CBS) models. We also analyze errors made by models trained on different percentages of the troll dataset (10% and 100%). The error analysis is based on the validation dataset.

One "bot" user repeatedly tweets the time of day.

> Example: *"It's 5 o'clock in Auckland. It's 5 o'clock in Apia. It's 5 o'clock in Juneau. It's 5 o'clock in Seattle. It's 5 o'clock in San Rafael. It's 5 o'clock in Yanacancha..."*

For the CBS model, the number of Bot-related false positives did not increase after adding more troll-related data (i.e., from 10% to 100%). Suggesting that the stylistic and behavior feature are able to distinguish a bot from troll. Yet, a substantial group of errors are still bot-related. Therefore, we believe future work should jointly learn to classify bots and trolls.

Political. The second category of errors are labeled as "political". These tweets are not essentially leaning towards democratic or republican ideologies. Rather they are politically active users, that are criticizing various issues or posting political updates on current events. The topic of the tweets included, but were not limited to, healthcare, Medicaid, Obamacare, and war. Tweets mentioned several political figures such as Donald Trump, Barrack Obama, Ivanka Trump, Ted Cruz, and Jeb Bush. Likewise, politically active users that were misclassified as trolls also used terms such as debate, campaign, and president.

> Example: *"...The **GOP** asked her to endorse **Rubio** NBC/WSJ knows that their recent poll is a fraud. It would have been better to say **JEB** polls **Rubio** was leading the nation wide poll The **Gop** pundits keep saying..."*

We did find a few false positives were also related to sexual abuse. Overall, with the C model, the number of false positives increased after adding more troll data. For CBS, there was a slight increase in errors (10 to 13), but the increase was not as dramatic. This suggests that stylistic and behav-

ior information can distinguish between politically active users and trolls with a political agenda.

Unknown Characters. The third category only resulted in a few errors. We labeled this group as "unknown character" which groups users that have tweets with repetitive non-English characters along with repetitive mentions, in combination with shared links. Overall, because the content does not appear in or ngrams, the false positive is called because of the user's behavior (i.e., sharing many links).

> Example: "لصفلا نع اذه ثدحتسا بابحرم طباور دجتس سييب نو اجنام نم ٩٣٢ درجمب لفسلأاب ةدهاشملاو ليمحتلا يف لصفلا دعوم دجتسو لصفلا رودص لاقملا اذه. *https://t.co/XXXXXX"*

The CBS model only had 3 unknown character-related errors. Likewise, the number of errors did not increase, or decrease, by adding more trolls to the training dataset. Overall, many of the unknown characters are not in the top 5000 unigrams. Thus, we find that many of the false postives are caused by the behavior aspects of the tweets (e.g., sharing many hyperlinks).

Misc. The final category we developed for false positives are "misc." errors. These tweets did not contain political-related topics. The focus of the tweets ranged from religion to pop culture. Likewise, sometimes, users in this group shared links for marketing purposes. We find that this is the largest group of errors, and the number of misc-related errors increases dramatically as more troll data is added (e.g,. 11 to 29 for CBS). We observed a pattern in the ground-truth troll data in which they talk about Veterans Day, then heroes, Christmas, someone's birthday, and music. They then generally post a politically-related tweet.

Example: *"Specials 3/28/19 Sandwich: turkey, bacon, avocado aioli and greens ... Sad note, today is chef Laurette's last day ... Specials 3/29/19 Sandwich: Parmigiana chicken breast ... **Also contains 20+ urls**"*

Many of the errors are caused by the behavior of the user (e.g., sharing a large number of links). To fix these errors in future work, adding topic pattern over time could help. Intuitively, if a user never discusses any political topics, and is not likely to tweet one, based on temporal patterns that differ from known troll farms, then we may be able to reduce this group of false positives.

6.1.2 False Negatives

In Table 4b we display the counts of false negatives that fall into one of five groups: Support, Discord, Political Concealment, Unknown Character, and Misc. Overall, for both C and CBS, and unlike false positives, we find that the number of false negatives decreases as more data is added. This pattern is also evident in Figure 2 by the nearly linear increase recall as more data is added.

Discord. The model failed to detect Russian troll tweets gave an impression of "discord"—in our work we labeled accounts that were attempting discord about certain topics, e.g. black lives matter, immigration ban on Muslims, and racial degradation/issues.

Example: *"@EdwardNiam Namaste Cops getting away with murder. Once again #TamirRice #Justice4Tamir #BlackLivesMatters #policebrutality https://t.co/XXXXX Love my city! #Cleveland #Blackycleveland #streetart #graffiti https://t.co/XXXXXX ... **Also contains 10+ urls** "*

For C, the number of errors dropped from 14 to 10 by adding more data. Likewise, for CBS, the errors dropped from 13 to 7. We find that behavioral and stylistic information takes better advantage of more data, with a nearly 50% drop in discord errors. Intuitively, CBS improves by a lot because many of the discord text contain many hyperlinks which the model correlates with troll behavior. Moreover, common topics are captured by the top 5000 ngrams as more troll data is added.

Political with Concealment. We refer to next group of errors as "political with concealment". The models failed to identify trolls that posted a large number of tweets that were not related to politics, compared to the political-related tweets.

Examples of non-political topics include tweets about the Kardashians and Pamela Anderson. Generally, we found the transition into a political post are quite sudden. Political concealment is a major tactic used by troll organizations to masquerade themselves as US citizens. While CBS performed slightly better with more data (12 to 9) than C (12 to 10), political concealment errors still make up a large proportion of the false negatives.

Example: *"... I was supposed to be flying from NY to San Antonio on business, but my wife got hurt the day before and I canceled my trip. #My911Story ...**Poland bans Russian "journalist"** from entering Schengen zone until 2020 https://t.co/XXXXX via .... RT @EjHirschberger: This is my daughter, Elizabeth Thomas, missing since Monday, March 13th. Please help me find..."*

Support. The "support" category is similar to political false negatives. Except, most of the tweets for a user consisted of messages which that heavily support Donald Trump, but they do not directly refer to him. The tweets mentioned anti-Muslim and anti-Hillary posts.

Example: *"We don't allow "refugees" into this country until we help our homeless first #IslamKills"*

Generally, adding more data solves this issue. This suggests that the training data is not large enough to capture all the topics discussed by Russian trolls.

Misc. The largest portion false negatives are caused by users that either did not not tweet any political issues or tweeted political issues that are not common, thus not captured by the 5000 most frequent unigrams. We labeled this category as "misc". Most of these tweets did not have any specific focus which seemed to repeat. The length of the tweets was not long. Two uncommon political subjects kept recurring are about nuclear explosions and chemicals. For example, many of these users tweeted about #FukushimaAgain or #Fukushima2015, a nuclear disaster that occurred in Japan.

Example: *"... **#FukushimaAgain** Ukrainians say it was the new Chernobyl! They are afraid! I wanna drown my sorrow http://t.co/XXXXX ... Bitterness is like drinking poison Chernobyl's reactor is going to explode again!..."*

Compared to the misc group for false positives, we found that the misc examples for false negatives did not always contain many distinguishing behavior or stylistic characteristics. Therefore, a large number of false negatives are produced by both the C (23 false negatives) and CBS (20 false negatives) models.

Unknown Character. Finally, we also have a category called "unknown character" for false negatives. Often those were related to non-English characters that are not commonly occurring within the continental US. Examples include Unicode characters from the Russian alphabet.

> Example: "Ковер на стене и бесконечные тосты. Что удивляет испанку в русских: *https://t.co/XXXXX*"

We find that most of these errors are handled by adding more troll data. For instance, CBS errors were reduced from 19 to 5 by increasing the troll data from 10% to 100%. We find that the behavior and stylistic features are important to handle the unknown character error type.

6.1.3 Error Analysis Discussion

Overall, we believe temporal patterns of topics could further reduce false negatives. For example, if we analyze a user's tweets over time, we may find that they repeatedly discuss the following topics in temporally: 1. pop culture 2. birthday wish 3. political 4. pop culture. Thus, temporal-topic patterns can be used as auxiliary features. If we use neural networks, the patterns can be used by a recurrent neural network. The topics can be learned automatically using topic modeling.

6.2 Limitations

There are two limitations to this study. First, the control dataset is not guaranteed to be troll-free. While we did not find any obvious trolls in our error analysis of false positives, this does not stop them from being part of the training, test, or unlabeled datasets. This can result in sub-optimal performance, either by incorrectly reported test results, or because of noisy training data. Second, the training dataset consisted of Twitter accounts that have selected English as their primary language. Thus, given the limitations, future work should provide more varied datasets. Specifically, data should be collected carefully to avoid contamination. Also, larger collections of bots and politically active users should be added to the dataset to increase the difficulty of the task. Furthermore, normal users that discuss non-political topics similar to the topics discussed by the trolls should be targeted to include in a new dataset. Finally, while we found that stylistic and behavior information can improve classification performance, sometimes this information resulted in more false positives (e.g., Misc false positives).

7 Conclusion

Social media platforms are likely to play a more important role in political discourse for both democratic and authoritative nations, as evidenced by recent world events. Hence, it is important that we develop approaches to identify malicious actors seeking to influence the outcomes or decision making of various stakeholders by manipulating social media platforms. Therefore, in this paper we presented a novel troll detection method, based on state-of-the-art stylometric and behavioral information. Moreover, because it is challenging to collect real troll accounts, we analyzed the use of self-supervision to automatically annotate unlabeled collections of data. Specifically, we showed that self-supervision improves detection performance with as few as 100 training users and with nearly 1,000 annotated trolls. Finally, we performed a detailed error analysis that provides insight for future model development. Future research includes, but is not limited to, new dataset development, detecting both bots and trolls, expanding the stylistic/behavioral features, and introducing temporal topic patterns as features.

Also, it is important to study the ethical implications of this technology, such as asking the question, "How could false positives, or false negatives, adversely impact real people?" Moreover, should black box models be used by government agencies, or social media companies, to monitor Russian troll activity? It is important to understand each of these questions before putting this work into production.

References

Ahmed Abbasi and Hsinchun Chen. 2008. Writeprints: A stylometric approach to identity-level identification and similarity detection in cyberspace. *ACM Transactions on Information Systems (TOIS)*, 26(2):7.

Monica Anderson, Skye Toor, Lee Rainie, and Aaron Smith. 2018. Activism in the social media age.

Washington, DC: Pew Internet & American Life Project. Retrieved July, 11:2018.

Ahmer Arif, Leo Graiden Stewart, and Kate Starbird. 2018. Acting the part: Examining information operations within# blacklivesmatter discourse. *Proceedings of the ACM on Human-Computer Interaction*, 2(CSCW):20.

Adam Badawy, Emilio Ferrara, and Kristina Lerman. 2018. Analyzing the digital traces of political manipulation: the 2016 russian interference twitter campaign. In *2018 IEEE/ACM International Conference on Advances in Social Networks Analysis and Mining (ASONAM)*, pages 258–265. IEEE.

SG BIRD and E LOPER. 2004. Nltk: The natural language toolkit. Association for Computational Linguistics.

David A Broniatowski, Amelia M Jamison, SiHua Qi, Lulwah AlKulaib, Tao Chen, Adrian Benton, Sandra C Quinn, and Mark Dredze. 2018. Weaponized health communication: Twitter bots and russian trolls amplify the vaccine debate. *American journal of public health*, 108(10):1378–1384.

Dorothy Elizabeth Robling Denning. 1999. *Information warfare and security*, volume 4. Addison-Wesley Reading, MA.

Ivan Habernal and Iryna Gurevych. 2015. Exploiting debate portals for semi-supervised argumentation mining in user-generated web discourse. In *Proceedings of the 2015 conference on empirical methods in natural language processing*, pages 2127–2137.

Jane Im, Eshwar Chandrasekharan, Jackson Sargent, Paige Lighthammer, Taylor Denby, Ankit Bhargava, Libby Hemphill, David Jurgens, and Eric Gilbert. 2019. Still out there: Modeling and identifying russian troll accounts on twitter. *arXiv preprint arXiv:1901.11162*.

Armand Joulin, Edouard Grave, Piotr Bojanowski, and Tomas Mikolov. 2016. Bag of tricks for efficient text classification. *arXiv preprint arXiv:1607.01759*.

Vaibhavi Kalgutkar, Ratinder Kaur, Hugo Gonzalez, Natalia Stakhanova, and Alina Matyukhina. 2019. Code authorship attribution: Methods and challenges. *ACM Computing Surveys*, 52(1):3:1–3:36.

Yoon Kim. 2014. Convolutional neural networks for sentence classification. In *Proceedings of the 2014 Conference on Empirical Methods in Natural Language Processing (EMNLP)*, pages 1746–1751.

Yanchao Li, Yong li Wang, Dong-Jun Yu, Ye Ning, Peng Hu, and Ruxin Zhao. 2019. Ascent: Active supervision for semi-supervised learning. *IEEE Transactions on Knowledge and Data Engineering*.

Clare Llewellyn, Laura Cram, Adrian Favero, and Robin L Hill. 2018. Russian troll hunting in a brexit twitter archive. In *Proceedings of the 18th ACM/IEEE on Joint Conference on Digital Libraries*, pages 361–362. ACM.

Neil Mallinar, Abhishek Shah, Rajendra Ugrani, Ayush Gupta, Manikandan Gurusankar, Tin Kam Ho, Q. Vera Liao, Yunfeng Zhang, Rachel K. E. Bellamy, Robert Yates, Chris Desmarais, and Blake McGregor. 2019. Bootstrapping conversational agents with weak supervision. In *The Thirty-Third AAAI Conference on Artificial Intelligence, AAAI 2019, The Thirty-First Innovative Applications of Artificial Intelligence Conference, IAAI 2019, The Ninth AAAI Symposium on Educational Advances in Artificial Intelligence, EAAI 2019, Honolulu, Hawaii, USA, January 27 - February 1, 2019.*, pages 9528–9533.

Panagiotis T Metaxas and Eni Mustafaraj. 2012. Social media and the elections. *Science*, 338(6106):472–473.

RS Mueller. 2019. Report on the investigation into russian interference in the 2016 presidential election. *US Department of Justice*.

Christopher Paul and Miriam Matthews. 2016. The russian "firehose of falsehood" propaganda model. *Rand Corporation*, pages 2–7.

Jian Peng, Sam Detchon, Kim-Kwang Raymond Choo, and Helen Ashman. 2017. Astroturfing detection in social media: a binary n-gram-based approach. *Concurrency and Computation: Practice and Experience*, 29(17).

Pavithra Rajendran, Danushka Bollegala, and Simon Parsons. 2016. Contextual stance classification of opinions: A step towards enthymeme reconstruction in online reviews. In *Proceedings of the Third Workshop on Argument Mining (ArgMining2016)*, pages 31–39.

Pavithra Rajendran, Danushka Bollegala, and Simon Parsons. 2018. Is something better than nothing? automatically predicting stance-based arguments using deep learning and small labelled dataset. In *Proceedings of the 2018 Conference of the North American Chapter of the Association for Computational Linguistics: Human Language Technologies, Volume 2 (Short Papers)*, pages 28–34.

Takeshi Sakaki, Makoto Okazaki, and Yutaka Matsuo. 2010. Earthquake shakes twitter users: real-time event detection by social sensors. In *Proceedings of the 19th international conference on World wide web*, pages 851–860. ACM.

Yunita Sari, Mark Stevenson, and Andreas Vlachos. 2018. Topic or style? exploring the most useful features for authorship attribution. In *Proceedings of the 27th International Conference on Computational Linguistics*, pages 343–353.

Roy Schwartz, Jesse Dodge, Noah A Smith, and Oren Etzioni. 2019. Green ai. *arXiv preprint arXiv:1907.10597*.

Efstathios Stamatatos. 2009. A survey of modern authorship attribution methods. *Journal of the American Society for information Science and Technology*, 60(3):538–556.

Leo G Stewart, Ahmer Arif, and Kate Starbird. 2018. Examining trolls and polarization with a retweet network. In *Proc. ACM WSDM, Workshop on Misinformation and Misbehavior Mining on the Web*.

Stefan Stieglitz and Linh Dang-Xuan. 2013. Emotions and information diffusion in social media—sentiment of microblogs and sharing behavior. *Journal of management information systems*, 29(4):217–248.

Emma Strubell, Ananya Ganesh, and Andrew McCallum. 2019. Energy and policy considerations for deep learning in nlp. *arXiv preprint arXiv:1906.02243*.

Meng Wang, Xian-Sheng Hua, Tao Mei, Richang Hong, Guojun Qi, Yan Song, and Li-Rong Dai. 2009. Semi-supervised kernel density estimation for video annotation. *Computer Vision and Image Understanding*, 113(3):384–396.

Zichao Yang, Diyi Yang, Chris Dyer, Xiaodong He, Alex Smola, and Eduard Hovy. 2016. Hierarchical attention networks for document classification. In *Proceedings of the 2016 conference of the North American chapter of the association for computational linguistics: human language technologies*, pages 1480–1489.

Jie Yin, Sarvnaz Karimi, Andrew Lampert, Mark Cameron, Bella Robinson, and Robert Power. 2015. Using social media to enhance emergency situation awareness. In *Twenty-fourth international joint conference on artificial intelligence*.

Savvas Zannettou, Tristan Caulfield, William Setzer, Michael Sirivianos, Gianluca Stringhini, and Jeremy Blackburn. 2019. Who let the trolls out?: Towards understanding state-sponsored trolls. In *Proceedings of the 10th ACM Conference on Web Science*, pages 353–362. ACM.

Yubao Zhang, Xin Ruan, Haining Wang, Hui Wang, and Su He. 2016. Twitter trends manipulation: a first look inside the security of twitter trending. *IEEE Transactions on Information Forensics and Security*, 12(1):144–156.

Identifying Nuances in Fake News vs. Satire:
Using Semantic and Linguistic Cues

Or Levi[1,*], **Pedram Hosseini**[2,*], **Mona Diab**[2,3] and **David A. Broniatowski**[2]

[1]AdVerifai

[2]The George Washington University, Washington DC, USA

[3]Amazon AWS AI, Seattle, USA

`or@adverifai.com, phosseini@gwu.edu`

Abstract

The blurry line between nefarious fake news and protected-speech satire has been a notorious struggle for social media platforms. Further to the efforts of reducing exposure to misinformation on social media, purveyors of fake news have begun to masquerade as satire sites to avoid being demoted. In this work, we address the challenge of automatically classifying fake news versus satire. Previous work have studied whether fake news and satire can be distinguished based on language differences. Contrary to fake news, satire stories are usually humorous and carry some political or social message. We hypothesize that these nuances could be identified using semantic and linguistic cues. Consequently, we train a machine learning method using semantic representation, with a state-of-the-art contextual language model, and with linguistic features based on textual coherence metrics. Empirical evaluation attests to the merits of our approach compared to the language-based baseline and sheds light on the nuances between fake news and satire. As avenues for future work, we consider studying additional linguistic features related to the humor aspect, and enriching the data with current news events, to help identify a political or social message.

1 Introduction

The efforts by social media platforms to reduce the exposure of users to misinformation have resulted, on several occasions, in flagging legitimate satire stories. To avoid penalizing publishers of satire, which is a protected form of speech, the platforms have begun to add more nuance to their flagging systems. Facebook, for instance, added an option to mark content items as "Satire", if "the content is posted by a page or domain that is a known satire publication, or a reasonable person would understand the content to be irony or humor with a social message" (Facebook). This notion of humor and social message is also echoed in the definition of satire by Oxford dictionary as "the use of humour, irony, exaggeration, or ridicule to expose and criticize people's stupidity or vices, particularly in the context of contemporary politics and other topical issues".

The distinction between fake news and satire carries implications with regard to the exposure of content on social media platforms. While fake news stories are algorithmically suppressed in the news feed, the satire label does not decrease the reach of such posts. This also has an effect on the experience of users and publishers. For users, incorrectly classifying satire as fake news may deprive them from desirable entertainment content, while identifying a fake news story as legitimate satire may expose them to misinformation. For publishers, the distribution of a story has an impact on their ability to monetize content.

Moreover, in response to these efforts to demote misinformation, fake news purveyors have begun to masquerade as legitimate satire sites, for instance, carrying small badges at the footer of each page denoting the content as satire (Jennifer Golbeck, 2018). The disclaimers are usually small such that the stories are still being spread as though they were real news (Funke, 2019).

This gives rise to the challenge of classifying fake news versus satire based on the content of a story. While previous work (Jennifer Golbeck, 2018) have shown that satire and fake news can be distinguished with a word-based classification approach, our work is focused on the semantic and linguistic properties of the content. Inspired by the distinctive aspects of satire with regard to humor and social message, our hypothesis is that using semantic and linguistic cues can help to capture

---

Proceedings of the 2nd Workshop on NLP for Internet Freedom: Censorship, Disinformation, and Propaganda, pages 31–35

Hong Kong, China, November 4, 2019 ©2019 Association for Computational Linguistics

these nuances.

Our main research questions are therefore, RQ1) are there semantic and linguistic differences between fake news and satire stories that can help to tell them apart?; and RQ2) can these semantic and linguistic differences contribute to the understanding of nuances between fake news and satire beyond differences in the language being used?

The rest of paper is organized as follows: in section 2, we briefly review studies on fake news and satire articles which are the most relevant to our work. In section 3, we present the methods we use to investigate semantic and linguistic differences between fake and satire articles. Next, we evaluate these methods and share insights on nuances between fake news and satire in section 4. Finally, we conclude the paper in section 5 and outline next steps and future work.

2   Related Work

Previous work addressed the challenge of identifying fake news (Niall J. Conroy, 2015; Kai Shu and Liu, 2017), or identifying satire (Clint Burfoot, 2009; Aishwarya N. Reganti, 2016; Victoria Rubin, 2016), in isolation, compared to real news stories.

The most relevant work to ours is that of Golbeck et al. (Jennifer Golbeck, 2018). They introduced a dataset of fake news and satirical articles, which we also employ in this work. The dataset includes the full text of 283 fake news stories and 203 satirical stories, that were verified manually, and such that each fake news article is paired with a rebutting article from a reliable source. Albeit relatively small, this data carries two desirable properties. First, the labeling is based on the content and not the source, and the stories spread across a diverse set of sources. Second, both fake news and satire articles focus on American politics and were posted between January 2016 and October 2017, minimizing the possibility that the topic of the article will influence the classification.

In their work, Golbeck et al. studied whether there are differences in the language of fake news and satirical articles on the same topic that could be utilized with a word-based classification approach. A model using the Naive Bayes Multinomial algorithm is proposed in their paper which serves as the baseline in our experiments.

3   Method

In the following subsections, we investigate the semantic and linguistic differences of satire and fake news articles.[1]

3.1   Semantic Representation with BERT

To study the semantic nuances between fake news and satire, we use BERT (Devlin et al., 2018), which stands for Bidirectional Encoder Representations from Transformers, and represents a state-of-the-art contextual language model. BERT is a method for pre-training language representations, meaning that it is pre-trained on a large text corpus and then used for downstream NLP tasks. Word2Vec (Tomas Mikolov, 2013) showed that we can use vectors to properly represent words in a way that captures semantic or meaning-related relationships. While Word2Vec is a context-free model that generates a single word-embedding for each word in the vocabulary, BERT generates a representation of each word that is based on the other words in the sentence. It was built upon recent work in pre-training contextual representations, such as ELMo (Matthew E. Peters, 2018) and ULMFit (Jeremy Howard, 2018), and is deeply bidirectional, representing each word using both its left and right context. We use the pre-trained models of BERT and fine-tune it on the dataset of fake news and satire articles using Adam optimizer with 3 types of decay and 0.01 decay rate. Our BERT-based binary classifier is created by adding a single new layer in BERT's neural network architecture that will be trained to fine-tune BERT to our task of classifying fake news and satire articles.

3.2   Linguistic Analysis with Coh-Metrix

Inspired by previous work on satire detection, and specifically Rubin et al. (Victoria Rubin, 2016) who studied the humor and absurdity aspects of satire by comparing the final sentence of a story to the first one, and to the rest of the story - we hypothesize that metrics of text coherence will be useful to capture similar aspects of semantic relatedness between different sentences of a story.

Consequently, we use the set of text coherence metrics as implemented by Coh-Metrix (McNamara et al., 2010). Coh-Metrix is a tool for producing linguistic and discourse representations of

---

[1]Reproducibility report, including codes and results, is available at: https://github.com/adverifai/Satire_vs_Fake

	PCA Component	Description	estimate	std.error	statistic	
Satire associated	**RC19**	First person singular pronoun incidence	1.80	0.41	4.38	***
	RC5	Sentence length, number of words	0.66	0.18	3.68	***
	RC15	Estimates of hypernymy for nouns	0.61	0.19	3.18	**
	RC49	Word Concreteness	0.54	0.17	3.18	**
	RC35	Ratio of casual particles to causal verbs	0.56	0.18	3.10	**
	RC91	Text Easability PC Referential cohesion	0.45	0.16	2.89	**
	RC20	Incidence score of gerunds	0.43	0.16	2.77	**
	RC32	Expanded temporal connectives incidence	0.44	0.16	2.75	**
	RC9	Third person singular pronoun incidence	0.44	0.16	2.67	**
	RC43	Word length, number of letters	0.45	0.20	2.27	*
	RC46	Verb phrase density	0.37	0.16	2.25	*
	RC97	Coh-Metrix L2 Readability	0.34	0.16	2.16	*
	RC61	Average word frequency for all words	0.50	0.24	2.13	*
	RC84	The average givenness of each sentence	0.37	0.18	2.11	*
	RC65	Text Easability PC Syntactic simplicity	0.38	0.18	2.08	*
	RC50	Lexical diversity	0.37	0.18	2.05	*
Fake news associated	**RC30**	Agentless passive voice density	-1.05	0.21	-4.96	***
	RC73	Average word frequency for content words	-0.72	0.20	-3.68	***
	RC59	Adverb incidence	-0.62	0.18	-3.43	***
	RC55	Number of sentences	-0.79	0.26	-3.09	**
	RC62	Causal and intentional connectives	-0.42	0.15	-2.72	**
	RC34	LSA overlap between verbs	-0.35	0.16	-2.22	*
	RC44	LSA overlap, adjacent sentences	-0.36	0.16	-2.16	*
	RC47	Sentence length, number of words	-0.36	0.18	-2.03	*
	RC89	LSA overlap, all sentences in paragraph	-0.34	0.17	-1.97	*
	(Intercept)		-0.54	0.19	-2.91	

Table 1: Significant components of our logistic regression model using the Coh-Metrix features. Variables are also separated by their association with either satire or fake news. **Bold**: the remaining features following the step-wise backward elimination. *Note*: *** $p < 0.001$, ** $p < 0.01$, * $p < 0.05$.

a text. As a result of applying the Coh-Metrix to the input documents, we have 108 indices related to text statistics, such as the number of words and sentences; referential cohesion, which refers to overlap in content words between sentences; various text readability formulas; different types of connective words and more. To account for multicollinearity among the different features, we first run a Principal Component Analysis (PCA) on the set of Coh-Metrix indices. Note that we do not apply dimensionality reduction, such that the features still correspond to the Coh-Metrix indices and are thus explainable. Then, we use the PCA scores as independent variables in a logistic regression model with the fake and satire labels as our dependent variable. Significant features of the logistic regression model are shown in Table 1 with the respective significance levels. We also run a step-wise backward elimination regression.

Those components that are also significant in the step-wise model appear in bold.

4 Evaluation

In the following sub sections, we evaluate our classification model and share insights on the nuances between fake news and satire, while addressing our two research questions.

4.1 Classification Between Fake News and Satire

We evaluate the performance of our method based on the dataset of fake news and satire articles and using the F1 score with a ten-fold cross-validation as in the baseline work (Jennifer Golbeck, 2018).

First, we consider the semantic representation with BERT. Our experiments included multiple pre-trained models of BERT with different sizes and cases sensitivity, among which the large un-

Model	P	R	F1
Headline only	0.46	0.89	0.61
Text body only	0.78	0.52	0.62
Headline + text body	**0.81**	**0.75**	**0.78**

Table 2: Results of classification between fake news and satire articles using BERT pre-trained models, based on the headline, body and full text. **Bold**: best performing model. *P*: Precision, and *R*: Recall

Method	P	R	F1
Baseline	0.70	0.64	0.67
Coh-Metrix	0.72	0.66	0.74*
Pre-trained BERT	**0.81**	**0.75**	**0.78***

Table 3: Summary of results of classification between fake news and satire articles using the baseline Multinomial Naive Bayes method, the linguistic cues of text coherence and semantic representation with a pre-trained BERT model. Statistically significant differences with the baseline are marked with '*'. **Bold**: best performing model. *P*: Precision, and *R*: Recall

cased model, **bert_uncased_L-24_H-1024_A-16**, gave the best results. We use the recommended settings of hyper-parameters in BERT's Github repository and use the fake news and satire data to fine-tune the model. Furthermore, we tested separate models based on the headline and body text of a story, and in combination. Results are shown in Table 2. The models based on the headline and text body give a similar F1 score. However, while the headline model performs poorly on precision, perhaps due to the short text, the model based on the text body performs poorly on recall. The model based on the full text of headline and body gives the best performance.

To investigate the predictive power of the linguistic cues, we use those Coh-Metrix indices that were significant in both the logistic and step-wise backward elimination regression models, and train a classifier on fake news and satire articles. We tested a few classification models, including Naive Bayes, Support Vector Machine (SVM), logistic regression, and gradient boosting - among which the SVM classifier gave the best results.

Table 3 provides a summary of the results. We compare the results of our methods of the pre-trained BERT, using both the headline and text body, and the Coh-Mertix approach, to the language-based baseline with Multinomial Naive Bayes from (Jennifer Golbeck, 2018). Both the semantic cues with BERT and the linguistic cues with Coh-Metrix significantly outperform the baseline on the F1 score. The two-tailed paired t-test with a 0.05 significance level was used for testing statistical significance of performance differences. The best result is given by the BERT model. Overall, these results provide an answer to research question RQ1 regarding the existence of semantic and linguistic difference between fake news and satire.

4.2 Insights on Linguistic Nuances

With regard to research question RQ2 on the understanding of semantic and linguistic nuances between fake news and satire - a key advantage of studying the coherence metrics is explainability. While the pre-trained model of BERT gives the best result, it is not easily interpretable. The coherence metrics allow us to study the differences between fake news and satire in a straightforward manner.

Observing the significant features, in bold in Table 1, we see a combination of surface level related features, such as sentence length and average word frequency, as well as semantic features including LSA (Latent Semantic Analysis) overlaps between verbs and between adjacent sentences. Semantic features which are associated with the gist representation of content are particularly interesting to see among the predictors since based on Fuzzy-trace theory (Reyna, 2012), a well-known theory of decision making under risk, gist representation of content drives individual's decision to spread misinformation online. Also among the significant features, we observe the causal connectives, that are proven to be important in text comprehension, and two indices related to the text easability and readability, both suggesting that satire articles are more sophisticated, or less easy to read, than fake news articles.

5 Conclusion and Future Work

We addressed the challenge of identifying nuances between fake news and satire. Inspired by the humor and social message aspects of satire articles, we tested two classification approaches based on a state-of-the-art contextual language model, and linguistic features of textual coherence. Evaluation of our methods pointed to the existence of semantic and linguistic differences between fake news and satire. In particular, both methods achieved a significantly better performance than the baseline language-based method. Lastly, we studied the feature importance of our linguistic-based method to help shed light on the nuances between fake news and satire. For instance, we observed that satire articles are more sophisticated, or less easy to read, than fake news articles.

Overall, our contributions, with the improved classification accuracy and towards the understanding of nuances between fake news and satire, carry great implications with regard to the delicate balance of fighting misinformation while protecting free speech.

For future work, we plan to study additional linguistic cues, and specifically humor related features, such as absurdity and incongruity, which were shown to be good indicators of satire in previous work. Another interesting line of research would be to investigate techniques of identifying whether a story carries a political or social message, for example, by comparing it with timely news information.

References

Upendra Kumar Amitava Das Rajiv Bajpai Aishwarya N. Reganti, Tushar Maheshwari. 2016. Modeling satire in english text for automatic detection. *IEEE 16th International Conference on Data Mining Workshops (ICDMW)*.

Timothy Baldwin Clint Burfoot. 2009. Automatic satire detection: Are you having a laugh? *Proceedings of the ACL-IJCNLP Conference Short Papers*.

Jacob Devlin, Ming-Wei Chang, Kenton Lee, and Kristina Toutanova. 2018. Bert: Pre-training of deep bidirectional transformers for language understanding. *arXiv preprint arXiv:1810.04805*.

Facebook. Fact-checking on facebook: What publishers should know. `https://www.facebook.com/help/publisher/182222309230722`. [Online].

Daniel Funke. 2019. Facebooks fact-checking project sometimes forces hoaxers to change their content. `http://bit.ly/2m89KNr`. [Online].

Brooke Auxier Jennifer Golbeck, Matthew Mauriello. 2018. Fake news vs satire: A dataset and analysis. *Proceedings of the 10th ACM Conference on Web Science*.

Sebastian Ruder Jeremy Howard. 2018. Universal language model fine-tuning for text classification. *Proceedings of the 56th Annual Meeting of the Association for Computational Linguistics*.

Suhang Wang Jiliang Tang Kai Shu, Amy Sliva and Huan Liu. 2017. Fake news detection on social media: A data mining perspective. *ACM SIGKDD Explorations Newsletter*.

Mohit Iyyer Matt Gardner Christopher Clark Kenton Lee Luke Zettlemoyer Matthew E. Peters, Mark Neumann. 2018. Deep contextualized word representations. *NAACL*.

Danielle S McNamara, Max M Louwerse, Philip M McCarthy, and Arthur C Graesser. 2010. Cohmetrix: Capturing linguistic features of cohesion. *Discourse Processes*, 47(4):292–330.

Yimin Chen Niall J. Conroy, Victoria L. Rubin. 2015. Automatic deception detection: methods for finding fake news. *Proceedings of the 78th ASIST Annual Meeting*.

Valerie F Reyna. 2012. A new intuitionism: Meaning, memory, and development in fuzzy-trace theory. *Judgment and Decision making*.

Kai Chen Greg Corrado Jeffrey Dean Tomas Mikolov, Ilya Sutskever. 2013. Distributed representations of words and phrases and their compositionality. *Proceedings of the 26th International Conference on Neural Information Processing Systems*.

Yimin Chen Sarah Cornwell Victoria Rubin, Niall Conroy. 2016. Fake news or truth? using satirical cues to detect potentially misleading news. *Proceedings of the Second Workshop on Computational Approaches to Deception Detection*.

Calls to Action on Social Media:
Potential for Censorship and Social Impact

Anna Rogers, Olga Kovaleva, Anna Rumshisky
Department of Computer Science
University of Massachusetts Lowell
Lowell, MA 01854, USA
{arogers, okovaleva, arum}@cs.uml.edu

Abstract

Calls to action on social media are known to
be effective means of mobilization in social
movements, and a frequent target of censorship. We investigate the possibility of their automatic detection and their potential for predicting real-world protest events, on historical data of Bolotnaya protests in Russia (2011-
2013). We find that political calls to action can
be annotated and detected with relatively high
accuracy, and that in our sample their volume
has a moderate positive correlation with rally
attendance.

1 Introduction

Calls to action (CTAs) are known to be effective means of mobilization in social networks
(P.D. Guidry et al., 2014; Savage et al., 2016), and
they are also known to be a target for censorship
by authoritarian states (King et al., 2013, 2014).
However, to the best of our knowledge, they have
not been systematically evaluated for their potential for automatic detection and predicting offline
protest events.

We contribute a case study on political CTAs
in historical data on Bolotnaya protests in Russia (2011-2013). We identify 14 core and borderline types of political CTAs, and we show that
they are relatively easy both to annotate (with IAA
0.78) and to classify (F1 of 0.77, even with a small
amount of annotated data). All of that puts them at
high risk for censorship, but also opens the possibilities to track such censorship. We also find that
in Bolotnaya data, the volume of CTAs on social
media has a moderate positive correlation with actual rally attendance.

2 Related Work

2.1 Prediction of social unrest with social media data

Social movements differ in their goals (reforms or
preservation of status quo), size of the group they
are targeting, methods, and other factors (Snow
et al., 2004), but their success always ultimately
depends on successful mobilization of new participants. The role of social media in that has been
clear since the Arab Spring (Dewey et al., 2012).
Social media fundamentally changed the social
movements, enabling new formats of protest, a
new model of power, and greater activity outside
of formal social organizations (Earl et al., 2015).

Expert judgement is famously unreliable for
predicting political events (Tetlock, 2017). So, if
social media play such an important role in social
movements, can they also be used to track and perhaps predict the real-world events? By now hundreds of studies explored various kinds of forecasting based on social media (Phillips et al., 2017;
Agarwal and Sureka, 2015), from economic factors to civil unrest. Most of them show that their
techniques do have predictive merits, although
some skepticism is warranted (Gayo-Avello et al.,
2013).

Most of the civil unrest prediction work is
done on Twitter and news, sometimes in combination with other sources such as blogs and various
economic indicators (Ramakrishnan et al., 2014;
Manrique et al., 2013). The basic instrument of
analysis in most of these studies is time series of
social media activity on a given topic (Hua et al.,
2013). Data filtering is typically performed via
protest-related keywords, hashtags, geolocation or
known activist accounts. Many studies also rely on
some combination of spatiotemporal features (e.g.
Ertugrul et al. (2019); Zhao et al. (2015)). The
texts of posts could be mined for extracting struc-

Proceedings of the 2nd Workshop on NLP for Internet Freedom: Censorship, Disinformation, and Propaganda, pages 36–44
Hong Kong, China, November 4, 2019 ©2019 Association for Computational Linguistics

tured event-related information, or dense meaning representations could be used without identifying specific features, such as doc2vec representations of news articles and social media streams (Ning et al., 2016). Additionally, social network structure (Renaud et al., 2019) and activity cascades (Cadena et al., 2015) were also found useful, as well as mining and incorporating demographic information (Compton et al., 2014).

The typically-used features that are extracted from social media text include time, date, and place mentions, sentiment polarity of the post, and presence of violent words (Benkhelifa et al., 2014; Bahrami et al., 2018). Another popular approach relies on manually created lexicons of protest-related vocabulary (such as "police", "molotov", "corruption", etc.) combined with event-specific names of politicians, activists etc. (Spangler and Smith, 2019; Mishler et al., 2017). Korolov et al. (2016) identifies possible stages of mobilization in a social movement (sympathy, awareness, motivation, ability to take part). To the best of our knowledge, CTAs have not been systematically investigated for their predictive potential.

2.2 Censorship in social media

Similarly to the systems used to predict offline events, many current censorship systems seem to rely on keywords (MacKinnon, 2009; Verkamp and Gupta, 2012; Chaabane et al., 2014; Zhu et al., 2013). However, it is highly likely that states engaging in suppression of collective action are researching more sophisticated options, and it is therefore imperative that censorship monitors also have better tools to monitor what gets deleted.

Much of research on Internet censorship focuses on China, where there does not seem to be a single policy enforced everywhere: local organizations and companies show significant variation in their implementations (Knockel et al., 2017; Miller, 2018; Knockel, 2018). This depends on only on the goals of the platform, its ties or dependence on the government, but also the market forces: a competing platform that would find a way to censor less would be more attractive for the users (Ling, 2010). The actual process also varies based on the available resources: it is likely that larger companies have significant censor staff (Li and Rajagopalan, 2013), while others might rely only rely on simple keyword filtering. Finally, even at government level not all criticism is disal-

lowed: a significant degree of freedom seems to be allowed with respect to local social movements that are unlikely to become a threat to the regime (Qin et al., 2017).

Calls to action seem to be an obvious candidate for types of verbal messages strongly associated with social movements, and they are known to be effective means of mobilization in social networks (P.D. Guidry et al., 2014; Savage et al., 2016). In particular, King et al. (2013, 2014) report that sometimes the censors let through materials that are simply critical of government, but flag materials with collective action potential (such as calls to attend a rally or support opposition). The effort to shut down the collective action is clear, for example, from the fact that Instagram was simply shut down for 4 days while photos of Hong Kong protests were trending (Ma, 2016).

To the best of our knowledge, the censorship potential of CTAs has also not been specifically addressed in the context of political protests.

3 Case study: Bolotnaya protests, Russia

Our case study is the 2011–2013 Russian protests, of which the best known is the "March of the Millions" on May 6, 2012 in the Bolotnaya square in Moscow. The movement was widespread, with protests in many smaller Russian cities and towns. The protesters were opposing fraudulent elections and government corruption. This was the largest protest movement in Russia since 1990s.

The experiments discussed below rely on the "Bolotnaya" dataset that contains posts, likes and groups of users from VKontakte, the largest Russian social network. The main statistics for the dataset are shown in Table 1. It was created by the New Media Center (Moscow, Russia) in 2014 on the basis of a list of 476 protest groups, which was compiled by Yandex (the largest Russian search engine). The data is used by an agreement with New Media Center.

Enikolopov et al. (2018) report that the number of users of VK social network in different locations was in itself associated with higher protest activity, and locations where the user base was fractured between VKontakte and Facebook had fewer protests, which overall suggests that the main role of social media was the ease of coordination (rather than actual spreading of information critical of the government). This is consistent with the reported role of Facebook in Egypt's

Protest groups	476
Posts in the protest groups	196017
Protest groups' members	221813
Posts posted by the group	77604
Posts shared from other groups	81403
Time frame covered	08.2010 - 10.2014
Users liking the posts by the protest groups	57754

Table 1: Basic statistics on the Bolotnaya dataset

Tahrir Square protests (Tufekci and Wilson, 2012). If these conclusions are correct, then higher volume of CTA should in itself also be a factor in higher protest attendance.

4 Defining Calls to Action

Prototypical CTAs are imperatives prompting the addressee to perform some action, such as *"Don't let the government tell you what to think!"*. This seems like a straightforward category to annotate, but in reality CTAs may be expressed in various ways, including both direct and indirect speech acts. There are many borderline cases that would in the absence of clear guidelines decrease inter-annotator agreement (IAA). There is relevant work on the task of identification of requests in emails (Lampert et al., 2010) and intention classification for dialogue agents (Quinn and Zaiane, 2014), but, to the best of our knowledge, this work is the first to create a detailed schema for CTA annotation in the context of a political protest.

The current work on censorship is concerned not so much with CTAs in particular, but with a broader category of "material with collective action potential". King et al. (2013) defines such materials as those that '(a) involve protest or organized crowd formation outside the Internet; (b) related to individuals who have organized or incited collective action on the ground in the past; or (c) relate to nationalism or nationalist sentiment that have incited protest or collective action in the past.' In other words, this definition only concerns offline events, and does not include various forms of "crowd protesting" such as calls to share information critical of the government.

Based on extensive manual analysis of samples from Bolotnaya dataset, we identified 5 core and 9 borderline cases for political CTAs, shown in Figure 2. Since we were interested in CTAs for social movements, we excluded any other CTAs that would formally fit the criteria, such as invitations, marketing CTAs etc. We also excluded

any other protest-related posts, such as reports of protest events. Of the core and borderline CTA cases, we chose to consider 8 as CTAs.

This choice does not have a firm theoretical underpinning and would vary depending on the researcher's perspective and the case study. For example, in our Bolotnaya data we opted to not include broad rhetorical questions like *"For how much longer shall we put up with this?"*, but in a different context (especially in a different culture) they could be key. Inter-annotator agreement depends on how the guidelines' describing the chosen policy explicitly.

5 Annotation study

Pilot data analysis made it clear that the CTA and non-CTA classes were not balanced. Since CTAs overall constitute a small portion of all posts, we pre-selected the data for annotation using a manually created seed list of 155 protest-related keywords and phrases, such as "participate", "share", "join", "fair elections", etc.

We used our schema to develop detailed annotation guidelines for an annotation study on 1000 VKontakte posts from Russian Bolotnaya data. The annotation was performed on the level of full post, not individual sentences. We considered a post as CTA if it included even one instance of a political CTA as defined above. Ambiguous cases were treated as political CTA, as long as they *could* function as such: for example, *Join us tomorrow!* could refer to both a protest or a birthday party.

Each post was annotated by 3 native Russian speakers, using the classification interface of Prodigy[1] annotation tool. The inter-annotator agreement as estimated by Krippendorf's alpha was .78. In the end, we obtained 871 posts on which at least 2 annotators agreed. 300 of them were identified as CTAs, and 571 - as non-CTAs. This was used as the training dataset for the work to be described in subsequent sections.

6 Classification

In our experiments, we randomly split the collected CTA dataset into the train and test parts in the 80/20% ratio. We selected Logistic Regression (LR) and Support Vector Machine classifier with a linear kernel (SVC) as our baseline models. Both models were used as implemented in the

---

[1] https://prodi.gy/

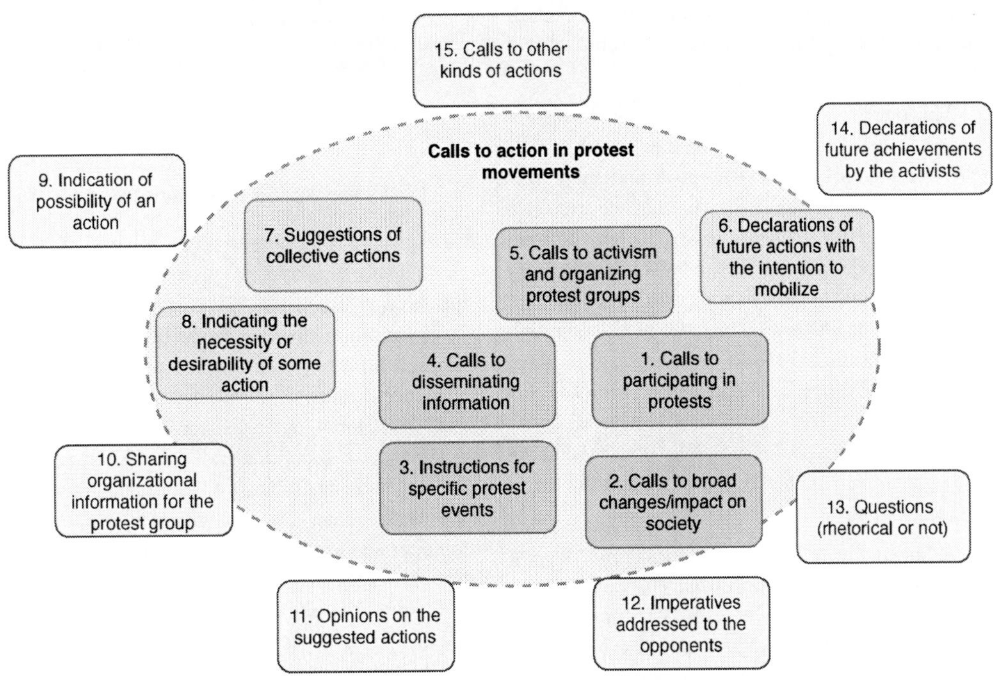

Figure 1: The core and peripheral cases of political CTAs. This study focuses on types 1-8.

Examples for each type:

1. Everybody, join us tomorrow in Sakharov square!
2. If you love Russia, if you love your home city of Smolensk, start the fight with the crooks and thieves!
3. Do not form a line or arrange to meet in a specific place.
4. Invite foreign press and TV – let them see what is going on in our capital!
5. Observers in Kaluga, please respond!
6. That's ok, we will tell them what we think of them even in the square in front of the Central market!
7. I suggest we put on white stripes on our arms as a symbol of honest elections. That's easy to do!
8. On the 10th of March we should come in large numbers!
9. You can download the leaflet with the invitation here.
10. This is the beginning! We will start activities when we will have 50 members. We repeat, participation in this group can only be active.
11. I do like the idea of the government's resignation, but I think your slogans are too emotional. Furthermore, I'm against calling an early election.
12. Out with you, McFaul! And take Putin and Medvedev with you, together with Nemtsov and Chirikova!
13. Is THAT really our choice? (rhetorical)
Today at 10 pm Vlad and I are going to post the leaflets around the city. Who wants to help us? (factual)
14. Together we will get rid of Putin's lies and dictatorship!
15. Everybody, come to my birthday party on Saturday!

Figure 2: Types of calls to actions in Russian social networks, with examples `scikit-learn`[2] library. In both cases we used TF-IDF representations of both original posts and posts lemmatized with `pymorphy`[3] library (Korobov, 2015). We picked the best regularization hyperparameters for each model through cross-validation based on the average F1 score over 5 folds.

The current state-of-the-art deep learning approaches rely on large Transformer-based models pre-trained on large text corpora and then fine-tuned for a given task. In particular, we tried two versions of BERT (Devlin et al., 2019): the multilingual model released in the PyTorch repository of BERT [4], and the Russian version (RuBERT) released by DeepPavlov[5]. The latter model is initialized as multilingual BERT and further fine-tuned on Russian Wikipedia and news corpora (Kuratov and Arkhipov, 2019). Both models have 12 layers and 180M parameters. We trained both models for 40 epochs with the batch size of 32 and the learning rate of $5e^{-5}$.

Additionally to BERT representations, we experimented with the contextual embedder of the ELMo model (Peters et al., 2018) pre-trained for Russian and released by DeepPavlov[6]. The posts were split into sentences using the NLTK library[7] and each sentence token was encoded by the ELMo embedder into a 1024-dimensional vector. The classification was performed by a standard LSTM network (Hochreiter and Schmidhuber, 1997) with a hidden size of 256 units followed by a linear layer. We trained the network for 25 epochs and with the learning rate of 0.001.

The results of all the classification experiments are shown in Table 2. The best performance was achieved by RuBERT, with LSTM on ELMo close second. The effect of lemmatization with linear classifiers is inconsistent. It is interesting that simple logistic regression with lemmatizatized TF-IDF representation of the posts is only 4 F1 points below ELMo, which suggests that the overall classification task is not very difficult.

---

[2]https://scikit-learn.org
[3]https://github.com/kmike/pymorphy2/
[4]https://github.com/huggingface/
pytorch-transformers
[5]http://docs.deeppavlov.ai/en/master/
components/bert.html
[6]https://github.com/deepmipt/
DeepPavlov/tree/master/deeppavlov
[7]https://www.nltk.org/

Classifier	Acc.	F1
LR (no lemmatization)	0.78	0.67
LR (lemmatization)	0.82	0.71
SVC (no lemmatization)	0.80	0.68
SVC (lemmatization)	0.78	0.65
BERT multilingual	0.8	0.73
RuBERT	0.86	0.78
LSTM on ELMo	0.83	0.75

Table 2: CTA classification results

7 CTAs for Predicting social unrest

To estimate the potential usefulness of CTAs as indicators of offline protest events, we ran the trained RuBERT CTA classifier over 91K posts falling in the date range between Dec 2011 through Jul 2013 from the Bolotnaya dataset.

Figure 3 shows the volume of posts identified as CTAs, plotted against the Wikipedia data about attendance of individual rallies[8]. When no attendance data is available, we assume that there were 0 protest events. The two green lines correspond to upper and lower attendance estimates. The blue line shows the detected CTAs.

Despite the noisiness and incompleteness of the available protest data (see subsection 9.1), the Pearson's correlation between attendance estimates and the number of detected CTAs is about 0.4, which is considered to be "moderate". This could make CTAs a useful additional factor to systems based on spatiotemporal, demographic, and/or network activity features.

---

[8]Russian Wikipedia, Protest movement in Russia (2011-2013): https://tinyurl.com/y46qyb9w.

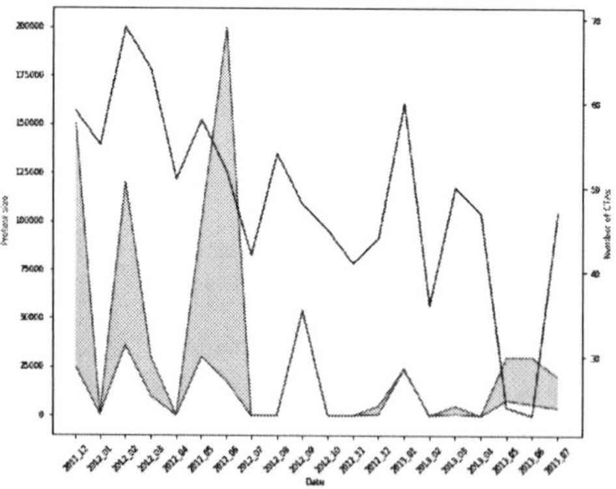

Figure 3: The correlation between the detected CTAs (blue) and the rally attendance (green) per month. The two green lines reflect the upper and lower attendance estimates depending on the source of data used.

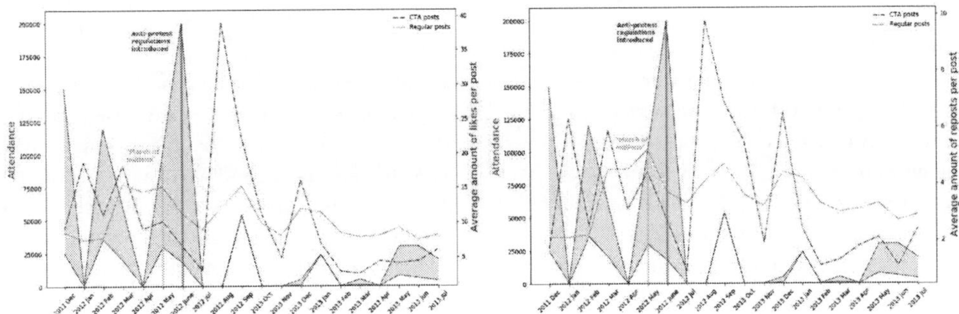

Figure 4: Average number of likes and reposts on CTA and non-CTA posts vs rally attendance

We also conducted experiments to estimate the real-world effect of likes and reposts of CTA posts. Intuitively, one would expect that a higher number of likes and reposts of CTA posts should result in higher attendance for protest rallies. To see whether that was the case for Bolotnaya data we calculated the number of shares and likes on posts detected as CTAs by our classifier, and all other posts in the sample. Figure 4 shows these numbers plotted against the attendance of the protest events.

The pattern we actually observed in Bolotnaya data is different: before the March of the Millions the average number of both reposts and likes is spiking before a protest event, and going down after it. This corresponds to preparation and the aftermath of a major event. Interestingly, after the March of the Millions there was much like/repost activity which did *not* result in any larger events. This can be attributed to the introduction of the anti-protest laws that effectively stifled the movement: the link between social media and real-world activity clearly becomes weaker.

8 Discussion

8.1 Censoring CTAs

Our annotated dataset is quite small (only 871 posts), and this is on purpose: our point is that even with such a small (and unbalanced) dataset it is already possible to obtain a reasonably good classifier (and its performance would likely improve with more data). This is an additional factor in censorship potential: if a system for detecting CTAs could be built quickly and cheaply, it is highly likely that such systems are already being developed by the well-sponsored research teams employed by the authoritarian states. Our study should at least level the playing field for censor-

ship monitors, as will be discussed below. The guidelines we developed will be made available on request by researchers.

The data specific to our Bolotnaya case study would not be openly released because, 8 years after the events, the issues that were driving them continue to be the key factors in the activities of the Russian opposition movements. In particular, Russia has just experienced a new wave of protests estimated to be the largest since 2012 (Wilpert, 2019), also driven by the issues of corruption and fair elections, and resulting in hundreds of arrests (BBC, 2019a,b). Many of the key political figures on both sides are also the same. All this makes our Bolotnaya data potentially useful for censoring new protests.

The situation actually became worse for the protesters because since 2011 a range of new laws went into action to restrict activity on social media. The social network users and popular bloggers are personally identifiable (via their phone numbers), VPNs are illegal, and social network operators are obliged to store activity data for 6 months and decrypt them for authorities (House, 2018; Wesolowsky, 2019). Activists can be imprisoned for sharing "inauthentic and illegal information of social importance", a broad formulation that is interpreted freely by the authorities (Schreck, 2017).

9 Web monitoring potential

As discussed above, materials with collective action potential are already undergoing active censorship in authoritarian states, and it is highly likely that classifiers similar to ours are actually already in place. We hope that our study would somewhat level the playing field for those who combat the censorship.

In particular, if authoritarian states are able to detect CTAs for censorship, it is equally possible to use CTA classifiers in monitoring systems that would scan the web for content that is removed, and report on the ongoing censorship. At present monitoring efforts rely on manual and keyword analysis (MacKinnon, 2009; Verkamp and Gupta, 2012; Chaabane et al., 2014; Zhu et al., 2013). Note that if data on what is being censored were continually collected, the censors would actually "help" the monitoring efforts: by flagging and removing content they would essentially be providing free annotation.

One more use of CTA classifiers would be to help the protesters to find new creative ways of expressing their views that would pass the automatic filters, such as the Chinese egao phenomenon (Horsburgh, 2014; Yates and Hasmath, 2017). Providing an independent web-service with which the activists could check how easy their message is to flag would arguably boost such creativity and provide the activists with their own weapons in the linguistic race against the authoritarian states.

9.1 Limitations

The present study is limited in several ways. First, the small size of annotated data ony provides a lower bound on the performance on CTA classifiers, which would likely increase with more annotated data. However, our point was not in achieving the best possible performance, but in showing that automatic detection of CTAs is possible even with relatively little data.

The second limitation comes from the lack of reliable attendance data for Bolotnaya protests - a situation pervasive in authoritarian states with tight control over media and civic organizations. For example, the official police report for the Kaluga square event stated 8,000 people, while opposition politicians reported 100-120,000. According to bloggers, there were 30,000 people, and a Russian parliamentarian estimated 50-60,000[9]. However, this limitation would impact any prediction method, and it arises precisely in the situations in which the most important protest activity is happening.

Last but not the least, the whole field of forecasting in with social media data is suffering from

the lack of common best practices, which is aggravated by the impossibility to replicate most of the results due to data sharing concerns (Phillips et al., 2017). This study is not an exception: Bolotnaya data in this study was used by an agreement with New Media Center, and we cannot release it publicly. Without major changes in accessibility of social network data for researchers, the only way forward in the field seems to be partial validation by similar patterns uncovered in other case studies.

10 Conclusion

Calls to action are a vital part of mobilization effort in social movements, but, to the best of our knowledge, their potential for censorship and predicting offline protest events has not yet been evaluated.

We examine political calls to action in a case study on historical data on Bolotnaya protests in Russia (2011-2013). We identify 14 core and borderline types of political CTAs, and we show that they are relatively easy to annotate (with IAA 0.78) and detect automatically (F1 of 0.77, even with a small amount of annotated data), which puts them at high risk for censorship in authoritarian states. We also find that in Bolotnaya data, the volume of CTAs on social media has a moderate positive correlation with actual rally attendance.

11 Acknowledgements

We thank Viktoria Khaitchuk, Gregory Smelkov (University of Massachusetts Lowell), and Mikhail Gronas (Dartmouth College) for their help in developing the annotation schema and the training set. We also thank the anonymous reviewers for their valuable feedback. This work was supported in part by the U.S. Army Research Office under Grant No. W911NF-16-1-0174.

References

Swati Agarwal and Ashish Sureka. 2015. Applying Social Media Intelligence for Predicting and Identifying On-line Radicalization and Civil Unrest Oriented Threats. *arXiv:1511.06858 [cs]*.

Mohsen Bahrami, Yasin Findik, Burcin Bozkaya, and Selim Balcisoy. 2018. Twitter Reveals: Using Twitter Analytics to Predict Public Protests. *arXiv:1805.00358 [cs]*.

BBC. 2019a. More than 600 detained in banned Russian protest. *BBC News*.

---

[9]Russian Wikipedia, Protest movement in Russia (2011-2013): https://tinyurl.com/y46qyb9w.

BBC. 2019b. Thousand arrests at Moscow election protest. *BBC News*.

E. Benkhelifa, E. Rowe, R. Kinmond, O. A. Adedugbe, and T. Welsh. 2014. Exploiting Social Networks for the Prediction of Social and Civil Unrest: A Cloud Based Framework. In *2014 International Conference on Future Internet of Things and Cloud*, pages 565–572.

Jose Cadena, Gizem Korkmaz, Chris J. Kuhlman, Achla Marathe, Naren Ramakrishnan, and Anil Vullikanti. 2015. Forecasting social unrest using activity cascades. *PloS one*, 10(6):e0128879.

Abdelberi Chaabane, Terence Chen, Mathieu Cunche, Emiliano De Cristofaro, Arik Friedman, and Mohamed Ali Kaafar. 2014. Censorship in the wild: Analyzing Internet filtering in Syria. In *Proceedings of the 2014 Conference on Internet Measurement*, pages 285–298.

Ryan Compton, Craig Lee, Jiejun Xu, Luis Artieda-Moncada, Tsai-Ching Lu, Lalindra De Silva, and Michael Macy. 2014. Using publicly visible social media to build detailed forecasts of civil unrest. *Security Informatics*, 3(1):4.

Jacob Devlin, Ming-Wei Chang, Kenton Lee, and Kristina Toutanova. 2019. BERT: Pre-training of Deep Bidirectional Transformers for Language Understanding. In *Proceedings of the 2019 NAACL-HLT*, pages 4171–4186.

Taylor Dewey, Juliane Kaden, Miriam Marks, Shun Matsushima, and Beijing Zhu. 2012. The impact of social media on social unrest in the Arab Spring. Technical report, Defense Intelligence Agency, Stanford University.

Jennifer Earl, Jayson Hunt, R. Kelly Garrett, and Aysenur Dal. 2015. New technologies and social movements. *The Oxford handbook of social movements*, pages 355–366.

Ruben Enikolopov, Alexey Makarin, and Maria Petrova. 2018. Social Media and Protest Participation: Evidence from Russia. SSRN Scholarly Paper ID 2696236, Social Science Research Network, Rochester, NY.

Ali Mert Ertugrul, Yu-Ru Lin, Wen-Ting Chung, Muheng Yan, and Ang Li. 2019. Activism via attention: Interpretable spatiotemporal learning to forecast protest activities. *EPJ Data Science*, 8(1):5.

Daniel Gayo-Avello, Panagiotis Takis Metaxas, Eni Mustafaraj, Markus Strohmaier, Harald Schoen, Peter Gloor, Evangelos Kalampokis, Efthimios Tambouris, and Konstantinos Tarabanis. 2013. Understanding the predictive power of social media. *Internet Research*.

Sepp Hochreiter and Jürgen Schmidhuber. 1997. Long Short-Term Memory. *Neural Computation*, 9(8):1735–1780.

Nicola Horsburgh. 2014. *Chinese Politics and International Relations: Innovation and Invention*, 1 edition.

Freedom House. 2018. Freedom on the Net 2018: Russia.

T. Hua, C. Lu, N. Ramakrishnan, F. Chen, J. Arredondo, D. Mares, and K. Summers. 2013. Analyzing Civil Unrest through Social Media. *Computer*, 46(12):80–84.

Gary King, Jennifer Pan, and Margaret E. Roberts. 2013. How Censorship in China Allows Government Criticism but Silences Collective Expression. *American Political Science Review*, 107(2):326–343.

Gary King, Jennifer Pan, and Margaret E. Roberts. 2014. Reverse-engineering censorship in China: Randomized experimentation and participant observation. 345(6199):1251722.

Jeffrey Knockel. 2018. *Measuring Decentralization of Chinese Censorship in Three Industry Segments*. Ph.D., The University of New Mexico.

Jeffrey Knockel, Lotus Ruan, and Masashi Crete-Nishihata. 2017. Measuring Decentralization of Chinese Keyword Censorship via Mobile Games. In *7th USENIX Workshop on Free and Open Communications on the Internet (FOCI 17)*.

Mikhail Korobov. 2015. Morphological Analyzer and Generator for Russian and Ukrainian Languages. In *Analysis of Images, Social Networks and Texts*, Communications in Computer and Information Science, pages 320–332. Springer.

R. Korolov, D. Lu, J. Wang, G. Zhou, C. Bonial, C. Voss, L. Kaplan, W. Wallace, J. Han, and H. Ji. 2016. On predicting social unrest using social media. In *ASONAM 2016*, pages 89–95.

Yuri Kuratov and Mikhail Arkhipov. 2019. Adaptation of deep bidirectional multilingual transformers for russian language. *arXiv preprint arXiv:1905.07213*.

Andrew Lampert, Robert Dale, and Cecile Paris. 2010. Detecting Emails Containing Requests for Action. In *Proceedings of NAACL-HLT*, pages 984–992, Los Angeles, California. ACL.

Hui Li and Megha Rajagopalan. 2013. At Sina Weibo's censorship hub, China's Little Brothers cleanse online chatter.

Yutian Ling. 2010. Upholding Free Speech and Privacy Online: A Legal-Based and Market-Based Approach for Internet Companies in China. *Santa Clara Computer & High Technology Law Journal*, (1):175–218.

Veronica Ma. 2016. Propaganda and Censorship: Adapting to the Modern Age. *Harvard International Review; Cambridge*, 37(2):46–50.

Rebecca MacKinnon. 2009. China's censorship 2.0: How companies censor bloggers. *First Monday*, 14(2).

P. Manrique, H. Qi, A. Morgenstern, N. Velásquez, T. Lu, and N. Johnson. 2013. Context matters: Improving the uses of big data for forecasting civil unrest: Emerging phenomena and big data. In *2013 IEEE International Conference on Intelligence and Security Informatics*, pages 169–172.

Blake Andrew Phillip Miller. 2018. The limits of commercialized censorship in China.

A. Mishler, K. Wonus, W. Chambers, and M. Bloodgood. 2017. Filtering Tweets for Social Unrest. In *2017 IEEE 11th International Conference on Semantic Computing (ICSC)*, pages 17–23.

Yue Ning, Sathappan Muthiah, Huzefa Rangwala, and Naren Ramakrishnan. 2016. Modeling precursors for event forecasting via nested multi-instance learning. In *Proceedings of the 22nd ACM SIGKDD International Conference on Knowledge Discovery and Data Mining*, pages 1095–1104. ACM.

Jeanine P.D. Guidry, Richard D. Waters, and Gregory D. Saxton. 2014. Moving social marketing beyond personal change to social change: Strategically using Twitter to mobilize supporters into vocal advocates. *Journal of Social Marketing*, 4(3):240–260.

Matthew Peters, Mark Neumann, Mohit Iyyer, Matt Gardner, Christopher Clark, Kenton Lee, and Luke Zettlemoyer. 2018. Deep Contextualized Word Representations. In *Proceedings of NAACL-HLT*, pages 2227–2237.

Lawrence Phillips, Chase Dowling, Kyle Shaffer, Nathan Hodas, and Svitlana Volkova. 2017. Using Social Media to Predict the Future: A Systematic Literature Review. *arXiv:1706.06134 [cs]*.

Bei Qin, David Strömberg, and Yanhui Wu. 2017. Why Does China Allow Freer Social Media? Protests versus Surveillance and Propaganda. *Journal of Economic Perspectives*, 31(1):117–140.

Kevin Quinn and Osmar Zaiane. 2014. Identifying questions & requests in conversation. In *Proceedings of the 2014 International C* Conference on Computer Science & Software Engineering*, page 10. ACM.

Naren Ramakrishnan, Patrick Butler, Sathappan Muthiah, Nathan Self, Rupinder Khandpur, Parang Saraf, Wei Wang, Jose Cadena, Anil Vullikanti, Gizem Korkmaz, Chris Kuhlman, Achla Marathe, Liang Zhao, Ting Hua, Feng Chen, Chang Tien Lu, Bert Huang, Aravind Srinivasan, Khoa Trinh, Lise Getoor, Graham Katz, Andy Doyle, Chris Ackermann, Ilya Zavorin, Jim Ford, Kristen Summers, Youssef Fayed, Jaime Arredondo, Dipak Gupta, and David Mares. 2014. 'Beating the News' with EMBERS: Forecasting Civil Unrest Using Open Source Indicators. In *Proceedings of the 20th ACM SIGKDD International Conference on Knowledge Discovery and Data Mining*, KDD '14, pages 1799–1808, New York, NY, USA. ACM.

Molly Renaud, Rostyslav Korolov, David Mendonça, and William Wallace. 2019. Social Network Structure as a Predictor of Social Behavior: The Case of Protest in the 2016 US Presidential Election. In *Recent Developments in Data Science and Intelligent Analysis of Information*, Advances in Intelligent Systems and Computing, pages 267–278. Springer International Publishing.

Saiph Savage, Andrés Monroy-Hernández, and Tobias Hollerer. 2016. Botivist: Calling Volunteers to Action using Online Bots. In *19th ACM Conference on Computer-Supported Cooperative Work and Social Computing*. ACM.

Carl Schreck. 2017. Russian Activist Convicted For Repost...About Repost He Was Convicted For.

David A. Snow, Sarah A. Soule, and Hanspeter Kriesi. 2004. Mapping the Terrain. In *The Blackwell Companion to Social Movements*, pages 3–16. Blackwell Pub. Ltd.

Ethan Spangler and Ben Smith. 2019. Let Them Tweet Cake: Estimating Public Dissent using Twitter. SSRN Scholarly Paper ID 3418050, Social Science Research Network, Rochester, NY.

Philip E. Tetlock. 2017. *Expert Political Judgment: How Good Is It? How Can We Know?*, new edition edition. Princeton University Press, Princeton Oxford.

Zeynep Tufekci and Christopher Wilson. 2012. Social Media and the Decision to Participate in Political Protest: Observations From Tahrir Square. *Journal of Communication*, 62(2):363–379.

John-Paul Verkamp and Minaxi Gupta. 2012. Inferring Mechanics of Web Censorship Around the World.

Tony Wesolowsky. 2019. Six Steps Russia Is Taking Toward Restricting Its Internet.

Greg Wilpert. 2019. Russia's Anti-Gov't Protests Draw Large Crowds, but Putin Remains Secure.

Mathew Yates and Reza Hasmath. 2017. When a joke is more than a joke: Humor as a form of networked practice in the Chinese cyber public sphere. *The Journal of Chinese Sociology*, 4(1):17.

Liang Zhao, Feng Chen, Chang-Tien Lu, and Naren Ramakrishnan. 2015. Spatiotemporal event forecasting in social media. In *Proceedings of the 2015 SIAM International Conference on Data Mining*, pages 963–971. SIAM.

Tao Zhu, David Phipps, Adam Pridgen, Jedidiah R. Crandall, and Dan S. Wallach. 2013. The velocity of censorship: High-fidelity detection of microblog post deletions. In *Presented as Part of the 22nd USENIX Security Symposium (USENIX Security 13)*, pages 227–240.

Mapping (Dis-)Information Flow about the MH17 Plane Crash

Mareike Hartmann
Dep. of Computer Science
University of Copenhagen
Denmark
hartmann@di.ku.dk

Yevgeniy Golovchenko
Dep. of Political Science
University of Copenhagen
Denmark
yg@ifs.ku.dk

Isabelle Augenstein
Dep. of Computer Science
University of Copenhagen
Denmark
augenstein@di.ku.dk

Abstract

Digital media enables not only fast sharing of information, but also disinformation. One prominent case of an event leading to circulation of disinformation on social media is the MH17 plane crash. Studies analysing the spread of information about this event on Twitter have focused on small, manually annotated datasets, or used proxys for data annotation. In this work, we examine to what extent text classifiers can be used to label data for subsequent content analysis, in particular we focus on predicting pro-Russian and pro-Ukrainian Twitter content related to the MH17 plane crash. Even though we find that a neural classifier improves over a hashtag based baseline, labeling pro-Russian and pro-Ukrainian content with high precision remains a challenging problem. We provide an error analysis underlining the difficulty of the task and identify factors that might help improve classification in future work. Finally, we show how the classifier can facilitate the annotation task for human annotators.

1 Introduction

Digital media enables fast sharing of information, including various forms of false or deceptive information. Hence, besides bringing the obvious advantage of broadening information access for everyone, digital media can also be misused for campaigns that spread disinformation about specific events, or campaigns that are targeted at specific individuals or governments. Disinformation, in this case, refers to intentionally misleading content (Fallis, 2015).

A prominent case of a disinformation campaign are the efforts of the Russian government to control information during the Russia-Ukraine crisis (Pomerantsev and Weiss, 2014). One of the most important events during the crisis was the crash of Malaysian Airlines (MH17) flight on July 17, 2014. The plane crashed on its way from Amsterdam to Kuala Lumpur over Ukrainian territory, causing the death of 298 civilians. The event immediately led to the circulation of competing narratives about who was responsible for the crash (see Section 2), with the two most prominent narratives being that the plane was either shot down by the Ukrainian military, or by Russian separatists in Ukraine supported by the Russian government (Oates, 2016). The latter theory was confirmed by findings of an international investigation team. In this work, information that opposes these findings by promoting other theories about the crash is considered disinformation. When studying disinformation, however, it is important to acknowledge that our fact checkers (in this case the international investigation team) may be wrong, which is why we focus on both of the narratives in our study.

MH17 is a highly important case in the context of international relations, because the tragedy has not only increased Western, political pressure against Russia, but may also continue putting the government's global image at stake. In 2020, at least four individuals connected to the Russian separatist movement will face murder charges for their involvement in the MH17 crash (Harding, 2019), which is why one can expect the waves of disinformation about MH17 to continue spreading. The purpose of this work is to develop an approach that may help both practitioners and scholars of political science, international relations and political communication to detect and measure the scope of MH17-related disinformation.

Several studies analyse the framing of the crash and the spread of (dis)information about the event in terms of pro-Russian or pro-Ukrainian framing. These studies analyse information based on manually labeled content, such as television transcripts (Oates, 2016) or tweets (Golovchenko

Proceedings of the 2nd Workshop on NLP for Internet Freedom: Censorship, Disinformation, and Propaganda, pages 45–55
Hong Kong, China, November 4, 2019 ©2019 Association for Computational Linguistics

et al., 2018; Hjorth and Adler-Nissen, 2019). Restricting the analysis to manually labeled content ensures a high quality of annotations, but prohibits analysis from being extended to the full amount of available data. Another widely used method for classifying misleading content is to use distant annotations, for example to classify a tweet based on the domain of a URL that is shared by the tweet, or a hashtag that is contained in the tweet (Guess et al., 2019; Gallacher et al., 2018; Grinberg et al., 2019). Often, this approach treats content from uncredible sources as misleading (e.g. misinformation, disinformation or fake news). This methods enables researchers to scale up the number of observations without having to evaluate the fact value of each piece of content from low-quality sources. However, the approach fails to address an important issue: Not all content from uncredible sources is necessarily misleading or false and not all content from credible sources is true. As often emphasized in the propaganda literature, established media outlets too are vulnerable to state-driven disinformation campaigns, even if they are regarded as credible sources (Jowett and O'donnell, 2014; Taylor, 2003; Chomsky and Herman, 1988)[1].

In order to scale annotations that go beyond metadata to larger datasets, Natural Language Processing (NLP) models can be used to automatically label text content. For example, several works developed classifiers for annotating text content with frame labels that can subsequently be used for large-scale content analysis (Boydstun et al., 2014; Tsur et al., 2015; Card et al., 2015; Johnson et al., 2017; Ji and Smith, 2017; Naderi and Hirst, 2017; Field et al., 2018; Hartmann et al., 2019). Similarly, automatically labeling attitudes expressed in text (Walker et al., 2012; Hasan and Ng, 2013; Augenstein et al., 2016; Zubiaga et al., 2018) can aid the analysis of disinformation and misinformation spread (Zubiaga et al., 2016). In this work, we examine to which extent such classifiers can be used to detect pro-Russian framing related to the MH17 crash, and to which extent classifier predictions can be relied on for analysing information flow on Twitter.

MH17 Related (Dis-)Information Flow on Twitter We focus our classification efforts on a Twitter dataset introduced in Golovchenko et al. (2018), that was collected to investigate the flow of MH17-related information on Twitter, focusing on the question who is distributing (dis-)information. In their analysis, the authors found that citizens are active distributors, which contradicts the widely adopted view that the information campaign is only driven by the state and that citizens do not have an active role.

To arrive at this conclusion, the authors manually labeled a subset of the tweets in the dataset with pro-Russian/pro-Ukrainian frames and build a retweet network, which has Twitter users as nodes and edges between two nodes if a retweet occurred between the two associated users. An edge was considered as *polarized* (either pro-Russian or pro-Ukrainian), if at least one retweet between the two users connected by the edge was pro-Russian/pro-Ukrainian. Then, the amount of polarized edges between users with different profiles (e.g. citizen, journalist, state organ) was computed.

Labeling more data via automatic classification (or computer-assisted annotation) of tweets could serve an analysis as the one presented in Golovchenko et al. (2018) in two ways. First, more edges could be labeled.[2] Second, edges could be labeled with higher precision, i.e. by taking more tweets comprised by the edge into account. For example, one could decide to only label an edge as polarized if at least half of the retweets between the users were pro-Ukrainian/pro-Russian.

Contributions We evaluate different classifiers that predict frames for unlabeled tweets in Golovchenko et al. (2018)'s dataset, in order to increase the number of polarized edges in the retweet network derived from the data. This is challenging due to a skewed data distribution and the small amount of training data for the pro-Russian class. We try to combat the data sparsity using a data augmentation approach, but have to report a negative result as we find that data augmentation in this particular case does not improve classification results. While our best neural classifier clearly outperforms a hashtag-based baseline, generating high quality predictions for the pro-

---

[1]The U.S. media coverage of weapons of mass destruction in Iraq stands as one of the most prominent examples of how generally credible sources can be exploited by state authorities.

[2]Only 26% of the available tweets in Golovchenko et al. (2018)'s dataset are manually labeled.

Russian class is difficult: In order to make predictions at a precision level of 80%, recall has to be decreased to 23%. Finally, we examine the applicability of the classifier for finding new polarized edges in a retweet network and show how, with manual filtering, the number of pro-Russian edges can be increased by 29%. We make our code, trained models and predictions publicly available[3].

2 Competing Narratives about the MH17 Crash

We briefly summarize the timeline around the crash of MH17 and some of the dominant narratives present in the dataset. On July 17, 2014, the MH17 flight crashed over Donetsk Oblast in Ukraine. The region was at that time part of an armed conflict between pro-Russian separatists and the Ukrainian military, one of the unrests following the Ukrainian revolution and the annexation of Crimea by the Russian government. The territory in which the plane fell down was controlled by pro-Russian separatists.

Right after the crash, two main narratives were propagated: Western media claimed that the plane was shot down by pro-Russian separatists, whereas the Russian government claimed that the Ukrainian military was responsible. Two organisations were tasked with investigating the causes of the crash, the Dutch Safety Board (DSB) and the Dutch-led joint investigation team (JIT). Their final reports were released in October 2015 and September 2016, respectively, and conclude that the plane had been shot down by a missile launched by a BUK surface-to-air system. The BUK was stationed in an area controlled by pro-Russian separatists when the missile was launched, and had been transported there from Russia and returned to Russia after the incident. These findings are denied by the Russian government until now. There are several other crash-related reports that are frequently mentioned throughout the dataset. One is a report by Almaz-Antey, the Russian company that manufactured the BUK, which rejects the DSB findings based on mismatch of technical evidence. Several reports backing up the Dutch findings were released by the investigative journalism website Bellingcat.[4]

The crash also sparked the circulation of several alternative theories, many of them promoted in Russian media (Oates, 2016), e.g. that the plane was downed by Ukrainian SU25 military jets, that the plane attack was meant to hit Putin's plane that was allegedly traveling the same route earlier that day, and that the bodies found in the plane had already been dead before the crash.

3 Dataset

For our classification experiments, we use the MH17 Twitter dataset introduced by Golovchenko et al. (2018), a dataset collected in order to study the flow of (dis)information about the MH17 plane crash on Twitter. It contains tweets collected based on keyword search[5] that were posted between July 17, 2014 (the day of the plane crash) and December 9, 2016.

Golovchenko et al. (2018) provide annotations for a subset of the English tweets contained in the dataset. A tweet is annotated with one of three classes that indicate the framing of the tweet with respect to responsibility for the plane crash. A tweet can either be *pro-Russian* (Ukrainian authorities, NATO or EU countries are explicitly or implicitly held responsible, or the tweet states that Russia is not responsible), *pro-Ukrainian* (the Russian Federation or Russian separatists in Ukraine are explicitly or implicitly held responsible, or the tweet states that Ukraine is not responsible) or *neutral* (neither Ukraine nor Russia or any others are blamed). Example tweets for each category can be found in Table 2. These examples illustrate that the framing annotations do not reflect general polarity, but polarity with respect to responsibility to the crash. For example, even though the last example in the table is in general pro-Ukrainian, as it displays the separatists in a bad light, the tweet does not focus on responsibility for the crash. Hence the it is labeled as neutral.

Table 1 shows the label distribution of the annotated portion of the data as well as the total amount of original tweets, and original tweets plus their retweets/duplicates in the network. A *retweet* is a repost of another user's original tweet, indicated by a specific syntax (RT @username:). We consider as *duplicate* a tweet with text that is identical to an original tweet after preprocessing (see Section 5.1). For our classification experiments,

---

[3] https://github.com/coastalcph/mh17
[4] https://www.bellingcat.com/

[5] These keywords were: MH17, Malazijskij [and] Boeing (in Russian), #MH17, #Pray4MH17, #PrayforMH17. The dataset was collected using the Twitter *Garden hose*, which means that it contains a 10% of all tweets within the specified period that matched the search criterion.

	Label	Original	All
	Pro-Russian	512	4,829
Labeled	Pro-Ukrainian	910	12,343
	Neutral	6,923	118,196
Unlabeled	-		192,003 377,679
Total	-		200,348 513,047

Table 1: Label distribution and dataset sizes. Tweets are considered *original* if their preprocessed text is unique. *All* tweets comprise original tweets, retweets and duplicates.

we exclusively consider original tweets, but model predictions can then be propagated to retweets and duplicates.

4 Classification Models

For our classification experiments, we compare three classifiers, a hashtag-based baseline, a logistic regression classifier and a convolutional neural network (CNN).

Hashtag-Based Baseline Hashtags are often used as a means to assess the content of a tweet (Efron, 2010; Godin et al., 2013; Dhingra et al., 2016). We identify hashtags indicative of a class in the annotated dataset using the pointwise mutual information (pmi) between a hashtag hs and a class c, which is defined as

$$\mathrm{pmi}(hs, c) = \log \frac{\mathrm{p}(hs, c)}{\mathrm{p}(hs)\,\mathrm{p}(c)} \qquad (1)$$

We then predict the class for unseen tweets as the class that has the highest pmi score for the hashtags contained in the tweet. Tweets without hashtag (5% of the tweets in the development set) or with multiple hashtags leading to conflicting predictions (5% of the tweets in the development set) are labeled randomly. We refer to to this baseline as HS_PMI.

Logistic Regression Classifier As non-neural baseline we use a logistic regression model.[6] We compute input representations for tweets as the average over pre-trained word embedding vectors for all words in the tweet. We use fasttext embeddings (Bojanowski et al., 2017) that were pre-trained on Wikipedia.[7]

Convolutional Neural Network Classifier As neural classification model, we use a convolutional neural network (CNN) (Kim, 2014), which has previously shown good results for tweet classification (dos Santos and Gatti, 2014; Dhingra et al., 2016).[8] The model performs 1d convolutions over a sequence of word embeddings. We use the same pre-trained fasttext embeddings as for the logistic regression model. We use a model with one convolutional layer and a relu activation function, and one max pooling layer. The number of filters is 100 and the filter size is set to 4.

5 Experimental Setup

We evaluate the classification models using 10-fold cross validation, i.e. we produce 10 different datasplits by randomly sampling 60% of the data for training, 20% for development and 20% for testing. For each fold, we train each of the models described in Section 4 on the training set and measure performance on the test set. For the CNN and LOGREG models, we upsample the training examples such that each class has as many instances as the largest class (Neutral). The final reported scores are averages over the 10 splits.[9]

5.1 Tweet Preprocessing

Before embedding the tweets, we replace urls, retweet syntax (RT @user_name:) and @mentions (@user_name) by placeholders. We lowercase all text and tokenize sentences using the StandfordNLP pipeline (Qi et al., 2018). If a tweet contains multiple sentences, these are concatenated. Finally, we remove all tokens that contain non-alphanumeric symbols (except for dashes and hashtags) and strip the hashtags from each token, in order to increase the number of words that are represented by a pre-trained word embedding.

5.2 Evaluation Metrics

We report performance as F1-scores, which is the harmonic mean between precision and recall. As the class distribution is highly skewed and we

---

[6]As non-neural alternative, we also experimented with SVMs. These showed inferior performance to the regression model.

[7]In particular, with cross-lingual experiments in mind (see Section 7), we used embeddings that are pre-aligned between languages available here https://fasttext.cc/docs/en/aligned-vectors.html

[8]We also ran intitial experiments with recurrent neural networks (RNNs), but found that results were comparable with those achieved by the CNN architecture, which runs considerably faster.

[9]We train with the same hyperparameters on all splits, these hyperparameters were chosen according to the best macro f score averaged over 3 runs with different random seeds on *one* of the splits.

Label	Example tweet
Pro-Ukrainian	Video - Missile that downed MH17 'was brought in from Russia' @peterlane5news RT @mashable: Ukraine: Audio recordings show pro-Russian rebels tried to hide #MH17 black boxes. Russia Calls For New Probe Into MH17 Crash. Russia needs to say, ok we fucked up.. Rather than play games @IamMH17 STOP LYING! You have ZERO PROOF to falsely blame UKR for #MH17 atrocity. You will need to apologize.
Pro-Russian	Why the USA and Ukraine, NOT Russia, were probably behind the shooting down of flight #MH17 RT @Bayard_1967: UKRAINE Eyewitness Confirm Military Jet Flew Besides MH17 Airliner: BBC ... RT @GrahamWP_UK: Just read through #MH17 @bellingcat report, what to say - written by frauds, believed by the gullible. Just that.
Neutral	#PrayForMH17 :(RT @deserto_fox: Russian terrorist stole wedding ring from dead passenger #MH17

Table 2: Example tweets for each of the three classes.

are mainly interested in accurately classifying the classes with low support (pro-Russian and pro-Ukrainian), we report macro-averages over the classes. In addition to F1-scores, we report the area under the precision-recall curve (AUC).[10] We compute an AUC score for each class by converting the classification task into a one-vs-all classification task.

6 Results

The results of our classification experiments are presented in Table 3. Figure 1 shows the per-class precision-recall curves for the LOGREG and CNN models as well as the confusion matrices between classes.[11]

Comparison Between Models We observe that the hashtag baseline performs poorly and does not improve over the random baseline. The CNN classifier outperforms the baselines as well as the LOGREG model. It shows the highest improvement over the LOGREG for the pro-Russian class. Looking at the confusion matrices, we observe that for the LOGREG model, the fraction of True Positives is equal between the pro-Russian and the pro-Ukrainian class. The CNN model produces a higher amount of correct predictions for the pro-Ukrainian than for the pro-Russian class. The absolute number of pro-Russian True Positives is lower for the CNN, but so is in return the amount of misclassifications between the pro-Russian and pro-Ukrainian class.

Per-Class Performance With respect to the per-class performance, we observe a similar trend across models, which is that the models perform best for the neutral class, whereas performance is lower for the pro-Ukrainian and pro-Russian classes. All models perform worst on the pro-Russian class, which might be due to the fact that it is the class with the fewest instances in the dataset.

Considering these results, we conclude that the CNN is the best performing model and also the classifier that best serves our goals, as we want to produce accurate predictions for the pro-Russian and pro-Ukrainian class without confusing between them. Even though the CNN can improve over the other models, the classification performance for the pro-Russian and pro-Ukrainian class is rather low. One obvious reason for this might be the small amount of training data, in particular for the pro-Russian class.

In the following, we briefly report a negative result on an attempt to combat the data sparseness with cross-lingual transfer. We then perform an error analysis on the CNN classifications to shed light on the difficulties of the task.

7 Data Augmentation Experiments using Cross-Lingual Transfer

The annotations in the MH17 dataset are highly imbalanced, with as few as 512 annotated examples for the pro-Russian class. As the annotated examples were sampled from the dataset at random, we assume that there are only few tweets with pro-Russian stance in the dataset. This observation is in line with studies that showed that the amount of disinformation on Twitter is in fact small (Guess et al., 2019; Grinberg et al., 2019). In order to find more pro-Russian training examples, we turn to a resource that we expect to contain large amounts of pro-Russian (dis)information. The *Elections integrity dataset*[12] was released by Twitter in 2018 and contains the tweets and ac-

---

[10]The AUC is computed according to the trapezoidal rule, as implemented in the sklearn package (Pedregosa et al., 2011)

[11]Both the precision-recall curves and the confusion matrices were computed by concatenating the test sets of all 10 datasplits

[12]https://about.twitter.com/en_us/values/elections-integrity.html#data

Model	Macro-avg		Pro-Russian		Pro-Ukrainian		Neutral	
	F1	AUC	F1	AUC	F1	AUC	F1	AUC
RANDOM	0.25	-	0.10	-	0.16	-	0.47	-
HS_PMI	0.25	-	0.10	-	0.16	-	0.48	-
LOGREG	0.59	0.53	0.38	0.34	0.51	0.41	0.88	0.86
CNN	**0.69**	**0.71**	**0.55**	**0.57**	**0.59**	**0.60**	**0.93**	**0.94**

Table 3: Classification results on the English MH17 dataset measured as F1 and area under the precision-recall curve (AUC).

count information for 3,841 accounts that are believed to be Russian trolls financed by the Russian government. While most tweets posted after late 2014 are in English language and focus on topics around the US elections, the earlier tweets in the dataset are primarily in Russian language and focus on the Ukraine crisis (Howard et al., 2018). One feature of the dataset observed by Howard et al. (2018) is that several hashtags show high peakedness (Kelly et al., 2012), i.e. they are posted with high frequency but only during short intervals, while others are persistent during time.

We find two hashtags in the Elections integrity dataset with high peakedness that were exclusively posted within 2 days after the MH17 crash and that seem to be pro-Russian in the context of responsibility for the MH17 crash: #КиевСкажиПравду (*Kiew tell the truth*) and #Киевсбилбоинг (*Kiew made the plane go down*). We collect all tweets with these two hashtags, resulting in 9,809 Russian tweets that we try to use as additional training data for the pro-Russian class in the MH17 dataset. We experiment with cross-lingual transfer by embedding tweets via aligned English and Russian word embeddings.[13] However, so far results for the cross-lingual models do not improve over the CNN model trained on only English data. This might be due to the fact that the additional Russian tweets rather contain a general pro-Russian frame than specifically talking about the crash, but needs further investigation.

8 Error Analysis

In order to integrate automatically labeled examples into a network analysis that studies the flow of polarized information in the network, we need to produce high precision predictions for the pro-

Russian and the pro-Ukrainian class. Polarized tweets that are incorrectly classified as neutral will hurt an analysis much less than neutral tweets that are erroneously classified as pro-Russian or pro-Ukrainian. However, the worst type of confusion is between the pro-Russian and pro-Ukrainian class. In order to gain insights into why these confusions happen, we manually inspect incorrectly predicted examples that are confused between the pro-Russian and pro-Ukrainian class. We analyse the misclassifications in the development set of all 10 runs, which results in 73 False Positives of pro-Ukrainian tweets being classified as pro-Russian (referred to as *pro-Russian False Positives*), and 88 False Positives of pro-Russian tweets being classified as pro-Ukrainian (referred to as *pro-Ukrainian False Positives*). We can identify three main cases for which the model produces an error:

1. the correct class can be directly inferred from the text content easily, even without background knowledge

2. the correct class can be inferred from the text content, given that event-specific knowledge is provided

3. the correct class can be inferred from the text content if the text is interpreted correctly

For the pro-Russian False Positives, we find that 42% of the errors are category I and II errors, respectively, and 15% of category III. For the pro-Ukrainian False Positives, we find 48% category I errors, 33% category II errors and and 13% category III errors. Table 4 presents examples for each of the error categories in both sets which we will discuss in the following.

Category I Errors Category I errors could easily be classified by humans following the annotation guidelines (see Section 3). One difficulty can

---

[13]We use two sets of monolingual fasttext embeddings trained on Wikipedia (Bojanowski et al., 2017) that were aligned relying on a seed lexicon of 5000 words via the RC-SLS method (Joulin et al., 2018)

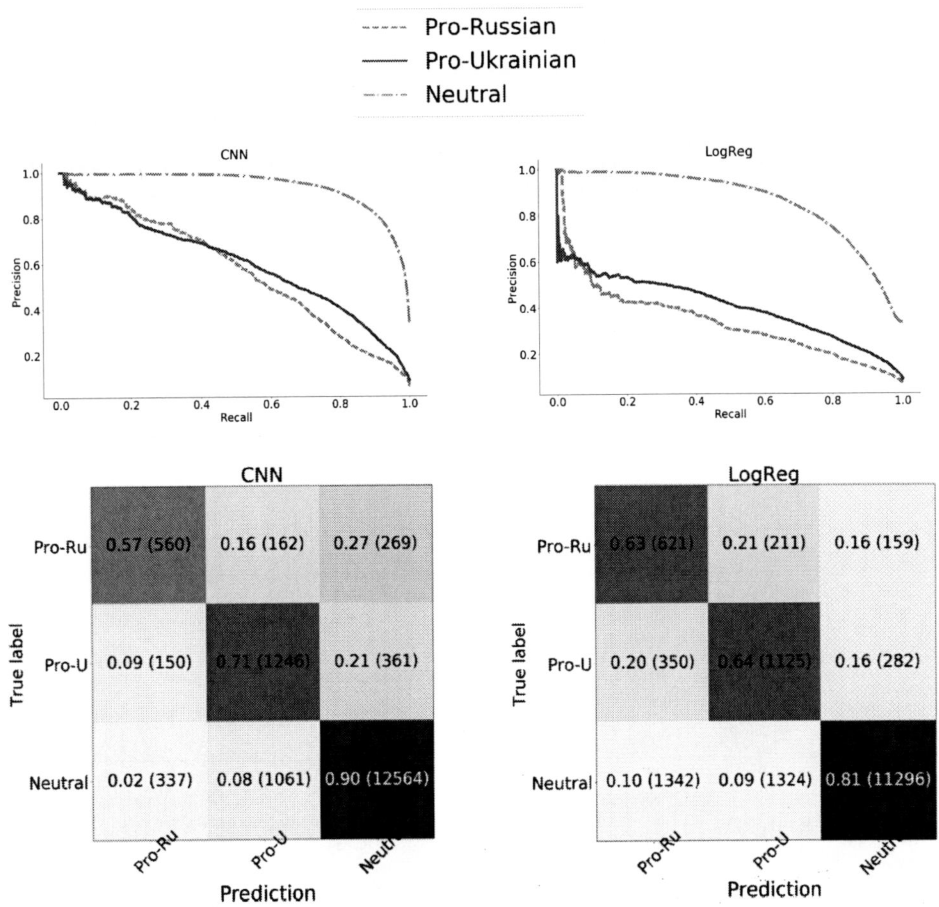

Figure 1: Confusion matrices for the CNN (left) and the logistic regression model (right). The y-axis shows the true label while the x-axis shows the model prediction.

be seen in example f). Even though no background knowledge is needed to interpret the content, interpretation is difficult because of the convoluted syntax of the tweet. For the other examples it is unclear why the model would have difficulties with classifying them.

Category II Errors Category II errors can only be classified with event-specific background knowledge. Examples g), i) and k) relate to the theory that a Ukrainian SU25 fighter jet shot down the plane in air. Correct interpretation of these tweets depends on knowledge about the SU25 fighter jet. In order to correctly interpret example j) as pro-Russian, it has to be known that the bellingcat report is pro-Ukrainian. Example l) relates to the theory that the shoot down was a false flag operation run by Western countries and the bodies in the plane were already dead before the

crash. In order to correctly interpret example m), the identity of *Kolomoisky* has to be known. He is an anti-separatist Ukrainian billionaire, hence his involvement points to the Ukrainian government being responsible for the crash.

Category III Errors Category III errors occur for examples that can only be classified by correctly interpreting the tweet authors' intention. Interpretation is difficult due to phenomena such as irony as in examples n) and o). While the irony is indicated in example n) through the use of the hashtag *#LOL*, there is no explicit indication in example o).

Interpretation of example q) is conditioned on world knowledge as well as the understanding of the speakers beliefs. Example r) is pro-Russian as it questions the validity of the assumption AC360 is making, but we only know that because we

Error cat.	True class	Model prediction	id	Tweet
I	Pro-U	Pro-R	a)	RT @ChadPergram: Hill intel sources say Russia has the capability to potentially shoot down a #MH17 but not Ukraine.
			b)	RT @C4ADS: .@bellingcat's new report says #Russia used fake evidence for #MH17 case to blame #Ukraine URL
			c)	The international investigation blames Russia for MH17 crash URL #KievReporter #MH17 #Russia #terror #Ukraine #news #war
	Pro-R	Pro-U	d)	RT @RT_com: BREAKING: No evidence of direct Russian link to #MH17 - US URL URL
			e)	RT @truthhonour: Yes Washington was behind Eukraine jets that shot down MH17 as pretext to conflict with Russia. No secrets there
			f)	Ukraine Media Falsely Claim Dutch Prosecutors Accuse Russia of Downing MH17: Dutch prosecutors de URL #MH17 #alert
II	Pro-U	Pro-R	g)	@Werteverwalter @Ian56789 @ClarkeMicah no SU-25 re #MH17 believer has ever been able to explain it,facts always get in their way
			h)	Rebel theories on #MH17 "total nonsense", Ukrainian Amb to U.S. Olexander Motsyk interviewed by @jaketapper via @cnn
			i)	Ukrainian Pres. says it's false "@cnnbrk: Russia says records indicate Ukrainian warplane was flying within 5 km of #MH17 on day of crash.
	Pro-R	Pro-U	j)	Russia has released some solid evidence to contradict @EliotHiggins + @bellingcat's #MH17 report. http://t.co/3leYfSoLJ3
			k)	RT @masamikuramoto: @MJoyce2244 The jets were seen by Russian military radar and Ukrainian eyewitnesses. #MH17 @Fossibilities @irina
			l)	RT @katehodal: Pro-Russia separatist says #MH17 bodies "weren't fresh" when found in Ukraine field,suggesting already dead b4takeoff
			m)	RT @NinaByzantina: #MH17 redux: 1) #Kolomoisky admits involvement URL 2) gets $1.8B of #Ukraine's bailout funds
III	Pro-U	Pro-R	n)	#Russia again claiming that #MH17 was shot down by air-to-air missile, which of course wasn't russian-made. #LOL URL
			o)	RT @20committee: New Moscow line is #MH17 was shot down by a Ukrainian fighter. With an LGBT pilot, no doubt.
	Pro-R	Pro-U	q)	RT @merahza: If you believe the pro Russia rebels shot #MH17 then you'll believe Justine Bieber is the next US President and that Coke is a
			q)	So what @AC360 is implying is that #US imposed sanctions on #Russia, so in turn they shot down a #Malaysia jet carrying #Dutch people? #MH17
			r)	RT @GrahamWP_UK: #MH17 1. A man on sofa watching YouTube thinks it was a 'separatist BUK'. 2. Man on site for over 25 hours doesn't.

Table 4: Examples for the different error categories. Error category I are cases where the correct class can easily be inferred from the text. For error category II, the correct class can be inferred from the text with event-specific knowledge. For error category III, it is necessary to resolve humour/satire in order to infer the intended meaning that the speaker wants to communicate.

know that the assumption is absurd. Example s) requires to evaluate that the speaker thinks people on site are trusted more than people at home.

From the error analysis, we conclude that category I errors need further investigation, as here the model makes mistakes on seemingly easy instances. This might be due to the model not being able to correctly represent Twitter specific language or unknown words, such as *Eukraine* in example e). Category II and III errors are harder to avoid and could be improved by applying reasoning (Wang and Cohen, 2015) or irony detection methods (Van Hee et al., 2018).

9 Integrating Automatic Predictions into the Retweet Network

Finally, we apply the CNN classifier to label new edges in Golovchenko et al. (2018)'s retweet network, which is shown in Figure 2. The retweet network is a graph that contains users as nodes and an edge between two users if the users are retweeting each other.[14] In order to track the flow of polarized information, Golovchenko et al. (2018) label an edge as polarized if at least one tweet contained in the edge was manually annotated as

[14]Golovchenko et al. (2018) use the k10 core of the network, which is the maximal subset of nodes and edges, such that all included nodes are connected to at least k other nodes (Seidman, 1983), i.e. all users in the network have interacted with at least 10 other users.

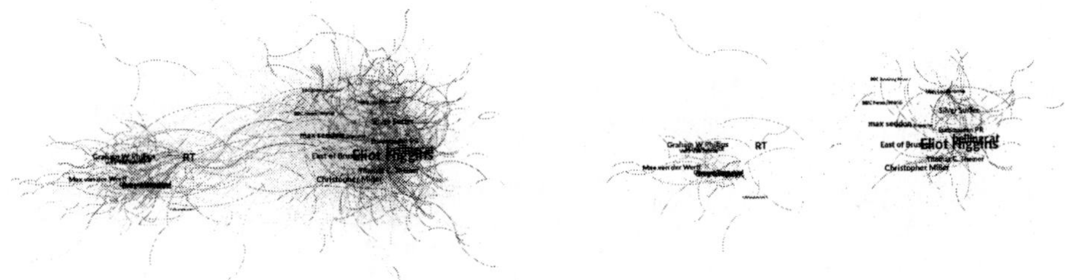

Figure 2: The left plot shows the original k10 retweet network as computed by Golovchenko et al. (2018) together with the new edges that were added after manually re-annotating the classifier predictions. The right plot only visualizes the new edges that we could add by filtering the classifier predictions. Pro-Russian edges are colored in red, pro-Ukrainian edges are colored in dark blue and neutral edges are colored in grey. Both plots were made using The Force Atlas 2 layout in gephi (Bastian et al., 2009).

pro-Russian or pro-Ukrainian. While the network shows a clear polarization, only a small subset of the edges present in the network are labeled (see Table 5).

Automatic polarity prediction of tweets can help the analysis in two ways. Either, we can label a previously unlabeled edge, or we can verify/confirm the manual labeling of an edge, by labeling additional tweets that are comprised in the edge.

9.1 Predicting Polarized Edges

In order to get high precision predictions for unlabeled tweets, we choose the probability thresholds for predicting a pro-Russian or pro-Ukrainian tweet such that the classifier would achieve 80% precision on the test splits (recall at this precision level is 23%). Table 5 shows the amount of polarized edges we can predict at this precision level. Upon manual inspection, we however find that the quality of predictions is lower than estimated. Hence, we manually re-annotate the pro-Russian and pro-Ukrainian predictions according to the official annotation guidelines used by (Golovchenko et al., 2018). This way, we can label 77 new pro-Russian edges by looking at 415 tweets, which means that 19% of the candidates are hits. For the pro-Ukrainian class, we can label 110 new edges by looking at 611 tweets (18% hits). Hence even though the quality of the classifier predictions is too low to be integrated into the network analysis right away, the classifier drastically facilitates the annotation process for human annotators compared to annotating unfiltered tweets (from the original labels we infer that for unfiltered tweets, only 6% are hits for the pro-Russian class, and 11% for the pro-Ukrainian class).

	Pro-R	Pro-U	Neutral	Total
# labeled edges in k10	270	678	2193	3141
# candidate edges	349	488	-	873
# added after filtering predictions	**77**	**110**	-	187

Table 5: Number of labeled edges in the k10 network before and after augmentation with predicted labels. Candidates are previously unlabeled edges for which the model makes a confident prediction. The total number of edges in the network is 24,602.

10   Conclusion

In this work, we investigated the usefulness of text classifiers to detect pro-Russian and pro-Ukrainian framing in tweets related to the MH17 crash, and to which extent classifier predictions can be relied on for producing high quality annotations. From our classification experiments, we conclude that the real-world applicability of text classifiers for labeling polarized tweets in a retweet network is restricted to pre-filtering tweets for manual annotation. However, if used as a filter, the classifier can significantly speed up the annotation process, making large-scale content analysis more feasible.

Acknowledgements

We thank the anonymous reviewers for their helpful comments. The research was carried out as part of the 'Digital Disinformation' project, which was directed by Rebecca Adler-Nissen and funded by the Carlsberg Foundation (project number CF16-0012).

References

Isabelle Augenstein, Tim Rocktäschel, Andreas Vlachos, and Kalina Bontcheva. 2016. Stance Detection with Bidirectional Conditional Encoding. In *Proceedings of EMNLP*.

Mathieu Bastian, Sebastien Heymann, and Mathieu Jacomy. 2009. Gephi: An open source software for exploring and manipulating networks.

Piotr Bojanowski, Edouard Grave, Armand Joulin, and Tomas Mikolov. 2017. Enriching word vectors with subword information. *Transactions of the Association for Computational Linguistics*, 5:135–146.

Amber E. Boydstun, Dallas Card, Justin H. Gross, Philip Resnik, and Noah A. Smith. 2014. Tracking the Development of Media Frames within and across Policy Issues. In *Proceedings of APSA*.

Dallas Card, Amber E. Boydstun, Justin H. Gross, Philip Resnik, and Noah A. Smith. 2015. The Media Frames Corpus: Annotations of Frames Across Issues. In *Proceedings of ACL*, pages 438–444.

Noam Chomsky and Edward Herman. 1988. Manufacturing Consent New York. *Pantheon*.

Bhuwan Dhingra, Zhong Zhou, Dylan Fitzpatrick, Michael Muehl, and William Cohen. 2016. Tweet2Vec: Character-Based Distributed Representations for Social Media. In *Proceedings of the 54th Annual Meeting of the Association for Computational Linguistics (Volume 2: Short Papers)*, pages 269–274, Berlin, Germany. Association for Computational Linguistics.

Miles Efron. 2010. Hashtag retrieval in a microblogging environment. In *Proceedings of the 33rd international ACM SIGIR conference on Research and development in information retrieval*, pages 787–788. ACM.

Don Fallis. 2015. What is disinformation? *Library Trends*, 63(3):401–426.

Anjalie Field, Doron Kliger, Shuly Wintner, Jennifer Pan, Dan Jurafsky, and Yulia Tsvetkov. 2018. Framing and Agenda-setting in Russian News: a Computational Analysis of Intricate Political Strategies. In *Proceedings of EMNLP*, pages 3570–3580. Association for Computational Linguistics.

John D. Gallacher, Vlad Barash, Philip N. Howard, and John Kelly. 2018. Junk news on military affairs and national security: Social media disinformation campaigns against us military personnel and veterans. *ArXiv*, abs/1802.03572.

Fréderic Godin, Viktor Slavkovikj, Wesley De Neve, Benjamin Schrauwen, and Rik Van de Walle. 2013. Using topic models for twitter hashtag recommendation. In *Proceedings of the 22nd International Conference on World Wide Web*, pages 593–596. ACM.

Yevgeniy Golovchenko, Mareike Hartmann, and Rebecca Adler-Nissen. 2018. State, media and civil society in the information warfare over Ukraine: citizen curators of digital disinformation. *International Affairs*, 94(5):975–994.

Nir Grinberg, Kenneth Joseph, Lisa Friedland, Briony Swire, and David Lazer. 2019. Fake news on twitter during the 2016 u.s. presidential election. *Science*, 363:374–378.

Andrew Guess, Jonathan Nagler, and Joshua Tucker. 2019. Less than you think: Prevalence and predictors of fake news dissemination on facebook. In *Science advances*.

Like Harding. 2019. Three Russians and one Ukrainian to face MH17 murder charges. *The Guardian*.

Mareike Hartmann, Tallulah Jansen, Isabelle Augenstein, and Anders Søgaard. 2019. Issue Framing in Online Discussion Fora. In *Proceedings of the 2019 Conference of the North American Chapter of the Association for Computational Linguistics: Human Language Technologies, Volume 1 (Long and Short Papers)*, pages 1401–1407.

Kazi Saidul Hasan and Vincent Ng. 2013. Stance Classification of Ideological Debates: Data, Models, Features, and Constraints. In *Proceedings of the Sixth International Joint Conference on Natural Language Processing*, pages 1348–1356, Nagoya, Japan. Asian Federation of Natural Language Processing.

Frederik Hjorth and Rebecca Adler-Nissen. 2019. Ideological Asymmetry in the Reach of Pro-Russian Digital Disinformation to United States Audiences. *Journal of Communication*, 69(2):168–192.

Philip N Howard, Bharath Ganesh, Dimitra Liotsiou, John Kelly, and Camille François. 2018. *The IRA, social media and political polarization in the United States, 2012-2018*. University of Oxford.

Yangfeng Ji and Noah Smith. 2017. Neural Discourse Structure for Text Categorization. In *Proceedings of ACL*.

Kristen Johnson, Di Jin, and Dan Goldwasser. 2017. Leveraging Behavioral and Social Information for Weakly Supervised Collective Classification of Political Discourse on Twitter. In *Proceedings of ACL*.

Armand Joulin, Piotr Bojanowski, Tomas Mikolov, Hervé Jégou, and Edouard Grave. 2018. Loss in translation: Learning bilingual word mapping with a retrieval criterion. In *Proceedings of the 2018 Conference on Empirical Methods in Natural Language Processing*.

Garth S. Jowett and Victoria O'donnell. 2014. *Propaganda & persuasion*. Sage.

John Kelly, Vladimir Barash, Karina Alexanyan, Bruce Etling, Robert Faris, Urs Gasser, and John G Palfrey. 2012. Mapping Russian Twitter. *Berkman Center Research Publication*, (2012-3).

Yoon Kim. 2014. Convolutional Neural Networks for Sentence Classification. In *Proceedings of the 2014 Conference on Empirical Methods in Natural Language Processing (EMNLP)*, pages 1746–1751.

Nona Naderi and Graeme Hirst. 2017. Classifying Frames at the Sentence Level in News Articles. In *Proceedings of RANLP*, pages 536–542.

Sarah Oates. 2016. Russian media in the digital age: Propaganda rewired. *Russian Politics*, 1(4):398–417.

F. Pedregosa, G. Varoquaux, A. Gramfort, V. Michel, B. Thirion, O. Grisel, M. Blondel, P. Prettenhofer, R. Weiss, V. Dubourg, J. Vanderplas, A. Passos, D. Cournapeau, M. Brucher, M. Perrot, and E. Duchesnay. 2011. Scikit-learn: Machine Learning in Python. *Journal of Machine Learning Research*, 12:2825–2830.

Peter Pomerantsev and Michael Weiss. 2014. *The menace of unreality: How the Kremlin weaponizes information, culture and money.*

Peng Qi, Timothy Dozat, Yuhao Zhang, and Christopher D Manning. 2018. Universal Dependency Parsing from Scratch. In *Proceedings of the {CoNLL} 2018 Shared Task: Multilingual Parsing from Raw Text to Universal Dependencies*, pages 160–170, Brussels, Belgium. Association for Computational Linguistics.

Cícero dos Santos and Maíra Gatti. 2014. Deep Convolutional Neural Networks for Sentiment Analysis of Short Texts. In *Proceedings of COLING 2014, the 25th International Conference on Computational Linguistics: Technical Papers*, pages 69–78, Dublin, Ireland. Dublin City University and Association for Computational Linguistics.

Stephen B. Seidman. 1983. Network structure and minimum degree. *Social Networks*, 5(3):269 – 287.

Philip M. Taylor. 2003. Munitions of the Mind. *A history of propaganda from the ancient world.*

Oren Tsur, Dan Calacci, and David Lazer. 2015. A Frame of Mind: Using Statistical Models for Detection of Framing and Agenda Setting Campaigns. In *Proceedings of ACL-IJCNLP*, pages 1629–1638. Association for Computational Linguistics.

Cynthia Van Hee, Els Lefever, and Véronique Hoste. 2018. SemEval-2018 Task 3: Irony Detection in English Tweets. In *Proceedings of The 12th International Workshop on Semantic Evaluation*, pages 39–50, New Orleans, Louisiana. Association for Computational Linguistics.

Marilyn Walker, Pranav Anand, Rob Abbott, and Ricky Grant. 2012. Stance Classification using Dialogic Properties of Persuasion. In *Proceedings of the 2012 Conference of the North American Chapter of the Association for Computational Linguistics: Human Language Technologies*, pages 592–596, Montréal, Canada. Association for Computational Linguistics.

William Yang Wang and William W Cohen. 2015. Joint information extraction and reasoning: A scalable statistical relational learning approach. In *Proceedings of the 53rd Annual Meeting of the Association for Computational Linguistics and the 7th International Joint Conference on Natural Language Processing (Volume 1: Long Papers)*, pages 355–364.

Arkaitz Zubiaga, Elena Kochkina, Maria Liakata, Rob Procter, Michal Lukasik, Kalina Bontcheva, Trevor Cohn, and Isabelle Augenstein. 2018. Discourse-aware rumour stance classification in social media using sequential classifiers. *Inf. Process. Manage.*, 54(2):273–290.

Arkaitz Zubiaga, Maria Liakata, Rob Procter, Geraldine Wong Sak Hoi, and Peter Tolmie. 2016. Analysing how people orient to and spread rumours in social media by looking at conversational threads. *PloS one*, 11(3):e0150989.

ArgDiver: Generating Sentential Arguments from Diverse Perspectives on Controversial Topic

ChaeHun Park   **Wonsuk Yang**   **Jong C. Park**[†]
School of Computing
Korea Advanced Institute of Science and Technology
{ddehun, derrick0511, park}@nlp.kaist.ac.kr

Abstract

Considering diverse aspects of an argumentative issue is an essential step for mitigating a biased opinion and making reasonable decisions. A related generation model can produce flexible results that cover a wide range of topics, compared to the retrieval-based method that may show unstable performance for unseen data. In this paper, we study the problem of generating sentential arguments from multiple perspectives, and propose a neural method to address this problem. Our model, ArgDiver (Argument generation model from <u>Diver</u>se perspectives), in a way a conversational system, successfully generates high-quality sentential arguments. At the same time, the automatically generated arguments by our model show a higher diversity than those generated by any other baseline models. We believe that our work provides evidence for the potential of a good generation model in providing diverse perspectives on a controversial topic.

1 Introduction

If one wants to address a potentially controversial issue, it is important to consider all of its aspects. When there are many such issues, some means of automating the process are called for. Automatically providing diverse aspects of an argumentative topic has thus received much attention. For instance, Wachsmuth et al. (2017) and Stab et al. (2018) developed a search engine for various arguments, while distinguishing the stance of each for a given claim. Ajjour et al. (2018) retrieved related arguments on a given topic, mapped the arguments to a topic space, and visualized such arguments within the topic space according to their distribution and their topical tendency.

These researches on a retrieval-based system have been very active, such as retrieving claims

from documents (Levy et al., 2014; Lippi and Torroni, 2015, 2016) and discovering multiple viewpoints from an online debate (Trabelsi and Zaiane, 2018). As the outputs of these retrieval-based systems are based on sentences originally written by a human writer (as implied in the name "retrieval"), their outputs are often quite diverse and of high-quality.

However, a retrieval-based system does not have sufficient flexibility towards input with missing keywords or topics unseen to the database on which the system is based. Therefore, the performance of a retrieval-based system is bound by the coverage of the database. In response, a generation system has recently been looked into for argument mining. Wang and Ling (2016) summarized arguments to show only important contents in large text. Hua and Wang (2018) and Hua et al. (2019) generated counter-arguments for a given statement. Hidey and McKeown (2019) edited an original claim from the Reddit comments to generate contrastive claims. Online review generation, taking into account the personality of each e-commerce user, has also been actively studied (Ni and McAuley, 2018; Li et al., 2019). Well-trained generation-based systems could generate the results relatively independent of the coverage of the training data, since these systems could be generalized easily for an unseen dataset.

Still, a common problem that generation-based systems suffer from is that they often provide too generic output regardless of the input text (e.g., "I don't know.", "I don't agree with you."). Also, a popular sequence-to-sequence (Seq2Seq) framework (Sutskever et al., 2014) for various text generation tasks is designed to generate only one output from an input (*one-to-one*). Therefore, it is hard to model a *one-to-many* relationship, which is arguably more suitable for argument generation as a real-world argument may have multiple per-

---

[†] Corresponding author

Proceedings of the 2nd Workshop on NLP for Internet Freedom: Censorship, Disinformation, and Propaganda, pages 56–65
Hong Kong, China, November 4, 2019 ©2019 Association for Computational Linguistics

Claim	This House believes university education should be free.
Sentential argument 1	Individuals have a right to the experience of higher education.
Sentential argument 2	The state benefits from the skills of a university educated populace.
Sentential argument 3	The cost to the state is far too great to sustain universal free education.
Sentential argument 4	State control of acceptance and curriculum criteria has negative effects.

Table 1: Example of a claim and its diverse sentential arguments.

spectives.

In this paper, we describe a model called ArgDiver, which stands for Argument generation model from Diverse perspectives, to overcome the limitations above of a generation-based argumentation system. For a given claim, ArgDiver generates multiple sentential arguments that cover diverse perspectives on the given claim. Table 1 shows an example[1] of the input and outputs of our system. More specifically, given a claim in favor of free university education, sentential arguments 1 and 2 support the claim, considering the right for higher education and benefits of the state, respectively. On the other hand, sentential arguments 3 and 4 are against the claim, considering the financial burden of the state and the negative effects of the intervention by the state, respectively. We understand that diverse perspectives of this kind should be provided with deep and varied stances, not only with a binary stance, towards given claims.

Our model adopts a Seq2Seq framework and introduces latent mechanisms based on the hypothesis that each latent mechanism may be matched with one perspective (Zhou et al., 2017, 2018; Tao et al., 2018; Gao et al., 2019; Chen et al., 2019a). We present a model that is trained by simply selecting a latent mechanism to optimize the model towards each target argument. Our model can avoid the generation of redundant outputs and be trained with a more accurate optimization strategy.

We use the PERSPECTRUM dataset proposed by Chen et al. (2019b). This dataset consists of pairs of one claim sentence (e.g., "Animals should have lawful rights.") and more than one cluster of

sentential arguments (e.g., "Animals are equal to human beings.", "Animals have no interest or rationality."). Each cluster contains more than one sentential argument that share the same perspective within the cluster. In our research, we use a claim sentence as the input sequence of the model and each sentential argument as a target sequence of the model.

We evaluate our model with two measures, a) the quality of each of the generated sentential arguments, and b) their diversities. For the generation quality, we use BLEU score (Papineni et al., 2002) and three word embedding based metrics (Liu et al., 2016). For diversity, we use Dist-1/2 metric (Li et al., 2016) and a newly proposed metric. Experimental results show that our model generates sentential arguments of quality comparable to that of strong baseline models. Furthermore, our model generates more diverse sentential arguments than the baseline models.

The rest of this paper is organized as follows. We describe the related work in Section 2 and present our neural model in Section 3. We then describe the experimental settings and results in Sections 4 and 5, respectively. Finally, we conclude our work in Section 6.

2 Related Work

2.1 Argumentative Text Generation

Argumentative text generation is an active research area. Paul and Girju (2010) detected various contrastive viewpoints from an argumentative text by summarization. Le et al. (2018) proposed a chatbot to interact and debate with people with both retrieval-based and generation-based methods. Hua and Wang (2018) and Hua et al. (2019) generated counter-arguments given a statement on a controversial topic. They used an external knowledge (e.g., Wikipedia) to enrich their model. Hidey and McKeown (2019) edited the original claim semantically to generate a contrastive claim. Wachsmuth et al. (2018) and Khatib et al. (2017) discovered effective strategies and patterns that enhance persuasive argumentation. The most relevant work to the present research would be a retrieval-based system by Sato et al. (2015) that collects relevant sentences with frequently mentioned topics for debate (e.g., pollution, disease, poverty), and reorders them to offer related arguments. However, their system requires a pre-defined topic, a dictionary, and rules,

---

[1] https://idebate.org/debatabase

unlike ours.

2.2 Response Generation

Recently, neural generation models built upon a Seq2Seq framework (Sutskever et al., 2014) have been widely used in many text generation tasks, such as machine translation, document summarization and response generation (Bahdanau et al., 2015; Luong et al., 2015; Vinyals and Le, 2015; Nallapati et al., 2016; Xing et al., 2017). A few of them incorporate latent mechanisms to model the diversity of acceptable responses and one-to-many relationships. (Zhou et al., 2017, 2018) proposed an augmented Seq2Seq model with multiple latent mechanism embedding. Gao et al. (2019) used latent keywords as an additional factor to generate multiple responses and trained a model using a reinforcement learning algorithm. Tao et al. (2018) proposed a multi-head attention mechanism with a Seq2Seq model to attend various semantic aspects of an input text, using the heads to generate multiple responses. Chen et al. (2019a) claimed the importance of accurate optimization using a latent mechanism while proposing a posterior mapping selection that considers both the input text and target responses.

3 Method

3.1 Overview of ArgDiver

Our model is based on a neural Seq2Seq model with attention mechanism (Sutskever et al., 2014; Bahdanau et al., 2015). We extend this framework by inserting N different latent mechanisms to model the *one-to-many* relationship. Our model is trained to generate an independent sentential argument for a latent mechanism. In training, our model generates N different candidate arguments for a claim and uses only one of them using the minimum negative log-likelihood (NLL) for optimization. By this, our model can avoid general and redundant responses and each latent mechanism can help generate diverse arguments. In testing, each latent mechanism is utilized to generate a sentential argument. Our model may be understood as an extension of the model suggested by Zhou et al. (2017), in using latent mechanisms. Our model selects proper latent mechanisms to increase the diversity of the arguments that it generates.

3.2 Proposed Model

Assume a claim X and a group of related arguments P_1, P_2, P_3. Our proposed model takes a sequence of tokens within the claim $X = (x_1, x_2 \ldots, x_{|X|})$ as input, where x_i is a token at timestep i and $|X|$ is the length of the claim. Each token is passed to the word embedding layer and transformed into a fixed size word embedding vector $e(x_i)$. Each word embedding vector is then transformed into a hidden state h_i by one-layer bidirectional GRU (bi-GRU) encoder (Cho et al., 2014) as follows:

$$h_i = [\overrightarrow{h_i}; \overleftarrow{h_i}] \tag{1}$$

$$\overrightarrow{h_i} = GRU(\overrightarrow{h_{i-1}}, e(x_i)) \tag{2}$$

$$\overleftarrow{h_i} = GRU(\overleftarrow{h_{i+1}}, e(x_i)) \tag{3}$$

where $[\overrightarrow{h_i}; \overleftarrow{h_i}]]$ denotes the concatenation of forward and backward hidden states at timestep i, $\overrightarrow{h_i}$ and $\overleftarrow{h_i}$ are the forward and backward hidden states at timestep i, respectively. The last hidden states of both directions are then concatenated into $h = [\overrightarrow{h_{|x|}}; \overleftarrow{h_1}]]$. This vector is used as the final semantic representation of the input claim.

Our model uses one-layer unidirectional GRU as the decoder. The semantic representation of the claim is concatenated with randomly initialized N different latent mechanisms $M = (m_1, m_2 \ldots, m_N)$, to make N different semantic representations $H = ([h; m_1], [h; m_2], \ldots, [h; m_N])$. These concatenated representations are then used independently as N different initial states of the decoder.

The hidden state of the decoder is updated by an attention mechanism as proposed by Bahdanau et al. (2015):

$$s_{kt} = GRU(s_{kt-1}, c_{kt-1}, e(y_{t-1})); s_{k1} = h_k \tag{4}$$

$$c_{kt} = \sum_{i=1}^{|X|} a_{kti} h_i \tag{5}$$

$$a_{kti} = \frac{\exp(e_{kti})}{\sum_{j=1}^{|X|} \exp(e_{ktj})} \tag{6}$$

$$e_{kti} = v^T \tanh(W_h[s_{kt}; h_i]) \tag{7}$$

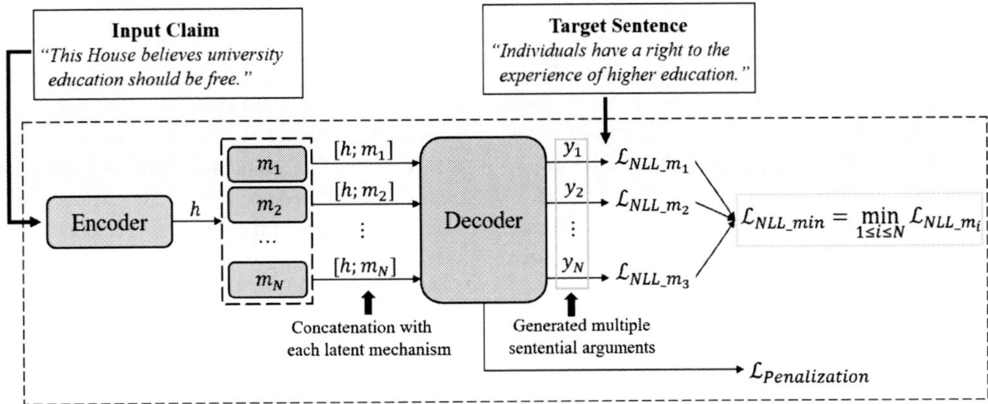

Figure 1: Overview of our sentential arguments generation model.

where s_{kt} denotes the hidden state at timestep t with the kth latent mechanism, and W_h and v^T are learnable parameters. $e(y_{t-1})$ is the word embedding vector of the target token at timestep $t - 1$. c_{kt-1} is the context vector at timestep $t - 1$ with the kth latent mechanism, which is the weighted sum of the hidden states of the encoder.

3.3 Objective Function

The remaining part of the model architecture is choosing the proper objective function to train our model for one target and multiple generated results. A general and typical approach in this case is calculating all losses of each generated argument and averaging them:

$$\mathcal{L}_{\text{NLL\_avg}} = -\frac{1}{N} \sum_{i=1}^{N} \log P(Y|X, m_i) \quad (8)$$

where NLL means negative log-likelihood and $P(Y|X, m_i)$ is the conditional probability that the model generates the target argument Y when input claim X and latent mechanism m_i are given. However, a naïve and rough optimization that does not select the appropriate latent mechanism to generate the given target argument may result in poor and redundant performance (Gao et al., 2019; Chen et al., 2019a). To avoid this, we select only one generated argument that shows minimum NLL for the given target argument to optimize our model, following Gao et al. (2019):

$$\mathcal{L}_{\text{NLL\_min}} = \min(\{-\log P(Y|X, m_1), \\ \ldots, -\log P(Y|X, m_N)\}) \quad (9)$$

This is based on the hypothesis that the most appropriate latent mechanism to generate the target

sentential argument would generate the best result with target (minimum NLL), compared with other generated results using other latent mechanisms. We compare the impacts of two different objective functions on performance in Section 5.2.

3.4 Penalty Term

We introduce an additional penalty term into the objective function, to regularize each latent mechanism to attend different semantic aspects of the input claim and avoid redundant outcomes within different latent mechanisms. We follow the work by Lin et al. (2017) and Tao et al. (2018), to encourage each latent mechanism to focus consistently on different and diverse semantic aspects of the input text. We accumulate the attention distribution of the decoder for each decoder timestep per latent mechanism, and normalize it by the length of the target sequence. We then concatenate them to make an $N \times |X|$ dimension matrix as follows:

$$A_k = \frac{\sum_{i=1}^{|Y|} a_{kti}}{|Y|} \in \mathbb{R}^{1 \times |X|} \quad (10)$$

$$A = \{A_1||A_2||\ldots||A_N\} \in \mathbb{R}^{N \times |X|} \quad (11)$$

where A_k is the result of mean pooling across the decoding timestep, where $\sum A_k$ is 1. We then introduce a Frobenius norm after dot product between A and A^T, and subtract an identity matrix from it:

$$\mathcal{L}_{\text{penalization}} = \left\| AA^T - I \right\|_F^2 \quad (12)$$

where $\|\cdot\|_F^2$ is the square after standard Frobenius norm and I is an identity matrix. Note that each element $AA^T[i, j]$ is the summation after element-wise product of the two attention distributions A_i and A_j. To minimize the term above, the diagonal elements and other elements of AA^T should be approximated to 1 and 0, respectively. This makes two attention distributions by different latent mechanisms to become more orthogonal to each other on the semantic space, encouraging each attention distribution to become more sparse.

The final objective function of our model is defined as:

$$\mathcal{L}_{\text{total}} = \lambda \mathcal{L}_{\text{NLL\_min}} + (1 - \lambda) \mathcal{L}_{\text{penalization}} \quad (13)$$

where $\mathcal{L}_{\text{NLL\_min}}$ is negative log likelihood that is defined in Equation 9 and $\mathcal{L}_{\text{penalization}}$ is defined in Equation 12. λ is the hyperparameter that controls the weight of two loss terms.

4 Experiments

4.1 Dataset

We use the PERSPECTRUM dataset (Chen et al., 2019b), which consists of a sentence that corresponds to a claim (e.g., "Animals should have lawful rights.") and more than one group of sentential arguments. Each argument group contains diverse sentential arguments regarding the claim (e.g., "Animals are equal to human beings.", "Animals have no interest or rationality."), and sentences in the same group share the same perspective towards the claim. We use the claim sentence as an input sequence and each sentence of every sentence group as the target sequence of our model. The dataset contains 907 claims and 11,164 related sentential arguments. We split the dataset into 541, 139, and 227 claims (and the corresponding sentential arguments) for training, validation, and testing, respectively. We use the split guidelines from Chen et al. (2019b), making sure that claims on the same topic are in the same partition. The split guidelines are to prevent the model from overfitting to a fixed set of keywords.

4.2 Compared Method

We compare our proposed model with several neural response generation models.

Seq2Seq + attention (Bahdanau et al., 2015): The standard sequence-to-sequence architecture with soft attention mechanism.

MMI-bidi (Li et al., 2016): Beam search using Maximum Mutual Information (MMI) to generate diverse outputs, by using both input sequence to output sequence and vice versa. We train another Seq2Seq model that generates input sequence from output sequence. We used the hyperparameters of λ=0.5, γ=1 and beam size=100.

MARM (Zhou et al., 2017): This model augments the Seq2Seq model with latent mechanism embedding to model the diversity of responding mechanisms. The number of latent mechanisms is set to 5.

CMHAM (Tao et al., 2018): This model uses multi-head attention with a Seq2Seq architecture and introduces a penalty term to encourage diverse attentions over different heads. We used 5 heads in our experiments.

MMPMS (Chen et al., 2019a): This model maps the semantic representation of the input text into multiple semantic spaces, and selects an appropriate mapping using both the input text and a target response. We set the number of mappings to 12.

ArgDiver: We use a model that is trained with the objective function in Equation 9 as our proposed model (**ArgDiver**). In addition, we compare our model with a variant that is trained with the objective function in Equation 8 (**ArgDiver**$_{\text{avg}}$) as described in Section 5.2.

4.3 Evaluation

We evaluate the models with two critics, the quality and the diversity of the generated sentential arguments for each.

For the quality, we use the following metrics. For the evaluation of a multiple argument generation system, we measure the score of each generated argument and report their average score.

BLEU-1/2 (Papineni et al., 2002): A widely used metric for the text generation task by measuring n-gram precision. We regard the target arguments that correspond to an input claim as the multiple references to calculate the score.

Embedding Average/Greedy/Extreme (Liu et al., 2016): These metrics evaluate results based on the semantic similarity between hypothesis and references, using a semantic representation by word embedding. These metrics take into account the diversity of a possible hypothesis and have been adopted for the evaluation of a conversation system (Xu et al., 2017; Tao et al., 2018).

For the diversity, we use the following metrics.

Dist-1/2 (Li et al., 2016): The number of unique unigrams/bigrams within a sentence normalized

Method	BLEU-1	BLEU-2	Embedding Average	Embedding Greedy	Embedding Extreme
Seq2Seq	0.3189	0.0947	<u>0.8489</u>	0.6198	0.4142
MMI-bidi	0.2263	0.0755	**0.8660**	0.6507	0.3971
MARM	0.2352	0.0099	0.7875	**0.6707**	**0.4497**
CMHAM	<u>0.3227</u>	**0.1009**	0.8334	0.6192	0.4069
MMPMS	0.2676	0.0725	0.8162	<u>0.6256</u>	<u>0.4186</u>
ArgDiver	**0.3268**	<u>0.0964</u>	0.8107	0.6002	0.4146

Table 2: Automatic evaluation results on generation quality. The highest and second highest scores are highlighted by bold and underline, respectively, for each metric.

Method	Dist-1	Dist-2	Dist-1-within	Dist-2-within
Seq2Seq	0.1230	0.2697	0.1624	0.2903
MMI-bidi	0.0707	0.2014	0.0868	0.1757
MARM	0.0456	0.0753	0.0377	0.1200
CMHAM	<u>0.1418</u>	**0.3236**	<u>0.3222</u>	<u>0.5412</u>
MMPMS	0.0650	0.1376	0.1485	0.3389
ArgDiver	**0.1585**	<u>0.2909</u>	**0.3645**	**0.6134**

Table 3: Automatic evaluation results on diversity of generation. The highest and second highest scores are highlighted by bold and underline, respectively, for each metric.

by the total number of unigrams/bigrams.

Dist-1/2-within: To the best of our knowledge, there has been no widely used metric to measure the diversity among multiple generated texts. We propose a simple metric to measure the diversity within the generated texts from the given input text, namely, Dist-1/2-within. To this end, this metric is calculated by *(The sum of the numbers of unique n-grams for each result that does not occur in other results) / (The sum of all generated numbers of unigrams/bigrams).*

4.4 Implementation Details

We use a Tensorflow framework (Abadi et al., 2016) to implement our model and baselines. We adopt the pre-trained 300-dimensional Glove word embedding (Pennington et al., 2014) for the word embedding layer of each model. The vocabulary size is the same for all models and set as 50K. Stanford CoreNLP (Manning et al., 2014) is used to tokenize our dataset. We use 256-dimensional hidden states for encoder and 384-dimensional hidden states for decoder. We use a dropout on the GRU cells with a probability of 0.2 (Srivastava et al., 2014), and apply gradient clipping (Pascanu et al., 2013) with a maximum norm of 3. The maximum numbers of tokens for encoder and decoder are set both to 50 and the batch size is set to 16 for all models. We use Adam optimizer (Kingma and Ba, 2015), with the initial learning rate set to 0.0005. In our model, the number and the dimen-

sion of the latent mechanism are set to 5 and 128, respectively. We initialized each of the vectors that represent latent mechanisms to a uniform distribution over [-0.001, 0.001]. We use beam search for generation, where the beam size is set to 10, except for the MMI-bidi model. We pre-train the weights of our encoder and decoder with the Wikitext 103 dataset proposed by Merity et al. (2017), and use it to initialize the weights of all baseline models and ours. We set λ in Equation 13 as 0.5.

5 Results

5.1 Overall Performance

Table 2 shows the evaluation results of each model in terms of generation quality using BLEU score and word embedding based metrics. We can see that our model achieves competitive performance in nearly all metrics. In BLEU score, our model ArgDiver and CMHAM outperform other baseline models. For the word embedding metrics, however, the two models show relatively low performance.

The evaluation results about the diversity of the generation are shown in Table 3. We see that ArgDiver achieves the best performance in three metrics (Dist-1, Dist-1/2-within), and the second performance in one metric (Dist-2). Except for our model, CMHAM outperforms other baselines in all metrics. By this, we can see that our model can generate diverse and multiple arguments to ex-

Method	BLEU-1	BLEU-2	Embedding Average	Embedding Greedy	Embedding Extreme
ArgDiver$_{\text{avg}}$	0.3376	0.1100	0.8561	0.6335	0.4270
ArgDiver	0.3268	0.0964	0.8107	0.6002	0.4146

Table 4: Automatic evaluation results on generation quality with different objective functions.

Method	Dist-1	Dist-2	Dist-1-within	Dist-2-within
ArgDiver$_{\text{avg}}$	0.0976	0.1611	0.0159	0.0261
ArgDiver	0.1585	0.2909	0.3645	0.6134

Table 5: Automatic evaluation results on diversity of generation with different objective functions.

amine diverse aspects of a given claim.

5.2 Effect of Objective Function

As we described in Section 3.3, we compare the impact on performance of two different objective functions. Table 4 and Table 5 show the evaluation results of our models in terms of quality and diversity of generated text, respectively. In terms of the generation quality, ArgDiver$_{\text{avg}}$ shows similar but slightly better performance than ArgDiver. Meanwhile, ArgDiver shows more promising results than ArgDiver$_{\text{avg}}$ against the diversity metric. In particular, we see that each latent mechanism generates exactly the same texts to the given claim about 74% for ArgDiver$_{\text{avg}}$, though only about 6% for ArgDiver. These results indicate that ArgDiver$_{\text{avg}}$ fails to utilize the full capacity of latent mechanisms, and goes back to the vanilla Seq2Seq model. By this, we postulate that the accurate optimization of a model considering the difference of each latent mechanism is the key for generating truly diverse arguments.

5.3 Case Study

The sample generated sentential arguments by each model and by a human are displayed in Table 6. The human-generated arguments are from the PERSPECTRUM dataset. The results of Seq2Seq model begin with the same phrase, and make a difference by selecting different words at the ending steps of decoding. In case of the MMPMS model, some of the mappings generate meaningless and repeated results. This may be due to the absence of a posterior mapping selection as it requires the target argument for the generation to proceed, which is absent in the testing scenario. CMHAM model and ArgDiver generate diverse and high quality multiple arguments. Including the CMHAM model and our proposed model, exactly the same texts with different latent mecha-

nisms are often found in the results. This may point out the limitation of a small size of the dataset and the necessity of advanced approaches, which is left for future work.

5.4 Limitations and Future Work

In this subsection, we discuss the limitations of the current work and possible ways to improve our proposal as future work.

For the prior distribution of latent mechanisms, our current model uses all latent mechanisms to generate individual sentential arguments for all kinds of claim. It is yet reasonable to posit that the appropriate degree of each latent mechanism for its use in generation may depend on the topic of the given claim. As future work, we plan to devise a model which considers the probability by which each latent mechanism would be used to generate sentential arguments with the given claim.

For the low interpretability of latent mechanism, ideal results of our model would be that there exist shared characteristics in the generated sentential arguments with the same latent mechanism and a different input claim. However, it is hard to observe these characteristics within the generated results of our model. In addition, the latent mechanism sometimes tends to generate the output by memorizing some of the frequent phrases in the dataset (e.g., "This is the right of (. . .).", "There is no need for compulsion."). One of the possible reasons is that each latent mechanism focuses on the syntactic difference of each sentential argument, rather than semantic differences such as topics or characteristics.

As future work, we plan to present an improved model to distinguish the semantic and syntactic factors of each perspective. One possibility is to model the latent personality in the sentential arguments. For instance, the person who is interested in environmental issues is more likely to have a

Claim	We should fear the power of government over the internet.
Human	Internet regulation is necessary to ensure a safe internet.
	Internet regulation is a euphemism for censorship.
	Internet governance is necessary to combat heinous crimes committed via the internet.
	Internet regulation is an attempt by big interest groups to regulate the internet in their favour.
Seq2Seq	There is no reason to have the negative impact on nationalist sentiment.
	There is no reason to have the negative impact on them.
	There is no reason to have the negative impact on politics.
	There is no reason to have the problems in the environment.
	There is no reason to have the negative impact on nationalist footprint.
CMHAM	Everyone should be allowed free speech.
	It is clear to impose their religion!
	The American people would be more accountable for the council.
	The American people would be more accountable for the council.
	This is a part of a crime and should not be the state.
MMPMS	The result of all should have the rights to have the right to have the right to all their own decisions.
	Domestic protect the vote.
	Make these equal off taken off against equal off countries would make all these rights as illegal as as as as (…)
	The freedom of the economy would have the freedom of the freedom of the freedom of the freedom of the (…)
	It would have a negative impact .
ArgDiver	National sovereignty would result in a government's freedom of expression.
	The government should not be celebrated.
	It is a necessary for national security.
	It's conceivable to the wrong hands.
	The government is a best way to have a universal right to have a universal right to practice.

Table 6: Sample arguments of a claim generated by human and models.

relatively predictable and specific perspective on certain topics than those who are not. The generation model considering these aspects could provide more human-like arguments with a wide coverage of many persons' characteristics.

Another possibility would be for our model to incorporate the background knowledge to generate the arguments. We believe that such an explicit provision of the background knowledge to the model can increase the informativeness and the relevance of the generated arguments to the input claim.

6 Conclusion

In this work, we looked into a new task that generates diverse and multiple sentential arguments with the given claim on a controversial topic. To address this task, we introduced a new model based on the Seq2Seq framework, called ArgDiver, to optimize each latent mechanism more properly and generate diverse outputs. Experimental results confirm that diverse sentential arguments could be generated with high quality, and that our model shows higher diversity than any other baseline models.

Acknowledgments

This work was supported by Institute for Information and communications Technology Promotion (IITP) grant funded by the Korea government MSIT) (No. 2018-0-00582-002, Prediction and augmentation of the credibility distribution via linguistic analysis and automated evidence document collection).

References

Martín Abadi, Paul Barham, Jianmin Chen, Zhifeng Chen, Andy Davis, Jeffrey Dean, Matthieu Devin, Sanjay Ghemawat, Geoffrey Irving, Michael Isard, et al. 2016. Tensorflow: A system for large-scale machine learning. In *12th USENIX Symposium on Operating Systems Design and Implementation (OSDI 16)*, pages 265–283.

Yamen Ajjour, Henning Wachsmuth, Dora Kiesel, Patrick Riehmann, Fan Fan, Giuliano Castiglia, Rosemary Adejoh, Bernd Fröhlich, and Benno Stein. 2018. Visualization of the topic space of argument search results in args. me. In *Proceedings of the EMNLP 2018: System Demonstrations*, pages 60–65.

Dzmitry Bahdanau, Kyunghyun Cho, and Yoshua Bengio. 2015. Neural machine translation by jointly learning to align and translate. In *Proceedings of the 3rd ICLR*.

Chaotao Chen, Jinhua Peng, Fan Wang, Jun Xu, and Hua Wu. 2019a. Generating multiple diverse responses with multi-mapping and posterior mapping selection. In *Proceedings of the 28th IJCAI*, pages 4918–4924.

Sihao Chen, Daniel Khashabi, Wenpeng Yin, Chris Callison-Burch, and Dan Roth. 2019b. Seeing things from a different angle: Discovering diverse perspectives about claims. In *Proceedings of the 17th NAACL-HLT*, pages 542–557.

Kyunghyun Cho, Bart van Merrienboer, Dzmitry Bahdanau, and Yoshua Bengio. 2014. On the properties of neural machine translation: Encoder-decoder approaches. In *Proceedings of SSST@EMNLP 2014, Eighth Workshop on Syntax, Semantics and Structure in Statistical Translation, Qatar, 25 October 2014*, pages 103–111.

Jun Gao, Wei Bi, Xiaojiang Liu, Junhui Li, and Shuming Shi. 2019. Generating multiple diverse responses for short-text conversation. In *Proceedings of the 33rd AAAI*, volume 33, pages 6383–6390.

Christopher Hidey and Kathy McKeown. 2019. Fixed that for you: Generating contrastive claims with semantic edits. In *Proceedings of the 17th NAACL-HLT*, pages 1756–1767.

Xinyu Hua, Zhe Hu, and Lu Wang. 2019. Argument generation with retrieval, planning, and realization. In *Proceedings of the 57th ACL*, pages 2661–2672, Florence, Italy.

Xinyu Hua and Lu Wang. 2018. Neural argument generation augmented with externally retrieved evidence. In *Proceedings of the 56th ACL*, pages 219–230.

Khalid Al Khatib, Henning Wachsmuth, Matthias Hagen, and Benno Stein. 2017. Patterns of argumentation strategies across topics. In *Proceedings of the EMNLP 2017*, pages 1351–1357.

Diederik P. Kingma and Jimmy Ba. 2015. Adam: A method for stochastic optimization. In *3rd International Conference on Learning Representations, ICLR 2015, San Diego, CA, USA, May 7-9, 2015, Conference Track Proceedings*.

Dieu-Thu Le, Cam Tu Nguyen, and Kim Anh Nguyen. 2018. Dave the debater: a retrieval-based and generative argumentative dialogue agent. In *Proceedings of the 5th Workshop on Argument Mining*, pages 121–130.

Ran Levy, Yonatan Bilu, Daniel Hershcovich, Ehud Aharoni, and Noam Slonim. 2014. Context dependent claim detection. In *Proceedings of the 25th COLING: Technical Papers*, pages 1489–1500.

Jiwei Li, Michel Galley, Chris Brockett, Jianfeng Gao, and Bill Dolan. 2016. A diversity-promoting objective function for neural conversation models. In *NAACL HLT, San Diego California, USA, June 12-17*, pages 110–119.

Piji Li, Zihao Wang, Lidong Bing, and Wai Lam. 2019. Persona-aware tips generation. In *Proceedings of the WWW 2019*, pages 1006–1016. ACM.

Zhouhan Lin, Minwei Feng, Cícero Nogueira dos Santos, Mo Yu, Bing Xiang, Bowen Zhou, and Yoshua Bengio. 2017. A structured self-attentive sentence embedding. In *5th ICLR, Toulon, France, April 24-26, 2017*.

Marco Lippi and Paolo Torroni. 2015. Context-independent claim detection for argument mining. In *Proceedings of the 24th IJCAI*.

Marco Lippi and Paolo Torroni. 2016. Argument mining from speech: Detecting claims in political debates. In *Proceedings of the 30th AAAI*.

Chia-Wei Liu, Ryan Lowe, Iulian Serban, Mike Noseworthy, Laurent Charlin, and Joelle Pineau. 2016. How not to evaluate your dialogue system: An empirical study of unsupervised evaluation metrics for dialogue response generation. In *Proceedings of the EMNLP 2016*, pages 2122–2132.

Thang Luong, Hieu Pham, and Christopher D. Manning. 2015. Effective approaches to attention-based neural machine translation. In *Proceedings of the EMNLP 2015*, pages 1412–1421.

Christopher D. Manning, Mihai Surdeanu, John Bauer, Jenny Finkel, Steven J. Bethard, and David McClosky. 2014. The Stanford CoreNLP natural language processing toolkit. In *ACL System Demonstrations*, pages 55–60.

Stephen Merity, Caiming Xiong, James Bradbury, and Richard Socher. 2017. Pointer sentinel mixture models. In *5th ICLR 2017, Toulon, France, April 24-26*.

Ramesh Nallapati, Bowen Zhou, Cicero dos Santos, Caglar Gulcehre, and Bing Xiang. 2016. Abstractive text summarization using sequence-to-sequence rnns and beyond. In *Proceedings of the 20th SIGNLL*, pages 280–290.

Jianmo Ni and Julian McAuley. 2018. Personalized review generation by expanding phrases and attending on aspect-aware representations. In *Proceedings of the 56th ACL*, pages 706–711.

Kishore Papineni, Salim Roukos, Todd Ward, and Wei-Jing Zhu. 2002. Bleu: a method for automatic evaluation of machine translation. In *Proceedings of the 40th ACL*, pages 311–318. Association for Computational Linguistics.

Razvan Pascanu, Tomas Mikolov, and Yoshua Bengio. 2013. On the difficulty of training recurrent neural networks. In *ICML*, pages 1310–1318.

Michael Paul and Roxana Girju. 2010. A two-dimensional topic-aspect model for discovering multi-faceted topics. In *Proceedings of the 24th AAAI*.

Jeffrey Pennington, Richard Socher, and Christopher D. Manning. 2014. Glove: Global vectors for word representation. In *Proceedings of the EMNLP 2014, October 25-29, 2014, Qatar*, pages 1532–1543.

Misa Sato, Kohsuke Yanai, Toshinori Miyoshi, Toshihiko Yanase, Makoto Iwayama, Qinghua Sun, and Yoshiki Niwa. 2015. End-to-end argument generation system in debating. In *Proceedings of the ACL-IJCNLP 2015: System Demonstrations*, pages 109–114.

Nitish Srivastava, Geoffrey E. Hinton, Alex Krizhevsky, Ilya Sutskever, and Ruslan Salakhutdinov. 2014. Dropout: a simple way to prevent neural networks from overfitting. *J. Mach. Learn. Res.*, 15(1):1929–1958.

Christian Stab, Johannes Daxenberger, Chris Stahlhut, Tristan Miller, Benjamin Schiller, Christopher Tauchmann, Steffen Eger, and Iryna Gurevych. 2018. Argumentext: Searching for arguments in heterogeneous sources. In *Proceedings of the 16th NAACL: Demonstrations*, pages 21–25.

Ilya Sutskever, Oriol Vinyals, and Quoc V Le. 2014. Sequence to sequence learning with neural networks. In *Proceedings of the 28th NIPS*, pages 3104–3112.

Chongyang Tao, Shen Gao, Mingyue Shang, Wei Wu, Dongyan Zhao, and Rui Yan. 2018. Get the point of my utterance! learning towards effective responses with multi-head attention mechanism. In *Proceedings of the 27th IJCAI*, pages 4418–4424.

Amine Trabelsi and Osmar R Zaiane. 2018. Unsupervised model for topic viewpoint discovery in online debates leveraging author interactions. In *Proceedings of the 12th ICWSM*.

Oriol Vinyals and Quoc V. Le. 2015. A neural conversational model. *CoRR*.

Henning Wachsmuth, Martin Potthast, Khalid Al Khatib, Yamen Ajjour, Jana Puschmann, Jiani Qu, Jonas Dorsch, Viorel Morari, Janek Bevendorff, and Benno Stein. 2017. Building an argument search engine for the web. In *Proceedings of the 4th Workshop on Argument Mining*, pages 49–59.

Henning Wachsmuth, Manfred Stede, Roxanne El Baff, Khalid Al Khatib, Maria Skeppstedt, and Benno Stein. 2018. Argumentation synthesis following rhetorical strategies. In *Proceedings of the 27th ICCL*, pages 3753–3765.

Lu Wang and Wang Ling. 2016. Neural network-based abstract generation for opinions and arguments. In *Proceedings of the 15th NAACL-HLT 2016*, pages 47–57.

Chen Xing, Wei Wu, Yu Wu, Jie Liu, Yalou Huang, Ming Zhou, and Wei-Ying Ma. 2017. Topic aware neural response generation. In *Proceedings of the 31st AAAI*.

Zhen Xu, Bingquan Liu, Baoxun Wang, Chengjie Sun, Xiaolong Wang, Zhuoran Wang, and Chao Qi. 2017. Neural response generation via GAN with an approximate embedding layer. In *Proceedings of the EMNLP 2017, Copenhagen, Denmark, September 9-11, 2017*, pages 617–626.

Ganbin Zhou, Ping Luo, Rongyu Cao, Fen Lin, Bo Chen, and Qing He. 2017. Mechanism-aware neural machine for dialogue response generation. In *Proceedings of the 31st AAAI*.

Ganbin Zhou, Ping Luo, Yijun Xiao, Fen Lin, Bo Chen, and Qing He. 2018. Elastic responding machine for dialog generation with dynamically mechanism selecting. In *Proceedings of the 32nd AAAI*.

Rumor Detection on Social Media: Datasets, Methods and Opportunities

Quanzhi Li, Qiong Zhang, Luo Si, Yingchi Liu
Alibaba Group, US
Bellevue, WA, USA
{quanzhi.li, qz.zhang, luo.si, yingchi.liu}@alibaba-inc.com

Abstract

Social media platforms have been used for information and news gathering, and they are very valuable in many applications. However, they also lead to the spreading of rumors and fake news. Many efforts have been taken to detect and debunk rumors on social media by analyzing their content and social context using machine learning techniques. This paper gives an overview of the recent studies in the rumor detection field. It provides a comprehensive list of datasets used for rumor detection, and reviews the important studies based on what types of information they exploit and the approaches they take. And more importantly, we also present several new directions for future research.

1 Introduction

Rumors sometimes may spread very quickly over social media platforms, and rumor detection has gained great interest in both academia and industry recently. Government authorities and social media platforms are also taking efforts to defeat the negative impacts of rumors. In the following sub sections, we first introduce the rumor detection definition, the problem statement, and user stance, an important concept for the rest of this paper.

1.1 Rumor Detection

Different publications may have different definitions for rumor. It is hard to do a head-to-head comparison between existing methods due to the lack of consistency. In this survey, a rumor is defined as a statement whose truth value is *true, unverified* or *false* (Qazvinian et al., 2011). When a rumor's veracity value is *false*, some studies call it *"false rumor"* or *"fake news"*. However, many previous studies give *"fake news"* a stricter definition: fake news is a news article published by a news outlet that is intentionally and verifiably false (Vosoughi et al., 2018; Shu et al.,

2017a; Cao et al., 2018). The focus of this study is rumor on social media, not fake news. There are also different definitions for *rumor detection*. In some studies, rumor detection is defined as determining if a story or online post is a rumor or non-rumor (i.e. a real story, a news article), and the task of determining the veracity of a rumor (*true, false* or *unverified*) is defined as rumor verification (Zubiaga et al., 2016; Kochkina et al., 2018). But in this survey paper, as well as in (Ma et al., 2016; Cao et al., 2018; Shu et al, 2017; Zhou et al., 2018), *rumor detection* is defined as determining the veracity value of a rumor. This means it is the same as *rumor verification* defined in some other studies.

1.2 Problem Statement

The rumor detection problem is defined as follow: A story x is defined as a set of n pieces of related messages $M = \{m_1, m_2, ..., m_n\}$. m_1 is the source message (post) that initiated the message chain, which could be a tree-structure having multiple branches. For each message m_i, it has attributes representing its content, such as text and image. Each message is also associated with a user who posted it. The user also has a set of attributes, including name, description, avatar image, past posts, etc. The rumor detection task is then defined as: Given a story x with its message set M and user set U, the rumor detection task aims to determine whether this story is *true, false* or *unverified* (or just *true* or *false* for datasets having just two labels). This definition formulates the rumor detection task as a veracity classification task. The definition is the same as the definition used in many studies (Cao et al., 2018; Shu et al, 2017b; Ma et al., 2016; Zhou et al., 2018).

1.3 User Stance

User responses to a source post (the first message) have been exploited in some rumor detection models. Most studies use four stance categories:

Proceedings of the 2nd Workshop on NLP for Internet Freedom: Censorship, Disinformation, and Propaganda, pages 66–75
Hong Kong, China, November 4, 2019 ©2019 Association for Computational Linguistics

Dataset	Total rumors (claims)	Text	User info	Time stamp	Propagation info	Platform	Description
PHEME-R	330	y	y	y	y	Twitter	Tweets from [Zubiaga et al., 2016]
PHEME	6425	y	y	y	y	Twitter	Tweets from [Kochkina et al., 2018]
Ma-Twitter	992	y	y	y		Twitter	Tweets from [Ma et al., 2016]
Ma-Weibo	4,664	y	y	y		Weibo	Weibo data from [Ma et al., 2016]
Twitter15	1,490	y	y	y	y	Twitter	Tweets from [Liu et al., 2015; Ma et al.,2016]
Twitter16	818	y	y	y	y	Twitter	Tweets from [Ma et al., 2017b]
BuzzFeedNews	2,282	y				Facebook	Facebook data from [Silverman et al., 2016]
SemEval19	325	y	y	y	y	Twitter, Reddit	SemEval 2019 Task 7 data set.
Kaggle Emergent	2145	y				Twitter, Facebook	Kaggle rumors based on Emergent.info
Kaggle Snopes	16.9K	y				Twitter, Facebook	Kaggle rumors based on Snopes.com
Facebook Hoax	15.5K	y	y	y		Facebook	Facebook data from [Tacchini et al., 2017]
Kaggle PolitiFact	2923	y	y	y	y	Twitter	Kaggle rumors based on PolitiFact
FakeNewsNet	23,196	y	y	y	y	Twitter	Dataset from [Shu et al., 2019], enhanced from PolitiFact and GossipCop

Table 1: Datasets for rumor detection and their properties

supporting, denying, querying and *commenting*. Some studies have explicitly used stance information in their rumor detection model, and have shown big performance improvement (Liu et al., 2015; Enayet and El-Beltagy, 2017; Ma et al., 2018a; Kochkina et al., 2018), including the two systems, (Enayet and El-Beltagy, 2017) and (Li et al., 2019a), that were ranked No. 1 in SemEval 2017 and SemEval 2019 rumor detection tasks, respectively. Stance detection is not the focus of this paper, but stance information has been used explicitly or implicitly in many rumor detection models, and in the next section we will also discuss some multi-task learning approaches that jointly learn stance detection and rumor detection models.

In the following sections, we will *1.* introduce a comprehensive list of datasets for rumor detection, *2.* discuss the research efforts categorized by the information and approaches they use, and *3.* present several directions for future research

2 Datasets and Evaluation Metrics

2.1 Datasets

Datasets could vary depending on what platforms the data are collected from, what types of contents are included, whether propagation information is recorded, and so on. Table 1 lists the datasets for rumor detection. There are also other datasets for fake news detection. Because this paper focuses on rumor detection on social media, and those datasets are only for fake news detection and do not have social context information (e.g. user responses, user data, and propagation information), so we did not list them here. The data of datasets in Table 1 are collected from four social media platforms: Twitter, Facebook, Reddit and Weibo. Weibo is a Chinese social media platform with over 400 million users, and it is very similar to Twitter. More than half of these datasets have three veracity labels: *true, false* and *unverified*. Others have only two labels: *true* and *false*. Among these datasets, PHEME-R has been used by SemEval 2017 rumor detection task and SemEval19 has been used by SemEval 2019 rumor detection task (Gorrell et al., 2019). The dataset links are listed below:

- *PHEME-R*:
  https://figshare.com/articles/PHEME_rumour_scheme_da taset_journalism_use_case/2068650
- *PHEME*:
  https://figshare.com/articles/PHEME_dataset_for_Rumou r_Detection_and_Veracity_Classification/6392078
- *Ma-Twitter*: http://alt.qcri.org/~wgao/data/rumdect.zip
- *Ma-Weibo*: http://alt.qcri.org/~wgao/data/rumdect.zip
- *Twitter15*:
  https://www.dropbox.com/s/7ewzdrbelpmrnxu/rumdetect 2017.zip?dl=0
- *Twitter16*:
  https://www.dropbox.com/s/7ewzdrbelpmrnxu/rumdetect 2017.zip?dl=0
- *BuzzFeedNews*: https://github.com/BuzzFeedNews/2016-10-fac\ebook-fact-check

- *SemEval19*:
  https://competitions.codalab.org/competitions/19938#lear n_the_details-overview
- *Kaggle Emergent*:
  https://www.kaggle.com/arminehn/rumor-citation
- *Kaggle Snopes*:
  https://www.kaggle.com/arminehn/rumor-citation
- *Facebook Hoax*: https://github.com/gabll/some-like-it-hoax/tree/master/dataset
- *Kaggle PolitiFact*:
  https://www.kaggle.com/arminehn/rumor-citation
- *FakeNewsNet*:
  https://github.com/KaiDMML/FakeNewsNet

2.2   Evaluation Metrics

Most existing approaches consider rumor detection as a classification problem. Usually it is either a binary (*true* or *false*) or a multi-class (*true, false* or *unverified*) classification problem. The evaluation metrics used the most are precision, recall, *F1* and accuracy measures. Because some datasets are skewed, Macro *F1* measure will provide a better view on the algorithm performance over all classes. Here we briefly describe them. For each class *C*, we calculate its precision (*p*), recall (*r*) and *F1* score as follow:

$$p = \frac{\text{no. of rumors predicetd as C correctly}}{\text{no. of rumors predicted as C}} \quad (1)$$

$$r = \frac{\text{no. of rumors predicetd as C correctly}}{\text{no. of rumors annotated as C}} \quad (2)$$

$$F1 = \frac{2*p*r}{p+r} \quad (3)$$

Consider all the classes together, then the Macro *F1* score is:

$$Macro\ F1 = \frac{1}{n} \sum_{i=1}^{n} F1_i \quad (4)$$

where *n* is the number of classes, and $F1_i$ is the score for class *i*. The overall accuracy for all the rumor types is:

$$accuracy = \frac{\text{no. of rumors predicetd correctly}}{\text{no. of rumors}} \quad (5)$$

3   Features and Approaches

In this section, we review previous studies based on the type of information they exploited in their models. The information for rumor detection can be categorized from several information dimensions: content, user, propagation path, and network. We will also give a brief overview for studies employing multi-task learning for stance detection and rumor detection, and introduce the contests for rumor detection. Table 2 presents the studies and their related information. From this table we can see that most studies have exploited text content, user information and propagation path. A few of them also explicitly incorporate user stance in their models. It also shows that almost all the most recent studies utilized neural networks in their models. Due to the space limitation, we just describe the representative studies in this paper.

3.1   Approaches Using Content Information

Textual Content. Text content is utilized by almost all the previous studies on rumor detection. It includes the source post and all user replies. According to deception style theory, the content style of deceptive information that aims to deceive readers should be somewhat different from that of the truth, e.g., using exaggerated expressions or strong emotions. And from user response text, we can also explore stance and opinion of users towards rumors.

Generally, text features can be grouped into attribute-based or structure-based features (Zhou and Zafarani, 2018). Attribute-based features include quantity (word, noun, verb, phrase, etc.), uncertainty (number of question mark, quantifiers, tentative terms, modal terms), subjectivity (percentage of subjective verbs, imperative commands), sentiment (positive/negative words, exclamation marks), diversity (unique content words, unique function words), and readability. Structure-based features include lexicon, syntax, semantic and discourse information, such as part-of-speech taggers, context-free grammar, and Linguistic Inquiry and Word Count (LIWC).

An early study from (Castillo et al., 2011) uses many text features in their model, such as the fraction of tweets with hashtags. These features and other additional text features are also used in other studies (Liu et al., 2015; Enayet and El-Beltagy, 2017; Li et al., 2019a; Ma et al., 2017; Li et al., 2019b). Kwon et al. (2013) also use LIWC dictionaries. Chua and Banerjee (2016) analyzed six categories of features: comprehensibility, sentiment, time orientation, quantitative details, writing style, and topic. Some important features reported were: negation words, past, present, future POS in the tweets, discrepancy, sweat and exclusion features. Textual content plays an important role in rumor detection, but most studies show that just utilizing text content is not enough.

Visual Content: Visual features (images or videos) have been shown to be an important indicator for rumor detection (Jin et al., 2017a; Jin

Study	Information Used						Approach
	Text	Visual	User	Propagation	Network	Explicitly using user stance	
[Castillo et al., 2011]	y		y	y			DT
[Chang et al., 2016]	y	y	y				Clustering
[Chen et al., 2016]	y		y	y		y	Anomaly detection, KNN
[Chua and Banerjee, 2016]	y						LR
[Enayet and El-Beltagy, 2017]	y		y			y	SVM
[Giasemidis et al., 2016]	y		y		y		DT
[Gupta et al., 2012]	y		y		y		Graph
[Gupta et al., 2013]		y	y		y		DT, Graph
[Jin et al., 2016]	y		y		y	y	Graph, LDA
[Kwon et al., 2013]	y		y	y			SVM, RF, LR
[Kwon et al., 2017]	y		y	y			SpikeM
[Li et al., 2016]	y		y	y			SVM
[Li et al., 2019]	y	y	y	y		y	Deep NN, LSTM
[Liu et al., 2015]	y	y	y			y	SVM
[Liu and Wu, 2018]	y			y			CNN, RNN
[Ma et al., 2017]	y			y			NN
[Ma et al., 2015]	y						SVM, RF, DT
[Ma et al., 2018a]	y			y			LSTM, multi-task
[Ma et al., 2018b]	y			y			Recursive NN
[Qin et al., 2016]	y						SVM
[Shu et al., 2017b]	y		y		y		NN
[Vosoughi, 2015]	y		y	y			HMM
[Wang and Terano, 2015]	y		y		y	y	Graph
[Wang et al., 2018]	y	y					CNN, Adversarial NN
[Wu et al., 2015]	y		y	y			SVM
[Yang et al., 2012]	y		y				SVM
[Yang et al., 2015]	y		y		y		Graph
[Yang et al., 2018]	y			y			CNN
[Zhang et al., 2018]	y		y		y		RNN

Table 2: Previous studies, used information, and methods. Note: SVM - support vector machine, RF - random forest, DT- decision tree, LR – logistic regression, KNN – k nearest neighbor, NN – neural network, HMM – hidden Markov model.

et al., 2017b; Shu et al., 2017a; Wang et al., 2018). Rumors exploit the individual vulnerabilities and often use sensational or fake images to provoke emotional user responses. There are two visual feature types: statistical features and content features. Statistical features include image/video count, image ratio, etc. (Gupta et al., 2013; Jin et al., 2017a; Jin et al., 2017b; Shu et al., 2017a; Liu et al., 2015; Li et al., 2019a; Li et al., 2019b; Shu et al., 2017). Visual content features include clarity score, coherence score, diversity score, similarity distribution histogram, etc. (Wang et al., 2018; Shu et al., 2017). Jin et al. (2017a; 2017b) use various visual content and statistical features for rumor detection. Wang et al. (2018) employ a multi-modal feature extractor to extract the textual and visual features from posts, and then the textual feature representation and visual feature representation are concatenated together to form the multi-modal feature representation.

3.2 Approaches Exploiting User Information

Users engage in rumor dissemination in multiple ways, such as sharing, liking, forwarding and reviewing. Many previous studies have shown that user credibility information is very important in rumor verification (Castillo et al., 2011; Yang et al., 2012; Gupta et al., 2012; Liu et al., 2015; Vosoughi, 2015; Shu et al., 2017b; Zhang et al., 2018; Liu and Wu, 2018; Li et al., 2019a; Li et al., 2019b). Based on 421 false rumors and 1.47 million related tweets, Li et al. (2016) study various semantic aspects of false rumors, and analyze their spread and user characteristics. Some findings are: when people do not have clarity about the veracity of a rumor, they usually just spread it without adding their opinions; credible users are less likely to support rumors, while low credibility accounts provide the most support; in terms of supporting or debunking a rumor, credible users are much more stringent, and hence a more trustworthy source than their corresponding counterparts.

Hand-crafted user features like registration age of users, number of followers, the number of posts the user had authored, and the like, are leveraged along with other textual and propagation features in Castillo et al. (2011) and other studies (Liu et al., 2015; Enayet and El-Beltagy, 2017; Li et al., 2019a; Li et al., 2019b). Liu and Wu (2018) construct user representations using network embedding approaches on the social network graph. There has been evidence that lots of rumors come from either fake news websites or hyper-partisan websites (Silverman, 2016; Li et al., 2016; Liu et al., 2015).

3.3 Approaches Based on Propagation Path and Network

Rumors spread through social media in the form of shares and re-shares of the source post and shared posts, resulting in a diffusion cascade or tree. The path of re-shares and other propagation dynamics are utilized for rumor detection. We group current studies into (1) cascade-based rumor detection techniques, which take direct advantage of rumor propagation paths, and (2) network-based detection methods, which construct a flexible network from cascades, from which rumors are indirectly detected.

Propagation-based: When using cascades to detect rumors, one either distinguishes them by computing the similarity of its cascade to that of other true/false rumors, or by generating a cascade representation that facilitates distinguishing false and true rumors. Ma et al. (2018b) construct a tree-structured neural network, based on fake news cascades, for rumor detection. Liu and Wu (2018) employ propagation path classification with RNN for early rumor detection. Zubiaga et al. (2018b) propose a method based on an LSTM layer followed by several dense ReLU layers. Other studies utilizing propagation path are (Kwon et al., 2017; Wu et al., 2015; Chen et al., 2016; Yang et al., 2018; Li et al., 2019a; Li et al., 2019b). Experiments from these studies show that models employing propagation path perform better than

the feature-based algorithms. But we should keep in mind that we usually do not have much propagation information at the early stage of a rumor spread, and early detection is especially critical for a real-time rumor detection system. The study from (Vosoughi et al., 2018) shows that unconfirmed news tends to exhibit multiple and periodic discussion spikes, whereas confirmed news typically has a single prominent spike, and false rumor spreads farther, faster, and more widely than true news.

Network-based: Network-based rumor detection constructs flexible networks to indirectly capture rumor propagation information. The constructed networks can be homogeneous, heterogeneous, or hierarchical. Gupta et al. (2012) construct a network consisting of users, messages and events, using PageRank-like algorithm to compute event credibility. Yang et al. (2015) incorporate network features derived from comments, and they said that when the network feature was added to the traditional features, the results improved substantially. Wang and Terano (2015) propose social graphs to model the interaction between users and identify influential rumor spreaders. Heterogeneous networks have multiple types of nodes or edges. An example is the tri-relationship network among news creators, the rumors, and users (Shu et al., 2017b), which uses entity embedding and relation modeling to build a hybrid framework for rumor detection. In (Zhang et al., 2018), an RNN model is designed to detect rumors through exploring creators, contents, subjects and their relationships.

3.4 Joint Learning for User Stance and Rumor Detection

User stance plays an important role in rumor detection. Recent works have employed multi-task learning approaches to jointly learn stance detection and veracity prediction, in order to improve classification accuracy by utilizing the interdependence between them. Ma et al. (2018a) jointly learn the stance detection and the veracity prediction tasks, where each task has a task-specific GRU layer, and the tasks also share a GRU layer. The shared layer is to capture patterns common to both tasks, and the task specific layer is to capture the patterns that are more important to that task. In the rumor detection task, the hidden state at the last time step is used for prediction through a fully-connected output layer.

Ma et al. found that joint learning improves the performance of individual tasks, and utilizing shared and task-specific parameters is more beneficial than using only the shared parameters without the task-specific layer. Kochkina et al. (2018) propose a multi-task method without task specific layer for rumor verification. Both approaches do not employ attention in their models, and user information is not used. Li et al. (2019b) exploit both user credibility information and attention mechanism in their joint learning approach.

3.5 Rumor Detection Contests

There are two contests for rumor detection: 1. SemEval-2017 Task 8: Determining rumor veracity and support for rumors (Derczynski et al., 2017). The approach from (Enayet and El-Beltagy, 2017) was ranked No. 1 for the rumor detection task. 2. SemEval-2019 Task 7: Determining rumor veracity and support for rumors (Gorrell et al., 2019). The approach from (Li et al., 2019a) was ranked No. 1 for the rumor detection task. The datasets used in these two tasks are listed in Table 1. Both (Enayet and El-Beltagy, 2017) and (Li et al., 2019a) exploited content, user and propagation information. They also utilized user stance directly in their models. The main difference between them are that Li et al. (2019a) used neural networks, while Enayet and El-Beltagy (2017) employed an SVM model.

There are also two contests related to fake news, but actually both of them are about stance detection, not fake news detection. They are the *Fake News Challenge* at: http://www.fakenewschallenge.org, and the *WSDM 2019 cup: classification of fake news article* at: https://www.kaggle.com/c/fake-news-pair-classification-challenge

4 Future Research Directions

Although significant advances have been made in debunking rumors on social media, nevertheless, there remain many challenges to overcome. Based on the review of previous studies and also our experiences in both research and practical system implementation of rumor detection, here we present several directions for future rumor detection research.

4.1 Knowledge Base

Knowledge base (KB) is very helpful for fake news detection (Hassan et al., 2017). There have been some studies on employing KB for fake news detection, but very few or none on rumor detection over social media. One reason is that for rumors on social media, we already have much information, especially the social context information, to exploit and do research on. Another reason is that, compared to fake news detection which mainly deals with news articles, rumors on social media are about various topics, and it is hard to build appropriate KBs that cover them. Therefore, most previous studies on rumor detection have not paid attention to exploiting KB for debunking rumors.

The automatic fact-checking process aims to assess the claim by comparing the knowledge extracted from rumor text to known facts (true knowledge) stored in the constructed KB or knowledge graph. One advantage of utilizing KB for debunking rumor on social media is that the source posts (claims) are usually short, and it is easier to extract the main claim from the short message, compared to analyzing a long news article which might have several claims. Research from (Kwon et al., 2017) shows that text features are very important when we want to detect rumor at its very early stage, since there is no propagation information or very few feedbacks from users when a rumor just emerges. By extracting knowledge from rumor text, we hypothesize that the KB-based approach would be especially helpful for the rumor early detection. As a starting point, the initial research effort can focus on the topic areas of popular rumors, and the approaches that are already effective in fake news detection can be explored first. We think how effective KBs can help in rumor detection and how we can integrate it with other social context information will be an interesting research topic.

4.2 Target of User Response

User responses are quite informative for rumor detection. Usually false rumors will receive more negative and questioning responses, which can be leveraged for rumor detection. Each source message (rumor claim) has many replies, and they are either direct replies, or replies to other messages in the conversion thread. The structure of the conversion thread is important for understanding the real stance of the user of a reply. For example, given a message "This is fake" and a reply to it "I totally agree", if we do not consider that the reply is towards "This is fake", then we will give a wrong stance label, "support", to this reply. But actually, this response is denying the rumor claim. Although the neural network models based on propagation analysis may partially learn this information, we think explicitly handle this situation would improve rumor detection performance.

Another issue with the user response target is that sometimes the user response is not towards the claim of the source message, but certain aspects of the rumor story. For example, this is a false rumor in SemEval19 rumor detection task: "National Geographic channel has reportedly paid $ 1 million for this daring video. https://t.co/CDbjf65bKG." Many responses towards this rumor are talking about how great the video is or how brave the goat in the video is, e.g. "Perseverance and fighting spirit!!" and "Nice one!!!!!!". For a stance detection algorithm, it is very possible to predict this type of responses as "support", due to their positive sentiment. This obviously will also mislead the rumor detection algorithm. We think it is worthwhile to research on the intent of user responses, to better understand the actual target of a user comment.

4.3 Cross-domain and Cross-language

Most previous studies emphasize on distinguishing false rumors from truth with experimental settings that are generally limited to a specific social media platform, or certain topic domains, such as politics. Analyzing rumors across topics or platforms would let us gain deeper understanding of rumors and discover their unique characteristics that can further assist debunking them across domains (topic and platform).

Recently, we have seen rumors spreading across languages, especially rumors involving topics on politics, investment, business and finance. Often times, a rumor is already debunked in one language, but it is still spreading in another language, due to the language barrier and the lack of cross-language rumor detection tool. This is quite true for some rumors in Chinese on Weibo and WeChat, a social media platform similar to Facebook. These rumors are usually about politics, world affairs, business and health/medical topics.

For example, in WeChat, there are many rumors about some supplements, claiming they are good for certain diseases and also presenting certain fake evidences citing some foreign studies. This type of rumors is very hard for ordinary users to verify, especially the elder people who are the main group who are interested in rumors related to healthcare, medicine, and longevity. This has becoming more serious in the last couple of years, since more people in the rural areas start to use smart phone and social media. How to deal with this type of cross-language and cross-platform rumor detection problem would also be an interesting research topic.

4.4 Explanatory Detection

Most rumor detection approaches only predict the veracity of a rumor, and very little information is revealed why it is a false rumor. Finding the evidences supporting the prediction and presenting them to users would be very beneficial, since it helps users to debunk rumors by themselves. Making the result explanatory has attracted research in other areas, such as explanatory recommendation, but it is still a new topic in rumor detection field. This may become harder as more models are using deep learning techniques nowadays. However, as AI techniques are used in more applications, the demands for result explanation from users are also increasing. For example, now we are designing and implementing a rumor detection system for an Alibaba product, and one important product feature required by the product designers and users is to provide explanation for the veracity prediction result.

4.5 Integrating User Stance and User Credibility Together

Several studies have shown that both user stance and user credibility information help improve rumor detection performance (Liu et al., 2015; Enayet and El-Beltagy, 2017; Li et al., 2019b). However, these studies just treat the stance label and the features reflecting user credibility, such as no. of followers and user account age, as separate features in the overall prediction model. None of them has tried to integrate these two types of information together systematically, to get a unified indicator to reflect how important a response is for determining the veracity of a rumor. For example, we want to clearly differentiate these two different situations: an authoritative and credible user, such as a credible news agency or government agent, debunks or supports a claim, and a low credible user, e.g. a malicious account, debunks or supports a claim. And as explained in the "Target of User Response" section, we also need to take the real target into consideration when designing the integration model.

4.6 Utilizing External Textual Information

Besides KBs mentioned before, other types of external information may also help rumor detection, such as articles from credible new agency websites, announcements or documents from governments and authorities, official announcements from involved parties, past rumors that have been verified, etc. We can compare the current rumor with these external text data, to gain more insights on the rumor. This sounds like a boring idea and an old information retrieval and text matching problem, but actually it will have very practical impact on rumor detection, especially for a real rumor detection system. Many rumors are just resurfacing of old ones, or their variants. And for a human, when we verify a rumor, one of the things we will do is also to check relevant website to see if there is any relevant information about this rumor, such as official announcement. The study from (Qin et al. 2016) shows that this approach is very effective when detecting rumors that have variants in the past at real-time. One system implementation challenge is to monitor these websites and scrape the relevant text information.

4.7 Multi-task Learning

Studies already show that jointly learning of stance detection and rumor detection improves the performance of rumor detection (Kochkina et al., 2018; Ma et al., 2018a). In the rumor detection workflow, depending on the algorithms, the following tasks might be involved: user credibility evaluation, source credibility evaluation, knowledge extraction, etc. If there are appropriate datasets with annotations for these data types, one research direction is to explore multi-task learning for these tasks, in addition to the user stance and rumor detection tasks. We expect it will benefit the rumor veracity prediction task, at least.

4.8 Rumor Early Detection

Rumor early detection is to detect a rumor at its early stage before it wide-spreads on social media, so that one can take appropriate actions earlier. Early detection is especially important for a real-time system, since the more a rumor spreads, the more damages it causes, and more likely for people to trust it. This is a very challenging task, since at its early stage a rumor has little propagation information and very few user responses. The algorithm has to primarily rely on the content and external knowledge, such as KB. Several studies have tested their algorithms on the early stage of rumors (Liu et al., 2015, Ma et al., 2016; Kwon et al., 2017; Liu and Wu, 2018). Kwon et al. (2017) analyzed feature stability over time and reported that user and linguistic features are better than structured and propagation features for determining the veracity of a rumor at its early stage. Although there are already some studies on this direction, more research efforts are still needed, due to its importance in the real systems.

4.9 Framework for a Real Rumor Detection System

Although there are many studies on rumor detection, most of them focus on models that utilize only part of the available information and test them on datasets that are platform or domain-specific. Very few of them are designed for real-time systems (Liu et al., 2015; Liu et al., 2016). A framework for a practical rumor detection system should try to exploit all the available information, and apply these information and models appropriately for different situations that might involve multiple factors, such as platforms, rumor stages, topics, languages, and content types (text, video or image). From the exploiting information point of view, we think the following information or data are worth to explore: text content (lexical, syntactical, semantic, writing style, etc.), visual content (video, image), rumor topics, knowledge bases, external documents, old rumors, propagation information, user features, source credibility, user credibility, heterogenous and homogeneous network structures, cross-platform information, and cross-language information.

References

Juan Cao, Junbo Guo, Xirong Li, Zhiwei Jin, Han Guo, and Jintao Li, Automatic Rumor Detection on Microblogs, 2018, https://arxiv.org/abs/1807.03505

Carlos Castillo, M. Mendoza, and B. Poblete. Information credibility on twitter. WWW 2011.

Cheng Chang, Yihong Zhang, Claudia Szabo, and Quan Z. Sheng. 2016. Extreme user and political rumor detection on twitter. ADMA 2016.

Weiling Chen, Chai Kiat Yeo, Chiew Tong Lau, and Bu Sung Lee. 2016. Behavior deviation: An anomaly detection view of rumor preemption. 2016 IEEE IEMCON

Alton Y. K. Chua and Snehasish Banerjee. 2016. Linguistic predictors of rumor veracity on the internet. 2016 MCECS.

L. Derczynski, K. Bontcheva, M. Liakata, R. Procter, G. W. S. Hoi, and A. Zubiaga, Semeval-2017 task 8: Rumoureval: Determining rumour veracity and support for rumours, SemEval 2017

Omar Enayet and Samhaa R El-Beltagy. 2017. Niletmrg at semeval-2017 task 8: Determining rumour and veracity support for rumours on twitter. SemEval17

Genevieve Gorrell, Kalina Bontcheva, Leon Derczynski, Elena Kochkina, Maria Liakata, and Arkaitz Zubiaga, RumourEval 2019: Determining Rumour Veracity and Support for Rumours. SemEval 2019

Manish Gupta, Peixiang Zhao, and Jiawei Han. 2012. Evaluating event credibility on twitter. 2012 SIAM ICDM

Gupta, H. Lamba, P. Kumaraguru, and A. Joshi. Faking sandy: characterizing and identifying fake images on twitter during hurricane sandy. WWW 2013

Naeemul Hassan, Fatma Arslan, Chengkai Li, and Mark Tremayne. 2017. Toward automated fact-checking: Detecting check-worthy factual claims by ClaimBuster. KDD

Zhiwei Jin, Juan Cao, Yongdong Zhang, and Jiebo Luo. 2016. News Verification by Exploiting Conflicting Social Viewpoints in Microblogs. AAAI 2016

Zhiwei Jin, Juan Cao, Han Guo, Yongdong Zhang, and Jiebo Luo. 2017a. Multimodal fusion with recurrent neural networks for rumor detection on microblogs. ACM MC

Zhiwei Jin, Juan Cao, Yongdong Zhang, Jianshe Zhou, and Qi Tian. Novel visual and statistical image features for microblogs news verification. IEEE transactions on multimedia

Elena Kochkina, Maria Liakata, Isabelle Augenstein, Turing at SemEval-2017: Sequential Approach to Rumour Stance Classification with Branch-LSTM, SemEval 2017

Elena Kochkina, Maria Liakata, Arkaitz Zubiaga, All-in-one: Multi-task Learning for Rumour Verification, COLING 2018

Sejeong Kwon, Meeyoung Cha, Kyomin Jung, Wei Chen, and Yajun Wang. 2013. Prominent features of rumor propagation in online social media. ICDM.

Sejeong Kwon, Meeyoung Cha, and Kyomin Jung. 2017. Rumor detection over varying time windows. PloS

Quanzhi Li, Xiaomo Liu, Rui Fang, Armineh Nourbakhsh, Sameena Shah, User Behaviors in Newsworthy Rumors: A Case Study of Twitter. ICWSM 2016

Quanzhi Li, Armineh Nourbakhsh, Sameena Shah, Xiaomo Liu, Real-Time Novel Event Detection from Social Media, IEEE ICDE 2017

Quanzhi Li, Qiong Zhang, Luo Si, 2019a, eventAI at SemEval-2019 Task 7: Rumor Detection by Exploiting Information from Multiple Dimensions, SemEval 2019.

Quanzhi Li, Qiong Zhang, Luo Si, 2019b, Rumor Detection by Exploiting User Credibility Information, Attention and Multi-task Learning, ACL 2019.

Xiaomo Liu, Armineh Nourbakhsh, Quanzhi Li, Rui Fang, Sameena Shah, 2015, Real-time Rumor Debunking on Twitter, CIKM 2015

Xiaomo Liu, Quanzhi Li, Armineh Nourbakhsh, et al. Reuters Tracer: A Large Scale System of Detecting & Verifying Real-Time News Events from Twitter. CIKM 2016

Xiaomo Liu, Armineh Nourbakhsh, Quanzhi Li, Sameena Shah, et al., Reuters tracer: Toward automated news production using large scale social media data. IEEE BigData 2017

Yang Liu and Yi-fang Brook Wu. 2018. Early Detection of Fake News on Social Media Through Propagation Path Classification with CNN. AAAI 2018

Jing Ma, Wei Gao, Prasenjit Mitra, Sejeong Kwon, et al., 2016. Detecting rumors from microblogs with recurrent neural networks. IJCAI 2016.

Jing Ma, Wei Gao, Kam-Fai Wong, Detect rumors in microblog posts using propagation structure via kernel learning, ACL 2017

Jing Ma, Wei Gao, Kam-Fai Wong, Detect Rumor and Stance Jointly by Neural Multi-task Learning, WWW 2018

Jing Ma, Wei Gao, Kam-Fai Wong, Rumor Detection on Twitter with Tree-structured Recursive Neural Networks, ACL 2018

V. Qazvinian, E. Rosengren, D. R. Radev, and Q. Mei. Rumor has it: Identifying misinformation in microblogs. EMNLP 2011.

Yumeng Qin, Dominik Wurzer, Victor Lavrenko, and Cunchen Tang. 2016. Spotting rumors via novelty detection. arXiv:16 11.06322 (2016).

RumourEval 2019, https://competitions.codalab.org/competitions/19938

Craig Silverman, Lauren Strapagiel, Hamza Shaban, et al. Hyperpartisan Facebook pages are publishing false and misleading information at an alarming rate. Buzzfeed News.

Kai Shu, H Russell Bernard, and Huan Liu. 2018. Studying Fake News via Network Analysis: Detection and Mitigation. arXiv preprint arXiv:1804.10233 (2018).

Kai Shu, Amy Sliva, Suhang Wang, Jiliang Tang, and Huan Liu. 2017a. Fake news detection on social media: A data mining perspective. SIGKDD Explorations Newsletter

Kai Shu, Suhang Wang, and Huan Liu. 2017b. Exploiting tri-relationship for fake news detection. arXiv preprint arXiv:1712.07709 (2017).

Kai Shu, Deepak Mahudeswaran, Suhang Wang, Dongwon Lee, Huan Liu, FakeNewsNet: A Data Repository with News Content, Social Context and Spatial temporal Information for Studying Fake News on Social Media, 2019, https://arxiv.org/abs/1809.01286

Eugenio Tacchini, Gabriele Ballarin, Marco L, et al. Some Like it Hoax: Automated Fake News Detection in Social Networks. arXiv preprint arXiv:1704.07506 (2017).

Soroush Vosoughi. 2015. Automatic Detection and Verification of Rumors on Twitter. Ph.D. Dissertation.

Shihan Wang and Takao Terano. 2015. Detecting rumor patterns in streaming social media. BigData.

Yaqing Wang, Fenglong Ma, Zhiwei Jin, et al. 2018. EANN: Event Adversarial Neural Networks for Multi-Modal Fake News Detection. ACM SIGKDD

K. Wu, S. Yang, and K. Q. Zhu. False rumors detection on sina weibo by propagation structures. ICDE 2015.

Fan Yang, Yang Liu, Xiaohui Yu, and Min Yang. 2012. Automatic detection of rumor on sina weibo. ACM SIGKDD Workshop on Mining Data Semantics.

YeKang Yang, Kai Niu, and ZhiQiang He. 2015. Exploiting the topology property of social network for rumor detection. JCSSE'15

Xinyi Zhou, Reza Zafarani, Fake news: research, detection methods, and opportunities, https://arxiv.org/abs/1812.00315 2018

Arkaitz Zubiaga, Maria Liakata, Rob Procter, et al. Analysing how people orient to and spread rumours in social media by looking at conversational threads. PloS one

Arkaitz Zubiaga, Ahmet Aker, Kalina Bontcheva, Maria Liakata, and Rob Procter. Detection and resolution of rumours in social media: A survey. ACM Comput. Survey.

Arkaitz Zubiaga, Elena Kochkina, Maria Liakata, Rob Procter, Michal Lukasik, et al. 2018b. Discourse-aware rumour stance classification in social media using sequential classifiers. IPM.

Unraveling the Search Space of Abusive Language in Wikipedia
with Dynamic Lexicon Acquisition

Wei-Fan Chen
Bauhaus-Universität Weimar
`wei-fan.chen@uni-weimar.de`

Khalid Al-Khatib
Bauhaus-Universität Weimar
`khalid.alkhatib@uni-weimar.de`

Matthias Hagen
Martin-Luther-Universität
Halle-Wittenberg
`matthias.hagen@informatik`
`.uni-halle.de`

Henning Wachsmuth
Paderborn University
`henningw@upb.de`

Benno Stein
Bauhaus-Universität Weimar
`benno.stein@uni-weimar.de`

Abstract

Many discussions on online platforms suffer from users offending others by using abusive terminology, threatening each other, or being sarcastic. Since an automatic detection of abusive language can support human moderators of online discussion platforms, detecting abusiveness has recently received increased attention. However, the existing approaches simply train one classifier for the whole variety of abusiveness. In contrast, our approach is to distinguish explicitly abusive cases from the more "shadowed" ones. By dynamically extending a lexicon of abusive terms (e.g., including new obfuscations of abusive terms), our approach can support a moderator with explicit unraveled explanations for why something was flagged as abusive: due to known explicitly abusive terms, due to newly detected (obfuscated) terms, or due to shadowed cases.

1 Introduction

The web has become the primary medium for people to share and discuss their opinions, stances, and knowledge. But not all people behave ethically on the respective online platforms: different types of abusive language have widely spread on the web. Systems that (semi-)automatically detect abusive language have gained quite some attention in the recent years. Such tools could support human moderators who try to protect online platforms from abusive language and to maintain high-quality user-generated content.

People use various ways to offend others. On one hand, they either *directly* offend the recipient of a text (direct recipient) or *indirectly* offend some other person, entity, or group (other recipient). On the other hand, abusive words and phrases may be used *explicitly* (e.g., "asshole!"), possibly in obfuscated form (e.g., "a$$h0le"), or abusiveness can also happen *implicitly* via sarcasm (e.g., "go back to school, whatever you learned didn't stick") or via new racist or abusive codes (e.g., on the platform *4chan*, "Google" is used as a slur for black people, "skittle" for Arabs, and "butterfly" for gays).[1]

Some recent studies have pointed to different types and to the importance of separating them, especially (Waseem et al., 2017). However, the distinction between the different offending dimensions has hardly been investigated for the development of abusive language classifiers (Schmidt and Wiegand, 2017). Accordingly, existing approaches consider the language of all abusive texts irrespective of their offending dimensions as one single search space. They simply train one machine learning model with different linguistic features on this space in order to classify unseen text as being abusive or not. Due to the diversity of language in offending dimensions, we expect such models to often result in limited effectiveness in practice. The reason is that, when learning to detect abusive texts following one way, for instance, the inclusion of training texts following other ways induces noise that diminishes the visibility of discriminative patterns.

As a solution, we propose to unravel the search space of abusive language via a three-stage classification approach. First, utilizing an abusive lexicon, we split the search space into two subspaces: texts with abusive words or phrases from the lexicon,

---

[1]`https://mic.com/articles/155739`

Proceedings of the 2nd Workshop on NLP for Internet Freedom: Censorship, Disinformation, and Propaganda, pages 76–82
Hong Kong, China, November 4, 2019 ©2019 Association for Computational Linguistics

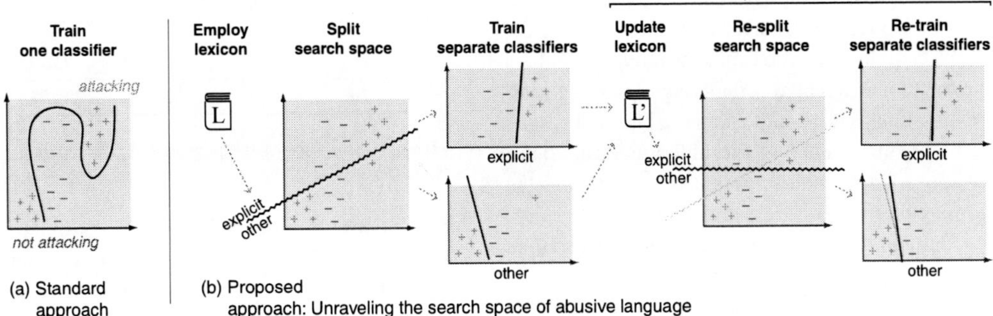

Figure 1: (a) Standard abusive language detection: Train a single classifier on all instances. (b) Proposed approach: Iteratively split the search space based on the offending dimension and train classifiers for each subspace.

and texts without such words. Second, we train a distinct classifier for each subspace. Third, using the predictions of the two classifiers, we perform an ablation test to discover new abusive terms from the subspaces. The found abusive words are added to the abusive lexicon that can serve as a dynamic source of explanations for a moderator that questions the detectors decision to flag a text as abusive. Figure 1 compares our approach to the "standard" single-search-space method.

To evaluate our approach to abusive language detection, we carried out several experiments using the *personal attacks corpus* of Wulczyn et al. (2017). The corpus consists of more than 100,000 comments from Wikipedia talk pages, each labeled as being a personal attack or not. In addition, the corpus includes manual labels for the target of attack, i.e., being the direct recipient or a third party.

The experimental results show that our search space unraveling slightly improves over state-of-the-art single-space classifiers with the additional bonus of a dynamic abusiveness lexicon that can help to explain the classifier's decisions.

The contribution of this paper is three-fold:

- We investigate how to unravel the search space of abusive language based on the underlying offending way.

- We develop computational approach that performs the unraveling in practice, and we evaluate it for the classification of Wikipedia talk page comments as being abusive or not.

- We dynamically develop a new lexicon for new abusive terms.

The developed resources are freely available on `https://webis.de`.

2 Related Work

The automatic detection of abusive language has been studied extensively in the last years. Proposed approaches target different types of abusive language, ranging from hate speech (Warner and Hirschberg, 2012) and cyberbullying (Nitta et al., 2013) to profanity (Sood et al., 2012) and personal attacks (Wulczyn et al., 2017).

Despite the importance of labeled data for abusive language detection, only few datasets are available so far for this task. Most of them come from large online platforms, such as Twitter (Waseem and Hovy, 2016), Yahoo (Nobata et al., 2016), and Wikipedia (Wulczyn et al., 2017). In terms of the number of labeled texts, the latter is the biggest, consisting of more than 100,000 Wikipedia talk page comments. We use this dataset for the evaluation of our approach.

Abusive (or offensive) language detection usually follows a supervised learning paradigm with either binary or multi-class classifiers. While existing abusiveness classifiers exploit a variety of lexical, syntactic, semantic, and knowledge-based features, one study showed character n-grams alone to be very good features (Mehdad and Tetreault, 2016). Until recently, the most effective overall approaches rely on neural network architectures such as CNN and RNN (Badjatiya et al., 2017; Pavlopoulos et al., 2017). On the personal attacks corpus, Pavlopoulos et al. (2017) have developed several very effective deep learning models with word embedding features. We employ the best-performing neural model, but we analyze the effect of adding our new approach (i.e., to unravel the abusiveness search space) that simultaneously helps to improve lexicon-based explainability.

An approach somewhat comparable to ours has been proposed by Dinakar et al. (2011) to detect cyberbullying on YouTube: different classifiers trained for different cyberbullying topics (e.g., sexuality, intelligence, and culture). The best results come from combining the individual classifiers, while a single multi-class classifier (mixing the different topics) was less effective.

Our approach is also related to co-training (Blum and Mitchell, 1998) and iterative feature selection/discovery (Liu et al., 2003; Xiang et al., 2012). In co-training, a labeled training set is extended by iteratively adding trustful instances from an unlabeled set based on the predictions of the classifier. Similarly, our approach extends its abusiveness lexicon iteratively. The iterative feature selection/discovery aims at finding new discriminating features to train the classifiers. This is in line with the third stage of our approach where new abusive terms are learned based on the predictions of the classifiers. The dynamically-updated lexicon can then serve as a good source for explaining many classifier decisions on the in-lexicon cases.

3 Data

In this section, we detail the data that we employ for the implementation and evaluation of our approach. Specifically, we describe the Wikipedia personal attack corpus (Wulczyn et al., 2017) and the abusive language lexicon of Wiegand et al. (2018).

3.1 Wikipedia Personal Attack Corpus

Wikipedia is one of the online platforms suffering from abusive language, especially from personal attacks (Shachaf and Hara, 2010). In particular, each Wikipedia article is associated to a so called *talk page*, where users are solicited to write comments in order to discuss and improve the quality of the article's content. While the large majority of comments is valuable, some users attack others with texts comprising hate speech and harassment, among others.

Our analysis and evaluation are based on the personal attack corpus (Wulczyn et al., 2017) that includes 115,864 comments extracted from Wikipedia talk page comments. Each comment has been labeled by at least ten crowdsourced annotators as an 'attack' (i.e., being abusive) or 'not-attack' (i.e., non-abusive) with an inter-annotator agreement of 0.45 in terms of Krippendorff's α. The label of each comment was aggregated based

	Train	Validation	Test
Attack	8,079	2,755	2,880
Not-attack	61,447	20,405	20,298
All	69,526	23,160	23,178

Table 1: Statistics of the personal attacks corpus.

on the distribution of the labels and the majority vote (about 12% are attacks). The corpus comes with a 60-20-20 split into training, validation, and test set (see Table 1 for corpus statistics).

3.2 Abusive Language Lexicon

To carry out our approach, we employ the lexicon of Wiegand et al. (2018). This lexicon has been built through an in-depth examination of negative polar expressions. To this end, a set of candidate abusive words has been collected from the negative polar expressions from the 'subjectivity lexicon' of (Wilson et al., 2005) as well as the frequently listed abusive words in the lexicons surveyed by Schmidt and Wiegand (2017). The expressions in this set have been manually labeled into abusive and non-abusive using a crowdsourcing setting. Based on the resulting labels, a new supervised classifier that distinguishes between abusive and non-abusive expressions has been developed. This classifier, then, has been applied to a large number of negative polar expressions derived from Wiktionary, in order to label them into abusive and non-abusive.

Accordingly, two versions of the lexicon have been created: (1) *the base lexicon* which comprises the manually labeled expressions, and (2) *the expanded lexicon* which includes the automatically labeled expressions in accordance with the predictions of the developed classifier. The first lexicon contains 1650 words and expressions in which 551 of them are abusive, while the second contains 8478 words and expressions with 2989 abusive ones.

The results of using the lexicon for detecting the abusive language in micro-posts demonstrate high effectiveness, particularly in cross-domain settings.

4 Approach

Our approach unravels the search space based on the hypothesis that the differences of abusive texts with and without explicit abusive words are reflected in varying, possibly opposite feature distributions on the lexical, syntactic, semantic, or pragmatic level. In an iterative ablation test step, more domain-specific abusive words are detected.

4.1 Unraveling the Search Space

In contrast to standard approaches training abusiveness classifiers on all examples at once, we propose to apply a three-stage approach.

1) Splitting the Search Space Using an abusive lexicon, we split the training and validation sets into two subspaces of texts containing explicit abusive terms and other texts (see Figure 1(b)).

2) Training Two Abusiveness Classifiers On each training set of the two resulting subspaces (*explicit / other*), a distinct classifier is trained to predict the 'not-attack' probability.

3) Collecting New Abusive Terms Each of the two classifiers is run on 100 random attack and 100 random not-attack texts from the respective validation set ('attack' / 'not-attack' according to ground-truth majority vote). In an ablation test, each word from these selected texts is iteratively removed and the probability of the text to be 'not-attack' is compared to the prediction with that word. The words are then ordered by their "abusiveness" (i.e., words are ranked higher the more their removal raises the 'not-attack' score). Ideally, obfuscated abusive words and sarcastic expressions will be ranked high. The top-k "new" abusive words for each subset (*explicit / other*) and each ground-truth label ('attack' / 'not-attack') are added to the lexicon ($\leq 4k$ words at most per iteration, k being set to 20 after pilot experiments).

4.2 Iterative Unraveling

At the end of an iteration (i.e., splitting the datasets, training two classifiers, and collecting new abusive words), the effectiveness of the classifiers is tested on the validation set. When there is no improvement for three iterations, the process stops.

4.3 Abusiveness Classification

Given an unknown text (e.g., in the test set), we check whether it contains an explicit abusive word from the developed lexicon, and select the appropriate classifier accordingly.

5 Experiments and Results

We compare our approach to the state of the art on the personal attack corpus, following the original suggestion of using the 2-class area under the ROC curve (AUC) and Spearman rank correlation as the evaluation metrics (AUC computed between derived 'attack' probabilities and the corpus majority vote while Spearman considers the fraction of corpus votes agreeing with a prediction).

5.1 Experimental Setup

To represent the state of the art, we employ the best-performing model on the personal attack corpus proposed by Pavlopoulos et al. (2017): an RNN model where the basic cell is a GRU. An embedding layer transforms an input word sequence into a word embedding sequence. Then, the model learns a hidden state from the word embeddings. The hidden state is employed to predict the probability of 'not-attack' using a linear regression layer.

We use 300-dimensional word embeddings (Pennington et al., 2014) pre-trained on the Common Crawl with 840 billion tokens and a vocabulary size of 2.2 million. Out-of-vocabulary words are mapped to one random vector. We use Glorot (Glorot and Bengio, 2010) to initialize the model, with mean-square error as loss function, Adam for optimization (Kingma and Ba, 2014), a learning rate of 0.001, and a batch size of 128.

The initial abusive lexicon used for splitting the search space is the complete set of words in the *base lexicon* of Wiegand et al. (2018) containing 1650 negative polar expressions. This lexicon performed better in our pilot experiments compared to the weakly labeled set of expressions in the *expanded lexicon*.

5.2 Results

On the personal attacks corpus, we compare our approach to the effectiveness reported by Wulczyn et al. (2017) and Pavlopoulos et al. (2017), and to our re-implementation of the RNN model of Pavlopoulos et al. (2017) that forms the basis of our approach (some implementation details missing in the original paper).

As can be seen in Table 2, our approach is slightly better than the re-implementation in terms of AUC and Spearman in both splits and the whole test set. Our approach is on a par with the previous best approach reported (slight AUC improvement to 97.80, but slightly lower Spearman score). The fact that the concatenation of *explicit* and *other* yields a higher AUC than any subspace is a result of the substantially lower predicted probabilities of attack on the *other* set as well as of the highly imbalanced distribution of 'attack' in the two sets.

<table>
<tr><th></th><th>First Iteration</th><th>Second Iteration</th></tr>
<tr><td>Explicit</td><td>why are you such an idiot
You re fuck of bitch</td><td>why are you such an idiot
You re fuck of bitch</td></tr>
<tr><td>Other</td><td>Stop erasing my work you MF Douche bag
Go fuk your Momma Rancie</td><td>Stop erasing my work you MF Douche bag
Go fuk your Momma Rancie</td></tr>
</table>

Figure 2: The abusiveness of words in texts with explicit abusive terms (above the line) and without abusive terms (below the line) in the first two iterations. Darker color indicates a higher abusiveness.

Approach	AUC	Spearman
Our proposed approach		
- all cases	**97.80**	70.26
- explicit	97.69	78.06
- other	97.05	55.37
Reimplementation		
- all cases	97.17	67.98
- explicit	97.08	75.45
- other	96.38	52.06
Pavlopoulos et al. (2017)	97.71	**72.79**
Wulczyn et al. (2017)	96.59	68.17

Table 2: Effectiveness on the test set of the personal attacks corpus (AUC and Spearman coefficients): our proposed approach, the previous state of the art (Pavlopoulos et al., 2017), our reimplementation of it, and the "standard" approach by Wulczyn et al. (2017).

Measure	1	2	3	4	5
AUC - Valid. all	97.17	**97.46**	97.40	97.34	97.33
AUC - Valid. explicit	96.94	**97.40**	97.21	97.25	97.14
AUC - Valid. other	**97.63**	96.58	96.36	95.46	95.32
AUC - Test all	97.58	**97.80**	97.74	97.68	97.69
AUC - Test explicit	97.25	**97.69**	97.51	97.55	97.55
AUC - Test other	**97.29**	97.05	96.94	94.14	96.15
Spearman - Valid. all	69.19	70.26	70.40	70.25	**70.41**
Spearman - Valid. explicit	76.67	77.43	78.05	**78.47**	78.46
Spearman - Valid. other	**56.88**	54.62	51.64	49.21	47.73
Spearman - Test all	69.73	71.07	71.26	70.87	**71.26**
Spearman - Test explicit	77.38	78.06	78.47	**78.79**	78.59
Spearman - Test other	**57.10**	55.37	53.37	50.50	50.14

Table 3: Effectiveness (AUC values and Spearman coefficients) of our approach's first five iterations.

	1	2	3	4	5
Size	1650	1725	1780	1829	1875
Increment		+75	+55	+49	+46
Partially abusive		+20	+30	+24	+18
Abusive		+14	+13	+18	+21
Non-abusive		+41	+12	+ 7	+ 7

Table 4: Increment and of the abusive lexicon in the first five iterations of our approach. The rows *partially abusive*, *abusive*, and *non-abusive* indicate the numbers of abusive words agreed by *one of*, *both*, *none of* the experts in the newly added words respectively.

Table 3 shows the AUC values and Spearman coefficients for the first five iterations of our approach on the unraveled validation and test set. The approach stops at the fifth iteration since the highest AUC performance (our target evaluation measure) on *all* and the *explicit* subspace of the validation set was obtained in the second iteration (three failed improvement attempts). The highest AUC for the *other* subspace is achieved in the first iteration, though. The Spearman values increase after each iteration, except again for the *other* subspace where the first iteration works best.

The expansion rates of the abusive lexicon are shown in Table 4. Fewer and fewer terms are added in later iterations since it becomes increasingly less likely for the ablation test to discover important new abusive words. Additionally, we asked two experts to also check the newly added words; they confirmed that more and more abusive terms are added (inter-annotator agreement of 0.59).

Our approach iteratively identifies new "highly abusive" words and moves the respective texts from the *other* subspace to the *explicit* subspace. Since the abusive terms are important clues for the classification, this will force the model for the *other* subspace to utilize new features. As a result, the texts without explicit abusive terms become more "difficult", such that the effectiveness in the *other* subspace decreases over time.

Table 5 shows the newly found words in each of the first iterations. For every iteration, we show words labeled as 'abusive' (two experts both agree they are abusive), 'partial abusive' (one of the experts agreed they are abusive) and 'non-abusive' (none of two experts both agrees they are abusive). For each label and each iteration, we select three words which have the highest 'abusiveness' (see the definition of 'abusiveness' in section 4.1). We found that our approach can find unusual abusive words (such as 'faggots') and also obfuscated/misspelled abusive words (such as 'fvck').

Figure 2 illustrates some texts with the abusive-

Iteration	Abusive	Partially abusive	Non-abusive
2	jerk	masturbating	headline
	fuckheads	freak	heck
	douchebag	clowns	nightmare
3	fucking	rudely	hometown
	fvck	dunce	lifetime
	bastard	pederast	imature
4	bithces	filthy	policemans
	sissy	lame	foot
	fuk	harrassing	die
5	niggers	nazi	pint
	faggots	hypocritical	boss
	fuckers	imposter	pay

Table 5: The newly added abusive words in the first iterations. By 'abusive', we refer to the words that both experts label as abusive. By 'partially abusive', we refer to the words that only one of the experts labels as abusive, and by 'non-abusive', we refer to the words that both experts label as non-abusive.

ness of each word in the first and second iteration. The classifier for the *explicit* subspace learns to emphasize the explicit abusive words (e.g., the more important "fuck" or "bitch" and the less important "are" or "an" in the second iteration) while the classifier for the *other* subspace identifies "new" abusive terms (e.g., "Douche" or "fuk") to be added to the lexicon.

6 Conclusion

Abusive language has become a ubiquitous problem on online platforms. Previous work aimed to train detectors on a single search space of potentially abusive texts. In contrast, we suggest to divide the search space into texts containing explicit abusive words (according to a dynamic lexicon) and texts that do not contain such terms. For each subspace, a different classifier is trained.

In an online scenario of consistently running our approach on new comments (some users may report offensive ones, etc.) to support human moderators on online platforms, newly "emerging" obfuscated offensive terms will quickly be spotted and are not "lost" in the dominating space of explicit abusiveness. The iterative extension of the lexicon also helps to increase effectiveness in our experiments showing our approach to be on a par with the previous state of the art on the personal attacks corpus.

Besides matching the previous state-of-the-art "black box" classification performance, our new approach with its dynamic lexicon comes with the benefit of an improved explainability that a human moderator may appreciate for the in-lexicon cases. For the human-in-the-loop platform moderation scenario, we plan a user study also including a functionality to manually add or blacklist terms from the lexicon in each iteration.

References

Pinkesh Badjatiya, Shashank Gupta, Manish Gupta, and Vasudeva Varma. 2017. Deep learning for hate speech detection in tweets. In *Proceedings of the 26th International Conference on World Wide Web Companion*, WWW '17 Companion, pages 759–760. International World Wide Web Conferences Steering Committee.

Avrim Blum and Tom Mitchell. 1998. Combining labeled and unlabeled data with co-training. In *Proceedings of the eleventh annual conference on Computational learning theory*, pages 92–100. ACM.

Karthik Dinakar, Roi Reichart, and Henry Lieberman. 2011. Modeling the detection of textual cyberbullying.

Xavier Glorot and Yoshua Bengio. 2010. Understanding the difficulty of training deep feedforward neural networks. In *Proceedings of the thirteenth international conference on artificial intelligence and statistics*, pages 249–256.

Diederik P Kingma and Jimmy Ba. 2014. Adam: A method for stochastic optimization. In *Proceedings of the 3rd International Conference on Learning Representations (ICLR)*.

Tao Liu, Shengping Liu, Zheng Chen, and Wei-Ying Ma. 2003. An evaluation on feature selection for text clustering. In *Proceedings of the 20th international conference on machine learning (ICML-03)*, pages 488–495.

Yashar Mehdad and Joel R. Tetreault. 2016. Do characters abuse more than words? In *SIGDIAL Conference*, pages 299–303.

Taisei Nitta, Fumito Masui, Michal Ptaszynski, Yasutomo Kimura, Rafal Rzepka, and Kenji Araki. 2013. Detecting cyberbullying entries on informal school websites based on category relevance maximization. In *Proceedings of the Sixth International Joint Conference on Natural Language Processing*, pages 579–586. Asian Federation of Natural Language Processing.

Chikashi Nobata, Joel Tetreault, Achint Thomas, Yashar Mehdad, and Yi Chang. 2016. Abusive language detection in online user content. In *Proceedings of the 25th International Conference on World Wide Web*, WWW '16, pages 145–153. International World Wide Web Conferences Steering Committee.

John Pavlopoulos, Prodromos Malakasiotis, and Ion Androutsopoulos. 2017. Deeper Attention to Abusive User Content Moderation. In *Proceedings of the 2017 Conference on Empirical Methods in Natural Language Processing, EMNLP 2017*, pages 1125–1135.

Jeffrey Pennington, Richard Socher, and Christopher Manning. 2014. Glove: Global vectors for word representation. In *Proceedings of the 2014 conference on empirical methods in natural language processing (EMNLP)*, pages 1532–1543.

Anna Schmidt and Michael Wiegand. 2017. A survey on hate speech detection using natural language processing. In *Proceedings of the Fifth International Workshop on Natural Language Processing for Social Media*, pages 1–10. Association for Computational Linguistics.

Pnina Shachaf and Noriko Hara. 2010. Beyond vandalism: Wikipedia trolls. *Journal of Information Science*, 36(3):357–370.

Sara Sood, Judd Antin, and Elizabeth Churchill. 2012. Profanity use in online communities. In *Proceedings of the SIGCHI Conference on Human Factors in Computing Systems*, pages 1481–1490. ACM.

William Warner and Julia Hirschberg. 2012. Detecting hate speech on the world wide web. In *Proceedings of the Second Workshop on Language in Social Media*, LSM '12, pages 19–26. Association for Computational Linguistics.

Zeerak Waseem and Dirk Hovy. 2016. Hateful symbols or hateful people? predictive features for hate speech detection on twitter. In *Proceedings of the NAACL Student Research Workshop*, pages 88–93. Association for Computational Linguistics.

Zeerak Waseem, Thomas, Dana Warmsley, and Ingmar Weber. 2017. Understanding Abuse: A Typology of Abusive Language Detection Subtasks. *CoRR*, abs/1705.09899.

Michael Wiegand, Josef Ruppenhofer, Anna Schmidt, and Clayton Greenberg. 2018. Inducing a lexicon of abusive words–a feature-based approach. In *Proceedings of the 2018 Conference of the North American Chapter of the Association for Computational Linguistics: Human Language Technologies*, volume 1, pages 1046–1056.

Theresa Wilson, Janyce Wiebe, and Paul Hoffmann. 2005. Recognizing contextual polarity in phrase-level sentiment analysis. In *Proceedings of the Conference on Human Language Technology and Empirical Methods in Natural Language Processing*, HLT '05, pages 347–354. Association for Computational Linguistics.

Ellery Wulczyn, Nithum Thain, and Lucas Dixon. 2017. Ex machina: Personal attacks seen at scale. *WWW '17 Proceedings of the 26th International Conference on World Wide Web*, pages 1391–1399.

Guang Xiang, Bin Fan, Ling Wang, Jason Hong, and Carolyn Rose. 2012. Detecting offensive tweets via topical feature discovery over a large scale twitter corpus. In *Proceedings of the 21st ACM international conference on Information and knowledge management*, pages 1980–1984. ACM.

Sentence-Level Propaganda Detection Using BERT with Context-Dependent Input Pairs

Wenjun Hou, Ying Chen

College of Information and Electrical Engineering, China Agricultural University, China
{houwenjun, chenying}@cau.edu.cn

Abstract

The goal of fine-grained propaganda detection is to determine whether a given sentence uses propaganda techniques (sentence-level) or to recognize which techniques are used (fragment-level). This paper presents the system of our participation in the sentence-level subtask of the propaganda detection shared task. In order to better utilize the document information, we construct context-dependent input pairs (sentence-title pair and sentence-context pair) to fine-tune the pretrained BERT, and we also use the undersampling method to tackle the problem of imbalanced data[1].

1 Introduction

Propaganda detection is a process of determining whether a news article or a sentence is misleading. Several research works have been proposed to detect propaganda on document-level (Rashkin et al., 2017; Barrón-Cedeño et al., 2019b), sentence-level and fragment-level (Da San Martino et al., 2019). Sentence-level detection or classification (SLC) is to determine whether a given sentence is propagandistic and it is a special binary classification problem, while the goal of fragment-level classification (FLC) is to extract fragments and assign with given labels such as *loaded language*, *flag-waving* and *causal oversimplification*, and it could be treated as a sequence labeling problem.

Compared with document-level, sentence-level and fragment-level detection are much more helpful, since detection on sentences and fragments are more practical for real-life applications. However, these fine-grained tasks are more challenging. Although Da San Martino et al. (2019) indicates that multi-task learning of both the SLC and the FLC could be beneficial for the SLC, in this paper, we

---

[1]Code is available at https://github.com/Wenjun-Hou/Propaganda-Detection-SLC

only focus on the SLC task so as to better investigate whether context information could improve the performance of our system. Since several pretrained language models (Devlin et al., 2019; Liu et al., 2019) have been proved to be effective for text classification and other natural language understanding tasks, we use the pretrained BERT (Devlin et al., 2019) for the SLC task. This paper elaborates our BERT-based system for which we construct sentence-title pairs and sentence-context pairs as input. In addition, in order to tackle the problem of imbalanced data, we apply the undersampling method (Zhou and Liu, 2006) to the training data, and we find that this method greatly boosts the performance of our system.

2 Related Work

Various methods have been proposed for propaganda detection. Rashkin et al. (2017) proposed to use LSTM and other machine learning methods for deception detection in different types of news, including *trusted*, *satire*, *hoax* and *propaganda*. Barrón-Cedeño et al. (2019b) proposed to use Maximum Entropy classifier (Berger et al., 1996) with different features replicating the same experimental setup of Rashkin et al. (2017) for two-way and four-way classifications. A fine-grained propaganda corpus was proposed in Da San Martino et al. (2019) which includes both sentence-level and fragment-level information. Based on this corpus and the pretrained BERT which is one of the most powerful pretrained language model, a multi-granularity BERT was proposed and it outperformed several strong BERT-based baselines.

3 Methodology

In our system, we utilize BERT as our base model and construct different kinds of input pairs to fine-tune it. When constructing the input representa-

Proceedings of the 2nd Workshop on NLP for Internet Freedom: Censorship, Disinformation, and Propaganda, pages 83–86
Hong Kong, China, November 4, 2019 ©2019 Association for Computational Linguistics

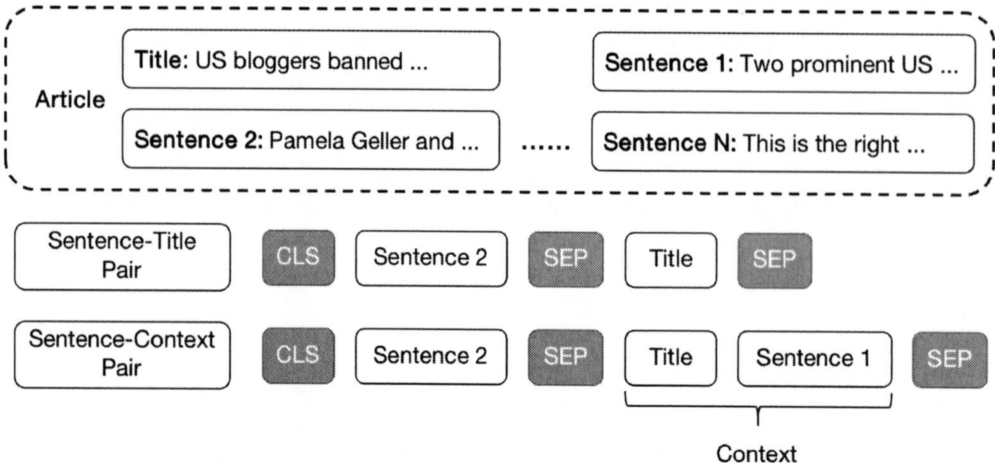

Figure 1: Two kinds of input pairs for BERT. [CLS] and [SEP] are two special tokens.

tion, a special token [CLS] is padded in front of every sentence and another token [SEP] is added at the end of it. In addition, for each input pair, a [SEP] is added between a sentence and its context or title. Finally, a linear layer and a *sigmoid* function are applied to the final representation of [CLS] to obtain the probability for classification. For comparison, we also use the official method (Random) as baseline which randomly labels sentences.

3.1 Data

The dataset is provided by NLP4IF 2019 Shared Task (Barrón-Cedeño et al., 2019a), and the training set, the development set, and the test set contain approximately 16,000, 2,000 and 3,400 sentences respectively. According to the statistics, only 29% of the training sentences are labeled as propaganda, and thus in this paper, we treat propaganda sentences as positive samples and non-propaganda sentences as negative samples. More details of the dataset could be found in Da San Martino et al. (2019).

3.2 Input pairs

Sentence Only: We only use the current sentence to fine-tune the model and models trained with this kind of input are used as baselines for those models trained with the following two kinds of input pairs.

Sentence-Title Pair: As described in Da San Martino et al. (2019), the source of the dataset that we use is news articles, and since the title is usually the summarization of a news article, we use the title as supplementary information.

Sentence-Context Pair: In addition to setting the title as the supplementary information, we construct the sentence-context pair which also includes preceding sentences as additional context, since preceding sentences usually convey the same or related events and this historical content is closely related to the current sentence. Figure 1. shows the details of this kind of input pair in which the preceding sentence and the title are directly concatenated.

3.3 Undersampling

As mentioned above, there are only 29% of training sentences labeled as propaganda (positive). In order to tackle the problem of imbalanced data, we first collect positive samples which size is S_{pos} and negative samples, then we resample S_{neg} (X percent of S_{pos}) from negative samples at the beginning of each training epoch. Finally, we combine and shuffle both positive samples and sampled negative samples as a new training set $S_{sampled}$.

$$S_{neg} = X * S_{pos} \tag{1}$$
$$S_{sampled} = S_{neg} + S_{pos} \tag{2}$$

3.4 Experiment Details

In this paper, we use the pretrained uncased version of $\text{BERT}_{\text{BASE}}$ and $\text{BERT}_{\text{LARGE}}$ [2] for the SLC, and more details of these two models could

---

[2] https://github.com/google-research/bert

Model	Input	Sample Rate	Precision	Recall	F_1
Random	-	-	44.38	50.74	47.35
BERT$_{\text{BASE}}$	Sentence Only	-	72.76	52.77	61.18
	Sentence-Title	-	70.54	56.70	62.87
		0.8	57.83	77.94	66.40
		0.9	60.77	70.64	65.33
		1.0	63.70	68.88	66.19
	Sentence-Context	-	71.10	54.94	61.98
		0.8	57.53	77.54	66.05
		0.9	60.95	73.07	66.46
		1.0	63.44	66.44	64.90
BERT$_{\text{LARGE}}$	Sentence Only	-	**73.19**	50.61	59.84
	Sentence-Title	-	71.23	54.26	61.60
		0.8	58.69	75.37	66.00
		0.9	61.89	64.82	63.31
		1.0	60.85	71.31	65.67
	Sentence-Context	-	71.88	49.12	58.36
		<u>0.8</u>	<u>59.43</u>	**<u>79.30</u>**	**<u>67.94</u>**
		0.9	63.73	66.58	65.12
		1.0	62.28	73.07	67.25

Table 1: Experiment results of different models on the SLC task, and the model with the highest F_1 score which has been underlined is chosen to be evaluated on the test set. '-' in sample rate means undersampling is not used.

Model	Data	Prec.	Rec.	F_1
Random	Dev.	44.38	50.74	47.35
	Test	38.80	49.42	43.47
BERT$_{\text{LARGE}}$	Dev.	59.43	79.30	67.94
	Test	51.81	74.44	61.10

Table 2: Experiment results of the chosen model and the random baseline for the SLC task.

be found in Devlin et al. (2019). Before fine-tuning, sentences are first converted to lower case and their maximum sequence length is set to 128. For a sentence-context pair, the maximum length of context is set to 100. If the sequence length of an input pair exceeds 128, then the context or title is truncated to meet the length.

When fine-tuning, we use the Adam (Kingma and Ba, 2014) with learning rate 2e-5 for 2 epochs, the batch size is 32 and the dropout probability is kept at 0.1. Since the title or context information could help improve the performance, we only apply the undersampling method to input pairs (sentence-title and sentence-context). For those models involved with undersampling, the sample rate X is set to 0.8, 0.9 or 1.0 empirically. During the training stage, all training samples are used.

We directly evaluate all the models on the development set, and the best model is chosen to generate predictions of the test data.

4 Result

Our approach is evaluated on Propaganda Detection@NLP4IF SLC dataset. In the development stage, we use three kinds of input and three different sample rates for BERT. Table 1. shows the results of the development set. From Table 1., without considering undersampling, we can see that using the sentence-title pair could boost the performance of BERT$_{\text{BASE}}$, compared with the model using only the current sentence and the random baseline. While using the sentence-context pair could improve the F_1 score of BERT$_{\text{BASE}}$ by 0.8% with precision rising to 71.10 and recall decreasing to 54.94, the performance of BERT$_{\text{BASE}}$ drops by around 1% with recall dropping significantly to 49.12.

We also observe that both performances of BERT$_{\text{BASE}}$ and BERT$_{\text{LARGE}}$ trained with original training sentences are competitive compared with the random baseline. However, the precision of BERT$_{\text{BASE}}$ at 70.54 and the one of BERT$_{\text{LARGE}}$ at 71.23 are significantly higher than the recall of both models, at 56.70 and at

54.26 respectively, and this may result from the problem of imbalanced instances. Thus, we introduce the undersampling technique using 0.8, 0.9 or 1.0 sample rate to tackle this issue. We observe from Table 1. that the F_1 score of $BERT_{BASE}$ with the sentence-title pair and 0.8 sample rate rises around by 5% and the same model using the sentence-context pair and 0.9 sample rate performs similarly. As for $BERT_{LARGE}$, while using the sentence-title pair has the similar performance as it is employed in the base version model, using the sentence-context pair strongly boosts the F_1 score, at 67.94 with 0.8 sample rate and at 67.25 with 1.0 sample rate. In addition, it is worth noting that there is a better trade-off between precision and recall with 1.0 sample rate than the one with 0.8.

In the test stage, since we are only allowed to submit a single run on the test set, we choose the model with the highest F_1 score (67.94) to generate predictions and the evaluated results are listed in Table 2. From Table 2., we can see that the recall raises by nearly 5% and the precision of it drops significantly, by around 7%, compared with the results on the development set, while the recall of Random Baseline also drops by approximately 5.5% and the precision of it remains nearly the same.

5 Conclusion and Future Work

In this paper, we examine capability of the context-dependent BERT model. In the sentence-level propaganda detection task, we construct sentence-title pairs and sentence-context pairs in order to better utilize context information to improve the performance of our system. Furthermore, the undersampling method is utilized to tackle the data imbalanced problem. Experiments show that both sentence-title/context pairs and the undersampling method could boost the performance of BERT on the SLC task.

In the future, we plan to apply multi-task learning to this context-dependent BERT, similar to the method mentioned in Da San Martino et al. (2019) or introducing other kinds of tasks, such as sentiment analysis or domain classification.

References

Alberto Barrón-Cedeño, Giovanni Da San Martino, and Preslav Nakov. 2019a. Findings of the nlp4if-2019 shared task on fine-grained propaganda detection. In *Proceedings of the 2nd Workshop on NLP for Internet Freedom (NLP4IF): Censorship, Disinformation, and Propaganda*, NLP4IF EMNLP 2019.

Alberto Barrón-Cedeño, Israa Jaradat, Giovanni Da San Martino, and Preslav Nakov. 2019b. Proppy: Organizing the news based on their propagandistic content. *Information Processing & Management*, 56(5):1849–1864.

Adam Berger, Stephen Della Pietra, and Vincent Della Pietra. 1996. A maximum entropy approach to natural language processing. *Computational Linguistics*.

Giovanni Da San Martino, Seunghak Yu, Alberto Barrón-Cedeño, Rostislav Petrov, and Preslav Nakov. 2019. Fine-grained analysis of propaganda in news articles. In *Proceedings of the 2019 Conference on Empirical Methods in Natural Language Processing and 9th International Joint Conference on Natural Language Processing*, EMNLP-IJCNLP 2019.

Jacob Devlin, Ming-Wei Chang, Kenton Lee, and Kristina Toutanova. 2019. Fine-grained analysis of propaganda in news articles. In *Proceedings of the 2019 Conference of the North American Chapter of the Association for Computational Linguistics: Human Language Technologies*, NAACL 2019.

Diederik P. Kingma and Jimmy Ba. 2014. Adam: A method for stochastic optimization. In *Proceedings of the 3rd International Conference for Learning Representations*, ICLR 2014.

Yinhan Liu, Myle Ott, Naman Goyal, Jingfei Du, Mandar Joshi, Danqi Chen, Omer Levy, Mike Lewis, Luke Zettlemoyer, and Veselin Stoyanov. 2019. Roberta: A robustly optimized bert pretraining approach. In *arXiv preprint arXiv:1409.0473*.

Hannah Rashkin, Eunsol Choi, Jin Yea Jang, Svitlana Volkova, and Yejin Choi. 2017. Truth of varying shades: Analyzing language in fake news and political fact-checking. In *Proceedings of the 2017 Conference on Empirical Methods in Natural Language Processing and 9th International Joint Conference on Natural Language Processing*, EMNLP 2017.

Zhi-Hua Zhou and Xu-Ying Liu. 2006. Training cost-sensitive neural networks with methods addressing the class imbalance problem. *IEEE Trans Knowledge and Data Engineering*, 18(1):63–77.

Fine-Grained Propaganda Detection with Fine-Tuned BERT

Shehel Yoosuf,
College of Science and Engineering
Hamad Bin Khalifa University
Doha, Qatar
syoosuf@mail.hbku.edu.qa

Yin "David" Yang
College of Science and Engineering
Hamad Bin Khalifa University
Doha, Qatar
yyang@hbku.edu.qa

Abstract

This paper presents the winning solution of the Fragment Level Classification (FLC) task in the Fine Grained Propaganda Detection competition at the NLP4IF'19 workshop. The goal of the FLC task is to detect and classify textual segments that correspond to one of the 18 given propaganda techniques in a news articles dataset. The main idea of our solution is to perform word-level classification using fine-tuned BERT, a popular pre-trained language model. Besides presenting the model and its evaluation results, we also investigate the attention heads in the model, which provide insights into what the model learns, as well as aspects for potential improvements.[1]

1 Introduction

Propaganda is a type of informative communication with the goal of serving the interest of the information giver (i.e., the propagandist), and not necessarily the recipient (Jowett and O'donnell, 2018). Recently, Da San Martino et al. compiled a new dataset for training machine learning models, containing labeled instances of several common types of propaganda techniques. Through such fine-grained labels, the authors aim to alleviate the issue of noise arising from classifying at a coarse level, e.g., the whole article, as attempted in previous works on propaganda classification (Barrón-Cedeño et al., 2019; Rashkin et al., 2017). Using this dataset, the Fragment Level Classification (FLC) task of the Fine-Grained Propaganda Detection Challenge in NLP4IF'19 requires detecting and classifying textual fragments that correspond to at least one of the 18 given propaganda techniques (Da San Martino et al., 2019a). For instance, given the sentence "Manchin says

---

[1]Code for reproducing the results can be found at `https://github.com/shehel/BERT_propaganda_detection`

Democrats acted like babies ...", the ground truth of FLC includes the detected propaganda technique for the fragment "babies", i.e., name-calling and labeling, as well as the start and end positions in the given text, i.e., from the 34th to the 39th characters in the sentence.

This paper describes the solution by the team "newspeak", which achieved the highest evaluation scores on both the development and test datasets of the FLC task. Our solution utilizes BERT (Devlin et al., 2018), a Transformer (Vaswani et al., 2017) based language model relying on multiheaded attention, and fine-tunes it for the purpose of the FLC task. One benefit of using the transformer architecture is that it leads to a more explainable model, especially with the fine grained information available through the dataset. We take a step in this direction by exploring the internals of the fine-tuned BERT model. To do so, we adapt the methods used in (Clark et al., 2019) and (Michel et al., 2019). In particular, we explore the average attention head distribution entropy, head importance, impact of masking out layers, and study the attention maps. The results reveal that the attention heads capture interpretable patterns, similar to ones observed in (Clark et al., 2019).

The rest of the paper is organized as follows. Section 2 presents our solution and elaborates on the architecture, training considerations and implementation details. Section 3 provides the results and analysis. Section 4 concludes with future directions.

2 Method

2.1 Solution Overview

We approach the problem by classifying each token in the input article into 20 token types, i.e., one for each of the 18 propaganda techniques,

Proceedings of the 2nd Workshop on NLP for Internet Freedom: Censorship, Disinformation, and Propaganda, pages 87–91
Hong Kong, China, November 4, 2019 ©2019 Association for Computational Linguistics

a "background" token type that signifies that the corresponding token is not part of a propaganda technique, and another "auxiliary" type to handle WordPiece tokenization (Devlin et al., 2018). For example, the word "Federalist" is converted to "Federal" and "ist" tokens after tokenization, and the latter would be assigned the auxiliary token type. Since the labels provided in the dataset are at character level, before training our classifier, we first perform a pre-processing step that converts these character level labels to token level, which is later reversed during post-processing to obtain the outputs at the character level. This is done by keeping track of character indices of every word in the sentence.

The token classifier is obtained by fine-tuning a pre-trained BERT model with the input dataset and the token-level labels from the pre-processing step. Specifically, we add a linear classification head to the last layer of BERT for token classification. To limit training costs, we split articles by sentence and process each sentence independently in the subsequent token classifier. The classification results are combined in the post-processing step to obtain the final predictions, as mentioned earlier.

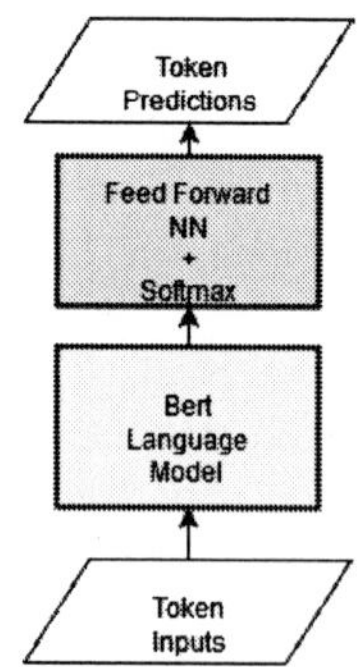

Figure 1: Architecture of our solution

2.2 Modeling

During the competition, we mainly explored three model architectures. The first is a simple scheme of fine-tuning a pre-trained BERT language model with a linear multilabel classification layer, as shown in Figure 1. The second performs unsupervised fine-tuning of the language model on the 1M news dataset (Corney et al., 2016) before supervised training on the competition dataset. This is motivated by the consideration of accounting for domain shift factors, since the BERT base model used in our solution was pretrained on BookCorpus and Wikipedia datasets (Devlin et al., 2018), whereas the dataset in this competition are news articles (Rietzler et al., 2019; Peters et al., 2019). Finally, the third model uses a single language model with 18 linear binary classification layers, one for each class. This is mainly to overcome the issue of overlapping labels, which is ignored in the former two model designs. Our final submission is based on the first architecture. Additionally, a fine-tuned BERT model with default parameters, i.e., the same setup described in the implementation section except for the learning rate schedule and sampling strategy, is used as a baseline for comparison in our experiments.

Preprocessing. Our solution performs token-level classification, while the data labels are at the character level. In our experiments, we observe that the conversion from character-level to token-level labels (for model fitting), as well as the reverse process (for prediction) incur a small performance penalty due to information lost in the conversion processes. Our final model in this competition does not consider overlapping labels, which occurs when one token belongs to multiple propaganda techniques simultaneously. Through experiments, we found that due to the above issues, the ground truth labels in the training data lead to an imperfect F1 score of 0.89 on the same dataset. This suggests that there is still much space for further improvement.

Dealing with Class Imbalance. The dataset provided in this competition is unbalanced with respect to propaganda classes. Some classes, such as "Strawmen", only have a few tens of training samples. To alleviate this problem, our solution employs two oversampling strategies: (i) weighting rarer classes with higher probability and (ii) sample propaganda sentences with a higher probability (say, 50% higher) than non-propaganda sentences. Such oversampling, however, also have adverse effects such as loss of precision and overfitting. Hence, the sampling method in our final submission strikes a balance through curriculum learning (Bengio et al., 2009), whereby an oversampling strategy is used in the first half of the training and sequential sampling is used in the second half.

Implementation. We trained all models on a machine with 4 Nvidia RTX 2080 Ti graphic cards. Our implementation is based on the Py-

Torch framework, using the pytorch-transformers package.[2] To accelerate training, all models were trained in mixed precision.

Our best models are based on the uncased base model of BERT which was found to work better than cased model, containing 12 transformer layers and 110 million parameters trained using the following hyper-parameters: batch size 64, sequence length 210, weight decay 0.01, and early stopping on F1 score on the validation set with patience value 7. Each model, including the final submission, was trained for 20 epochs. We used the Adam optimizer with a learning rate of 3e-5 and cosine annealing cycles with hard restarts and warmup of 10% of the total steps.

During the event, participants had only access to the training set labels which was split into a training set and a validation set with 30% of the articles chosen randomly. Models for submitting to the development set was chosen based on validation F1 scores, which in turn, informed the submissions for the test set.

2.3 Attention Analysis

We first measure the general change in behavior of the attention heads after finetuning on the dataset. We do this by visualizing the average entropy of each head's attention distribution before and after finetuning on the dataset. Intuitively, this measures how focused the attention weights of each of the heads are.

Next, we calculate head importance using

$$I_h = \mathbb{E}_{x \sim X} \left| \frac{\partial \mathcal{L}(x)}{\partial \xi_h} \right|, \tag{1}$$

where ξ_h is a binary mask applied to the multihead attention function to nullify it. X is the data distribution and $\mathcal{L}(x)$ is the loss on sample x. If I_h has a large value, it can be interpreted as an important head since changing it could also have a greater impact on the performance of the model. We use these scores to determine heads to visualize.

3 Results

The model that performed the best empirically was the BERT language model with a simple classifier, with parameter tuning, masked logits, cyclical learning rates and a sampling strategy. Table 1 shows the scores on the development set of

[2] https://github.com/huggingface/
pytorch-transformers

Model	F1	Precision	Recall
BERT-baseline	0.2214	0.252	0.1972
BERT-18 Binary	0.2273	0.2603	0.2017
BERT-1M News	0.2078	0.2671	0.17
BERT-submission	**0.242**	**0.289**	**0.208**

Table 1: Evaluation results on official development set

Technique	Dev F1	Test F1
Appeal-Authority	0	0
Appeal-Fear	0.3268	0.209
Bandwagon	0	0
Black-White-Fallacy	0	0.09
Casual-Oversimplification	0.05	0
Doubt	0.125	0.169
Exaggeration-Minimisation	0.276	0.159
Flag-Waving	0.409	0.438
Loaded-Language	0.4078	0.331
Namecalling-Labeling	0.2605	0.394
Obfuscation-Confusion	0	0
Red-Herring	0	0
Reductio-Hitlerum	0.206	0
Repetition	0.014	0.011
Slogans	0.153	0.1305
Strawmen	0	0
Thought-Cliches	0	0
Whataboutism	0.16	0

Table 2: Classwise F1 scores for final submission

the models we tried including the baseline BERT model. Retraining language model on 1M News dataset failed to match the performance of the original model. The model design with multiple binary classification linear layers (which is capable of predicting multiple labels for a token) obtained better results on some rarer classes; however, its performance on more common classes is lower, leading to a lower overall F1 score. However, we cannot draw conclusions on these approaches as we hypothesize that this could be improved by using a more optimal learning approach.

The model with the highest score based on BERT with a single multilabel token classification head was chosen as our submission to evaluate on the test set which yielded a test F1 score of 0.2488, 0.286 precision and 0.22 recall (see table 2 for class wise scores). This model won the competition.

We improved on the strong performance of baseline BERT model by firstly using an oversampling strategy where sentences with propaganda are weighted more, which in our final submission was 50%. Such an approach works because the number of sentences with no propaganda is much higher than that of ones with propaganda. Attempts at fixing the imbalance among propaganda techniques was found to be detrimental for the purpose of this competition, because the evaluation metric does not take into account this imbalance. Although oversampling helped the model

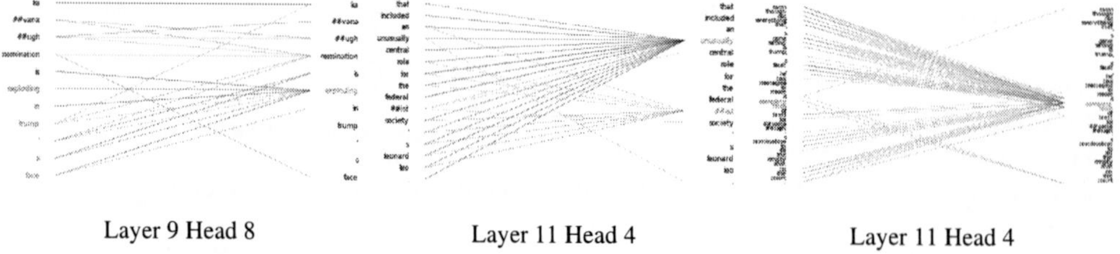

Layer 9 Head 8   Layer 11 Head 4   Layer 11 Head 4

Figure 2: Attention maps labeled by their layer and head number respectively. Green highlights propaganda fragment and red highlights the behaviour. The darkness of the line corresponds to the strength of the weight.

learn, we found that this led to overfitting and the model losing precision. Ablation studies showed that following oversampling with sequential sampling did indeed help improve the precision of the system. Second, we used an appropriate cyclic learning rate scheme to avoid poor local minima (Smith, 2017) as explained in previous section.

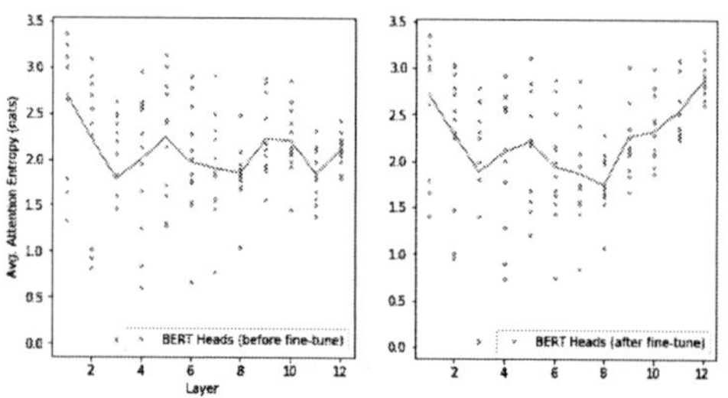

Figure 3: Average entropy of the attention weights of every attention head across layers

We examined attention heads from different layers based on their importance score. Excluding the linguistic patterns reported in (Clark et al., 2019), additional task specific patterns were observed indicating the model's ability to represent complex relationships (See Fig 2). For example, a number of heads appear to attend to adjectives and adverbs that could be useful for several propaganda techniques. Similarly, some heads pick out certain "loaded" words which all words in the sentence strongly attend to. However, it should be noted that the roles of attention heads are not clear cut, and further experimentation is required to further study this issue.

Next, we calculated the average entropy of the attention distribution of heads before and after fine-tuning. Fig 3 shows the entropy after the 8th layer increasing after fine-tuning while the earlier layers remain almost unchanged. It also happens that most of the high importance ranked heads are clustered between layers 5 and 8. We tried masking out the last 4 layers and fine-tuning the model giving an F1 score of 0.2 on the development set. This leads us to believe that BERT is still undertrained after fine-tuning as explored in (Liu et al., 2019) and requires better training strategies and hyperparameter selection schemes to fully utilize it.

4 Conclusion and Future Work

This paper describe our winning solution in the Fragment Level Classification (FLC) task of the Fine-Grained Propaganda Detection Challenge in NLP4IF'19. Our approach is based on the BERT language model, which exhibits strong performance out of the box. We explored several techniques and architectures to improve on the baseline, and performed attention analysis methods to explore the model. Our work highlights the difficulty of applying overparameterized models which can easily lead to sub-optimal utilization as shown in our analysis. The results confirm that language models are clearly a step forward for NLP in terms of linguistic modeling evident from its strong performance in detecting complex propaganda techniques.

Regarding future work, we plan to explore further methods for parameter efficient modeling which we hypothesize as being key for capturing interpretable linguistic patterns and consequently better representations. One related direction of research is spanBERT (Joshi et al., 2019), which includes a pretraining phase consisting of predicting spans instead of tokens which is inherently more suited for the propaganda dataset. Further, we plan to investigate methods and models that are capable of capturing features across multiple sentences, which are important for detecting some propaganda classes such as repetition. Finally, we also plan to look into visualizing and identifying additional patterns from the attention heads.

Acknowledgments

This publication was made possible by NPRP grant NPRP10-0208-170408 from the Qatar National Research Fund (a member of Qatar Foundation). The findings herein reflect the work, and are solely the responsibility, of the authors.

References

Alberto Barrón-Cedeño, Giovanni Da San Martino, Israa Jaradat, and Preslav Nakov. 2019. Proppy: A system to unmask propaganda in online news. In *Proceedings of the AAAI Conference on Artificial Intelligence*, volume 33, pages 9847–9848.

Yoshua Bengio, Jérôme Louradour, Ronan Collobert, and Jason Weston. 2009. Curriculum learning. In *Proceedings of the 26th annual international conference on machine learning*, pages 41–48. ACM.

Kevin Clark, Urvashi Khandelwal, Omer Levy, and Christopher D Manning. 2019. What does bert look at? an analysis of bert's attention. *arXiv preprint arXiv:1906.04341*.

David Corney, Dyaa Albakour, Miguel Martinez, and Samir Moussa. 2016. What do a million news articles look like? In *Proceedings of the First International Workshop on Recent Trends in News Information Retrieval co-located with 38th European Conference on Information Retrieval (ECIR 2016), Padua, Italy, March 20, 2016.*, pages 42–47.

Giovanni Da San Martino, Alberto Barron-Cedeno, and Preslav Nakov. 2019a. Findings of the nlp4if-2019 shared task on fine-grained propaganda detection. In *Proceedings of the 2nd Workshop on NLP for Internet Freedom (NLP4IF): Censorship, Disinformation, and Propaganda*, NLP4IFEMNLP '19, Hong Kong, China.

Giovanni Da San Martino, Seunghak Yu, Alberto Barrón-Cedeño, Rostislav Petrov, and Preslav Nakov. 2019b. Fine-grained analysis of propaganda in news articles. In *Proceedings of the 2019 Conference on Empirical Methods in Natural Language Processing and 9th International Joint Conference on Natural Language Processing, EMNLP-IJCNLP 2019, Hong Kong, China, November 3-7, 2019*, EMNLP-IJCNLP 2019, Hong Kong, China.

Jacob Devlin, Ming-Wei Chang, Kenton Lee, and Kristina Toutanova. 2018. Bert: Pre-training of deep bidirectional transformers for language understanding. *arXiv preprint arXiv:1810.04805*.

Mandar Joshi, Danqi Chen, Yinhan Liu, Daniel S Weld, Luke Zettlemoyer, and Omer Levy. 2019. Spanbert: Improving pre-training by representing and predicting spans. *arXiv preprint arXiv:1907.10529*.

Garth S Jowett and Victoria O'donnell. 2018. *Propaganda & persuasion*. Sage Publications.

Yinhan Liu, Myle Ott, Naman Goyal, Jingfei Du, Mandar Joshi, Danqi Chen, Omer Levy, Mike Lewis, Luke Zettlemoyer, and Veselin Stoyanov. 2019. Roberta: A robustly optimized bert pretraining approach. *arXiv preprint arXiv:1907.11692*.

Paul Michel, Omer Levy, and Graham Neubig. 2019. Are sixteen heads really better than one? *arXiv preprint arXiv:1905.10650*.

Matthew Peters, Sebastian Ruder, and Noah A Smith. 2019. To tune or not to tune? adapting pretrained representations to diverse tasks. *arXiv preprint arXiv:1903.05987*.

Hannah Rashkin, Eunsol Choi, Jin Yea Jang, Svitlana Volkova, and Yejin Choi. 2017. Truth of varying shades: Analyzing language in fake news and political fact-checking. In *Proceedings of the 2017 Conference on Empirical Methods in Natural Language Processing*, pages 2931–2937.

Alexander Rietzler, Sebastian Stabinger, Paul Opitz, and Stefan Engl. 2019. Adapt or get left behind: Domain adaptation through bert language model finetuning for aspect-target sentiment classification. *arXiv preprint arXiv:1908.11860*.

Leslie N Smith. 2017. Cyclical learning rates for training neural networks. In *2017 IEEE Winter Conference on Applications of Computer Vision (WACV)*, pages 464–472. IEEE.

Ashish Vaswani, Noam Shazeer, Niki Parmar, Jakob Uszkoreit, Llion Jones, Aidan N Gomez, Łukasz Kaiser, and Illia Polosukhin. 2017. Attention is all you need. In *Advances in neural information processing systems*, pages 5998–6008.

Neural Architectures for Fine-Grained Propaganda Detection in News

Pankaj Gupta[1,2], Khushbu Saxena[1], Usama Yaseen[1,2], Thomas Runkler[1], Hinrich Schütze[2]
[1]Corporate Technology, Machine-Intelligence (MIC-DE), Siemens AG Munich, Germany
[2]CIS, University of Munich (LMU) Munich, Germany
`pankaj.gupta@siemens.com` | `pankaj.gupta@campus.lmu.de`

Abstract

This paper describes our system (MIC-CIS) details and results of participation in the fine-grained propaganda detection shared task 2019. To address the tasks of sentence (SLC) and fragment level (FLC) propaganda detection, we explore different neural architectures (e.g., CNN, LSTM-CRF and BERT) and extract linguistic (e.g., part-of-speech, named entity, readability, sentiment, emotion, etc.), layout and topical features. Specifically, we have designed multi-granularity and multi-tasking neural architectures to jointly perform both the sentence and fragment level propaganda detection. Additionally, we investigate different ensemble schemes such as majority-voting, relax-voting, etc. to boost overall system performance. Compared to the other participating systems, our submissions are ranked 3rd and 4th in FLC and SLC tasks, respectively.

1 Introduction

In the age of information dissemination without quality control, it has enabled malicious users to spread misinformation via social media and aim individual users with propaganda campaigns to achieve political and financial gains as well as advance a specific agenda. Often disinformation is complied in the two major forms: fake news and propaganda, where they differ in the sense that the propaganda is possibly built upon true information (e.g., biased, loaded language, repetition, etc.).

Prior works (Rashkin et al., 2017; Habernal et al., 2017; Barrón-Cedeño et al., 2019) in detecting propaganda have focused primarily at document level, typically labeling all articles from a propagandistic news outlet as propaganda and thus, often non-propagandistic articles from the outlet are mislabeled. To this end, Da San Martino et al. (2019) focuses on analyzing the use of propaganda and detecting specific propagandistic

techniques in news articles at sentence and fragment level, respectively and thus, promotes explainable AI. For instance, the following text is a propaganda of type 'slogan'.

> Trump tweeted: ‘‘BUILD THE WALL!’’
> _{slogan}

Shared Task: This work addresses the two tasks in propaganda detection (Da San Martino et al., 2019) of different granularities: (1) *Sentence-level Classification* (SLC), a binary classification that predicts whether a sentence contains at least one propaganda technique, and (2) *Fragment-level Classification* (FLC), a token-level (multi-label) classification that identifies both the spans and the type of propaganda technique(s).

Contributions: **(1)** To address SLC, we design an ensemble of different classifiers based on Logistic Regression, CNN and BERT, and leverage transfer learning benefits using the pre-trained embeddings/models from FastText and BERT. We also employed different features such as linguistic (sentiment, readability, emotion, part-of-speech and named entity tags, etc.), layout, topics, etc. **(2)** To address FLC, we design a multi-task neural sequence tagger based on LSTM-CRF and linguistic features to jointly detect propagandistic fragments and its type. Moreover, we investigate performing FLC and SLC jointly in a multi-granularity network based on LSTM-CRF and BERT. **(3)** Our system (MIC-CIS) is ranked 3rd (out of 12 participants) and 4th (out of 25 participants) in FLC and SLC tasks, respectively.

2 System Description

2.1 Linguistic, Layout and Topical Features

Some of the propaganda techniques (Da San Martino et al., 2019) involve word and phrases that express strong emotional implications, exaggeration, minimization, doubt, national feeling, label-

Proceedings of the 2nd Workshop on NLP for Internet Freedom: Censorship, Disinformation, and Propaganda, pages 92–97
Hong Kong, China, November 4, 2019 ©2019 Association for Computational Linguistics

Category	Feature	Description
Linguistic	POS	part-of-speech tags using NLTk toolkit
	NER	named-entity tags using spacy toolkit, selected tags: {PERSON, NORP, FAC, ORG, GPE, LOC, EVENT, WORK_OF_ART, LAW, LANGUAGE}
	character analysis	count of question and exclamation marks in sentence capital features for each word: first-char-capital, all-char-capital, etc.
	readability	readability and complexity scores using measures from textstat API
	multi-meaning	sum of meanings of a word (grouped by POS) or its synonym nest in the sentence using WordNet
	sentiment	polarity (positive, negative, neural, compound) scores using spacy; subjectivity using TextBlob; max_pos: maximum of positive, max_neg: max of negative scores of each word in the sentence
	emotional	Emotion features (sadness, joy, fear, disgust, and anger) using IBM Watson NLU API
	loaded words	list of specific words and phrases with strong emotional implications (positive or negative)
Layout	sentence position	categorized as [FIRST, TOP, MIDDLE, BOTTOM, LAST], where, FIRST: 1st, TOP: $< 30\%$, Middle: between 30-70%, BOTTOM: $> 70\%$, LAST: last sentence of document
	sentence length (l)	categorized as $[= 2, 2 < l \leq 4, 4 < l \leq 8, 8 < l \leq 20, 20 < l \leq 40, 40 < l \leq 60, l > 60]$
Topical	topics	document-topic proportion using LDA, features derived using dominant topic (DT): [DT of current sentence == DT of document, DT of current sentence == DT of the next and previous sentences]
Representation	word vector	pre-trained word vectors from FastText (*FastTextWordEmb*) and BERT (*BERTWordEmb*)
	sentence vector	summing word vectors of the sentence to obtain *FastTextSentEmb* and *BERTSentEmb*
Decision	relax-boundary	(binary classification) Relax decision boundary and tag propaganda if prediction probability $\geq \tau$
Ensemble	majority-voting	Propaganda if majority says propaganda. In conflict, take prediction of the model with highest F1
	relax-voting	Propaganda if $\mathcal{M} \in [20\%, 30\%, 40\%]$ of models in the ensemble says propaganda.

Table 1: Features used in SLC and FLC tasks

ing , stereotyping, etc. This inspires[1] us in extracting different features (Table 1) including the complexity of text, sentiment, emotion, lexical (POS, NER, etc.), layout, etc. To further investigate, we use topical features (e.g., document-topic proportion) (Blei et al., 2003; Gupta et al., 2019a, 2018) at sentence and document levels in order to determine irrelevant themes, if introduced to the issue being discussed (e.g., *Red Herring*).

For word and sentence representations, we use pre-trained vectors from FastText (Bojanowski et al., 2017) and BERT (Devlin et al., 2019).

2.2 Sentence-level Propaganda Detection

Figure 1 (left) describes the three components of our system for SLC task: features, classifiers and ensemble. The arrows from features-to-classifier indicate that we investigate linguistic, layout and topical features in the two binary classifiers: LogisticRegression and CNN. For CNN, we follow the architecture of Kim (2014) for sentence-level classification, initializing the word vectors by FastText or BERT. We concatenate features in the last hidden layer before classification.

One of our strong classifiers includes BERT that has achieved state-of-the-art performance on multiple NLP benchmarks. Following Devlin et al. (2019), we fine-tune BERT for binary classification, initializing with a pre-trained model (i.e., *BERT-base, Cased*). Additionally, we apply a decision function (Table 1) such that a sentence is tagged as propaganda if prediction probability of the classifier is greater than a threshold (τ). We relax the binary decision boundary to boost recall, similar to Gupta et al. (2019b).

Ensemble of Logistic Regression, CNN and BERT: In the final component, we collect predictions (i.e., propaganda label) for each sentence from the three ($\mathcal{M} = 3$) classifiers and thus, obtain $\mathcal{M}$ number of predictions for each sentence. We explore two ensemble strategies (Table 1): majority-voting and relax-voting to boost precision and recall, respectively.

2.3 Fragment-level Propaganda Detection

Figure 1 (right) describes our system for FLC task, where we design sequence taggers (Vu et al., 2016; Gupta et al., 2016) in three modes: (1) *LSTM-CRF* (Lample et al., 2016) with word embeddings (w_e) and character embeddings c_e, token-level features (t_f) such as polarity, POS, NER, etc. (2) *LSTM-CRF+Multi-grain* that jointly performs FLC and SLC with FastTextWordEmb and BERTSentEmb, respectively. Here, we add binary

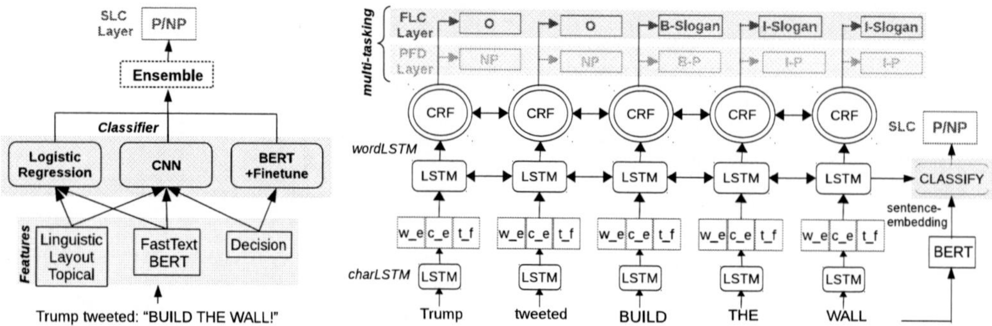

Figure 1: (Left): System description for SLC, including features, transfer learning using pre-trained word embeddings from FastText and BERT and classifiers: LogisticRegression, CNN and BERT fine-tuning. (Right): System description for FLC, including multi-tasking LSTM-CRF architecture consisting of Propaganda Fragment Detection (PFD) and FLC layers. Observe, a binary classification component at the last hidden layer in the recurrent architecture that jointly performs PFD, FLC and SLC tasks (i.e., multi-grained propaganda detection). Here, P: Propaganda, NP: Non-propaganda, B/I/O: Begin, Intermediate and Other tags of BIO tagging scheme.

sentence classification loss to sequence tagging weighted by a factor of α. (3) *LSTM-CRF+Multi-task* that performs propagandistic span/fragment detection (PFD) and FLC (fragment detection + 19-way classification).

Ensemble of Multi-grain, Multi-task LSTM-CRF with BERT: Here, we build an ensemble by considering propagandistic fragments (and its type) from each of the sequence taggers. In doing so, we first perform majority voting at the fragment level for the fragment where their spans exactly overlap. In case of non-overlapping fragments, we consider all. However, when the spans overlap (though with the same label), we consider the fragment with the largest span.

3 Experiments and Evaluation

Data: While the SLC task is binary, the FLC consists of 18 propaganda techniques (Da San Martino et al., 2019). We split (80-20%) the annotated corpus into 5-folds and 3-folds for SLC and FLC tasks, respectively. The development set of each the folds is represented by dev (internal); however, the un-annotated corpus used in leaderboard comparisons by dev (external). We remove empty and single token sentences after tokenization.

Experimental Setup: We use PyTorch framework for the pre-trained BERT model (*Bert-base-cased*[2]), fine-tuned for SLC task. In the multi-granularity loss, we set $\alpha = 0.1$ for sentence classification based on dev (internal, fold1) scores. We

[2] github.com/ThilinaRajapakse/
pytorch-transformers-classification

Task: **SLC** (25 participants)		Task: **FLC** (12 participants)	
Team	*F1 / P / R*	**Team**	*F1 / P / R*
ltuorp	**.6323** / .6028 / .6649	*newspeak*	**.2488** / .2863 / **.2201**
ProperGander	.6256 / .5649 / **.7009**	*Antiganda*	.2267 / **.2882** / .1869
YMJA	.6249 / **.6253** / .6246	**MIC-CIS**	.1999 / .2234 / .1808
MIC-CIS	.6231 / .5736 / .6819	*Stalin*	.1453 / .1921 / .1169
TeamOne	.6183 / .5779 / .6649	*TeamOne*	.1311 / .3235 / .0822

Table 2: Comparison of our system (MIC-CIS) with top-5 participants: Scores on Test set for SLC and FLC

use BIO tagging scheme of NER in FLC task. For CNN, we follow Kim (2014) with filter-sizes of [2, 3, 4, 5, 6], 128 filters and 16 batch-size. We compute binary-F1and macro-F1[3] (Tsai et al., 2006) in SLC and FLC, respectively on dev (internal). See Table 5 for hyper-parameter settings for FLC task using LSTM-CRF.

3.1 Results: Sentence-Level Propaganda

Table 3 shows the scores on dev (internal and external) for SLC task. Observe that the pre-trained embeddings (FastText or BERT) outperform TF-IDF vector representation. In row r2, we apply logistic regression classifier with *BERTSentEmb* that leads to improved scores over *FastTextSentEmb*. Subsequently, we augment the sentence vector with additional features that improves F1 on dev (external), however not dev (internal). Next, we initialize CNN by *FastTextWordEmb* or *BERT-WordEmb* and augment the last hidden layer (before classification) with *BERTSentEmb* and feature vectors, leading to gains in F1 for both the dev sets. Further, we fine-tune BERT and apply differ-

[3] evaluation measure with strict boundary detection

| | Dev (internal), Fold1 | | Dev (external) |
	Features	$F1 / P / R$	$F1 / P / R$
r1	*logisticReg* + TF-IDF	.569 / .542 / .598	.506 / .529 / .486
r2	*logisticReg* + FastTextSentEmb	.606 / .544 / .685	.614 / .595 / .635
	+ Linguistic	.605 / .553 / .667	.613 / .593 / .633
	+ Layout	.600 / .550 / .661	.611 / .591 / .633
	+ Topical	.603 / .552 / .664	.612 / .592 / .633
r3	*logisticReg* + BERTSentEmb	.614 / .560 / .679	.636 / .638 / .635
r4	+ Linguistic, Layout, Topical	.611 / .564 / .666	.643 / .641 / .644
r5	*CNN* + FastTextWordEmb	.616 / .685 / .559	.563 / .655 / .494
r6	+ BERTSentEmb	.612 / **.693** / .548	.568 / .673 / .491
r7	+ Linguistic, Layout, Topical	.648 / .630 / .668	.632 / .644 / .621
r8	*CNN* + BERTWordEmb	.610 / .688 / .549	.544 / .667 / .459
r9	+ Linguistic, Layout, Topical	.616 / .671 / .570	.555 / .662 / .478
r10	*BERT* + Fine-tune ($\tau \geq .50$)	.662 / .635 / .692	.639 / .653 / .625
r11	*BERT* + Fine-tune ($\tau \geq .40$)	.664 / .625 / .708	.649 / .651 / .647
r12	*BERT* + Fine-tune ($\tau \geq .35$)	.662 / .615 / .715	.650 / .647 / .654
Ensemble of (r3, r6, r12) within Fold1			
r15	majority-voting $|\mathcal{M}| > 50\%$	.666 / .663 / .671	.638 / .674 / .605
r16	relax-voting, $|\mathcal{M}| \geq 30\%$	.645 / .528 / .826	.676 / .592 / .788
Ensemble+ of (r3, r6, r12) from each **Fold1-5**, i.e., $|\mathcal{M}| = 15$			
r17	majority-voting $|\mathcal{M}| > 50\%$		.666 / **.683** / .649
r18	relax-voting, $|\mathcal{M}| \geq 40\%$		.670 / .646 / .696
r19	relax-voting, $|\mathcal{M}| \geq 30\%$		<u>.673</u> / .619 / <u>.737</u>
r20	+ postprocess (w=10, $\lambda \geq .99$)		.669 / .612 / .737
r21	+ postprocess (w=10, $\lambda \geq .95$)		.671 / .612 / .741
Ensemble of (r4, r7, r12) within Fold1			
r22	majority-voting $|\mathcal{M}| > 50\%$	**.669** / .641 / .699	.660 / .663 / .656
r23	relax-voting, $|\mathcal{M}| \geq 30\%$	.650 / .525 / **.852**	.674 / .584 / .797
Ensemble+ of (r4, r7, r12) from each **Fold1-5**, i.e., $|\mathcal{M}| = 15$			
r24	majority-voting $|\mathcal{M}| > 50\%$		.658 / .671 / .645
r25	relax-voting, $|\mathcal{M}| \geq 40\%$		.673 / .644 / .705
r26	relax-voting, $|\mathcal{M}| \geq 30\%$		**.679** / .622 / .747
r27	+ postprocess (w=10, $\lambda \geq .99$)		.674 / .615 / .747
r28	+ postprocess (w=10, $\lambda \geq .95$)		.676 / .615 / **.751**

Table 3: SLC: Scores on Dev (internal) of Fold1 and Dev (external) using different classifiers and features.

| | Dev (internal), Fold1 | | Dev (external) |
	Features	$F1 / P / R$	$F1 / P / R$
(I) *LSTM-CRF* + FastTextWordEmb		.153 / .228 / .115	.122 / .248 / .081
(II) + Polarity, POS, NER		.158 / .292 / .102	.101 / .286 / .061
(III) + Multi-grain (SLC+FLC)		.148 / .215 / .112	.119 / .200 / .085
(IV) + BERTSentEmb		.152 / .264 / .106	.099 / .248 / .062
(V) + Multi-task (PFD)		.144 / .187 / .117	.114 / .179 / .083
Ensemble of (II and IV) within **Fold1**			
+ postprocess			.116 / .221 / .076
Ensemble of (II and IV) within **Fold2**			
+ postprocess			.129 / .261 / .085
Ensemble of (II and IV) within **Fold3**			
+ postprocess			.133 / .220 / .095
Ensemble+ of (II and IV) from each **Fold1-3**, i.e., $|\mathcal{M}| = 6$			
+ postprocess			.164 / .182 / .150

Table 4: FLC: Scores on Dev (internal) of Fold1 and Dev (external) with different models, features and ensembles. PFD: Propaganda Fragment Detection.

r19 and r21, we observe a gain in recall, however an overall decrease in F1 applying *postprocess*.

Finally, we use the configuration of r19 on the test set. The ensemble+ of (r4, r7 r12) was analyzed after test submission. Table 2 (SLC) shows that our submission is ranked at 4th position.

3.2 Results: Fragment-Level Propaganda

Table 4 shows the scores on dev (internal and external) for FLC task. Observe that the features (i.e., polarity, POS and NER in row II) when introduced in LSTM-CRF improves F1. We run multi-grained LSTM-CRF without BERTSentEmb (i.e., row III) and with it (i.e., row IV), where the latter improves scores on dev (internal), however not on dev (external). Finally, we perform multi-tasking with another auxiliary task of PFD. Given the scores on dev (internal and external) using different configurations (rows I-V), it is difficult to infer the optimal configuration. Thus, we choose the two best configurations (II and IV) on dev (internal) set and build an ensemble+ of predictions (discussed in section 2.3), leading to a boost in recall and thus an improved F1 on dev (external).

Finally, we use the ensemble+ of (II and IV) from each of the folds 1-3, i.e., $|\mathcal{M}| = 6$ models to obtain predictions on test. Table 2 (FLC) shows that our submission is ranked at 3rd position.

4 Conclusion and Future Work

Our system (Team: MIC-CIS) explores different neural architectures (CNN, BERT and LSTM-CRF) with linguistic, layout and topical features

ent thresholds in relaxing the decision boundary, where $\tau \geq 0.35$ is found optimal.

We choose the three different models in the ensemble: Logistic Regression, CNN and BERT on fold1 and subsequently an ensemble+ of r3, r6 and r12 from each fold1-5 (i.e., 15 models) to obtain predictions for dev (external). We investigate different ensemble schemes (r17-r19), where we observe that the relax-voting improves recall and therefore, the higher F1 (i.e., 0.673). In *postprocess* step, we check for *repetition* propaganda technique by computing cosine similarity between the current sentence and its preceding $w = 10$ sentence vectors (i.e., BERTSentEmb) in the document. If the cosine-similarity is greater than $\lambda \in \{.99, .95\}$, then the current sentence is labeled as propaganda due to repetition. Comparing

Hyper-parameter	Value
learning rate	0.005
character (char) dimension	25
hidden unit::char LSTM	25
POS dimensions	25
hidden unit::word LSTM	200*, 100
word embeddings dimension	300
α	1.0, 0.1*

Table 5: Hyper-parameter settings for FLC task. * denotes the optimal parameters.

to address the tasks of fine-grained propaganda detection. We have demonstrated gains in performance due to the features, ensemble schemes, multi-tasking and multi-granularity architectures. Compared to the other participating systems, our submissions are ranked 3rd and 4th in FLC and SLC tasks, respectively.

In future, we would like to enrich BERT models with linguistic, layout and topical features during their fine-tuning. Further, we would also be interested in understanding and analyzing the neural network learning, i.e., extracting salient fragments (or key-phrases) in the sentence that generate propaganda, similar to Gupta and Schütze (2018) in order to promote explainable AI.

Acknowledgment

This research was supported by Bundeswirtschaftsministerium (bmwi.de), grant 01MD19003E (PLASS, plass.io) at Siemens AG - CT Machine Intelligence, Munich Germany.

References

Alberto Barrón-Cedeño, Giovanni Da San Martino, Israa Jaradat, and Preslav Nakov. 2019. Proppy: A system to unmask propaganda in online news. In *The Thirty-Third AAAI Conference on Artificial Intelligence, AAAI 2019, The Thirty-First Innovative Applications of Artificial Intelligence Conference, IAAI 2019, The Ninth AAAI Symposium on Educational Advances in Artificial Intelligence, EAAI 2019, Honolulu, Hawaii, USA, January 27 - February 1, 2019.*, pages 9847–9848.

David M. Blei, Andrew Y. Ng, and Michael I. Jordan. 2003. Latent dirichlet allocation. *J. Mach. Learn. Res.*, 3:993–1022.

Piotr Bojanowski, Edouard Grave, Armand Joulin, and Tomas Mikolov. 2017. Enriching word vectors with subword information. *TACL*, 5:135–146.

Giovanni Da San Martino, Seunghak Yu, Alberto Barrón-Cedeño, Rostislav Petrov, and Preslav Nakov. 2019. Fine-grained analysis of propaganda in news articles. In *Proceedings of the 2019 Conference on Empirical Methods in Natural Language Processing and 9th International Joint Conference on Natural Language Processing, EMNLP-IJCNLP 2019, Hong Kong, China, November 3-7, 2019*, EMNLP-IJCNLP 2019, Hong Kong, China.

Jacob Devlin, Ming-Wei Chang, Kenton Lee, and Kristina Toutanova. 2019. BERT: pre-training of deep bidirectional transformers for language understanding. In *Proceedings of the 2019 Conference of the North American Chapter of the Association for Computational Linguistics: Human Language Technologies, NAACL-HLT 2019, Minneapolis, MN, USA, June 2-7, 2019, Volume 1 (Long and Short Papers)*, pages 4171–4186.

Pankaj Gupta, Yatin Chaudhary, Florian Buettner, and Hinrich Schütze. 2019a. Document informed neural autoregressive topic models with distributional prior. In *The Thirty-Third AAAI Conference on Artificial Intelligence, AAAI 2019, The Thirty-First Innovative Applications of Artificial Intelligence Conference, IAAI 2019, The Ninth AAAI Symposium on Educational Advances in Artificial Intelligence, EAAI 2019, Honolulu, Hawaii, USA, January 27 - February 1, 2019.*, pages 6505–6512.

Pankaj Gupta, Subburam Rajaram, Hinrich Schütze, and Bernt Andrassy. 2018. Deep temporal-recurrent-replicated-softmax for topical trends over time. In *Proceedings of the 2018 Conference of the North American Chapter of the Association for Computational Linguistics: Human Language Technologies, NAACL-HLT 2018, New Orleans, Louisiana, USA, June 1-6, 2018, Volume 1 (Long Papers)*, pages 1079–1089.

Pankaj Gupta, Subburam Rajaram, Hinrich Schütze, and Thomas A. Runkler. 2019b. Neural relation extraction within and across sentence boundaries. In *The Thirty-Third AAAI Conference on Artificial Intelligence, AAAI 2019, The Thirty-First Innovative Applications of Artificial Intelligence Conference, IAAI 2019, The Ninth AAAI Symposium on Educational Advances in Artificial Intelligence, EAAI 2019, Honolulu, Hawaii, USA, January 27 - February 1, 2019.*, pages 6513–6520.

Pankaj Gupta and Hinrich Schütze. 2018. LISA: explaining recurrent neural network judgments via layer-wise semantic accumulation and example to pattern transformation. In *Proceedings of the Workshop: Analyzing and Interpreting Neural Networks for NLP, BlackboxNLP@EMNLP 2018, Brussels, Belgium, November 1, 2018*, pages 154–164.

Pankaj Gupta, Hinrich Schütze, and Bernt Andrassy. 2016. Table filling multi-task recurrent neural network for joint entity and relation extraction. In *COLING 2016, 26th International Conference on*

Computational Linguistics, Proceedings of the Conference: Technical Papers, December 11-16, 2016, Osaka, Japan, pages 2537–2547.

Ivan Habernal, Raffael Hannemann, Christian Pollak, Christopher Klamm, Patrick Pauli, and Iryna Gurevych. 2017. Argotario: Computational argumentation meets serious games. In *Proceedings of the 2017 Conference on Empirical Methods in Natural Language Processing, EMNLP 2017, Copenhagen, Denmark, September 9-11, 2017 - System Demonstrations*, pages 7–12.

Yoon Kim. 2014. Convolutional neural networks for sentence classification. In *Proceedings of the 2014 Conference on Empirical Methods in Natural Language Processing, EMNLP 2014, October 25-29, 2014, Doha, Qatar, A meeting of SIGDAT, a Special Interest Group of the ACL*, pages 1746–1751.

Guillaume Lample, Miguel Ballesteros, Sandeep Subramanian, Kazuya Kawakami, and Chris Dyer. 2016. Neural architectures for named entity recognition. In *NAACL HLT 2016, The 2016 Conference of the North American Chapter of the Association for Computational Linguistics: Human Language Technologies, San Diego California, USA, June 12-17, 2016*, pages 260–270.

Hannah Rashkin, Eunsol Choi, Jin Yea Jang, Svitlana Volkova, and Yejin Choi. 2017. Truth of varying shades: Analyzing language in fake news and political fact-checking. In *Proceedings of the 2017 Conference on Empirical Methods in Natural Language Processing, EMNLP 2017, Copenhagen, Denmark, September 9-11, 2017*, pages 2931–2937.

Richard Tzong-Han Tsai, Shih-Hung Wu, Wen-Chi Chou, Yu-Chun Lin, Ding He, Jieh Hsiang, Ting-Yi Sung, and Wen-Lian Hsu. 2006. Various criteria in the evaluation of biomedical named entity recognition. *BMC Bioinformatics*, 7:92.

Ngoc Thang Vu, Heike Adel, Pankaj Gupta, and Hinrich Schütze. 2016. Combining recurrent and convolutional neural networks for relation classification. In *Proceedings of the 2016 Conference of the North American Chapter of the Association for Computational Linguistics: Human Language Technologies*, pages 534–539. Association for Computational Linguistics.

Fine-Tuned Neural Models for Propaganda Detection at the Sentence and Fragment levels

Tariq Alhindi[†]   **Jonas Pfeiffer**[*]   **Smaranda Muresan**[††]

[†]Department of Computer Science, Columbia University
[‡]Data Science Institute, Columbia University
[*]Ubiquitous Knowledge Processing Lab, Technische Universitat Darmstadt
{tariq.a, smara}@columbia.edu
pfeiffer@ukp.informatik.tu-darmstadt.de

Abstract

This paper presents the CUNLP submission for the NLP4IF 2019 shared-task on Fine-Grained Propaganda Detection. Our system finished 5th out of 26 teams on the sentence-level classification task and 5th out of 11 teams on the fragment-level classification task based on our scores on the blind test set. We present our models, a discussion of our ablation studies and experiments, and an analysis of our performance on all eighteen propaganda techniques present in the corpus of the shared task.

1 Introduction

Propaganda aims at influencing a target audience with a specific group agenda using faulty reasoning and/or emotional appeals (Miller, 1939). Automatic detection of propaganda has been studied mainly at the article level (Rashkin et al., 2017; Barrón-Cedeño et al., 2019). However, in order to build computational models that can explain why an article is propagandistic, the model would need to detect specific techniques present at sentence or even token level.

The NLP4IF shared task on fine-grained propaganda detection aims to produce models capable of spotting propaganda techniques in sentences and text fragments in news articles (Da San Martino et al., 2019a). The data for this task consist of news articles that were labeled at the fragment level with one of eighteen propaganda techniques.

There are two sub-tasks in this shared task. The first one is a sentence classification task (SLC) to detect whether a sentence has a propaganda fragment or not. This binary classification task is evaluated based on the F1 score of the propaganda class which approximately represents one-third of the data. The second sub-task is a fragment level classification (FLC) task, in which a system needs to detect the type of propaganda technique expressed in a text fragment together with the beginning and the end of that text fragment. This task is evaluated based on the prediction of the type of propaganda technique and the intersection between the gold and the predicted spans. The details to the evaluation measure used for the FLC task are explained in Da San Martino et al. (2019a). Both sub-tasks were automatically evaluated on a unified development set. The system performance was centrally assessed without distributing the gold labels, however allowing for an unlimited number of submissions. The final performance on the test set was similarly evaluated, with the difference that the feedback was given only after the submission was closed, simultaneously concluding the shared-task.

In this paper, we describe the data in Section 2, our proposed methods for both sub-tasks in Section 3, and analyze the results and errors of our models in Section 4.

2 Data

The data for this shared task includes 350 articles in the training set, 61 articles in the development set, and 86 articles in the test set. The articles were taken from 48 news outlets; 13 propagandistic and 35 non-propagandistic as labeled by Media Bias/Fact Check[1]. These articles were annotated at the fragment level where each annotator was asked to tag the start and end of the propaganda text span as well as the type of propaganda technique. Table 1 lists all eighteen propaganda techniques and their frequencies in the training data. Since submissions to the development set were closed after the release of the test set, we divided the training set (350 articles) into a training set of 280 articles and a local dev set of 70 articles to continue to be able to perform ablation studies.

---

[1]https://mediabiasfactcheck.com/

Proceedings of the 2nd Workshop on NLP for Internet Freedom: Censorship, Disinformation, and Propaganda, pages 98–102
Hong Kong, China, November 4, 2019 ©2019 Association for Computational Linguistics

Propaganda Technique	Frequency
Loaded Language	2,115
Name Calling,Labeling	1,085
Repetition	571
Doubt	490
Exaggeration,Minimisation	479
Flag-Waving	240
Appeal to Fear/Prejudice	239
Causal Oversimplification	201
Slogans	136
Appeal to Authority	116
Black-and-White Fallacy	109
Thought-terminating Cliches	79
Whataboutism	57
Reductio ad hitlerum	54
Red Herring	33
Bandwagon	13
Straw Men	13
Obfuscation,Intentional Vagueness,Confusion	11
Total	**6,041**

Table 1: Frequency of all eighteen propaganda techniques in the training data

We also conduct our error analysis on the local dev set because we do not have access to the gold labels of the official dev and test sets of the shared task.

More details about the dataset and the annotation scheme for the eighteen propaganda techniques can be found in Da San Martino et al. (2019b). However, the results on the shared task data are not directly comparable as more articles were added to shared task's data. Da San Martino et al. (2019a) should be referred to for an accurate comparison between participants who all used the same development and test sets.

3 Methods

In the following we explain the details of our approach for the SLC and FLC tasks.

3.1 Sentence Level Classification (SLC)

We fine-tuned BERT (Devlin et al., 2019) for the binary sentence-level classification task of `propaganda` vs. `non-propaganda`. The training set has 16,298 sentences, out of which 4,720 are from the propaganda class. We used `bert-base-uncased` in our experiments as in preliminary results the cased version did not provide any improvements. The model was trained for 3 epochs using a learning rate of 2e-5, a maximum sequence length of 128, and a batch size of 16. We also experiment with a Logistic Regression Classifiers, where we used Linguistic Inquiry and Word Count (LIWC) features (Pen-

nebaker et al., 2001), punctuation features such as the existence of quotes or question marks, as well as BERT's prediction probabilities for each class. This gave some minor improvement on the development set of the shared-task. However, since we did not have access to the development set submission after the test set was released, we chose the final model based on the performance on the local development set. The final model used the fine-tuned BERT model mentioned above with a condition to predict `non-propaganda` only if the prediction probability is above 0.70 for the non-propaganda class. Otherwise the prediction of the sentence will be `propaganda` even if the majority of the prediction probability mass was for the `non-propaganda` class. This was a way to handle the unbalance in the training data without having to discard part of the data. The 0.70 threshold was chosen after elaborate experiments on both the local and the shared-task's development sets. This condition consistently provided an improvement of around 5 points in F1 score of the propaganda class on all experiments using different sets of features as shown in Table 2.

3.2 Fragment Level Classification (FLC)

Our architecture for the sequence labeling task builds on the flair framework (Akbik et al., 2018, 2019) that combines character level embeddings with different kinds of word embeddings as input to a BiLSTM-CRF model (Ma and Hovy, 2016; Lample et al., 2016). Akbik et al. (2018) have shown that stacking multiple pre-trained embeddings as input to the LSTM improves performance on the downstream sequence labeling task. We combine Glove embeddings (Pennington et al., 2014) with Urban Dictionary[2] embeddings[3].

Due to the small-size of our data set we additionally include one-hot-encoded features based on dictionary look-ups from the UBY dictionary provided by Gurevych et al. (2012). These features are based on concepts associated with the specific word such as *offensive, vulgar, coarse,* or *ethnic slur*. In total, 30 concept features were added as additional dimensions to the embedding representations.

We also experimented with stacking BERT embeddings with all or some of the embeddings mentioned above. However, this resulted on lower

---

[2]https://www.urbandictionary.com/
[3]https://data.world/jaredfern/urban-dictionary-embedding

scores on both the local and shared task development sets. The best model used urban-glove embeddings with concatenated one-hot encoded UBY features stacked with both forward and backward flair embeddings. The model was trained for a maximum of 150 epochs with early stopping using a learning rate of 0.1, a batch size of 32, and a BiLSTM with hidden size 256. The results of this model are shown in Table 5.

4 Results and Error Analysis

In this section we discuss the results of both subtasks on all three datasets: the local development set, the shared task development and test sets.

4.1 SLC Results

In SLC, we ran multiple experiments using BERT with and without additional features as shown in Table 2. The features include using the text passed as is to BERT without any preprocessing. Also, we experimented with adding the context which includes the two sentences that come before and after the target sentence. Context sentences were concatenated and passed as the second BERT input, while the target sentence was passed as the first BERT input. In addition, we experimented with using BERT logits (i.e., the probability predictions per class) as features in a Logistic Regression (LR) classifier concatenated with handcrafted features (e.g., LIWC, quotes, questions), and with predictions of our FLC classifier (tagged spans: whether the sentence has a propaganda fragment or not). However, none of these features added any statistically significant improvements. Therefore, we used BERT predictions for our final model with a condition to predict the majority class non-propaganda only if its prediction probability is more than 0.70 as shown in Table 3. This is a modified threshold as opposed to 0.80 in the experiments shown in Table 2 to avoid overfitting on a one dataset. The final threshold of 0.70 was chosen after experiments on both the local and shared task development sets, which also represents the ratio of the non-propaganda class in the training set.

Discussion of Propaganda Types: To further understand our model's performance in the SLC task, we looked at the accuracy of each propaganda techniques that occur more than 20 times in the local dev set as shown in Table 4.

Features	Model	Development		
		P	R	F
text	BERT	0.69	0.55	0.61
text	**BERT***	**0.57**	**0.79**	**0.66**
context	BERT	0.70	0.53	0.60
context	BERT*	0.63	0.67	0.65
BERT logits + handcrafted**	LR	0.70	0.56	0.61
BERT logits + handcrafted**	LR*	0.60	0.71	0.65
BERT logits + tagged spans	LR	0.70	0.53	0.60
BERT logits + tagged spans	LR*	0.61	0.71	0.66
BERT logits + all	LR	0.71	0.52	0.60
BERT logits + all	LR*	0.61	0.71	0.66

*Non-propaganda class is predicted only if its prediction probability is > 0.80
**handcrafted features include LIWC and presence of questions or quotes

Table 2: SLC experiments on different feature sets

Dataset	P	R	F
Local Dev	0.60	0.75	0.67
Development	0.62	0.68	0.65
Test	0.58	0.66	0.618

*Non-propaganda class is predicted only if its prediction probability is > 0.70

Table 3: SLC best model results on all three datasets

Repetition and Doubt are the two most challenging types for the classifier even though they are in the four most frequent techniques. It is expected for Repetition to be challenging as the classifier only looks at one sentence while Repetition occurs if a word (or more) is repeatedly mentioned in the article. Therefore, more information needs to be given to the classifier such as word counts across the document of all words in a given sentence. Due to time constrains, we did not test the effect of adding such features. Doubt on the other hand could have been challenging due to its very wide lexical coverage and variant sentence structure as doubt is expressed in many different words and forms in this corpus (e.g. "How is it possible the pope signed this decree?" and "I've seen little that has changed"). It is also among the types with high variance in length where one span sometimes go across multiple sentences.

4.2 FLC Results

In FLC, we only show the results of our best model in Table 5 to focus more on the differences between propaganda techniques. A more elaborate study of performance of different models should follow in future work. The best model is a BiLSTM-CRF with flair and urban glove embed-

Technique	Count	Accuracy
Loaded Language	299	71%
Name Calling,Labeling	163	69%
Repetition	124	44%
Doubt	71	40%
Exaggeration,Minimisation	63	67%
Flag-Waving	35	74%
Appeal to Fear/Prejudice	42	52%
Causal Oversimplification	24	58%
Slogans	24	54%

Table 4: SLC accuracy on frequent propaganda techniques in the local development set

dings with one hot encoded features as mentioned in Section 3.2.

Discussion of Propaganda Types: As we can see in Table 5, we can divide the propaganda techniques into three groups according to the model's performance on the development and test sets. The first group includes techniques with non-zero F1 scores on both datasets: `Flag-Waving`, `Loaded Language`, `Name Calling,Labeling` and `Slogans`. This group has techniques that appear frequently in the data and/or techniques with strong lexical signals (e.g. "American People" in `Flag-Waving`) or punctuation signals (e.g. quotes in `Slogans`). The second group has the techniques with a non-zero F1 score on only one of the datasets but not the other, such as: `Appeal to Authority`, `Appeal to Fear`, `Doubt`, `Reduction`, and `Exaggeration,Minimisation`. Two out of these five techniques (`Appeal to Fear` and `Doubt`) have very small non-zero F1 on the development set which indicates that they are generally challenging on our model and were only tagged due to minor differences between the two datasets. However, the remaining three types show significant drops from development to test sets or vice-versa. This requires further analysis to understand why the model was able to do well on one dataset but get zero on the other dataset, which we leave for future work. The third group has the remaining nine techniques were our sequence tagger fails to correctly tag any text span on either dataset. This group has the most infrequent types as well as types beyond the ability for our tagger to spot by looking at the sentence only such as `Repetition`.

Precision and Recall: Overall, our model has the highest precision among all teams on both datasets, which could be due to adding the UBY

Propaganda Technique	Development			Test
	P	R	F	F
Appeal to Authority	0	0	0	0.212
Appeal to Fear/Prejudice	0.285	0.006	0.011	0
Bandwagon	0	0	0	0
Black-and-White Fallacy	0	0	0	0
Causal Oversimplification	0	0	0	0
Doubt	0.007	0.001	0.002	0
Exaggeration,Minimisation	0.833	0.085	0.154	0
Flag-Waving	0.534	0.102	0.171	0.195
Loaded Language	0.471	0.160	0.237	0.130
Name Calling,Labeling	0.270	0.112	0.158	0.150
O,IV,C	0	0	0	0
Red Herring	0	0	0	0
Reductio ad hitlerum	0.318	0.069	0.113	0
Repetition	0	0	0	0
Slogans	0.221	0.034	0.059	0.003
Straw Men	0	0	0	0
Thought-terminating Cliches	0	0	0	0
Whataboutism	0	0	0	0
Overall	0.365	0.073	0.122	0.131*

*Test set overall precision is 0.323 and recall is 0.082. Precision and recall per technique were not provided for the test set by the task organizers.

Table 5: Precision, recall and F1 scores of the FLC task on the development and test sets of the shared task.

one-hot encoded features that highlighted some strong signals for some propaganda types. This also could be the reason for our model to have the lowest recall among the top 7 teams on both datasets as having explicit handcrafted signals suffers from the usual sparseness that accompanies these kinds of representations which could have made the model more conservative in tagging text spans.

4.3 Remarks from Both Tasks

In light of our results on both sub-tasks, we notice that the BERT-based sentence classification model is performing well on some propaganda types such as `Loaded Language` and `Flag-Waving`. It would be interesting to test in future work if using BERT as a sequence tagger (and not BERT embeddings in a BiLSTM-CRF tagger like we tested) would help in improving the sequence tagging results on those particular types. Finally, we noticed two types of noise in the data; there were some duplicate articles, and in some articles the ads were crawled as part of the article and tagged as non-propaganda. These could have caused some errors in predictions and therefore investigating ways to further clean the data might be helpful.

5 Conclusion

Propaganda still remains challenging to detect with high precision at a fine-grained level. This task provided an opportunity to develop computational models that can detect propaganda techniques at sentence and fragment level. We presented our models for each sub-task and discussed challenges and limitations. For some propaganda techniques, it is not enough to only look at one sentence to make an accurate prediction (e.g. Repetition) and therefore including the whole article as context is needed. For future work, we want to experiment with using a BERT-based sequence tagger for the FLC task. In addition, we want to analyze the relationships between propaganda techniques to understand whether some techniques share common traits, which could be helpful for the classification and tagging tasks.

References

Alan Akbik, Tanja Bergmann, Duncan Blythe, Kashif Rasul, Stefan Schweter, and Roland Vollgraf. 2019. Flair: An easy-to-use framework for state-of-the-art nlp. In *Proceedings of the 2019 Conference of the North American Chapter of the Association for Computational Linguistics (Demonstrations)*, pages 54–59.

Alan Akbik, Duncan Blythe, and Roland Vollgraf. 2018. Contextual string embeddings for sequence labeling. In *COLING 2018, 27th International Conference on Computational Linguistics*, pages 1638–1649.

Alberto Barrón-Cedeño, Giovanni Da San Martino, Israa Jaradat, and Preslav Nakov. 2019. Proppy: A system to unmask propaganda in online news. In *Proceedings of the AAAI Conference on Artificial Intelligence*, volume 33, pages 9847–9848.

Giovanni Da San Martino, Alberto Barron-Cedeno, and Preslav Nakov. 2019a. Findings of the nlp4if-2019 shared task on fine-grained propaganda detection. In *Proceedings of the 2nd Workshop on NLP for Internet Freedom (NLP4IF): Censorship, Disinformation, and Propaganda*, NLP4IFEMNLP '19, Hong Kong, China.

Giovanni Da San Martino, Seunghak Yu, Alberto Barrón-Cedeño, Rostislav Petrov, and Preslav Nakov. 2019b. Fine-grained analysis of propaganda in news articles. In *Proceedings of the 2019 Conference on Empirical Methods in Natural Language Processing and 9th International Joint Conference on Natural Language Processing, EMNLP-IJCNLP 2019, Hong Kong, China, November 3-7, 2019*, EMNLP-IJCNLP 2019, Hong Kong, China.

Jacob Devlin, Ming-Wei Chang, Kenton Lee, and Kristina Toutanova. 2019. BERT: Pre-training of deep bidirectional transformers for language understanding. In *Proceedings of the 2019 Conference of the North American Chapter of the Association for Computational Linguistics: Human Language Technologies, Volume 1 (Long and Short Papers)*, pages 4171–4186, Minneapolis, Minnesota. Association for Computational Linguistics.

Iryna Gurevych, Judith Eckle-Kohler, Silvana Hartmann, Michael Matuschek, Christian M Meyer, and Christian Wirth. 2012. Uby: A large-scale unified lexical-semantic resource based on lmf. In *Proceedings of the 13th Conference of the European Chapter of the Association for Computational Linguistics*, pages 580–590. Association for Computational Linguistics.

Guillaume Lample, Miguel Ballesteros, Sandeep Subramanian, Kazuya Kawakami, and Chris Dyer. 2016. Neural architectures for named entity recognition. *arXiv preprint arXiv:1603.01360.*

Xuezhe Ma and Eduard Hovy. 2016. End-to-end sequence labeling via bi-directional lstm-cnns-crf. In *Proceedings of the 54th Annual Meeting of the Association for Computational Linguistics (Volume 1: Long Papers)*, pages 1064–1074.

Clyde R. Miller. 1939. *The Techniques of Propaganda. From How to Detect and Analyze Propaganda, an address given at Town Hall. The Center for learning.*

James W Pennebaker, Martha E Francis, and Roger J Booth. 2001. Linguistic inquiry and word count: Liwc 2001. *Mahway: Lawrence Erlbaum Associates*, 71(2001):2001.

Jeffrey Pennington, Richard Socher, and Christopher Manning. 2014. Glove: Global vectors for word representation. In *Proceedings of the 2014 conference on empirical methods in natural language processing (EMNLP)*, pages 1532–1543.

Hannah Rashkin, Eunsol Choi, Jin Yea Jang, Svitlana Volkova, and Yejin Choi. 2017. Truth of varying shades: Analyzing language in fake news and political fact-checking. In *Proceedings of the 2017 Conference on Empirical Methods in Natural Language Processing*, pages 2931–2937.

Divisive Language and Propaganda Detection using Multi-head Attention Transformers with Deep Learning BERT-based Language Models for Binary Classification

Norman John Mapes Jr., Anna White, Radhika Medury, Sumeet Dua
Louisiana Tech Office of Research and Partnerships

NLP4IF 2019 Shared Task - Team: ltuorp, Rank SLC #1

Abstract

On the NLP4IF 2019 sentence level propaganda classification task, we used a BERT language model that was pre-trained on Wikipedia and BookCorpus as team ltuorp ranking #1 of 26. It uses deep learning in the form of an attention transformer. We substituted the final layer of the neural network to a linear real valued output neuron from a layer of softmaxes. The backpropagation trained the entire neural network and not just the last layer. Training took 3 epochs and on our computation resources this took approximately one day. The pre-trained model consisted of uncased words and there were 12-layers, 768-hidden neurons with 12-heads for a total of 110 million parameters. The articles used in the training data promote divisive language similar to state-actor-funded influence operations on social media. Twitter shows state-sponsored examples designed to maximize division occurring across political lines, ranging from "Obama calls me a clinger, Hillary calls me deplorable, … and Trump calls me an American" oriented to the political right, to Russian propaganda featuring "Black Lives Matter" material with suggestions of institutional racism in US police forces oriented to the political left. We hope that raising awareness through our work will reduce the polarizing dialogue for the betterment of nations.

1 Introduction and Related Works

A question can be posed "What is an influence operation also known as?" Our system was trained to answer these questions but in the form of a cloze comprehension test "_____ is an influence operation." Likewise, Wikipedia and BookCorpus were used to develop an unsupervised language model built from the cloze questions by deleting 10% of the words from the corpora. Then the model was fed forward and a softmax output selected the most appropriate word, if this word was correct no training was done, if it was incorrect then the error was backpropagated through the network from the last layer's neurons to the first layer's word embeddings that were the inputs. Because an attention-based transformer can discern the difference between a river "bank" and a deposit "bank" depending on the context of the words, these word embeddings are considered dynamic. This contrasts with static word embeddings that were popularized by Mikolov et al. 2013, where bank has the same embedding regardless of context. Our model looks both to the left in the sentence and to the right and encodes the position of a word using a sinusoidal addition to the embeddings giving it awareness of the order of words. The model we based our approach on is called BERT by Google Research (Devlin et al. 2018). We independently discovered the value of using BERT like in D. Giovanni, 2019. BERT has undergone many changes to become RoBERTa (Liu et al. 2019) from Facebook. BERT and its related works have remained close to state of the art on tasks such as SQuAD (Rajpurkar et al. 2016). Although these results are less than a year old and nearly perform question answering better than humans, the superhuman level has been achieved recently in a very rapidly moving field. But it cannot be said this was unexpected given the results that IBM had when it bested the two strongest Jeopardy Champions (Markoff, 2011) for a million-dollar prize nearly 8 years ago.

2   Methodology

Our approach was based upon a very recent state-of-the-art release by Google Research (Github, 2019), we worked in the Python programming language to preprocess the data, set parameters, train, validate and predict propaganda. To accelerate the pace of our feedback loop (data to predictions to metric of success) we used a train/test split of 80/20 on the first 10% of the training data. We trained for optimal F1 score and noted Matthew's Correlation Coefficient, and ROC AUC for additional tuning. These values were optimized using a manual grid search for F1 score while monitoring the other metrics. If one of the monitored metrics performed particularly poorly, then we chose a model with more competitive values for all the metrics. We began with a robust model of TF-IDF and Random Forest to establish a baseline around which we can experiment with several other models. In the end we found the unsupervised language model BERT to be most effective after supervised re-training.

We will now discuss the parameters that we experimented with in our final model and chose according to performance on the validation set. The BERT parameter of sentence length was set to the first 50 words. If a sentence was longer than 50 words, then the 51st and beyond were discarded. Our batch size during training was 32 and 500 during prediction. Gradually increasing the training batch size usually improves performance. However, we were running at maximum memory on our computational resources and were unable to increase batch sizes. Our learning rate began at 1e-5 and gradually increased according to the default warm-up schedule.

Attention is defined as:

$$Attention(Q, K, V) = Softmax(QK^T)V \quad (1)$$

$$Softmax(X) = \frac{exp(X)}{\sum exp(X)} \quad (2)$$

Where softmax takes a vector X and Q, K, V are all embeddings of dimensionality 768. For a more detailed low-level understanding of attention see Vaswani et al. 2017. Because each time the neural network is initialized a new random number is used for the embeddings it is

useful to ensemble attention neural networks for multi-head results. Each head gives a generally unique interpretation of the sentences. In our case we used 12 attention heads and 12 transformer blocks. Attention gives a particularly interesting result, as it selects for words which have an additional significance when used together, effectively capturing the interaction and sending this signal through to the next layer. This interaction along with the position encoding give the transformer the ability to consider context. For more discussion of transformers see Devlin et al. 2018. The dataset used is described in D. Giovanni 2019.

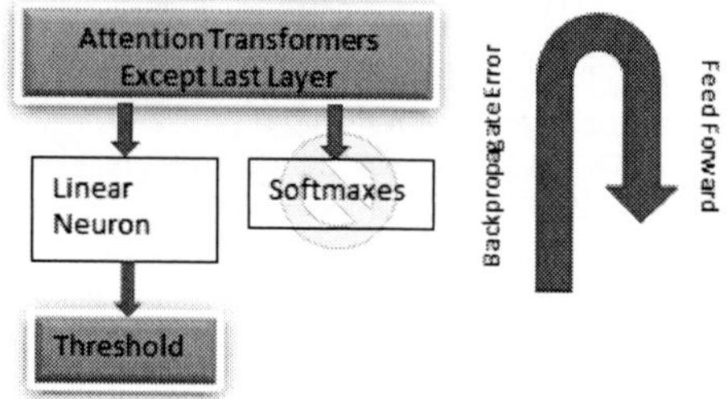

Figure 1 BERT-based attention transformer model with softmax layer substituted for a real valued neuron.

3   Results

On the development set we obtained two scores: one that was our internal 80/20 split on the 10% of the training data and the second that was based on the full set submissions to the webserver as team ltuorp. We selected the model parameters that were best for both. We found a threshold of 0.3 to classify propaganda was most effective for higher F1 scores. The threshold was selected using a manual grid search. By using a threshold, we formulated the problem as a regression problem. During training 0 was non-propaganda and 1 was propaganda. Then predictions were taken on the validation data and run through the regression model. If the predicted value was less than 0.3 it was classified as non-propaganda if it was equal to or greater than 0.3 it was classified as propaganda. We believe by having multiple datasets we were able to develop a better model. These datasets are both the language model that encompasses all of Wikipedia and BookCorpus and the partitioned training data. Had time allowed we would have used yet another frame of reference on the development set by performing 10 fold cross validation or leave one out validation.

A thought-provoking finding is that even though there are 18 categories of propaganda we were able to perform binary classification with a precision of 60.1, a recall of 66.5 and an F1 of 63.2 indicating that most of the propaganda follows a repeatable pattern in language and does not require human level intelligence or the need to recognize complex patterns to discern whether or not a sentence is propaganda. The baseline is 43.7, 38.8 and 49.4 respectively for comparison. The remaining 36.8 of F1 however would require a more complex model to classify. Because most propaganda follows a pattern it is possible to objectively and automatedly evaluate a publisher. For instance, news network X was found to have Y% more biased news than news network Z. Governments, critical readers, fact checking organizations, policy advisors, news companies, social media and internet companies can all make informed judgments based on the results of using these models.

4   Discussion and Future Work

The impact of our results cannot be overstated. Peer and near-peer competitors to the USA and allies spend money to influence US elections to a favorable outcome for the rival at the expense of US voters who potentially fail to secure a superior candidate. When analyzing home-grown propaganda, it is eerily similar, to the point of being indistinguishable from the foreign influence operations' divisive language that was found on social media such as Twitter and Facebook ads such as those in Figure 1. (Persily, 2017 and Twitter Data Release, 2019 and House Intelligence Committee 2017).

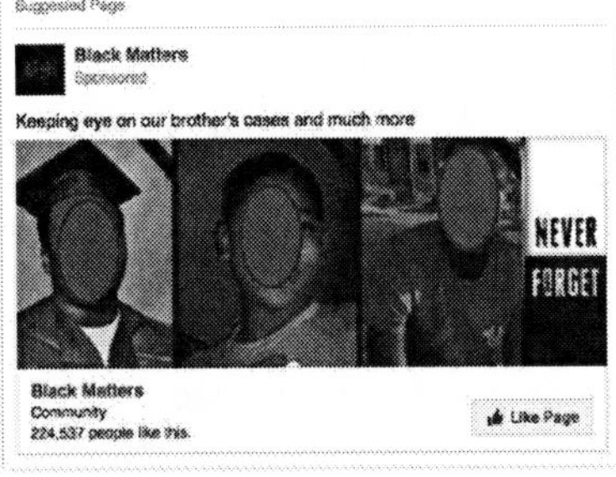

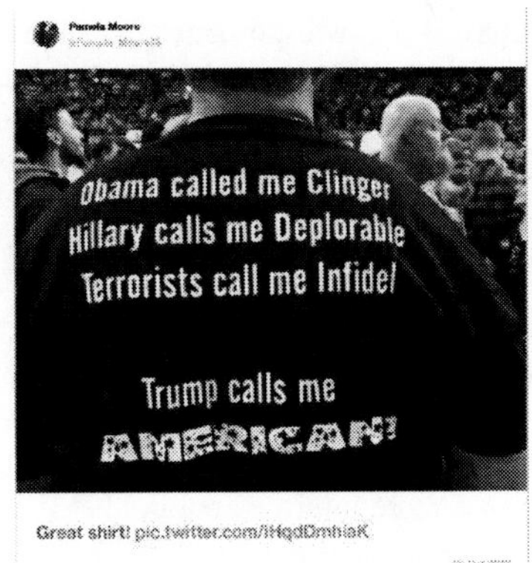

Figure 2 (Top Image) Russian propaganda using racially divisive content where 12,858 Rubles were spent. This is file P(1)0002156.pdf from the 2015-q2 archive in the citation above. Blue ovals have been placed to protect identities. 126 million Americans were exposed to organic content based on 3,393 Russian advertising campaigns. Any divisive topic was subject to use in these campaigns. (Bottom Image) Twitter based foreign information operations content.

In future works it would be significant to find divisive content such as those used in the Russian state-sponsored campaigns. It is often more subtle, image based, social media based and not found in traditional news sources. Also, it is usually disguised as counter-dialogue. However, this work and model gives a baseline upon which we can improve, using techniques such as the following.

We are very interested in the cloze question answering pre-training method that BERT uses. Perhaps in the future the model will be able to not penalize "good" answers. If there is a synonym that BERT predicts but it does not match the expected word, then it will train to reduce the probability of the acceptable but unexpected word occurring in that position.

Another future contribution will be the ability to reason using common sense. For example, in the Winograd Schema a question can be posed: "The city councilmen refused the demonstrators a permit because they [feared/advocated] violence." To answer the question the model must understand and have knowledge of the world and sentence structure to disambiguate the pronouns. It must also associate "councilmen refuse permit" as being incompatible with "councilmen fear". While "councilmen refuse permit" is compatible with "protesters who advocate violence". The best attempt only gets 70% accuracy on a default accuracy of 50%. (E. Davis 2019). This means that future works will no doubt raise the level of performance on Winograd Schema, a measure of commonsense reasoning and therefore likely, also the sentence level propaganda detection task.

5   Conclusion

We demonstrated good performance on classifying propaganda by attaining first place of 26 on the SLC task. It is our hope that the model and methods described in this paper will be used to create a more informed public that is resistant to divisive messages masked as counter-dialogue. One could conjecture that the motivation of foreign information operations is to sew discord and to reduce unity of a society's populace. We remain politically neutral with a hope that divisive language is not used intentionally to polarize others and in cases of legitimate promotion of already divisive topics, that polarization can be functionally minimized as opposed to unintentionally creating further division of an audience while advancing politically charged causes such as healthcare or social security reform (Howard, 2018). It may not be apparent how this happens, but common devices identified in the FLC portion of this competition such as flag waving i.e. conflating the opposing viewpoint with being unpatriotic, etc. is one example of many possible. While some propaganda has an element of truth, it is up to the reader to discern that they are being targeted to promote the cause of an information operation that often has a conflicting motivation with the reader's.

Acknowledgments

We would like to acknowledge the Propaganda Analysis Project and Twitter for providing relevant and high-quality datasets. Without these datasets we would have no empirical conclusions or be able to further the discussion to what to do with the results obtained and future directions.

References

Mikolov, Tomas, et al. "Efficient estimation of word representations in vector space." arXiv preprint arXiv:1301.3781 (2013).

Devlin, Jacob, et al. "Bert: Pre-training of deep bidirectional transformers for language understanding." arXiv preprint arXiv:1810.04805 (2018).

Da San Martino, Giovanni, Y. Seunghak, B. Alberto, P. Rotislav, N. Preslav "Fine-Grained Analysis of Propaganda in News Articles" EMNLP-IJCNLP 2019

Liu, Yinhan, et al. "RoBERTa: A Robustly Optimized BERT Pretraining Approach." arXiv preprint arXiv:1907.11692 (2019).

Rajpurkar, Pranav, et al. "Squad: 100,000+ questions for machine comprehension of text." arXiv preprint arXiv:1606.05250 (2016).

Markoff, John. "Computer wins on 'jeopardy!': trivial, it's not." New York Times 16 (2011).

Github "TensorFlow code and pre-trained models for BERT" https://github.com/google-research/bert 2019

Vaswani, Ashish, et al. "Attention is all you need." Advances in neural information processing systems. 2017.

Persily, Nathaniel. "The 2016 US Election: Can democracy survive the internet?." Journal of democracy 28.2 (2017): 63-76.

Twitter, "Election's Integrity Data Archive." https://about.twitter.com/en_us/values/elections-integrity.html#data (2019)

United State House Intelligence Committee "Exposing Russia's Effort to Sow Discord Online: The Internet Research Agency and Advertisements" https://intelligence.house.gov/social-media-content/ (2017)

E. Davis, L. Morgenstern and C. Ortiz "The Winograd Schema Challenge" New York University https://cs.nyu.edu/faculty/davise/papers/Winograd Schemas/WS.html (2019)

Howard, Philip N., et al. "Social media, news and political information during the US election: Was polarizing content concentrated in swing states?." arXiv preprint arXiv:1802.03573 (2018).

On Sentence Representations for Propaganda Detection:
From Handcrafted Features to Word Embeddings

André Ferreira Cruz and **Gil Rocha** and **Henrique Lopes Cardoso**
Laboratório de Inteligência Artificial e Ciências dos Computadores (LIACC)
Departamento de Engenharia Informática,
Faculdade de Engenharia da Universidade do Porto
Rua Dr. Roberto Frias, 4200-465 Porto, Portugal
{andre.ferreira.cruz, gil.rocha, hlc}@fe.up.pt

Abstract

Bias is ubiquitous in most online sources of natural language, from news media to social networks. Given the steady shift in news consumption behavior from traditional outlets to online sources, the automatic detection of propaganda, in which information is shaped to purposefully foster a predetermined agenda, is an increasingly crucial task. To this goal, we explore the task of *sentence-level propaganda detection*, and experiment with both handcrafted features and learned dense semantic representations. We also experiment with random undersampling of the majority class (non-propaganda) to curb the influence of class distribution on the system's performance, leading to marked improvements on the minority class (propaganda). Our best performing system uses pre-trained ELMo word embeddings, followed by a bidirectional LSTM and an attention layer. We have submitted a 5-model ensemble of our best performing system to the NLP4IF shared task on sentence-level propaganda detection (team *LIACC*), achieving rank 10 among 25 participants, with 59.5 F1-score.

1 Introduction

Propaganda shapes information in order to purposefully influence people's mindset and advance a predetermined agenda. The NLP4IF shared task on propaganda detection challenged participants to build systems capable of sentence-level (SLC) or fragment-level (FLC) detection of propagandistic texts (Da San Martino et al., 2019). We have participated on the SLC track, hence this will be the focus of this paper.

The rise of fake (Allcott and Gentzkow, 2017), hyperpartisan (Silverman et al., 2016), and propagandistic news on social media and online news outlets calls for improved automatic detection of bias in texts. However, any and all attempts at automated regulation of online content have freedom of speech implications, and risk unintended censorship (Akdeniz, 2010). Mindful of these considerations, we experiment with a set of handcrafted and interpretable stylometric features, together with a model based on Gradient Boosted Trees (Drucker and Cortes, 1996), thus facilitating inspection of what it is that the model has learned.

In addition, aiming for a better performance to the detriment of the model's interpretability, we experiment with deep neural networks, supplied with word embeddings learned on large external corpora, as this combination is the state-of-the-art for several natural language processing (NLP) tasks (Peters et al., 2018; Devlin et al., 2018; Akbik et al., 2019). Nonetheless, some degree of interpretability is maintained through the use of attention layers (Bahdanau et al., 2014), enabling inspection of which time-steps (words) the model is considering when making a prediction.

The provided train dataset consists of 350 articles, with a total of 16,965 sentences — 4,720 of which are labeled *propaganda*, and the remaining 12,245 labeled as *non-propaganda*. This class imbalance leads supervised learning models to favor predicting the majority class (*non-propaganda*), severely impacting performance on the minority class (Japkowicz and Stephen, 2002). In order to tackle this problem, we train all systems on a balanced version of the provided dataset, by means of random undersampling of the majority class, as this technique has been shown to have good results on several NLP tasks (Japkowicz and Stephen, 2002; Prusa et al., 2015).

The rest of the paper is organized as follows. Section 2 describes data pre-processing and feature selection, and details all tested models and their architectures. Section 3 analyzes our models' performance, analyzes attention-weight plots, and discusses results. Finally, Section 4 draws conclusions and sketches future work.

Proceedings of the 2nd Workshop on NLP for Internet Freedom: Censorship, Disinformation, and Propaganda, pages 107–112
Hong Kong, China, November 4, 2019 ©2019 Association for Computational Linguistics

2 System Description

We propose an approach based on a selection of handcrafted features paired with a Gradient Boosted Trees (GBT) model, as well as an approach based on learned dense semantic representations (word embeddings) paired with different deep-learning models. This Section describes the data pre-processing and feature selection, the choice of word embeddings, and the tested models and their hyperparameters.

2.1 Data Pre-processing

We tokenize sentences into words using *Spacy* (Honnibal and Montani, 2017). We standardize quotation marks (left and right, single and double), as well as single grave and acute accents, as all these characters may be represented by different unicode characters while portraying the same meaning.

2.2 Feature Selection

We use a small set of linguistically-inspired style and complexity features, already proven to have good performance on a similar bias-detection task – hyperpartisan news detection (Cruz et al., 2019). Some of the features portray the article in which each sentence is incorporated, while others portray the sentence itself. Our features are as follow:

- *num_sentences*: total number of sentences in the article;

- *avg_sent_char_len*: average character-length of article's sentences;

- *var_sent_char_len*: variance of character-length of the article's sentences;

- *actual_sent_char_len*: character-length of current sentence;

- *avg_word_len*: average of character-length of this sentence's words;

- *var_word_len*: variance of character-length of this sentence's words;

- *punct_freq*: this sentence's punctuation frequency;

- *capital_freq*: this sentence's capital-case frequency;

- *type-token-ratio* over lemmatized words — a measure of vocabulary diversity and richness (Johnson, 1944).

- TF-IDF (Robertson, 2004) vector for the 50 most frequent *unigrams* and *bi-grams*, whose document frequency does not exceed 95%.

2.3 Contextualized Word Representations

Deep-learning models proposed in this paper are supplied with dense word representations, generated from the pre-trained ELMo model (Peters et al., 2018). We use the *Flair* library (Akbik et al., 2019) to generate contextualized 3072-dimensional representations for each input word (concatenation of outputs from three 1024-dimensional layers). These embeddings are a function not only of the word itself but also of its context, enabling word disambiguation into different semantic representations.

We crop sentences to a maximum of 50 words, as a compromise between the representation's expressiveness and its computational cost (affecting only 3.7% of longer samples, see Figure 1). Shorter sentences are padded out with zeros.

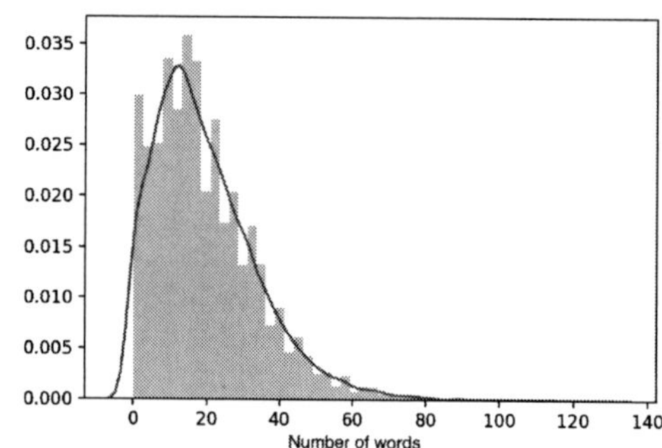

Figure 1: Distribution of sentence length.

2.4 Models & Architectures

As mentioned, we pair the data from handcrafted features with a Gradient Boosted Trees (GBT) model (Drucker and Cortes, 1996). Table 1 shows all hyperparameter values set for the GBT model. These values are the result of extensive grid searching, optimizing for F1-score (the task's official metric), and selecting the best performing model on 5-fold cross-validated results.

Additionally, we devise two deep-learning models to pair with word embedding representations.

estimators	100
learning-rate	0.1
loss	*exponential*
max. tree depth	10
min. samples at leaf	10
min. samples to split	2

Table 1: Hyperparameter values for GBT.

The *BiLSTM* model consists of a bidirectional long short-term memory layer (Gers et al., 2000). The last hidden time-step, concatenated from both directions, is then passed through a final fully connected layer followed by a sigmoid activation function. The *ABL* (**A**ttention-based **B**idirectional **L**STM) model is similar to the *BiLSTM* model, with an added attention layer (Bahdanau et al., 2014) operating over the hidden LSTM representations. Figure 2 shows this model's architecture. We use 40% dropout (Srivastava et al., 2014) on the initial embeddings, and 20% dropout on all remaining hidden-layers. All LSTM layers use 50 as the number of features of the hidden state.

For training, we use the Adam optimizer (Kingma and Ba, 2014) with default parameters, and Binary Cross-Entropy as the loss function. The batch size was set to 16, and training was stopped after 25 epochs, with early stopping upon 5 consecutive non-improving epochs on validation loss.

Deep-learning models were implemented using *PyTorch* (Paszke et al., 2017), and GBT using *scikit-learn* (Pedregosa et al., 2011).

3 Results and Discussion

Table 2 shows the results of all models over 5-fold cross-validation on the provided SLC training data. The top rows correspond to systems trained on a *balanced* version of the provided dataset, by means of random undersampling of the majority class (Japkowicz and Stephen, 2002), as an attempt to tackle the class imbalance on the original dataset (only 27.8% of which corresponds to *propaganda* sentences).

On the *balanced* dataset, the *ABL* model is the best-performing on both F1-score (official task metric) and accuracy, while *BiLSTM* achieved the best F1-score on the original data. *GBT* has a surprisingly inferior F1-score on the original data (32.6 points vs 53.0 points on the F1-metric for *BiLSTM*), but suffers the largest boost when com-

Model	*F1*	*P*	*R*	*A*
ABL *Balanced*	75.0	71.9	78.5	73.9
BiLSTM *Balanced*	74.7	69.5	80.7	72.6
GBT *Balanced*	67.7	65.8	69.6	66.7
BiLSTM	53.0	60.7	48.3	76.5
ABL	52.1	62.6	46.0	77.0
GBT	32.6	38.0	28.7	67.1

Table 2: Propaganda detection performance over 5-fold cross-validation. Models are ordered by decreasing F1-score (the task's official metric).

Model	*F1*	*P*	*R*
Best (team *ltuorp*)	63.2	60.3	66.5
Ours (ABL-*Balanced-Ens*)	59.5	50.9	71.6

Table 3: Official results for propaganda detection task (on withheld test data).

pared with its training on the *balanced* data (67.7 F1-score). Nonetheless, models based on word embeddings (*BiLSTM* & *ABL*) perform far better than those based on a handcrafted selection of features (*GBT*). This is expected, as *n-grams* fail to encode the text as a sequence, and fail to carry the meaning and relations between each word, which are known to be encoded in word embeddings (Peters et al., 2018).

Regarding the effectiveness of training on a balanced dataset, all systems saw dramatically increased performance on metrics relative to the positive class (labeled *propaganda*), accompanied by small decreases of overall accuracy. This is expected, as we are effectively depriving the model of useful samples from the majority class (labeled *non-propaganda*), but remarkably beneficial as can be seen by the improved F1-scores.

Our submission to the task was a 5-member *ABL* ensemble (ABL-*Balanced-Ens*), from 5 cross-validation iterations, trained on the *balanced* data. This system's predictions were the average of each model's independent prediction. This follows numerous works demonstrating consistent performance improvements when using ensembles of deep-learning classifiers (Peters et al., 2018).

Table 3 presents ours results on the official test data. Our system achieved 59.5 F1-score, ranking 10th among 25 participants, but lagging only 3.7 F1 points behind the best-performing system.

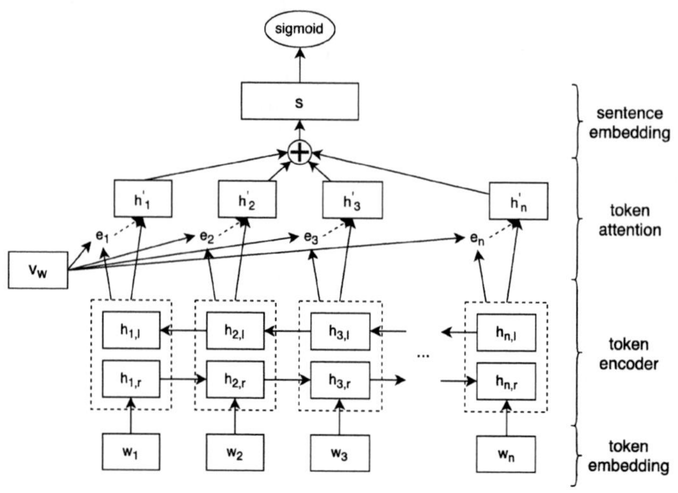

Figure 2: Visualization of ABL (bidirectional LSTM with attention).

3.1 Analyzing Attention Weights

Although the predictions of deep learning models are notoriously opaque, the attention layer present in *ABL* renders some degree of interpretability possible. By analyzing the attention energy associated with each word, we can intuitively extract conclusions regarding which parts of a sentence a model is taking into consideration.

Figure 3 shows a plot of attention energies over a sample article. The model seems to track writing style mostly through verb conjugations (*e.g.* 'needs', 'given', 'unprecedented'), as well as words with strong connotation which often portray the writer's opinion (*e.g.* 'wretched deals', 'machination', 'horrify').

From the sentences shown in Figure 3, the model incorrectly classifies the 4th and 5th sentences as *non-propaganda* (marked •), although with markedly low confidence (8% and 18% respectively). All remaining sentences are correctly classified. Through inspection of several attention-plots, intuitively, the model seems to pay close attention to a single opinion-inducing word when classifying a sentence as *propaganda*, while featuring a broader spread of attention weights when classifying a sentence as *non-propaganda*. The latter happens for both the 4th and 5th sentences.

•	He needs medical attention, the kind of treatment you get only in a hospital.
•	But it has been made clear to him that if he attempts to go to a hospital he will not be given free passage and he will be arrested.
+	His treatment amounts to the most unprecedented persecution.
•	Julian could leave the embassy if his own government, the government of his homeland, Australia, applied legitimate diplomatic pressure on behalf of its citizen.
•	We must ask ourselves why this hasn' t happened.
+	But that might be one of the so-called "wretched deals" that are being offered Assange.
•	Some very strange things are being said by senior members of these two governments.
+	The new foreign secretary of the United Kingdom, Jeremy Hunt, said sarcastically that the British police would offer Julian "a warm welcome" when he came out, when he would face serious charges.
•	Was Hunt referring to a deal which has already been done with the United States on extradition?
+	But this is the milieu of machination around someone who has the right of natural justice concerning his freedom.
+	Putting aside freedom of speech, the persecution of this man has been something that should horrify all free-thinking people.

Figure 3: Plots of attention-weights. Sentences are marked with + if **predicted** to be propaganda, and • otherwise. Symbol is colored red if prediction is wrong.

4 Conclusions and Future Work

We experimented with several models for sentence-level propaganda detection, exploring both handcrafted features and word embeddings. As expected, deep learning models improve performance to the detriment of feature interpretability. The best performing model is based on a bidirectional LSTM followed by an attention layer. We have submitted a 5-member ensemble of this model to the NLP4IF shared task, achieving 59.5 F1-score on the official test data, and ranking 10th among 25 participants.

Additionally, we have experimented with random undersampling to tackle the class imbalance on the provided training data. This lead to dramatic performance improvements on all models for metrics related to the minority class, accompanied by a small decrease in accuracy.

For future work, we intend to explore the integration of handcrafted features with word embeddings, to improve both model performance and transparency. We also intend to experiment with ensembles of independent classifiers, from independent feature-sets, in order to capture different facets of this complex problem.

Acknowledgments

André Ferreira Cruz is supported by the Calouste Gulbenkian Foundation, under grant number 226338. Gil Rocha is supported by a PhD studentship (with reference SFRH/BD/140125/2018) from Fundação para a Ciência e a Tecnologia (FCT). This research is partially supported by project DARGMINTS (POCI/01/0145/FEDER/031460), funded by FCT.

References

Alan Akbik, Tanja Bergmann, and Roland Vollgraf. 2019. Pooled contextualized embeddings for named entity recognition. In *NAACL 2019, 2019 Annual Conference of the North American Chapter of the Association for Computational Linguistics*, pages 724–728.

Yaman Akdeniz. 2010. To block or not to block: European approaches to content regulation, and implications for freedom of expression. *Computer Law & Security Review*, 26(3):260–272.

Hunt Allcott and Matthew Gentzkow. 2017. Social media and fake news in the 2016 election. *Journal of economic perspectives*, 31(2):211–36.

Dzmitry Bahdanau, Kyunghyun Cho, and Yoshua Bengio. 2014. Neural machine translation by jointly learning to align and translate. *arXiv preprint arXiv:1409.0473*.

André Ferreira Cruz, Gil Rocha, Rui Sousa-Silva, and Henrique Lopes Cardoso. 2019. Team fernandopessa at SemEval-2019 task 4: Back to basics in hyperpartisan news detection. In *Proceedings of the 13th International Workshop on Semantic Evaluation*, pages 999–1003, Minneapolis, Minnesota, USA. Association for Computational Linguistics.

Giovanni Da San Martino, Seunghak Yu, Alberto Barrón-Cedeño, Rostislav Petrov, and Preslav Nakov. 2019. Fine-grained analysis of propaganda in news articles. In *Proceedings of the 2019 Conference on Empirical Methods in Natural Language Processing and 9th International Joint Conference on Natural Language Processing, EMNLP-IJCNLP 2019*, EMNLP-IJCNLP 2019, Hong Kong, China.

Jacob Devlin, Ming-Wei Chang, Kenton Lee, and Kristina Toutanova. 2018. Bert: Pre-training of deep bidirectional transformers for language understanding. *arXiv preprint arXiv:1810.04805*.

Harris Drucker and Corinna Cortes. 1996. Boosting decision trees. In *Advances in neural information processing systems*, pages 479–485.

Felix A Gers, Jürgen Schmidhuber, and Fred Cummins. 2000. Learning to forget: Continual prediction with lstm. *Neural Computation*, 12(10):2451–2471.

Matthew Honnibal and Ines Montani. 2017. spaCy 2: Natural language understanding with Bloom embeddings, convolutional neural networks and incremental parsing. To appear.

Nathalie Japkowicz and Shaju Stephen. 2002. The class imbalance problem: A systematic study. *Intelligent data analysis*, 6(5):429–449.

Wendell Johnson. 1944. Studies in language behavior: A program of research. *Psychological Monographs*, 56(2):1–15.

Diederik P Kingma and Jimmy Ba. 2014. Adam: A method for stochastic optimization. *arXiv preprint arXiv:1412.6980*.

Adam Paszke, Sam Gross, Soumith Chintala, Gregory Chanan, Edward Yang, Zachary DeVito, Zeming Lin, Alban Desmaison, Luca Antiga, and Adam Lerer. 2017. Automatic differentiation in PyTorch. In *NIPS Autodiff Workshop*.

F. Pedregosa, G. Varoquaux, A. Gramfort, V. Michel, B. Thirion, O. Grisel, M. Blondel, P. Prettenhofer, R. Weiss, V. Dubourg, J. Vanderplas, A. Passos, D. Cournapeau, M. Brucher, M. Perrot, and E. Duchesnay. 2011. Scikit-learn: Machine learning in Python. *Journal of Machine Learning Research*, 12:2825–2830.

Matthew E. Peters, Mark Neumann, Mohit Iyyer, Matt Gardner, Christopher Clark, Kenton Lee, and Luke Zettlemoyer. 2018. Deep contextualized word representations. In *Proc. of NAACL*.

Joseph Prusa, Taghi M Khoshgoftaar, David J Dittman, and Amri Napolitano. 2015. Using random undersampling to alleviate class imbalance on tweet sentiment data. In *2015 IEEE international conference on information reuse and integration*, pages 197–202. IEEE.

Stephen Robertson. 2004. Understanding inverse document frequency: on theoretical arguments for idf. *Journal of documentation*, 60(5):503–520.

Craig Silverman, Lauren Strapagiel, Hamza Shaban, Ellie Hall, and Jeremy Singer-Vine. 2016. Hyperpartisan facebook pages are publishing false and misleading information at an alarming rate. *Buzzfeed News*.

Nitish Srivastava, Geoffrey Hinton, Alex Krizhevsky, Ilya Sutskever, and Ruslan Salakhutdinov. 2014. Dropout: a simple way to prevent neural networks from overfitting. *The journal of machine learning research*, 15(1):1929–1958.

JUSTDeep at NLP4IF 2019 Shared Task: Propaganda Detection using Ensemble Deep Learning Models

Hani Al-Omari
Jordan University of Science and Technology
Computer Science Department
Irbid, Jordan
alomarihani1997@gmail.com

Malak Abdullah
Jordan University of Science and Technology
Computer Science Department
Irbid, Jordan
mabdullah@just.edu.jo

Ola Al-Titi
Jordan University of Science and Technology
Computer Science Department
Irbid, Jordan
oaaltiti18@cit.just.edu.jo

Samira Shaikh
University of North Carolina at Charlotte
Computer Science Department
NC, USA
samirashaikh@uncc.edu

Abstract

The internet and the high use of social media have enabled the modern-day journalism to publish, share and spread news that is difficult to distinguish if it is true or fake. Defining "fake news" is not well established yet, however, it can be categorized under several labels: false, biased, or framed to mislead the readers that are characterized as propaganda. Digital content production technologies with logical fallacies and emotional language can be used as propaganda techniques to gain more readers or mislead the audience. Recently, several researchers have proposed deep learning (DL) models to address this issue. This research paper provides an ensemble deep learning model using BiLSTM, XGBoost, and BERT to detect propaganda. The proposed model has been applied on the dataset provided by the challenge NLP4IF 2019, Task 1 Sentence Level Classification (SLC) and it shows a significant performance over the baseline model.

1 Introduction

The spread of news has been transformed from traditional news distributors to social media feeds. However, content on social media is not properly monitored (Granik and Mesyura, 2017). It is difficult to distinguish trusted, credible news from untrustworthy news. This has raised questions about the quality of journalism and enabled the term "fake news". Identifying an article as fake news relies on the degree of falsity and intentionality of spreading the news. There are various types of fake or misleading news, such as publishing inaccurate news to reach a wide audience, publishing untruths with the intention to harm a person or organization, or publishing false news without checking all the facts. News with propaganda are called Propagandistic news articles, that are intentionally spread to mislead readers and influence their minds with a certain idea, for political, ideological, or business motivations (Tandoc Jr et al., 2018; Brennen, 2017).

Detecting fake news and propaganda is getting more attention recently (Jain and Kasbe, 2018; Helmstetter and Paulheim, 2018; Bourgonje et al., 2017), however, the limited resources and corpora is considered the biggest challenge for researchers in this field. In this work, we use the corpus provided by the shared task on fine-grained propaganda detection (NLP4IF 2019) (Da San Martino et al., 2019). The corpus consists of news articles in which the sentences are labeled as propagandistic or not. The goal of the challenge is to build automatic tools to detect propaganda. Knowing that deep learning is outperforming traditional machine learning techniques, we have proposed an ensemble deep learning model using BiLSTM, XGBoost, and BERT to address this challenge. Our proposed model shows a significant performance F1-score (0.6112) over the baseline model (0.4347). The key novelty of our work is using word embeddings and a unique set of semantic features, in a fully connected neural network architecture to determine the existence of propagandistic news in the article.

The remainder of this paper is organized as follows. Section 2 gives a brief description of the existing work in detecting fake news and propaganda. Section 3 provides a dataset description and the extracted features. Section 4 proposes the system architecture to determine the presence of propaganda in an article. Section 5 presents the evaluations and results. Finally, section 6 concludes with future directions for this research.

2 Related Work

Fake news and propaganda are hard challenges that face society and individuals. Detecting fake

Proceedings of the 2nd Workshop on NLP for Internet Freedom: Censorship, Disinformation, and Propaganda, pages 113–118
Hong Kong, China, November 4, 2019 ©2019 Association for Computational Linguistics

news and propaganda is increasingly motivating researchers (Jain and Kasbe, 2018; Helmstetter and Paulheim, 2018; Aphiwongsophon and Chongstitvatana, 2018; Barrón-Cedeño et al., 2019; Orlov and Litvak, 2018). The researchers in Jain and Kasbe (2018) proposed an approach for fake news detection using Naive Bayes classifier, where they applied the model on Facebook posts. The dataset was produced by GitHub that contains 6335 training samples. The results showed that using Naive Bayes classifier with n-gram is better than not using n-gram. Gilda (2017) explored Support Vector Machines, Stochastic Gradient Descent, Gradient Boosting, Bounded Decision Trees, and Random Forests to detect fake news. Their dataset was acquired from signal media and a list of sources from OpenSources.co, to predict whether the articles are truthful or fake.

In Helmstetter and Paulheim (2018), the researchers modeled the fake news problem as a two-class classification problem and their approach was a fake news detection system for Twitter using a weakly supervised approach. Naive Bayes, Decision Trees, Support Vector Machines (SVM), and Neural Networks had been used as basic classifiers with two ensemble methods, Random Forest and XG Boost, using parameter optimization on all of those approaches. In addition, the researchers in (Aphiwongsophon and Chongstitvatana, 2018) proposed a fake news detection model using Naive Bayes, Neural Network and SVM. The dataset collected by their team using TwitterAPI for a specified period between October 2017 to November 2017. The authors in (Bourgonje et al., 2017; Chaudhry et al., 2017) provided a platform to detect the stance of article titles based on their content on Fake News Challenge (FNC-1) dataset[1].

For identifying propagandistic news articles and reducing the impact of propaganda to the audience, (Barrón-Cedeño et al., 2019) provided the rst publicly available propaganda detection system called proppy, which is a real-world and real-time monitoring system to unmask propagandistic articles in online news. The system consists of four modules, which are article retrieval, event identication, deduplication and propaganda index computation. Moreover, (Gavrilenko et al., 2019) applied several neural network architectures such as Long Short-Term Memory(LSTM), hierarchical

bidirectional LSTM (H-LSTM) and Convolutional Neural Network (CNN) in order to classify the text into propaganda and non-propaganda. They have used different word representation models including word2vec, GloVe and TF-IDF (Pennington et al., 2014; Mikolov et al., 2013). The results showed that CNN with word2vec representation outperforms other models with accuracy equal to 88.2%. (Orlov and Litvak, 2018) provided an unsupervised approach for automatic identification of propagandists on Twitter using behavioral and text analysis of users accounts. Their proposed approach was applied on dataset that was retrieved from Twitter and collected using the Twitter stream API. Seven suspicious accounts were detected by the approach and it achieved 100% precision.

In contrast to these prior works reviewed, our work is different as we have investigated several Neural Network approaches to determine the most appropriate model for detecting propagandistic sentences in news article. We test the hypothesis that propagandistic news articles would contain emotional and affective words to a greater extent than other news articles.

3 Dataset and Extracted Features

The provided dataset for the NLP4IF 2019 Task 1 is described in (Da San Martino et al., 2019). The corpus consists of 350 articles for training and 61 articles for development for a total of 411 articles in plain text format. The title is followed by an empty row and the content of the article starting from the next row, one sentence per line. There are 16975 sentences in the training data, where 12244 are non-propaganda and 4721 are propaganda.

3.1 Data preprocessing

In our model, text preprocessing has been performed for each sentence of training and development set that includes: removing punctuation, cleaning text from special symbols, removing stop words, clean contractions, and correct some misspelled words.

3.2 Features

In our approach, we have 449 dimensions for our extracted features that are obtained as the following: Each line of text is represented as a 300-dimensional vector using the pretrained Glove embedding model (Pennington et al., 2014).

---

[1]http://www.fakenewschallenge.org

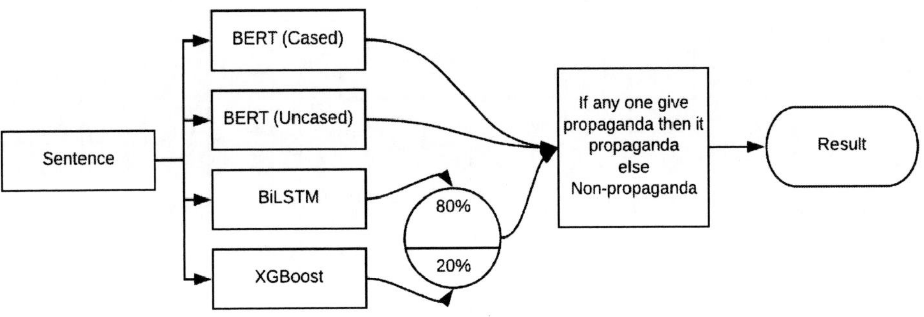

Figure 1: The architecture of our approach

It is worth mentioning that we have also experimented word2vec embedding model that is trained on Google News (Mikolov et al., 2013) but the results were not promising. Our hypothesis is that emotional and affective words will characterize fake news more strongly than neutral words. Accordingly, each line of text is represented as 149-dimensional vector by concatenating three vectors obtained from AffectiveTweets Weka-package (Mohammad and Bravo-Marquez, 2017; Bravo-Marquez et al., 2014), 43 features were extracted using the lexical resources; two-dimensional vector using the sentiments strength feature from the same package, and the final 100-dimensional vector is obtained by vectorizing the text into embeddings (c.f. Table 1).

Features	dimension
Glove	300
TweetToEmbeddings	100
TweetToInputLeixicon	4
TweetToLexicon	43
TweetToSentiStrength	2

Table 1: Features used in our approach

4 Our Approach

The architecture of our system consists of four sub-models: BiLSTM sub-model, XGBoost sub-model, BERT Cased and UnCased model (Figure 1). The description of these sub-models are in the following subsections, we have combined the Cased and UnCased Bert model in one subsection.

4.1 BiLSTM

In this sub-model, we have used use the Bidirectional Long Short-Term Memory (BiLSTM) (Schuster and Paliwal, 1997). The architecture of this sub-model as shown in Figure 2. There are two inputs that are feeding two different network architectures.

The first input is the encoded sentence to embedding layers, which is a lookup table that consists of 300-dimensional pretrained Glove vector to represent each word. This input goes into two BiLSTM layers each with 256 nodes and 0.2 dropout to avoid overfitting. Then, the output from BiLSTM layer is concatenated with Global Max Pooling and Global Average Pooling.

The second input is extracted using AffectiveTweets package as described earlier. The 145-dimensional vector feeds a fully connected neural network with four dense hidden layers of 512, 256, 128, 64 neurons, respectively. We found that the best activation function is ReLU (Goodfellow et al., 2013). A dropout of 0.2 has been added to avoid overfitting. After that we feed it into the previous concatenation layer. A fully connected neural network with four dense hidden layers of 512, 256, 128, 64 neurons for each layer has been applied after the concatenation layer. The activation function for each layer is ReLU, and between them there is a 0.2 dropout.

The output layer consists of 1-sigmoid neuron to predict the class of the sentence. For optimization, we have used Adam optimizer (Kingma and Ba, 2014) with 0.0001 learning rate and binary cross-entropy as a loss function. We have saved the output prediction weights to predict the testing datasets. The fit function uses number of epochs=

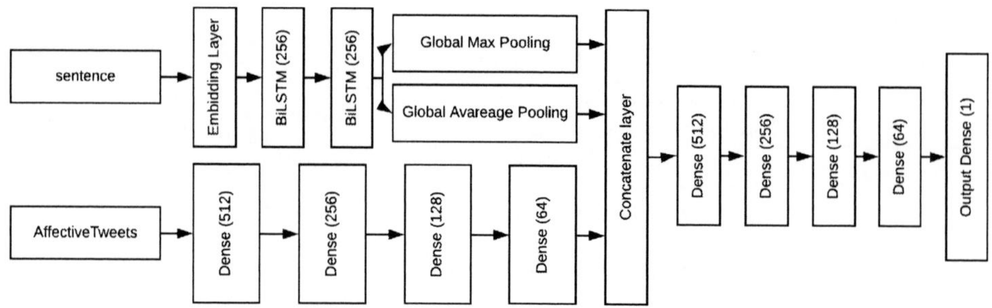

Figure 2: The architecture of BiLSTM sub-model

Features	StopWord	Cased	F1	Precision	Recall
Glove + AffectiveTweets	With	Yes	0.564600	0.630000	0.511502
Glove + AffectiveTweets	With	No	0.550273	0.648897	0.477673

Table 2: BiLSTM result on development data set

100, batch size= 512, validation split= 33% (See Table 2).

4.2 XGBoost

XGBoost (Chen and Guestrin, 2016) is a decision-tree ensemble machine learning algorithm that uses gradient boosting framework. It relies on an iterative method where new models are trained to correct previous model errors. Moreover, it is an optimized implementation of Gradient Boosting Decision Tree (GBDT) that provides a highly-efficient and parallel tree boosting. XGBoost has many hyperparameters that need tweaking. So, we have used Grid search to find the best values for the parameters. Also, we have chosen binary logistic as there are only two classes. Table 3 summarizes XGBoost hyperparameters. It is worth mentioning that we have handled the word embedding by summing words vectors in one sentence and feed it into XGBoost, see Table 4.

Hyperparameter	Value
Number of trees (n estimators)	1200
Learning Rate	0.1
Max Depth	3
Objective	binary:logistic
gamma	0.5
subsample	0.8

Table 3: XGBoost Hyperparameter

4.3 BERT

Bidirectional Encoder Representations from Transformers (BERT) (Devlin et al., 2018) is considered a new pretrained representations which obtains state-of-the-art results on wide variety of natural language processing tasks. BERT has many hyperparameters that need tweaking and after several experiments we adjust the best values for our model. There are two types of pretrained models, BERT-Base and BERT Large (we adopted the base model as it needs less memory). In each type, there are 5 pretrained models, however, we have used Uncased, Cased and Multilingual-Cased. We have noticed that using Uncased and Cased models with ensembling between them gives the best results (Table 5).

5 Results and Evaluation

One of the key findings is noticing that BERT model gives better prediction than the other models, which indicates that BERT can understand the text better than the other models.

In our experiments, we tried several combinations between sub-models. Using the predictions from the BiLSTM and XGBoost models for the development and test datasets, we noticed that the best results are performed with giving BiLSTM sub-model a weight of 0.8 and XGBoost sub-model a weight of 0.2. Combining both results with argmax the predictions to produce a partial result. Regarding the BERT cased and Uncased

Features	StopWord	Cased	F1	Precision	Recall
Glove (Common Crawl)	With	Yes	0.501667	0.652928	0.407307
Glove (Wiki-300)	With	No	0.498328	0.652079	0.403248
Glove+AffectiveTweets (Common Crawl)	With	Yes	0.479932	0.650463	0.380244
Glove+AffectiveTweets (Wiki-300)	With	No	0.480269	0.632743	0.387009

Table 4: XGBoost results on development dataset

Type	seq length	batch size	lr	epochs	StopWord	F1	Precision	Recall
Cased	400	4	1e-5	3	With	0.590288	0.671848	0.526387
Cased	**150**	**8**	**1e-5**	**3**	**With**	**0.600304**	**0.684575**	**0.534506**
Cased	150	8	1e-5	3	Without	0.563694	0.684720	0.479026
Uncased	**400**	**4**	**1e-5**	**3**	**With**	**0.622781**	**0.686786**	**0.569689**
Uncased	150	4	1e-5	3	With	0.573405	0.663701	0.504736
Uncased	150	4	1e-5	3	Without	0.570533	0.677840	0.492558

Table 5: BERT result on development dataset

	F1	Precision	Recall
BERT (Cased) + BERT (Uncased)	0.654671	0.669972	0.640054
BERT (Cased) + BERT (Uncased) + BiLSTM	0.665897	0.580483	0.780785
BERT (Cased) + BERT (Uncased) + BiLSTM (.8) + XGBoost (.2)	**0.674534**	**0.623421**	**0.734777**
BERT (Uncased) + BiLSTM (.5) + XGBoost (.5)	0.641975	0.650904	0.633288
BERT (Uncased) + BiLSTM (.8) + XGBoost (.2)	0.646542	0.543860	0.797023
BERT (Uncased) + BiLSTM	0.633787	0.545366	0.756428

Table 6: Ensembling result on development dataset

result, we have combined both of them together by checking if the 4 models predict that the sentence is non-propaganda then it will be labeled as non-propaganda, otherwise it will be labeled as Propaganda. Table 6 illustrates the best F1 score on the prediction.

6 Conclusion

In this paper, we have investigated several models and techniques to detect if a sentence in an article is propaganda or not. Experimental results showed that the ensemble of using BiLSTM, XGBoost, and BERT has achieved the best results. Also, the process of analyzing and extracting features, such as AffectiveTweets, has a major role in improving the BiLSTM model. The evaluations are performed using the dataset provided by NLP4IF Shared task. The proposed model has been ranked the seventh place among 26 teams. The F1-score that is achieved by our model is 0.6112 which outperformed the baseline model (0.4347) and it is (0.02) away from the first team. We strongly believe that the use of affectivetweets and the lexical features serve well to distinguish between propaganda vs. non-propaganda news.

References

Supanya Aphiwongsophon and Prabhas Chongstitvatana. 2018. Detecting fake news with machine learning method. In *2018 15th International Conference on Electrical Engineering/Electronics, Computer, Telecommunications and Information Technology (ECTI-CON)*, pages 528–531. IEEE.

Alberto Barrón-Cedeño, Giovanni Da San Martino, Israa Jaradat, and Preslav Nakov. 2019. Proppy: A system to unmask propaganda in online news. In *Proceedings of the AAAI Conference on Artificial Intelligence*, volume 33, pages 9847–9848.

Peter Bourgonje, Julian Moreno Schneider, and Georg Rehm. 2017. From clickbait to fake news detection: an approach based on detecting the stance of headlines to articles. In *Proceedings of the 2017 EMNLP Workshop: Natural Language Processing meets Journalism*, pages 84–89.

Felipe Bravo-Marquez, Marcelo Mendoza, and Barbara Poblete. 2014. Meta-level sentiment models for big social data analysis. *Knowledge-Based Systems*, 69:86–99.

Bonnie Brennen. 2017. Making sense of lies, deceptive propaganda, and fake news. *Journal of Media Ethics*, 32(3):179–181.

Ali K Chaudhry, Darren Baker, and Philipp Thun-Hohenstein. 2017. Stance detection for the fake news challenge: identifying textual relationships with deep neural nets. *CS224n: Natural Language Processing with Deep Learning*.

Tianqi Chen and Carlos Guestrin. 2016. Xgboost: A scalable tree boosting system. In *Proceedings of the 22nd acm sigkdd international conference on knowledge discovery and data mining*, pages 785–794. ACM.

Giovanni Da San Martino, Seunghak Yu, Alberto Barrón-Cedeño, Rostislav Petrov, and Preslav Nakov. 2019. Fine-grained analysis of propaganda in news articles. In *Proceedings of the 2019 Conference on Empirical Methods in Natural Language Processing and 9th International Joint Conference on Natural Language Processing, EMNLP-IJCNLP 2019, Hong Kong, China, November 3-7, 2019*, EMNLP-IJCNLP 2019, Hong Kong, China.

Jacob Devlin, Ming-Wei Chang, Kenton Lee, and Kristina Toutanova. 2018. Bert: Pre-training of deep bidirectional transformers for language understanding. *arXiv preprint arXiv:1810.04805*.

Olena Gavrilenko, Yurii Oliinyk, and Hanna Khanko. 2019. Analysis of propaganda elements detecting algorithms in text data. In *International Conference on Computer Science, Engineering and Education Applications*, pages 438–447. Springer.

Shlok Gilda. 2017. Evaluating machine learning algorithms for fake news detection. In *2017 IEEE 15th Student Conference on Research and Development (SCOReD)*, pages 110–115. IEEE.

Ian J Goodfellow, David Warde-Farley, Mehdi Mirza, Aaron Courville, and Yoshua Bengio. 2013. Maxout networks. *arXiv preprint arXiv:1302.4389*.

Mykhailo Granik and Volodymyr Mesyura. 2017. Fake news detection using naive bayes classifier. In *2017 IEEE First Ukraine Conference on Electrical and Computer Engineering (UKRCON)*, pages 900–903. IEEE.

Stefan Helmstetter and Heiko Paulheim. 2018. Weakly supervised learning for fake news detection on twitter. In *2018 IEEE/ACM International Conference on Advances in Social Networks Analysis and Mining (ASONAM)*, pages 274–277. IEEE.

Akshay Jain and Amey Kasbe. 2018. Fake news detection. In *2018 IEEE International Students' Conference on Electrical, Electronics and Computer Science (SCEECS)*, pages 1–5. IEEE.

Diederik P Kingma and Jimmy Ba. 2014. Adam: A method for stochastic optimization. *arXiv preprint arXiv:1412.6980*.

Tomas Mikolov, Ilya Sutskever, Kai Chen, Greg S Corrado, and Jeff Dean. 2013. Distributed representations of words and phrases and their compositionality. In *Advances in neural information processing systems*, pages 3111–3119.

Saif M Mohammad and Felipe Bravo-Marquez. 2017. Wassa-2017 shared task on emotion intensity. *arXiv preprint arXiv:1708.03700*.

Michael Orlov and Marina Litvak. 2018. Using behavior and text analysis to detect propagandists and misinformers on twitter. In *Annual International Symposium on Information Management and Big Data*, pages 67–74. Springer.

Jeffrey Pennington, Richard Socher, and Christopher Manning. 2014. Glove: Global vectors for word representation. In *Proceedings of the 2014 conference on empirical methods in natural language processing (EMNLP)*, pages 1532–1543.

Mike Schuster and Kuldip K Paliwal. 1997. Bidirectional recurrent neural networks. *IEEE Transactions on Signal Processing*, 45(11):2673–2681.

Edson C Tandoc Jr, Zheng Wei Lim, and Richard Ling. 2018. Defining fake news a typology of scholarly definitions. *Digital journalism*, 6(2):137–153.

Detection of Propaganda Using Logistic Regression

Jinfen Li
College of Arts and Sciences,
Syracuse University
jli284@syr.edu

Zhihao Ye
College of Information
Science and Engineering,
Hunan University
zhihaoye.chn@qq.com

Lu Xiao
School of Information Studies,
Syracuse University
lxiao04@syr.edu

Abstract

Various propaganda techniques are used to manipulate peoples perspectives in order to foster a predetermined agenda such as by the use of logical fallacies or appealing to the emotions of the audience. In this paper, we develop a Logistic Regression-based tool that automatically classifies whether a sentence is propagandistic or not. We utilize features like TF-IDF, BERT vector, sentence length, readability grade level, emotion feature, LIWC feature and emphatic content feature to help us differentiate these two categories. The linguistic and semantic features combination results in 66.16% of F1 score, which outperforms the baseline hugely.

1 Introduction

Attributes of social media communication make it challenging for a user to interpret someones comment and to examine the truthfulness of the information. For example, a social media message can be anonymous, from real people, or automatically generated, making it difficult to identify its source. Because of this challenge to interpret and evaluate a social media message, social media users are found to be persuaded by views that have no factual basis (Guo et al., 2018). They are influenced by misinformation and disinformation.

Various definitions are given in the literature to explain what propaganda is (for a list of such definitions, please see: https://publish.illinois.edu/ mirasotirovic/whatispropaganda). Focusing on the techniques in propaganda, we adopt Elluls definition that propaganda is "A set of methods employed by an organized group that wants to bring about the active or passive participation in its actions of a mass of individuals, psychologically unified through psychological manipulation and incorporated in an organization" (Ellul, 1966). People use propaganda techniques to purposely shape information and foster predetermined agenda (Miller, 1939; Weston, 2018). With the fast and wide spread of online news articles, it is much desired to have computing technologies that automatically detect propaganda in these texts.

This study presents our approach to a shared task that is aimed at detecting whether an given sentence from a news article is propagandistic. The shared tasks are part of 2019 Workshop on NLP4IF: censorship, disinformation, and propaganda , co-located with the EMNLP-IJCNLP conference. We focused on one of the task, which is referred to as SLC (Sentence- level Classification). In our approach, we came up with various features and classified the sentences using Logistic Regression.

2 Our Approach

Our model includes a list of linguistic features and semantic features extracted from BERT. After experiments on the BERT model and other machine learning models, we got the best performance using Logistic Regression.

2.1 Data

(Da San Martino et al., 2019a) provided with a corpus of about 500 news articles and splited the corpus into training, development and test, each containing 350, 61, 86 articles and 16,965, 2,235, 3,526 sentences. Each article has been retrieved with the newspaper3k library and sentence splitting has been performed automatically with NLTK sentence splitter (Da San Martino et al., 2019a).

2.2 Our Features

We identified a list of features and selected the top 98% using feature selection tool SelectKBest of Sklearn with score funtion of f_classif (https://scikit-learn.org/ stable/modules/generated/sklearn.

Proceedings of the 2nd Workshop on NLP for Internet Freedom: Censorship, Disinformation, and Propaganda, pages 119–124
Hong Kong, China, November 4, 2019 ©2019 Association for Computational Linguistics

`feature_selection.SelectKBest.
html`). Our final features including TF-IDF, length, readability grade level, emotion, LIWC and emphatic features, and the semantic features extracted from BERT.

2.2.1 TF-IDF

Term Frequency Inverse Document Frequency (TF-IDF) (Jones, 2004) gives us the information of term frequency through the proportion of inverse document frequency. Words that have small term frequency in each document but have high possibility to appear in documents with similar topics will have higher TF-IDF, while words like function words though frequently appear in every document will have low TF-IDF because of lower inverse document frequency. We used feature selection tool of sklearn based on ANOVA to select top 100 features from over 40,000 words.

2.2.2 Sentence Length

We found that the propagandistic sentences are more likely to be longer than the non-propagandistic ones, so we came up some features to capture this information. We have categorical feature **Short or Long Document** and used 1 to denote that it is a long document. A sentence belongs to a short document if it has less than eight tokens; otherwise, it belongs to a long document. We also have discrete features including **Text Length**(the number of characters in a sentence), **Word Count** and **Word Count Per Sentence**.

2.2.3 Readability Grade Level

We used The Flesch Grade Level readability formula, which is also commonly referred to as the Flesch-Kincaid Grade Level to calculate the readability grade of each text (Kincaid et al., 1975). The Flesch-Kincaid Grade Level outputs a U.S. school grade level, which indicates the average student in that grade level can read the text. For example, a score of 9.4 indicates that students in the ninth grade are able to read the document. The formula is as follow.

$$FKRA = (0.39 * ASL) + (11.8 * ASW) - 15.59$$

where, **FKRA** = Flesch-Kincaid Reading Age, **ASL** = Average Sentence Length (i.e., the number of words divided by the number of sentences), **ASW** = Average number of Syllable per Word (i.e., the number of syllables divided by the number of words). The average grade level is eighth and twelfth for non-propagandistic and propagandistic sentences, respectively.

2.2.4 Emotion Feature

Studies about the relationship between emotion and propaganda techniques are conducted. For example, (Kadir et al., 2016) found out that propaganda techniques in YouTube conjure peoples emotion that could affect unity. We took advantage of these studies by adding emotion features for SLC task.

- **NRC VAD Lexicon** (Mohammad, 2018); **NRC Emotion Lexicon** (Mohammad and Turney, 2013); **NRC Affect Intensity Lexicon** (Mohammad and Bravo-Marquez, 2017). We calculated the total score of the words listed in these lexicons respectively, and normalized the score between zero and one for each sentence.

- **MPQA** (Wilson et al., 2005), **Bing Liu** (Hu and Liu, 2004), and **AFINN** (Nielsen, 2011). We calculated the percentage of words with positive and negative emotions respectively in these lexicons for each sentence.

- **Insult** Noted that insult words are likely to be used in Name Calling and Labeling techniques, we refer to a lexicon that contains insult words from the `http://www.insult.wiki/wiki/Insult_List`. We calculated the count of insult words appearing in a sentence and normalized it by the token counts.

- **LIWC Emotion Lexicon**
  Affect the LIWC dictionary includes the overall affect including positive emotions, negative emotions, anxiety, anger and sadness; **Negative Emotions** it also includes negative emotion words correspond with human ratings of the writing excerpts (Alpers et al., 2005); **Anger** and some anger words without considering the context like 'hate, kill, annoyed'. We combined these three emotion information provided by LIWC emotion lexicon with the others provided by the lexicons mentioned above as the final emotion features.

2.2.5 LIWC Feature

- **Dictionary Words**: Percentage of all words captured by the dictionary, which refers to the collection of words that define one particular of the 80 categories (Tausczik and Pennebaker, 2010).

- **Article** The use of article can tell us some information about gender and the personality. (Newman et al., 2008) found that males had higher use of large words and articles than women. (Pennebaker and King, 1999) showed that articles were less frequent in the writing of people who scored high on extraversion.

- **Conjugations** Depth of thinking is reflected in complexity, and people use conjunctions to join multiple complex thoughts together to deepen their thoughts (Graesser et al., 2004).

- **Quote** The use of quote distracts us from the main body of the text to the content in the quotes. For example, ironic content (e.g. "A researcher with the organisation, Matthew Collins, said it was 'delighted' with the decision."), slogans (e.g. "Time for US to do the same.") and and loaded language (e.g. "Muslin Invaders") are put in the double quotes.

2.2.6 Emphatic Content in Double Quote

Researchers have identified many standard techniques (Koob, 2015; Zollmann, 2019) used in propaganda, such as slogans, name calling and loaded language, which often include the emphatic content in the title format(every word begins with capital letter) or every letter of the word is capitalized in the double quote. Therefore, our model includes a feature that reflects this aspect.

- **Slogans.** A slogan is a brief and striking phrase that may include labeling and stereotyping (Da San Martino et al., 2019b). Slogans tend to act as emotional appeals (Dan, 2015). Ex.: President Donald Trump Proposes "Simple Immigration Plan": Illegals Have To Go!

- **Name Calling.** Labeling the object of the propaganda campaign as either something the target audience fears, hates, finds undesirable or otherwise loves or praises (Miller, 1939).

Ex.: Democrats Friend Louis Farrakhan In Iran: "Death to America!" America Is The "Great Satan" Neither Manafort nor these "Russians" are in the visitor logs.

- **Loaded Language** Using words/phrases with strong emotional implications (positive or negative) to influence an audience (Weston, 2018). Ex.: Dem Candidate Ilhan Omar Defending Tweet On "The Evil Doings Of Israel" by Frank Camp, Daily Wire, October 28, 2018:

To translate the emphatic content in double quote into feature, we used a feature called "isEmphatic". If we found the stressed content in double quote in the format of title or upper letter in a sentence, we would use 1 to denote the sentence has emphatic content in it.

2.2.7 BERT Features

In order to further extract the semantic information of text, we apply sentence vectors generated by the state-of-the-art models, Bidirectional Encoder Representations from Transformers (BERT) (Devlin et al., 2018). Specifically, we use pretrained BERT model to predict text category, but we do not directly adopt BERT results as our final results because of the better performance of Logistic Regression. We use the vector obtained by BERT's hidden layer which can represent the semantic feature. The experimental result shows that BERT features can improve hugely on F1 score on the development dataset.

3 Experiment

3.1 Data Cleaning

For the input of BERT model, we removed the punctuation, and changed all the uppercase letters to lowercase. Also, we changed all clitics to full words (e.g. "isn't" becomes "is not"). For the linguistic features extraction part, we did not apply the same method as above, because uppercase letter and quotes are important features for this task.

3.2 Model

We used two models, one is the pretrained BERT model and the other is Logistic Regression. The architecture of our model is shown in Figure 1.

3.3 Model Setup

We used the pretrained uncased BERT-Base model and fine-tuned it using the following hyper-

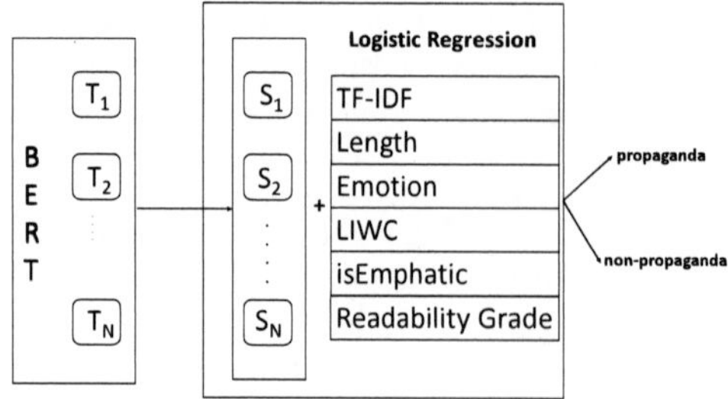

Figure 1: The architecture of our model

parameters: batch size of 16, sequence length of 70, weight decay of 0.01, and early stopping on validation F1 with patience of 7. For optimization, we used Adam with a learning rate of $2e - 5$. We tuned our models on the train dataset and we report results on the development dataset. For the Logistic Regression, we used the solver of LBFGS, penalty of l2, C of 1.0 and we used "balanced" mode to automatically adjust weights inversely proportional to class frequencies in the input data.

4   Results

Table 1 shows the ablation study results for the SLC task. We used the Logistic Regression with sentence length(the number of characters) feature to be the baseline. To test the importance of each individual feature in the classification, we applied them to Logistic Regression one at a time, including readability grade level, sentence length, LIWC, TF-IDF, emotion and BERT. Among these features, readability and sentence length increased 3.13% and 5.34% of F1 score, while LIWC, TF-IDF and emotion features increased 7.28%, 12.76% and 12.92% of F1 score respectively. These results suggest that the length and the complexity of a sentence is effective to differentiate propagandistic sentences from the non-propagandistic ones, but not as effective as LIWC, TF-IDF and emotion do. The implication is that while propaganda techniques are likely to appear in a complex and longer sentences, there are also long non-propagandistic sentences containing complex words. In addition, some propaganda techniques like slogan are not necessarily expressed in long sentences. The difference of language use, reflected by the words, punctuations (LIWC), term frequency inverse document frequency (TF-IDF) and the emotional expression (emotion) shapes a more fit boundary between propagandistic and non-propagandistic sentences.

We further explored the efficiency of semantic features extracted from BERT. The BERT feature improves the most among all the features in Logistic Regression by 18.05% of F1 score. This indicates that the higher granularity representation of a sentence better capture the presence of propaganda techniques. We conducted experiment using the pretrained and fine-tuned BERT and obtained huge improvements on the SLC task. As shown in Table 1, BERT performed better than LR_bert but worse than LR†‡, which indicates that the transfer learning when considering single semantic variable is not as effective as the combination with other linguistic features. Furthermore, we explored the effect of the isEmphatic feature introduced in Section 2.2.6. The isEmphatic feature is extremely sparse. We compared the performances of two classifiers that had the same feature set except the presence of isFmphatic, i.e., LR† and LR†‡ . The isEmpahtic feature improved the performance as evidenced by the slightly increase from 65.08% to 66.16%.

Model	Precision	Recall	F1
LR_base	38.80	49.42	43.47
LR_read	41.15	53.45	46.50
LR_length	42.49	57.38	48.82
LR_liwc	42.11	63.87	50.75
LR_tfidf	45.76	72.94	56.23
LR_emotion	49.58	65.36	56.39
LR_bert	55.50	69.01	61.52
BERT	67.00	63.19	65.04
LR†	57.10	75.64	65.08
LR†‡	58.00	77.00	**66.16**

Table 1: Sentence-level (SLC) results. † represents the inclusion of features other than isEmphatic into the model. ‡ represents the inclusion of isEmphatic features into the model

5   Related Work

There are a number of researchers applying machine learning to automatically identify Propagandistic news articles. (Barrón-Cedeño et al., 2019) presented PROPPY, the first publicly available real-world, real-time propaganda detection system for online news and they show that character n-grams and other style features outperform existing alternatives to identify propaganda based on word n-grams. (Ahmed et al., 2017) proposed a fake news(propagandistic news articles) detection model that use n-gram analysis and machine learning techniques. (Orlov and Litvak, 2018) presented an unsupervised approach using behavioral and text analysis of users and messages to identify groups of users who abuse the Twitter microblogging service to disseminate propaganda and misinformation.

Most relevant to our study, (Da San Martino et al., 2019b) proposed a BERT based technique to identify propaganda problems in the news articles. Specifically, the researchers trained a Multi-Granularity BERT model that includes multiple levels of semantic representations on two tasks. One task FLC identifies which of 18 propaganda techniques is/are present in the given fragment of the text. The other, namely, SLC is about classifying whether the given sentence is propagandistic. Different from their approach, we focused on the SLC task, and used the fine-tune BERT vectors combining various linguistic features, and fitted into a Logistic Regression model. Also, we only used the vectors extracted from the hidden layers of BERT to be part of our features. With a similar but smaller dataset, the researchers' model achieved 60.98% of F1 score, while ours is 66.16%. In this competition, our team ranked 9th out of 29 teams on the development set, with the F1 score of the top team being 2.7% higher than ours.

6 Conclusion and Future Work

In this paper, we focused on the sentence-level propaganda detection task and developed an automatic system based on some effective features. We got features including TF-IDF, length, emotion, readability level, LIWC, emphatic and BERT. Our ablation study shows that the length and complexity of sentence help to improve the performance slightly, comparing to the use of language reflected in specific term, frequency and emotional expression, which captures more propagandistic information. The semantic information extracted from BERT is crucial in detecting propaganda techniques, which improves the F1 score the most. The combination of these features and the BERT feature achieved the best performance with the Logistic Regression model. The F1 score is 66.16%.

Compared to (Da San Martino et al., 2019b), our approach focus more on the linguistic features combined with semantic features extracted from BERT, and use machine learning model , while they use the deep learning model with a high granularity task to improve performance on low granularity task.In terms of the performance, our F1 score is 66.16% whereas theirs is 60.98%. On the other hand, we noted that the two studies used different versions of the propaganda datasets, which may contribute to the observed difference in the performances.

In the future, we plan to embed the features we designed in the BERT model or studied more features from the propaganda techniques to improve the performance.

References

Hadeer Ahmed, Issa Traore, and Sherif Saad. 2017. Detection of online fake news using n-gram analysis and machine learning techniques. In *International Conference on Intelligent, Secure, and Dependable Systems in Distributed and Cloud Environments*, pages 127–138. Springer.

Georg W Alpers, Andrew J Winzelberg, Catherine Classen, Heidi Roberts, Parvati Dev, Cheryl Koopman, and C Barr Taylor. 2005. Evaluation of computerized text analysis in an internet breast cancer support group. *Computers in Human Behavior*, 21(2):361–376.

Alberto Barrón-Cedeño, Giovanni Da San Martino, Israa Jaradat, and Preslav Nakov. 2019. Proppy: A system to unmask propaganda in online news. In *Proceedings of the AAAI Conference on Artificial Intelligence*, volume 33, pages 9847–9848.

Giovanni Da San Martino, Alberto Barron-Cedeno, and Preslav Nakov. 2019a. Findings of the nlp4if-2019 shared task on fine-grained propaganda detection. In *Proceedings of the 2nd Workshop on NLP for Internet Freedom (NLP4IF): Censorship, Disinformation, and Propaganda*, NLP4IFEMNLP '19, Hong Kong, China.

Giovanni Da San Martino, Seunghak Yu, Alberto Barron-Cedeno, Rostislav Petrov, and Preslav Nakov. 2019b. Fine-grained analysis of propaganda in news articles. In *Proceedings of the 2019 Conference on Empirical Methods in Natural Language Processing*, EMNLP '19, Hong Kong, China.

Lavinia Dan. 2015. Techniques for the translation of advertising slogans. In *Proceedings of the International Conference Literature, Discourse and Multicultural Dialogue*, volume 3, pages 13–21.

Jacob Devlin, Ming-Wei Chang, Kenton Lee, and Kristina Toutanova. 2018. Bert: Pre-training of deep bidirectional transformers for language understanding. *arXiv preprint arXiv:1810.04805*.

Jacques Ellul. 1966. *Propaganda*. Knopf New York.

Arthur C Graesser, Danielle S McNamara, Max M Louwerse, and Zhiqiang Cai. 2004. Coh-metrix: Analysis of text on cohesion and language. *Behavior research methods, instruments, & computers*, 36(2):193–202.

Lei Guo, Jacob A Rohde, and H Denis Wu. 2018. Who is responsible for twitters echo chamber problem? evidence from 2016 us election networks. *Information, Communication & Society*, pages 1–18.

Minqing Hu and Bing Liu. 2004. Mining and summarizing customer reviews. In *Proceedings of the tenth ACM SIGKDD international conference on Knowledge discovery and data mining*, pages 168–177. ACM.

Karen Spärck Jones. 2004. A statistical interpretation of term specificity and its application in retrieval. *Journal of documentation*.

S Abd Kadir, A Mohd Lokman, and Toshio Tsuchiya. 2016. Emotion and techniques of propaganda in youtube videos. *Indian journal of science and technology*, 9:S1.

J Peter Kincaid, Robert P Fishburne Jr, Richard L Rogers, and Brad S Chissom. 1975. Derivation of new readability formulas (automated readability index, fog count and flesch reading ease formula) for navy enlisted personnel.

Jeff Koob. 2015. *Ad Nauseam: How Advertising and Public Relations Changed Everything*. iUniverse.

Clyde Raymond Miller. 1939. *How to detect and analyze propaganda*. Town Hall, Incorporated.

Saif Mohammad. 2018. Obtaining reliable human ratings of valence, arousal, and dominance for 20,000 english words. In *Proceedings of the 56th Annual Meeting of the Association for Computational Linguistics (Volume 1: Long Papers)*, pages 174–184.

Saif M Mohammad and Felipe Bravo-Marquez. 2017. Wassa-2017 shared task on emotion intensity. *arXiv preprint arXiv:1708.03700*.

Saif M Mohammad and Peter D Turney. 2013. Crowdsourcing a word–emotion association lexicon. *Computational Intelligence*, 29(3):436–465.

Matthew L Newman, Carla J Groom, Lori D Handelman, and James W Pennebaker. 2008. Gender differences in language use: An analysis of 14,000 text samples. *Discourse Processes*, 45(3):211–236.

FÅ Nielsen. 2011. A new anew: Evaluation of a word list for sentiment analysis in microblog,[in:] m. rowe et al. In *Proceedings of the ESWC2011 Workshop on Making Sense of Microposts: Big things come in small packages 718 in CEUR Workshop Proceedings*.

Michael Orlov and Marina Litvak. 2018. Using behavior and text analysis to detect propagandists and misinformers on twitter. In *Annual International Symposium on Information Management and Big Data*, pages 67–74. Springer.

James W Pennebaker and Laura A King. 1999. Linguistic styles: Language use as an individual difference. *Journal of personality and social psychology*, 77(6):1296.

Yla R Tausczik and James W Pennebaker. 2010. The psychological meaning of words: Liwc and computerized text analysis methods. *Journal of language and social psychology*, 29(1):24–54.

Anthony Weston. 2018. *A rulebook for arguments*. Hackett Publishing.

Theresa Wilson, Janyce Wiebe, and Paul Hoffmann. 2005. Recognizing contextual polarity in phrase-level sentiment analysis. In *Proceedings of Human Language Technology Conference and Conference on Empirical Methods in Natural Language Processing*.

Florian Zollmann. 2019. Bringing propaganda back into news media studies. *Critical Sociology*, 45(3):329–345.

Cost-Sensitive BERT for Generalisable Sentence Classification with Imbalanced Data

Harish Tayyar Madabushi[1] and **Elena Kochkina[2,3]** and **Michael Castelle[2,3]**

[1] University of Birmingham, UK
H.TayyarMadabushi.1@bham.ac.uk

[2]University of Warwick, UK
(E.Kochkina,M.Castelle.1)@warwick.ac.uk
[3]Alan Turing Institute, UK

Abstract

The automatic identification of propaganda has gained significance in recent years due to technological and social changes in the way news is generated and consumed. That this task can be addressed effectively using BERT, a powerful new architecture which can be fine-tuned for text classification tasks, is not surprising. However, propaganda detection, like other tasks that deal with news documents and other forms of decontextualized social communication (e.g. sentiment analysis), inherently deals with data whose categories are simultaneously imbalanced and dissimilar. We show that BERT, while capable of handling imbalanced classes with no additional data augmentation, does not generalise well when the training and test data are sufficiently dissimilar (as is often the case with news sources, whose topics evolve over time). We show how to address this problem by providing a statistical measure of similarity between datasets and a method of incorporating cost-weighting into BERT when the training and test sets are dissimilar. We test these methods on the Propaganda Techniques Corpus (PTC) and achieve the second highest score on sentence-level propaganda classification.

1 Introduction

The challenges of imbalanced classification—in which the proportion of elements in each class for a classification task significantly differ—and of the ability to generalise on dissimilar data have remained important problems in Natural Language Processing (NLP) and Machine Learning in general. Popular NLP tasks including sentiment analysis, propaganda detection, and event extraction from social media are all examples of imbalanced classification problems. In each case the number of elements in one of the classes (e.g. negative sentiment, propagandistic content, or specific events discussed on social media, respectively) is significantly lower than the number of elements in the other classes.

The recently introduced BERT language model for transfer learning (Devlin et al., 2018) uses a deep bidirectional transformer architecture to produce pre-trained context-dependent embeddings. It has proven to be powerful in solving many NLP tasks and, as we find, also appears to handle imbalanced classification well, thus removing the need to use standard methods of data augmentation to mitigate this problem (see Section 2.2.2 for related work and Section 4.1 for analysis).

BERT is credited with the ability to adapt to many tasks and data with very little training (Devlin et al., 2018). However, we show that BERT fails to perform well when the training and test data are significantly dissimilar, as is the case with several tasks that deal with social and news data. In these cases, the training data is necessarily a subset of past data, while the model is likely to be used on future data which deals with different topics. This work addresses this problem by incorporating cost-sensitivity (Section 4.2) into BERT.

We test these methods by participating in the Shared Task on Fine-Grained Propaganda Detection for the 2nd Workshop on NLP for Internet Freedom, for which we achieve the second rank on sentence-level classification of propaganda, confirming the importance of cost-sensitivity when the training and test sets are dissimilar.

1.1 Detecting Propaganda

The term 'propaganda' derives from *propagare* in post-classical Latin, as in "propagation of the faith" (Auerbach and Castronovo, 2014), and thus has from the beginning been associated with an intentional and potentially multicast communication; only later did it become a pejorative term. It was pragmatically defined in the World War II era as "the expression of an opinion or an action by individuals or groups deliberately designed to influence the opinions or the actions of other individuals or groups with reference to predetermined ends" (Institute for Propaganda Analysis, 1937).

For the philosopher and sociologist Jacques Ellul, however, in a society with mass communication, propaganda is *inevitable* and thus it is necessary to become more *aware* of it (Ellul, 1973); but whether or not to classify a given strip of text as propaganda depends not just on its content but on its *use* on the part of both addressers and addressees (Auerbach and Castronovo, 2014, 6), and this fact makes the automated detection of propaganda intrinsically challenging.

Despite this difficulty, interest in automatically detecting misinformation and/or propaganda has gained significance due to the exponential growth in online sources of information combined with the speed with which information is shared today. The sheer volume of social interactions makes it impossible to manually check the veracity of all information being shared. Automation thus remains a potentially viable method of ensuring that we continue to enjoy the benefits of a connected world without the spread of misinformation through either ignorance or malicious intent.

In the task introduced by Da San Martino et al. (2019), we are provided with articles tagged as propaganda at the sentence and fragment (or span) level and are tasked with making predictions on a development set followed by a final held-out test set. We note this gives us access to the articles in the development and test sets but not their labels.

We participated in this task under the team name *ProperGander* and were placed 2nd on the sentence level classification task where we make use of our methods of incorporating cost-sensitivity into BERT. We also participated in the fragment level task and were placed 7th. The significant contributions of this work are:

- We show that common ('easy') methods of data augmentation for dealing with class imbalance do not improve base BERT performance.

- We provide a statistical method of establishing the similarity of datasets.

- We incorporate cost-sensitivity into BERT to enable models to adapt to dissimilar datasets.

- We release all our program code on GitHub

and Google Colaboratory[1], so that other researchers can benefit from this work.

2 Related work

2.1 Propaganda detection

Most of the existing works on propaganda detection focus on identifying propaganda at the news article level, or even at the news outlet level with the assumption that each of the articles of the suspected propagandistic outlet are propaganda (Rashkin et al., 2017; Barrón-Cedeño et al., 2019).

Here we study two tasks that are more fine-grained, specifically propaganda detection at the sentence and phrase (fragment) levels (Da San Martino et al., 2019). This fine-grained setup aims to train models that identify linguistic propaganda techniques rather than distinguishing between the article source styles.

Da San Martino et al. (2019) were the first to propose this problem setup and release it as a shared task.[2] Along with the released dataset, Da San Martino et al. (2019) proposed a multi-granularity neural network, which uses the deep bidirectional transformer architecture known as BERT, which features pre-trained context-dependent embeddings (Devlin et al., 2018). Their system takes a joint learning approach to the sentence- and phrase-level tasks, concatenating the output representation of the less granular (sentence-level) task with the more fine-grained task using learned weights.

In this work we also take the BERT model as the basis of our approach and focus on the class imbalance as well as the lack of similarity between training and test data inherent to the task.

2.2 Class imbalance

A common issue for many Natural Language Processing (NLP) classification tasks is *class imbalance*, the situation where one of the class categories comprises a significantly larger proportion of the dataset than the other classes. It is especially prominent in real-world datasets and complicates classification when the identification of the minority class is of specific importance.

Models trained on the basis of minimising errors for imbalanced datasets tend to more fre-

---

[1] http://www.harishmadabushi.com/research/propaganda-detection/
[2] https://propaganda.qcri.org/nlp4if-shared-task/

quently predict the majority class; achieving high accuracy in such cases can be misleading. Because of this, the macro-averaged F-score, chosen for this competition, is a more suitable metric as it weights the performance on each class equally.

As class imbalance is a widespread issue, multiple techniques have been developed that help alleviate it (Buda et al., 2018; Haixiang et al., 2017), by either adjusting the model (e.g. changing the performance metric) or changing the data (e.g. oversampling the minority class or undersampling the majority class).

2.2.1 Cost-sensitive learning

Cost-sensitive classification can be used when the "cost" of mislabelling one class is higher than that of mislabelling other classes (Elkan, 2001; Kukar et al., 1998). For example, the real cost to a bank of miscategorising a large fraudulent transaction as authentic is potentially higher than miscategorising (perhaps only temporarily) a valid transaction as fraudulent. Cost-sensitive learning tackles the issue of class imbalance by changing the cost function of the model such that misclassification of training examples from the minority class carries more weight and is thus more 'expensive'. This is achieved by simply multiplying the loss of each example by a certain factor. This cost-sensitive learning technique takes misclassification costs into account during model training, and does not modify the imbalanced data distribution directly.

2.2.2 Data augmentation

Common methods that tackle the problem of class imbalance by modifying the data to create balanced datasets are undersampling and oversampling. Undersampling randomly removes instances from the majority class and is only suitable for problems with an abundance of data. Oversampling means creating more minority class instances to match the size of the majority class. Oversampling methods range from simple random oversampling, i.e. repeating the training procedure on instances from the minority class, chosen at random, to the more complex, which involves constructing synthetic minority-class samples. Random oversampling is similar to cost-sensitive learning as repeating the sample several times makes the cost of its mis-classification grow proportionally. Kolomiyets et al. (2011), Zhang et al. (2015), and Wang and Yang (2015) per-

form data augmentation using synonym replacement, i.e. replacing random words in sentences with their synonyms or nearest-neighbor embeddings, and show its effectiveness on multiple tasks and datasets. Wei et al. (2019) provide a great overview of 'easy' data augmentation (EDA) techniques for NLP, including synonym replacement as described above, and random deletion, i.e. removing words in the sentence at random with pre-defined probability. They show the effectiveness of EDA across five text classification tasks. However, they mention that EDA may not lead to substantial improvements when using pre-trained models. In this work we test this claim by comparing performance gains of using cost-sensitive learning versus two data augmentation methods, synonym replacement and random deletion, with a pre-trained BERT model.

More complex augmentation methods include back-translation (Sennrich et al., 2015), translational data augmentation (Fadaee et al., 2017), and noising (Xie et al., 2017), but these are out of the scope of this study.

3 Dataset

The Propaganda Techniques Corpus (PTC) dataset for the 2019 Shared Task on Fine-Grained Propaganda consists of a *training set* of 350 news articles, consisting of just over 16,965 total sentences, in which specifically propagandistic fragments have been manually spotted and labelled by experts. This is accompanied by a *development set* (or *dev set*) of 61 articles with 2,235 total sentences, whose labels are maintained by the shared task organisers; and two months after the release of this data, the organisers released a *test set* of 86 articles and 3,526 total sentences. In the training set, 4,720 ($\sim 28\%$) of the sentences have been assessed as containing propaganda, with 12,245 sentences ($\sim 72\%$) as non-propaganda, demonstrating a clear class imbalance.

In the binary *sentence-level classification* (SLC) task, a model is trained to detect whether each and every sentence is either 'propaganda' or 'non-propaganda'; in the more challenging *field-level classification* (FLC) task, a model is trained to detect one of 18 possible propaganda technique types in spans of characters *within* sentences. These propaganda types are listed in Da San Martino et al. (2019) and range from those which might be recognisable at the lexical level (e.g.

NAME_CALLING, REPETITION), and those which would likely need to incorporate semantic understanding (RED_HERRING, STRAW_MAN).[3]

For several example sentences from a sample document annotated with fragment-level classifications (FLC) (Figure 1). The corresponding sentence-level classification (SLC) labels would indicate that sentences 3, 4, and 7 are 'propaganda' while the the other sentences are 'non-propaganda'.

3.1 Data Distribution

One of the most interesting aspects of the data provided for this task is the notable difference between the training and the development/test sets. We emphasise that this difference is realistic and reflective of real world news data, in which major stories are often accompanied by the introduction of new terms, names, and even phrases. This is because the training data is a subset of past data while the model is to be used on future data which deals with different newsworthy topics.

We demonstrate this difference statistically by using a method for finding the similarity of corpora suggested by Kilgarriff (2001). We use the Wilcoxon signed-rank test (Wilcoxon, 1945) which compares the frequency counts of randomly sampled elements from different datasets to determine if those datasets have a statistically similar distribution of elements.

We implement this as follows. For each of the training, development and test sets, we extract all words (retaining the repeats) while ignoring a set of stopwords (identified through the Python Natural Language Toolkit). We then extract 10,000 samples (with replacements) for various pairs of these datasets (training, development, and test sets along with splits of each of these datasets). Finally, we use comparative word frequencies from the two sets to calculate the p-value using the Wilcoxon signed-rank test. Table 1 provides the minimum and maximum p-values and their interpretations for ten such runs of each pair reported. With p-value less than 0.05, we show that the train, development and test sets are self-similar and also significantly different from each other. In measuring self-similarity, we split each dataset after shuffling all sentences. While this comparison is made at the sentence level (as opposed to the arti-

---

³`https://propaganda.qcri.org/ annotations/` includes a flowchart instructing annotators to discover and isolate these 18 propaganda categories.

Set 1	Set 2	p-value (min)	p-value (max)	% Similar Tests
50% Train	50% Train	2.38E-01	9.11E-01	100
50% Dev	50% Dev	5.55E-01	9.96E-01	100
50% Test	50% Test	6.21E-01	8.88E-01	100
25% Dev	75% Dev	1.46E-01	5.72E-01	100
25% Test	75% Test	3.70E-02	7.55E-01	90
25% Train	75% Train	9.08E-02	9.66E-01	100
Train	Dev	2.05E-09	4.33E-05	0
Train	Test	8.37E-23	1.18E-14	0
Dev	Test	2.72E-04	2.11E-02	0

Table 1: p-values representing the similarity between (parts of) the train, test and development sets.

cle level), it is consistent with the granularity used for propaganda detection, which is also at the sentence level. We also perform measurements of self similarity after splitting the data at the article level and find that the conclusions of similarity between the sets hold with a p-value threshold of 0.001, where p-values for similarity between the training and dev/test sets are orders of magnitude lower compared to self-similarity. Since we use random sampling we run this test 10 times and present the both the maximum and minimum p-values. We include the similarity between 25% of a dataset and the remaining 75% of that set because that is the train/test ratio we use in our experiments, further described in our methodology (Section 4).

This analysis shows that while all splits of each of the datasets are statistically similar, the training set (and the split of the training set that we use for experimentation) are significantly different from the development and test sets. While our analysis does show that the development and the test sets are dissimilar, we note (based on the p-values) that they are significantly more similar to each other than they are to the training set.

4 Methodology

We were provided with two tasks: (1) propaganda fragment-level identification (FLC) and (2) propagandistic sentence-level identification (SLC). While we develop systems for both tasks, our main focus is toward the latter. Given the differences between the training, development, and test sets, we focus on methods for generalising our models. We note that propaganda identification is, in general, an imbalanced binary classification problem as most sentences are not propagandistic.

Due to the non-deterministic nature of fast GPU computations, we run each of our models three times and report the average of these three runs

Sentence 1:	The Senate Judiciary Committee voted 11-10 along party lines to advance the nomination of Judge Brett Kavanaugh out of committee to the Senate floor for a vote.
Sentence 2:	Of course, RINO Senator Jeff Flake (R-AZ) wanted to side with Senate Democrats in pushing for a FBI investigation into unsubstantiated allegations against Kavanaugh.
Sentence 3:	Outgoing Flake, and <LOADED_LANGUAGE> **good riddance** </LOADED_LANGUAGE>, said that he sided with his colleagues in having a "limited time and scope" investigation by the FBI into the allegations against Kavanaugh.
Sentence 4:	"<FLAG-WAVING> **This country is being ripped apart here, and we've got to make sure we do due diligence**</FLAG-WAVING>," Flake said.
Sentence 5:	He added that he would be more "comfortable" with an FBI investigation.
Sentence 6:	Comfort?
Sentence 7:	<WHATABOUTISM>**What about Judge Kavanaugh's comfort in being put through the ringer without a shred of evidence, Senator Flake**</WHATABOUTISM>?

Figure 1: Excerpt of an example (truncated) news document with three separate field-level classification (FLC) tags, for LOADED LANGUAGE, FLAG-WAVING, AND WHATABOUTISM.

through the rest of this section. When picking the model to use for our final submission, we pick the model that performs best on the development set.

When testing our models, we split the labelled training data into two non-overlapping parts: the first one, consisting of 75% of the training data is used to train models, whereas the other is used to test the effectiveness of the models. All models are trained and tested on the same split to ensure comparability. Similarly, to ensure that our models remain comparable, we continue to train on the same 75% of the training set even when testing on the development set.

Once the best model is found using these methods, we train that model on all of the training data available before then submitting the results on the development set to the leaderboard. These results are detailed in the section describing our results (Section 5).

4.1 Class Imbalance in Sentence Level Classification

The sentence level classification task is an imbalanced binary classification problem that we address using BERT (Devlin et al., 2018). We use BERT$_{BASE}$, uncased, which consists of 12 self-attention layers, and returns a 768-dimension vector that representation a sentence. So as to make use of BERT for sentence classification, we include a fully connected layer on top of the BERT self-attention layers, which classifies the sentence embedding provided by BERT into the two classes of interest (propaganda or non-propaganda).

We attempt to exploit various data augmentation techniques to address the problem of class imbalance. Table 2 shows the results of our experiments for different data augmentation techniques

when, after shuffling the training data, we train the model on 75% of the training data and test it on the remaining 25% of the training data and the development data.

Augmentation Technique	f1-score on 25% of Train	f1-score on Dev
None	0.7954	0.5803
Synonym Insertion	0.7889	0.5833
Dropping Words	0.7791	0.5445
Over Sampling	0.7843	0.6276

Table 2: F1 scores on an unseen (not used for training) part of the training set and the development set on BERT using different augmentation techniques.

We observe that BERT *without* augmentation consistently outperforms BERT with augmentation in the experiments when the model is trained on 75% of the training data and evaluated on the rest, i.e trained and evaluated on *similar data*, coming from the same distribution. This is consistent with observations by Wei et al. (2019) that contextual word embeddings do not gain from data augmentation. The fact that we shuffle the training data prior to splitting it into training and testing subsets could imply that the model is learning to associate topic words, such as 'Mueller', as propaganda. However, when we perform model evaluation using the development set, which is dissimilar to the training, we observe that synonym insertion and word dropping techniques also do not bring performance gains, while random oversampling increases performance over base BERT by 4%. Synonym insertion provides results very similar to base BERT, while random deletion harms model performance producing lower scores. We believe that this could be attributed to the fact that synonym insertion and random word dropping involve the introduction of noise to the data, while oversampling does not. As we are working with natural language data, this type of noise can in fact change the meaning of the sentence. Oversampling on the other hand purely increases the importance of the minority class by repeating training on the unchanged instances.

So as to better understand the aspects of oversampling that contribute to these gains, we perform a class-wise performance analysis of BERT with/without oversampling. The results of these experiments (Table 3) show that oversampling increases the overall recall while maintaining precision. This is achieved by significantly improving the recall of the minority class (propaganda) at the cost of the recall of the majority class.

	OS	No OS
precision	0.7967	0.7933
recall	0.7767	0.8000
f1-score	0.7843	0.7954
Non-Propaganda precision	0.8733	0.8467
Non-Propaganda recall	0.8100	0.8900
Non-Propaganda F1	0.8433	0.8667
Propaganda precision	0.5800	0.6600
Propaganda recall	0.6933	0.5533
Propaganda F1	0.6300	0.5533

Table 3: Class-wise precision and recall with and without oversampling (OS) achieved on unseen part of the training set.

So far we have been able to establish that **a)** the training and test sets are dissimilar, thus requiring us to generalise our model, **b)** oversampling provides a method of generalisation, and **c)** oversampling does this while maintaining recall on the minority (and thus more interesting) class.

Given this we explore alternative methods of increasing minority class recall without a significant drop in precision. One such method is cost-sensitive classification, which differs from random oversampling in that it provides a more continuous-valued and consistent method of weighting samples of imbalanced training data; for example, random oversampling will inevitably emphasise some training instances at the expense of others. We detail our methods of using cost-sensitive classification in the next section. Further experiments with oversampling might have provided insights into the relationships between these methods, which we leave for future exploration.

4.2 Cost-sensitive Classification

As discussed in Section 2.2.1, cost-sensitive classification can be performed by weighting the cost function. We increase the weight of incorrectly labelling a propagandistic sentence by altering the cost function of the training of the final fully connected layer of our model previously described in Section 4.1. We make these changes through the use of PyTorch (Paszke et al., 2017) which calculates the cross-entropy loss for a single prediction x, an array where the jth element represents the models prediction for class j, labelled with the class $class$ as given by Equation 1.

$$
\begin{aligned}
loss(x, class) &= -\log\left(\frac{\exp(x[class])}{\sum_j \exp(x[j])}\right) \\
&= -x[class] + \log\left(\sum_j \exp(x[j])\right)
\end{aligned}
\tag{1}
$$

The cross-entropy loss given in Equation 1 is modified to accommodate an array $weight$, the ith element of which represents the weight of the ith class, as described in Equation 2.

$$
loss(x, class) = weight[class]\Theta
$$

$$
\text{where, } \Theta = -x[class] + \log\left(\sum_j \exp(x[j])\right)
\tag{2}
$$

Intuitively, we increase the cost of getting the classification of an "important" class wrong and correspondingly decrees the cost of getting a less important class wrong. In our case, we increase the cost of mislabelling the minority class which is "propaganda" (as opposed to "non-propaganda").

We expect the effect of this to be similar to that of oversampling, in that it is likely to enable us to increase the recall of the minority class thus resulting in the decrease in recall of the overall model while maintaining high precision. We reiterate that this specific change to a model results in increasing the model's ability to better identify elements belonging to the minority class in *dissimilar* datasets when using BERT.

We explore the validity of this by performing several experiments with different weights assigned to the minority class. We note that in our experiments use significantly higher weights than the weights proportional to class frequencies in the

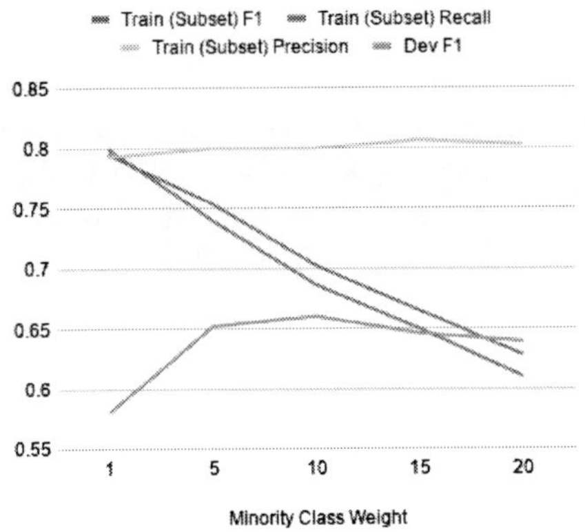

Figure 2: The impact of modifying the minority class weights on the performance on similar (subset of training set) and dissimilar (development) datasets. The method of increasing minority class weights is able to push the model towards generalisation while maintaining precision.

training data, that are common in literature (Ling and Sheng, 2011). Rather than directly using the class proportions of the training set, we show that tuning weights based on performance on the development set is more beneficial. Figure 2 shows the results of these experiments wherein we are able to maintain the precision on the subset of the training set used for testing while reducing its recall and thus generalising the model. The fact that the model is generalising on a dissimilar dataset is confirmed by the increase in the development set F1 score. We note that the gains are not infinite and that a balance must be struck based on the amount of generalisation and the corresponding loss in accuracy. The exact weight to use for the best transfer of classification accuracy is related to the dissimilarity of that other dataset and hence is to be obtained experimentally through hyperparameter search. Our experiments showed that a value of 4 is best suited for this task.

We do not include the complete results of our experiments here due to space constraints but include them along with charts and program code on our project website. Based on this exploration we find that the best weights for this particular dataset are *1* for non-propaganda and *4* for propaganda and we use this to train the final model used to submit results to the leaderboard. We also found that adding Part of Speech tags and Named Entity information to BERT embeddings by concatenating these one-hot vectors to the BERT embed-

dings does not improve model performance. We describe these results in Section 5.

4.3 Fragment-level classification (FLC)

In addition to participating in the Sentence Level Classification task we also participate in the Fragment Level Classification task. We note that extracting fragments that are propagandistic is similar to the task of Named Entity Recognition, in that they are both span extraction tasks, and so use a BERT based model designed for this task - We build on the work by Emelyanov and Artemova (2019) which makes use of Continuous Random Field stacked on top of an LSTM to predict spans. This architecture is standard amongst state of the art models that perform span identification.

While the same span of text cannot have multiple named entity labels, it can have different propaganda labels. We get around this problem by picking one of the labels at random. Additionally, so as to speed up training, we only train our model on those sentences that contain some propagandistic fragment. In hindsight, we note that both these decisions were not ideal and discuss what we might have otherwise done in Section 7.

5 Results

In this section, we show our rankings on the leaderboard on the test set. Unlike the previous exploratory sections, in which we trained our model on part of the training set, we train models described in this section on the complete training set.

5.1 Results on the SLC task

Our best performing model, selected on the basis of a systematic analysis of the relationship between cost weights and recall, places us second amongst the 25 teams that submitted their results on this task. We present our score on the test set alongside those of comparable teams in Table 4. We note that the task description paper (Da San Martino et al., 2019) describes a method of achieving an F1 score of 60.98% on a similar task although this reported score is not directly comparable to the results on this task because of the differences in testing sets.

5.2 Results on the FLC task

We train the model described in Section 4.3 on the complete training set before submitting to the leaderboard. Our best performing model was

Rank	Team	F1	Precision	Recall
1	ltuorp	0.632375	0.602885	0.664899
2	**Proper-Gander**	**0.625651**	**0.564957**	**0.564957**
3	YMJA	0.624934	0.625265	0.624602
...				
20	Baseline	0.434701	0.388010	0.494168

Table 4: Our results on the SLC task (2nd, in **bold**) alongside comparable results from the competition leaderboard.

placed 7th amongst the 13 teams that submitted results for this task. We present our score on the test set alongside those of comparable teams in Table 5. We note that the task description paper (Da San Martino et al., 2019) describes a method of achieving an F1 score of 22.58% on a similar task although, this reported score is not directly comparable to the results on this task.

Rank	Team	F1	Precision	Recall
1	newspeak	0.248849	0.286299	0.220063
2	Anti-ganda	0.226745	0.288213	0.186887
...				
6	aschern	0.109060	0.071528	0.229464
7	**Proper-Gander**	**0.098969**	**0.065167**	**0.205634**
...				
11	Baseline	0.000015	0.011628	0.000008

Table 5: Our results on the FLC task (7th, in **bold**) alongside those of better performing teams from the competition leaderboard.

One of the major setbacks to our method for identifying sentence fragments was the loss of training data as a result of randomly picking one label when the same fragment had multiple labels. This could have been avoided by training different models for each label and simply concatenating the results. Additionally, training on all sentences, including those that did not contain any fragments labelled as propagandistic would have likely improved our model performance. We intend to perform these experiments as part of our ongoing research.

6 Issues of Decontextualization in Automated Propaganda Detection

It is worth reflecting on the nature of the shared task dataset (PTC corpus) and its structural correspondence (or lack thereof) to some of the definitions of propaganda mentioned in the introduction. First, propaganda is a *social phenomenon* and takes place as an act of communication (O'Shaughnessy, 2005, 13-14), and so it is more than a simple information-theoretic *message* of zeros and ones—it also incorporates an addresser and addressee(s), each in phatic contact (typically via broadcast media), ideally with a shared denotational code and contextual surround(s) (Jakobson, 1960).

As such, a dataset of decontextualised documents with labelled sentences, devoid of authorial or publisher metadata, has taken us at some remove from even a simple everyday definition of propaganda. Our models for this shared task cannot easily incorporate information about the addresser or addressee; are left to assume a shared denotational code between author and reader (one perhaps simulated with the use of pre-trained word embeddings); and they are unaware of when or where the act(s) of propagandistic communication took place. This slipperiness is illustrated in our example document (Fig. 1): note that while Sentences 3 and 7, labelled as propaganda, reflect a propagandistic attitude on the part of the journalist and/or publisher, Sentence 4—also labelled as propaganda in the training data—instead reflects a "flag-waving" propagandistic attitude on the part of U.S. congressman Jeff Flake, via the conventions of *reported speech* (Vološinov, 1973, 115-130). While reported speech often is signaled by specific morphosyntactic patterns (e.g. the use of double-quotes and "Flake said") (Spronck and Nikitina, 2019), we argue that human readers routinely distinguish propagandistic reportage from the propagandastic speech acts of its subjects, and to conflate these categories in a propaganda detection corpus may contribute to the occurrence of false positives/negatives.

7 Conclusions and Future Work

In this work we have presented a method of incorporating cost-sensitivity into BERT to allow for better generalisation and additionally, we provide a simple measure of corpus similarity to determine when this method is likely to be useful. We intend to extend our analysis of the ability to generalise models to less similar data by experimenting on other datasets and models. We hope that the release of program code and documentation will allow the research community to help in this experimentation while exploiting these methods.

Acknowledgements

We would like to thank Dr Leandro Minku from the University of Birmingham for his insights into and help with the statistical analysis presented in this paper.

This work was also partially supported by The Alan Turing Institute under the EPSRC grant EP/N510129/1. Work by Elena Kochkina was partially supported by the Leverhulme Trust through the Bridges Programme and Warwick CDT for Urban Science & Progress under the EPSRC Grant Number EP/L016400/1.

References

Jonathan Auerbach and Russ Castronovo, editors. 2014. *The Oxford Handbook of Propaganda Studies*. Oxford Handbooks. Oxford University Press, Oxford, New York.

Alberto Barrón-Cedeño, Giovanni Da San Martino, Israa Jaradat, and Preslav Nakov. 2019. Proppy: A system to unmask propaganda in online news. In *Proceedings of the AAAI Conference on Artificial Intelligence*, volume 33, pages 9847–9848.

Mateusz Buda, Atsuto Maki, and Maciej A Mazurowski. 2018. A systematic study of the class imbalance problem in convolutional neural networks. *Neural Networks*, 106:249–259.

Giovanni Da San Martino, Seunghak Yu, Alberto Barrón-Cedeño, Rostislav Petrov, and Preslav Nakov. 2019. Fine-grained analysis of propaganda in news articles. In *Proceedings of the 2019 Conference on Empirical Methods in Natural Language Processing and 9th International Joint Conference on Natural Language Processing, EMNLP-IJCNLP 2019, Hong Kong, China, November 3-7, 2019*, EMNLP-IJCNLP 2019, Hong Kong, China.

Jacob Devlin, Ming-Wei Chang, Kenton Lee, and Kristina Toutanova. 2018. BERT: Pre-training of deep bidirectional transformers for language understanding. *arXiv preprint arXiv:1810.04805*.

Charles Elkan. 2001. The foundations of cost-sensitive learning. In *International joint conference on artificial intelligence*, volume 17, pages 973–978. Lawrence Erlbaum Associates Ltd.

Jacques Ellul. 1973. *Propaganda*. Random House USA Inc, New York.

Anton A. Emelyanov and Ekaterina Artemova. 2019. Multilingual named entity recognition using pretrained embeddings, attention mechanism and NCRF. *CoRR*, abs/1906.09978.

Marzieh Fadaee, Arianna Bisazza, and Christof Monz. 2017. Data augmentation for low-resource neural machine translation. *arXiv preprint arXiv:1705.00440*.

Guo Haixiang, Li Yijing, Jennifer Shang, Gu Mingyun, Huang Yuanyue, and Gong Bing. 2017. Learning from class-imbalanced data: Review of methods and applications. *Expert Systems with Applications*, 73:220–239.

Institute for Propaganda Analysis. 1937. How to detect propaganda. *Propaganda Analysis*, 1(2):5–8.

Roman Jakobson. 1960. Closing Statement: Linguistics and Poetics. In Thomas A. Sebeok, editor, *Style in Language*, pages 350–377. MIT Press, Cambridge, MA.

Adam Kilgarriff. 2001. Comparing corpora. *International Journal of Corpus Linguistics*, 6(1):97–133.

Oleksandr Kolomiyets, Steven Bethard, and Marie-Francine Moens. 2011. Model-portability experiments for textual temporal analysis. In *Proceedings of the 49th Annual Meeting of the Association for Computational Linguistics: Human Language Technologies: short papers-Volume 2*, pages 271–276. Association for Computational Linguistics.

Matjaz Kukar, Igor Kononenko, et al. 1998. Cost-sensitive learning with neural networks. In *ECAI*, pages 445–449.

CX Ling and VS Sheng. 2011. Cost-sensitive learning and the class imbalance problem. *Encyclopedia of Machine Learning: Springer*, 24.

Nicholas Jackson O'Shaughnessy. 2005. *Politics and Propaganda: Weapons of Mass Seduction*. University of Michigan Press, Ann Arbor.

Adam Paszke, Sam Gross, Soumith Chintala, Gregory Chanan, Edward Yang, Zachary DeVito, Zeming Lin, Alban Desmaison, Luca Antiga, and Adam Lerer. 2017. Automatic differentiation in PyTorch. In *NIPS Autodiff Workshop*.

Hannah Rashkin, Eunsol Choi, Jin Yea Jang, Svitlana Volkova, and Yejin Choi. 2017. Truth of varying shades: Analyzing language in fake news and political fact-checking. In *Proceedings of the 2017 Conference on Empirical Methods in Natural Language Processing*, pages 2931–2937.

Rico Sennrich, Barry Haddow, and Alexandra Birch. 2015. Improving neural machine translation models with monolingual data. *arXiv preprint arXiv:1511.06709*.

Stef Spronck and Tatiana Nikitina. 2019. Reported speech forms a dedicated syntactic domain. *Linguistic Typology*, 23(1):119–159.

V. N. Vološinov. 1973. *Marxism and the Philosophy of Language: Studies in Language*. Academic Press Inc, New York.

William Yang Wang and Diyi Yang. 2015. Thats so annoying!!!: A lexical and frame-semantic embedding based data augmentation approach to automatic categorization of annoying behaviors using# petpeeve tweets. In *Proceedings of the 2015 Conference on Empirical Methods in Natural Language Processing*, pages 2557–2563.

Jason W Wei and Kai Zou. 2019. Eda: Easy data augmentation techniques for boosting performance on text classification tasks. *arXiv preprint arXiv:1901.11196*.

Frank Wilcoxon. 1945. Individual comparisons by ranking methods. *Biometrics*, 1(6):80–83.

Ziang Xie, Sida I Wang, Jiwei Li, Daniel Lévy, Aiming Nie, Dan Jurafsky, and Andrew Y Ng. 2017. Data noising as smoothing in neural network language models. *arXiv preprint arXiv:1703.02573*.

Xiang Zhang, Junbo Zhao, and Yann LeCun. 2015. Character-level convolutional networks for text classification. In *Advances in neural information processing systems*, pages 649–657.

Understanding BERT Performance in Propaganda Analysis

Yiqing Hua
Cornell Tech
`yiqing@cs.cornell.edu`

Abstract

In this paper, we describe our system used in the shared task for fine-grained propaganda analysis at sentence level. Despite the challenging nature of the task, our pretrained BERT model (team YMJA) fine tuned on the training dataset provided by the shared task scored 0.62 F1 on the test set and ranked third among 25 teams who participated in the contest. We present a set of illustrative experiments to better understand the performance of our BERT model on this shared task. Further, we explore beyond the given dataset for false-positive cases that likely to be produced by our system. We show that despite the high performance on the given testset, our system may have the tendency of classifying opinion pieces as propaganda and cannot distinguish quotations of propaganda speech from actual usage of propaganda techniques.

1 Introduction

The NLP4IF shared task for 2019 consists of 451 newspaper articles from 48 news outlets that have been tagged for characteristics of 18 propaganda techniques (Da San Martino et al., 2019). The 18 propaganda techniques range from loaded language, name calling/labelling, repetition, to logical fallacies such as oversimplification, red herring, etc. Some of the techniques, by definition, require background knowledge to detect, such as the identification of slogans, which would first require one to know of the slogans.

The shared task consists of two subtasks, sentence level classification (SLC) and fragment level classification (FLC). In this paper, we focus our discussion on the sentence level classification. The subtask involves determining for each sentence, whether the text is 'propaganda' or not as a binary task. The definition of being 'propaganda' is that whether the utterance uses one of the 18 propaganda techniques listed in (Da San Martino et al., 2019).

In this paper, we describe our fine tuned BERT model used in the shared task. Our system (team YMJA) scored 0.62 F1 on the test set and ranked number third in the final competition for the SLC task. Further, we perform analyses in order to better understand the performance of our system. Specifically, we would like to understand if the model was able to identify propaganda given appearances of the defined propaganda techniques, or if it is exploiting obvious features that may lead to harmful false-positive examples.

Our results show that trained on the provided dataset from the shared task, our system may classify opinion pieces as propaganda and cannot distinguish quotation of propaganda speech from usage of propaganda techniques. We advise that future applications of propaganda analysis algorithms trained with similar definition of propaganda should be used with caution. We hope the insights gained from our study can help towards the design of a more robust system in propaganda analysis.

2 Related Work

Transformer based models (Vaswani et al., 2017) such as BERT (Devlin et al., 2018) have swept the field of natural language process and has led to reported improvements in virtually every task. The capacity of these models to capture long term dependencies and to represent context in ways useful for tagging is by now well established with multiple papers suggesting best practices (Sun et al., 2019).

Early works have applied machine learning techniques directly to the problem of propaganda labelling at article level (Rashkin et al., 2017; Volkova and Jang, 2018; Barrón-Cedeno et al.,

Proceedings of the 2nd Workshop on NLP for Internet Freedom: Censorship, Disinformation, and Propaganda, pages 135–138
Hong Kong, China, November 4, 2019 ©2019 Association for Computational Linguistics

2019), with varying definitions of propaganda. On the other hand, concerns have been raised regarding whether or not transformer based models themselves (Solaiman et al., 2019) will lead to propaganda generated by machines to deceive humans. However, others have argued (Zellers et al., 2019) that strong fake news generators are an essential part of detecting machine generated propaganda.

3 Fine Tuned BERT models

In principle, this tagging problem in the NLP4IF shared task is similar to the well studied problem of sentiment analysis for which there is ample literature. Our own model draws heavily from a Kaggle competitor's shared kernel (Reina, 2019) built upon the popular PyTorch Transformers libraries (Hugging Face, 2019). While that application in (Reina, 2019) is targeting toxicity in online comments, a change of labels is sufficient to make the same model apply to propaganda detection. The code of our implementation can be found in the published colab file[1].

We retrieved the uncased BERT-large model from github[2] and fine tuned the model on the training set. We used 10-fold cross validation to create an ensemble of models. The use of model ensemble techniques (Opitz and Maclin, 1999) to limit over-training and improve model performance on held out test data is a well established. This is a common feature of most Kaggle competitions, despite the fact that the resulting models consume substantially more resources.

We trained each model for 1 epoch, with batch size of 32, learning rate of 10^{-5}, decay of 0.01 and max sentence length of 129. Given the imbalance of positive and negative labels, we up-weight positive samples with a factor of 5 in the cross-entropy loss.

Our ensemble of models scored 0.62 F1 on the test set and ranked third among 25 teams, likely because the ensemble decreases the degree of overfitting.

4 Discussion

Recently, concerns have been raised (Niven and Kao, 2019) about the way that transformer based models encode information about the world.

There exists a very real possibility that the answers to questions about what statements are true or propaganda might have been identifications of trivial statistical cues that exist in the training data. Therefore, in this section, we perform the following analysis in order to better understand whether our system "understands" the true nature of propaganda.

The two largest categories of propaganda techniques being used are loaded language and name calling/labeling (51% according to (Da San Martino et al., 2019)). Since these two techniques are also often used in the scenario of online harassment and trolling, we experiment with tools specialized in online harassment detection in order to provide with a baseline. To this end, we use Perspective API [3]. Given an utterance and a defined attribute, the API returns a score between 0 to 1 as an estimate of the probability the utterance contains properties of the attribute. The attributes are toxicity, severe toxicity, identity attack, insult, profanity, threat, sexually explicit, flirtation, inflammatory, obscene, likely to reject (by New York Times moderators) and unsubstantial. The details of attributes' definitions are described at Perspective API website. We aggregate these scores as sentence-level features and train a logistic regression on top of them to predict the likelihood of the sentence being propaganda. As shown in Table 1, the Perspective-API baseline achieves 0.57 F1, with 0.54 precision and 0.60 recall on development set, better accuracy than the provided baseline using sentence length. Given that Perspective API was created for an unrelated task, the performance is surprisingly high and likely results from a high proportion of certain types of propaganda techniques in the dataset.

In the second analysis we investigate the unigrams and bigrams being labeled with highest likelihood of being propaganda by our trained BERT model. To this purpose, we fed all unigram and bigram combinations that appeared in the provided training set, development set and test set into our ensemble model to infer their likelihood of being propaganda. We list the top 20 unigrams and bigrams with highest probability of being propaganda determined by our system in Table 2. Many of the shown terms indicate uncivil usage (such as stupid, coward), or strong emotion (such as terri-

---

Method	F1	Precision	Recall
Perspective baseline	0.57	0.54	0.60
Sentence length baseline	0.47	0.44	0.51
BERT ensemble	0.66	0.63	0.69

Table 1: Performance of baselines on development set.

unigrams	devastating, cruel, vile, irrational, absurd, brutal, vicious, stupid, coward, awful, ignorant, unbelievable, doomed, idiot, terrifying, disgusting, horrible, hideous, horrific, pathetic
bigrams	shame less, totally insane, a horrible, utterly unacceptable, hysterical nonsense, the horrible, this horrific, absolutely disgusting, monumental stupidity, a pathetic, a disgusting, absolutely worthless, truly disgusting, utterly insane, this murderous, incredibly stupid, monstrous fraud, this lunatic, a disgrace, a hideous

Table 2: Top 20 unigrams and bigrams with highest likelihood of being propaganda.

fying, devastating, horrible). In fact, the inclusion of such words in sentences would often lead to the sentence being classified as propaganda. However, these combinations may as well be used in opinion pieces published in credible news sources. Indeed, our system predicts certain titles of opinion pieces as propaganda with high likelihood. For example, "Devastating news for America's intelligence"[4] published in Washington Post was scored with 0.85 probability of being propaganda by our system. Given the definition of this shared task, it could be the intended behavior that opinion pieces being considered as propaganda. Nevertheless, it is important to inform future users of this dataset and the resulting systems that opinion pieces are likely going to be classified as propaganda.

Another concern that this analysis raises is the limited capability of a system like this to distinguish quotations from actual usage of propaganda techniques. News articles often have the need to quote original speech from political figures or other events, who might use techniques of propaganda. Our analysis shows that the prediction of our system is not changed for a sentence when it is expressed as a quotation and that the mere presence of trigger words may lead to the classification of propaganda.

In conclusion, the shared task on fine-grained propaganda analysis at NLP4IF workshop raises an important problem and with its dataset provides a key tool to analyze and evaluate progress. However, as our analysis illustrated, there remains the challenge that the dataset appears unbalanced in that it focuses on loaded language and name calling/labelling. This makes it challenging for systems to capture signals of other more subtle or complex types of propaganda techniques. For example, despite its high performance on the given test set, our BERT ensemble model trained on this dataset has high likelihood of failing in a real world scenario, such as distinguishing quotations from actual propaganda. We hope this study can help inform a more refined definition and a more diverse dataset towards propaganda analysis.

5 Acknowledgement

We thank Jeffrey Sorensen and Andreas Veit for their helpful advices and proofreading. We thank the anonymous reviewer for their suggestions.

References

Alberto Barrón-Cedeno, Israa Jaradat, Giovanni Da San Martino, and Preslav Nakov. 2019. Proppy: Organizing the news based on their propagandistic content. *Information Processing & Management*.

Giovanni Da San Martino, Seunghak Yu, Alberto Barrón-Cedeño, Rostislav Petrov, and Preslav Nakov. 2019. Fine-grained analysis of propaganda in news articles. In *Proceedings of the 2019 Conference on Empirical Methods in Natural Language Processing and 9th International Joint Conference on Natural Language Processing*. Association for Computational Linguistics.

Jacob Devlin, Ming-Wei Chang, Kenton Lee, and Kristina Toutanova. 2018. BERT: pre-training of

---

[4]`https://www.washingtonpost.com/opinions/2019/08/02/devastating-news-americas-intelligence/`

deep bidirectional transformers for language understanding. In *Proceedings of the 2018 Annual Conference of the North American Chapter of the Association for Computational Linguistics: Human Language Technologies*. Association for Computational Linguistics.

Hugging Face. 2019. Pytorch transformers.

Timothy Niven and Hung-Yu Kao. 2019. Probing neural network comprehension of natural language arguments. *arXiv preprint arXiv:1907.07355*.

David Opitz and Richard Maclin. 1999. Popular ensemble methods: An empirical study. *Journal of artificial intelligence research*, 11:169–198.

Hannah Rashkin, Eunsol Choi, Jin Yea Jang, Svitlana Volkova, and Yejin Choi. 2017. Truth of varying shades: Analyzing language in fake news and political fact-checking. In *Proceedings of the 2017 Conference on Empirical Methods in Natural Language Processing*, pages 2931–2937. Association for Computational Linguistics.

Yuval Reina. 2019. Kernel for training bert using pytorch.

Irene Solaiman, Miles Brundage, Jack Clark, Amanda Askell, Ariel Herbert-Voss, Jeff Wu, Alec Radford, and Jasmine Wang. 2019. Release strategies and the social impacts of language models. *arXiv preprint arXiv:1908.09203*.

Chi Sun, Xipeng Qiu, Yige Xu, and Xuanjing Huang. 2019. How to fine-tune BERT for text classification? *arXiv preprint arXiv:1905.05583*.

Ashish Vaswani, Noam Shazeer, Niki Parmar, Jakob Uszkoreit, Llion Jones, Aidan N Gomez, Łukasz Kaiser, and Illia Polosukhin. 2017. Attention is all you need. In *Proceedings of the Advances in Neural Information Processing Systems*, pages 5998–6008.

Svitlana Volkova and Jin Yea Jang. 2018. Misleading or falsification: Inferring deceptive strategies and types in online news and social media. In *Companion Proceedings of the The Web Conference*, pages 575–583. International World Wide Web Conferences Steering Committee.

Rowan Zellers, Ari Holtzman, Hannah Rashkin, Yonatan Bisk, Ali Farhadi, Franziska Roesner, and Yejin Choi. 2019. Defending against neural fake news. *arXiv preprint arXiv:1905.12616*.

Pretrained Ensemble Learning for Fine-Grained Propaganda Detection

Ali Fadel, Ibraheem Tuffaha, and Mahmoud Al-Ayyoub

Jordan University of Science and Technology, Irbid, Jordan
{aliosm1997, bro.t.1996, malayyoub}@gmail.com

Abstract

In this paper, we describe our team's effort on the fine-grained propaganda detection on sentence level classification (SLC) task of NLP4IF 2019 workshop co-located with the EMNLP-IJCNLP 2019 conference. Our top performing system results come from applying ensemble average on three pretrained models to make their predictions. The first two models use the uncased and cased versions of Bidirectional Encoder Representations from Transformers (BERT) (Devlin et al., 2018) while the third model uses Universal Sentence Encoder (USE) (Cer et al., 2018). Out of 26 participating teams, our system is ranked in the first place with 68.8312 F1-score on the development dataset and in the sixth place with 61.3870 F1-score on the testing dataset.

1 Introduction

Propaganda is an information, particularly of a misleading or biased nature, used to promote certain causes or views influencing specific audiences agenda using incorrect claims that might include emotional delusions.

Thus, propaganda detection problem is a real-life challenge that can affect how people understand news. Despite the uniqueness of the propaganda detection problem where the sentence can be affected by the context of the news articles and biased by external influences like the author writing style, the problem can still be considered as a binary sentiment analysis task (Medhat et al., 2014). Given a sequence of tokens representing a sentence from an article, tag it with one of two classes: 0 for non-propaganda or 1 for propaganda.

A new task has been proposed by the Propaganda Analysis Project[1] with a new manually annotated dataset at Natural Language Processing for Internet Freedom 2019 (NLP4IF 2019) workshop co-located with EMNLP-IJCNLP 2019 conference. For the full task and dataset descriptions, readers can refer to (Da San Martino et al., 2019b).

In this paper, we describe our team's effort to tackle this problem. Without any preprocessing steps, we build several models. The first two use Bidirectional Encoder Representations from Transformers (BERT) (Devlin et al., 2018) (uncased and cased versions) to extract word embeddings, then feed them to a Recurrent Neural Network (RNN) based on Bidirectional Long Short-Term Memory (BiLSTM) (Hochreiter and Schmidhuber, 1997) cells. The third one uses Universal Sentence Encoder (USE) (Cer et al., 2018) to extract sentence embeddings, then feeds them to a shallow Feed-Forward Neural Network (FFNN). After that, an average ensemble is used to merge the models predictions. Our system is ranked in the first place with 68.8312 F1-score on the development dataset and in the sixth place with 61.3870 F1-score on the testing dataset out of participating 26 teams. More insights about the teams results can be found in (Da San Martino et al., 2019a).

The rest of this paper is organized as follows. In Section 2, we describe our methodology, including the pretrained models used and our models structures, while, in Section 3, we present our experimental results and discuss some insights from our models in Section 4. Finally, the paper is concluded in Section 5.

2 Methodology

In this section, we present a detailed description of the extraction procedure for the word and sentence embeddings using both BERT and USE pretrained models. We then discuss the neural network models built on top of the extracted representations.

---

[1] https://propaganda.qcri.org/index.html

Proceedings of the 2nd Workshop on NLP for Internet Freedom: Censorship, Disinformation, and Propaganda, pages 139–142
Hong Kong, China, November 4, 2019 ©2019 Association for Computational Linguistics

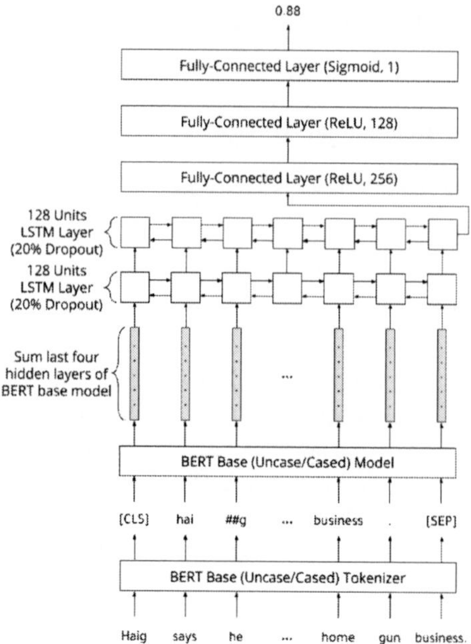

Figure 1: BERT-based models architecture

The implementation is available on a public repository.[2]

2.1 BERT-based Models

We use the small version of BERT (Base version) using each of the uncased and cased models provided by $pytorch - transformers$ Python package[3] to extract the word embeddings. The uncased and cased models are separately used to build two different models using the same RNN architecture. The usage of the cased version is to benefit from the cased words which mostly represent the named entities. As shown in Figure 1, the model can be divided into four layers/components:

1. Text Tokenization

   We use either the uncased or the cased BERT tokenizer (based on which model we want to train or inference) to tokenize text before feeding it to the BERT model. This step is important to run the BERT model and get the appropriate contextual words representations as the pretrained BERT model was trained on tokenized text (Devlin et al., 2018). The tokenizer applies several steps on the text to tokenize it. For example, it uses the Word-Piece tokenizer (Wu et al., 2016) to segment the words into subwords.

2. Embeddings Extraction

   After the tokenization step, the tokenized text runs through the BERT model while saving the outputs of the hidden layers. The final embedding vector for each token is the summation of the last four hidden layers of the BERT model.

3. RNN Component

   The contextual embedding vectors extracted from the BERT model are fed to two consecutive BiLSTM layers (Hochreiter and Schmidhuber, 1997) with 128 hidden units, each with 20% dropout rate (Srivastava et al., 2014).

4. Shallow Feed-Forward Neural Network Component

   The thought vector (which is the final state outputted from the last step by the RNN cell) taken from the second BiLSTM layer is used as a representation vector for the input sentence. The vector is used as an input to two fully-connected layers that have 256 and 128 hidden units, respectively, with ReLU as their activation function. These layers are followed by an output layer with a Sigmoid activation function.

The uncased and cased models are trained for 4 and 5 epochs, respectively, on an Nvidia GeForce GTX 970M GPU in less than 20 minutes to train each model using Adam optimization algorithm (Kingma and Ba, 2014) with 0.001 learning rate, 128 batch size, and binary cross-entropy loss function. As for the inference time on the development dataset, which contains 2235 sentences, it is 3.5 minutes with an average around 10 sentences per second.

2.2 USE-based Model

Without any preprocessing steps, we use the Transformer (Vaswani et al., 2017) version of the Universal Sentence Encoder (Cer et al., 2018) model to encode the input sentences into fixed length vectors of size 512. These vectors are used as an input to two fully-connected layers with the same structure as the one used in the BERT shallow feed-forward neural network component.

---

[2]Link removed to maintain anonymity

[3]https://github.com/huggingface/pytorch-transformers

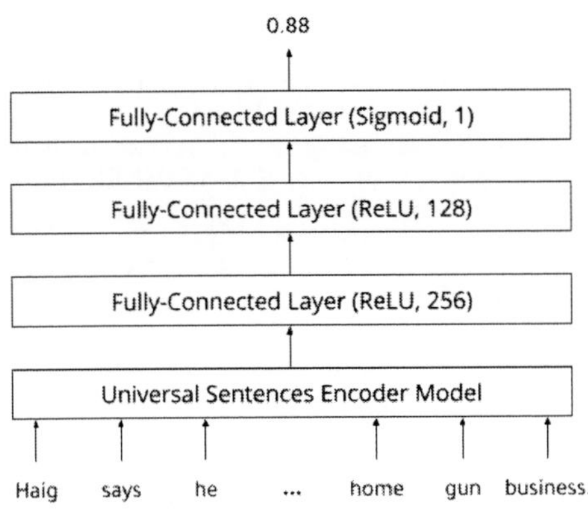

Figure 2: USE-based model architecture

This model is trained for 5 epochs on an Nvidia GeForce GTX 970M GPU in less than 5 minutes using Adam optimization algorithm (Kingma and Ba, 2014) with 0.001 learning rate, 32 batch size, and binary cross-entropy loss function. The inferencing time for this model is 30 seconds on the same development dataset with an average of 75 sentences per second.

3 Experimental Results

In this section, we present our experimental results by comparing our top performing system to several other attempts.

Our top performing system consists of three models. Two of these models are RNN models trained using contextual word embeddings extracted from BERT Base model using both uncased and cased versions. The uncased version achieves 66.1827 F1-score on the development dataset, while the cased version achieves 65.7849 F1-score on the development dataset. The ensemble average over these two models achieves 67.3279 F1-score on the same dataset. The third model, which is a shallow FFNN model that uses sentence embeddings extracted from Universal Sentences Encoder, achieves 63.7076 F1-score on the development dataset. Finally, the ensembling of the three models using average ensembing increases the results to 68.8312 F1-score on the development dataset, while the results decreased significantly on the testing dataset with 61.3870 F1-score. We adopted using 0.25 as our threshold for all experiments because using higher thresholds decreases the results significantly. For example, when using threshold 0.5 for the uncased

Table 1: Models results on development and testing datasets

Model	Dataset	F1-score
Uncased BERT	Dev	66.1827
Cased BERT	Dev	65.7849
Uncased BERT + Cased BERT	Dev	67.3279
USE	Dev	63.7076
Uncased BERT + Cased BERT + USE	Dev	68.8312
Uncased BERT + Cased BERT + USE	Test	61.3870

Table 2: Uncased BERT model experiments results on development datasets

Model	F1-score
More Training	60.6282
3 Fully-Connected Layers	63.3349
3 BiLSTM Layers	65.5619
Duplicating Hidden Units	65.5355
Weighted Attention	65.9804

BERT model, the results decreases to 58.1414 F1-score on the development dataset. Table 1 shows the models results on development and testing datasets.

We reach the previously mentioned uncased model that achieves 66.1827 F1-score after conducting several experiments to explore the effect of applying different techniques on the network structure. The first experiment was to train the model for 10 epochs instead of 5, which yielded 60.6282 F1-score. Secondly, 3 fully-connected layers were used in training instead of 2. This reduced the result to 63.3349 F1-score. Similarly, an extra BiLSTM layer was added to the model, which decreased the result to 65.5619 F1-score. Then, we tried to duplicate the number of hidden units in each layers, yielding 65.5355 F1-score. Finally, we applied a sequence weighted attention (Felbo et al., 2017) on the outputs of the second BiLSTM layer. The output attention vector was used as a sentence representation instead of the thought vector, but the results did not improve giving 65.9804 F1-score. Table 2 shows the uncased BERT model experiments results on developments dataset.

4 Discussion

Although the USE model did not perform well compared to either the uncased or the cased BERT models (with 63.7076 F1-score compared to 66.1827 and 65.7849, respectively), adding the USE model to the ensemble average on top of both BERT models increases the results on the development dataset by around 1.5 F1-score. This indicates that the sentences representations from USE model could have captured unique information from the sentences which BERT models missed. Similarly, BERT cased performs worse than BERT uncased, but it increases its results by about 1.15 F1-score as it can differentiate the named entities which highly affects the semantic meanings.

It is worth noting that the results for all the teams significantly decreased in the testing dataset compared to their corresponding results on the development dataset. This is probably due to the fact that the testing dataset has a different distribution from the development dataset, which makes it harder to predict the outcome from such difference especially given a relatively small training dataset.

5 Conclusion

In this paper, we present our work on propaganda detection on sentence level classification, where we implemented three different models, two are based on BERT with uncased and cased versions and the last one uses USE. All these models build useful sentence representation which are used to make predictions. The ensemble average of these models achieved the first place with 68.8312 F1-score on the development dataset and in the sixth place with 61.3870 F1-score on the testing dataset out of 26 participating teams.

Acknowledgments

We gratefully acknowledge the support of the Deanship of Research at the *Jordan University of Science and Technology* for supporting this work via Grant #20180193.

References

Daniel Cer, Yinfei Yang, Sheng-yi Kong, Nan Hua, Nicole Limtiaco, Rhomni St John, Noah Constant, Mario Guajardo-Cespedes, Steve Yuan, Chris Tar, et al. 2018. Universal sentence encoder. *arXiv preprint arXiv:1803.11175*.

Giovanni Da San Martino, Alberto Barron-Cedeno, and Preslav Nakov. 2019a. Findings of the nlp4if-2019 shared task on fine-grained propaganda detection. In *Proceedings of the 2nd Workshop on NLP for Internet Freedom (NLP4IF): Censorship, Disinformation, and Propaganda*, NLP4IFEMNLP '19, Hong Kong, China.

Giovanni Da San Martino, Seunghak Yu, Alberto Barrón-Cedeño, Rostislav Petrov, and Preslav Nakov. 2019b. Fine-grained analysis of propaganda in news articles. In *Proceedings of the 2019 Conference on Empirical Methods in Natural Language Processing and 9th International Joint Conference on Natural Language Processing, EMNLP-IJCNLP 2019, Hong Kong, China, November 3-7, 2019*, EMNLP-IJCNLP 2019, Hong Kong, China.

Jacob Devlin, Ming-Wei Chang, Kenton Lee, and Kristina Toutanova. 2018. Bert: Pre-training of deep bidirectional transformers for language understanding. *arXiv preprint arXiv:1810.04805*.

Bjarke Felbo, Alan Mislove, Anders Søgaard, Iyad Rahwan, and Sune Lehmann. 2017. Using millions of emoji occurrences to learn any-domain representations for detecting sentiment, emotion and sarcasm. *arXiv preprint arXiv:1708.00524*.

Sepp Hochreiter and Jürgen Schmidhuber. 1997. Long short-term memory. *Neural computation*, 9(8):1735–1780.

Diederik P Kingma and Jimmy Ba. 2014. Adam: A method for stochastic optimization. *arXiv preprint arXiv:1412.6980*.

Walaa Medhat, Ahmed Hassan, and Hoda Korashy. 2014. Sentiment analysis algorithms and applications: A survey. *Ain Shams engineering journal*, 5(4):1093–1113.

Nitish Srivastava, Geoffrey Hinton, Alex Krizhevsky, Ilya Sutskever, and Ruslan Salakhutdinov. 2014. Dropout: A simple way to prevent neural networks from overfitting. *Journal of Machine Learning Research*, 15:1929–1958.

Ashish Vaswani, Noam Shazeer, Niki Parmar, Jakob Uszkoreit, Llion Jones, Aidan N Gomez, Łukasz Kaiser, and Illia Polosukhin. 2017. Attention is all you need. In *Advances in neural information processing systems*, pages 5998–6008.

Yonghui Wu, Mike Schuster, Zhifeng Chen, Quoc V Le, Mohammad Norouzi, Wolfgang Macherey, Maxim Krikun, Yuan Cao, Qin Gao, Klaus Macherey, et al. 2016. Google's neural machine translation system: Bridging the gap between human and machine translation. *arXiv preprint arXiv:1609.08144*.

NSIT@NLP4IF-2019: Propaganda Detection from News Articles using Transfer Learning

Kartik Aggarwal[1] and **Anubhav Sadana**[2]

[1]Netaji Subhas Institute of Technology, Delhi, India
[1]*kartik.mp.16@nsit.net.in*
[2]SAP Labs
[2]*anubhav.sadana@sap.com*

Abstract

In this paper, we describe our approach and system description for NLP4IF 2019 Workshop: Shared Task on Fine-Grained Propaganda Detection. Given a sentence from a news article, the task is to detect whether the sentence contains a propagandistic agenda or not. The main contribution of our work is to evaluate the effectiveness of various transfer learning approaches like ELMo, BERT, and RoBERTa for propaganda detection. We show the use of Document Embeddings on the top of Stacked Embeddings combined with LSTM for identification of propagandistic context in the sentence. We further provide analysis of these models to show the effect of oversampling on the provided dataset. In the final test-set evaluation, our system ranked 21st with F_1-score of 0.43 in the SLC Task.

1 Introduction and Background

Propaganda is the deliberate spreading of ideas, facts or allegations with the aim of influencing the opinions or the actions of an individual or a group. Propaganda uses rhetorical and psychological techniques that are intended to go unnoticed to achieve maximum effect. Social media has contributed immensely in spreading these propagandistic articles reaching million users instantaneously. These articles may also lead to fake news circulation, election bias or misinformation thereby having adverse societal and political impact (Lewandowsky et al., 2017). Hence, there is an urgent need to detect these propagandistic articles and stop them from proliferating.

Propaganda Detection is the technique to automatically detect the use of propaganda in news articles. This will help to identify news outlets or articles that are biased and are trying to influence people's mindset and spread awareness limiting the impact of propaganda and help in fighting disinformation. Generally, propagandistic news articles use techniques like whataboutism, loaded-language, name-calling or bandwagon, etc (Da San Martino et al., 2019b). Detecting these techniques can help to easily identify propagandistic articles. This work aims to provide an approach that can accurately classify articles as Propagandistic or Non-Propagandistic.

Recently, there has been a lot of interest in studying bias and disinformation in news articles and social media (Baly et al., 2018; Gupta and Kumaraguru, 2018). Terms such as Propaganda detection, Fact-Checking, Fake News identification, etc. have started to gain huge attention in the domain of NLP (Rashkin et al., 2017; Volkova et al., 2017). Our work is an enhancement in this domain with the employment of recent state-of-the-art deep learning methods and architectures like ELMo (Peters et al., 2018) and BERT (Devlin et al., 2018).

Fine-Grained Analysis of propaganda in news articles (Da San Martino et al., 2019a) focuses on identifying the instances of use of specific propaganda techniques in the news article through a multi-granularity network. In this direction, Proppy - a system to unmask propaganda in online news (Barrón-Cedeño et al., 2019) was developed which monitors a number of news sources, deduplicates and clusters them into events on the basis of propagandistic content likelihood using various NLP techniques. With this motivation, two shared tasks for Fine-Grained Propaganda Detection were conducted as a part of *"Second Workshop on NLP for Internet Freedom (NLP4IF): Censorship, Dis-*

Proceedings of the 2nd Workshop on NLP for Internet Freedom: Censorship, Disinformation, and Propaganda, pages 143–147
Hong Kong, China, November 4, 2019 ©2019 Association for Computational Linguistics

information, and Propaganda", EMNLP-IJCNLP 2019 (Da San Martino et al., 2019a). Our team participated in the Sentence Level Classification (SLC) Task of the workshop. The details for the task is as follows:

Problem Definition SLC Task: Given a labelled training dataset D with a set of sentences, the objective of the task is to learn a binary classification/prediction function that predicts a label l, l ∈ {propaganda, non-propaganda} for a given sentence S, where propaganda: denotes the sentence containing propagandistic fragment and non-propaganda: denotes the sentence not containing any propagandistic fragment

Towards this objective we make the following contributions in this work:

1. We train transformer-based models like ELMo, BERT and RoBERTa with the provided dataset and show the effectiveness of transfer learning on downstream tasks in the domain of propaganda detection.

2. We show the use of document embeddings on a combination of multiple models for identifying whether the sentence contains propagandistic fragments or not.

3. We also show that these models do not perform very well on highly imbalanced datasets and thus require re-sampling techniques such as class oversampling to give better results on classification tasks.

4. We also present the comparison of these pre-trained transformer-based architectures with classical algorithms such as Naive Bayes, Logistic Regression and SVM.

Further, we have organised the paper as follows: In Section-2 we discuss the experimental setup adopted for this task. Section-3 details about the results for the experimented models followed by error analysis of the best model. Finally, Section-5 highlights the concluding remarks and the future work of the performed study.

2 Experimental Setup

This section provides an overview of the dataset used for training and evaluation along with the details of the various models used in this work.

Label	Train
Propaganda	4720
Non-Propaganda	12245

Table 1: Data Distribution

2.1 Dataset

The dataset for the SLC Task used in all of our experiments is provided by the organisers of NLP4IF. This data comes in the form of news articles given in TXT format. Each article starts with the title followed by an empty line and news-article body with the Labels for each article provided in a separate file.

The dataset is divided into training and development set where the labels are distributed as {*propaganda, non-propaganda*}. The training set consists of 16,965 examples of which 4,720 contain one or more propagandistic fragments and the remaining (12,245) do not. Figure 1 (Blue) exhibits the distribution of the data in the training set. The unlabelled development and test set were used for evaluation in our experiments. The standard evaluation measure for this task was F1-score even though precision and recall are reported.

As it is clearly evident from Fig.1 (Blue), there is a high imbalance between distribution of sentences that are propaganda and non-propaganda, which also happens in case of a real world dataset. We deal with this high data disproportion by the technique of class oversampling. For this, we just randomly select and duplicate the propaganda sentences so that the ratio changes from 3:1 to 3:2 approximately. Fig.1 (Red) shows the distribution between both the classes after oversampling.

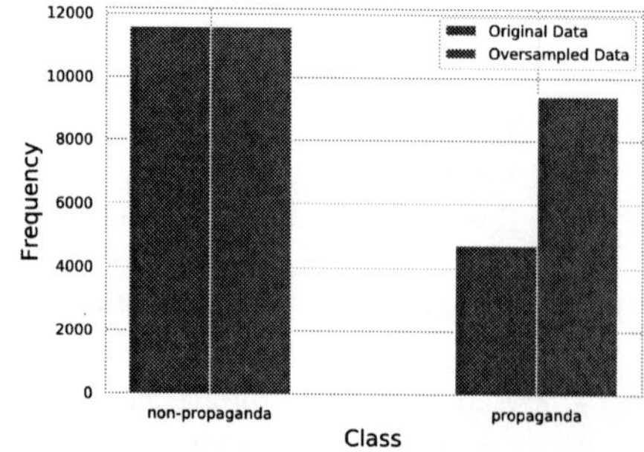

Figure 1: Distribution of Classes in Training Set

Table 2: Model Architectures used for training and their optimal hyperparameters

Model	Hyperparameters
BERT-1	BERT-Base-Uncased *batch-size=32, learning-rate=2e-5,epochs=3*
BERT-2	DocumentEmbeddings {Stacked Embeddings BERT + GRU + Dropout (p=0.5)} *batch-size=32, learning-rate=0.01,epochs=2, anneal-factor=0.5, patience=5*
ELMo-1	DocumentEmbeddings {Stacked Embeddings ELMo + GRU + Dropout (p=0.5)} *batch-size=64, learning-rate=1e-1,epochs=2, anneal-factor=0.5, patience=5*
ELMo-2	DocumentEmbeddings {Stacked Embeddings ELMo + FLAIR Embeddings (forward + backward) + GRU + Dropout (p=0.5)} *batch-size=64, learning-rate=0.001,epochs=3, anneal-factor=0.5, patience=5*
RoBERTa	DocumentEmbeddings {Stacked Embeddings RoBERTa + GRU + Dropout(p=0.5)} *batch-size=64, learning-rate=0.001,epochs=2, anneal-factor=0.5, patience=5*

2.2 Training Models

Transfer Learning has recently been one of the most effective methods in NLP. The key idea is to use a language model pretrained on a large corpus to transfer the information onto a downstream task. Fine-tuning these large pre-trained models produce very good results especially when there are small datasets available for training. Hence, for this task, we mainly use transformer-based models such as RoBERTa (Liu et al., 2019), BERT and ELMo models as they have shown great success in handling language based tasks across various domains. Training was largely done using Flair framework[1] (Akbik et al., 2019) along with AllenNLP library[2] (Gardner et al., 2018). Pretrained Stacked Embeddings are used to combine embeddings from multiple models. Document representation is then generated by applying LSTM over the stacked word embeddings in the document. Now we describe each of the models in brief:

Embeddings from Language Model (ELMo): We use the FLAIR implementation of ELMo by fine-tuning the pretrained stacked weights on Document Embeddings (ELMo-1). ELMo goes beyond the traditional word embeddings approach by producing context-sensitive features in a bi-directional manner. Left-to-right and right-to-left representations are concatenated to form an immediate word vector which are then fed to subsequent layers. Thus, ELMo can be effective for detecting words with propagandist context in the sentence even though the word by itself does not contain any propagandistic sentiment. We find the optimal parameters and train the model over original and oversampled dataset. Apart from this, we also experiment with a combination of Pretrained ELMo embeddings with FLAIR word-embeddings (ELMo-2).

Bidirectional Encoder Representations from Transformers (BERT) outperformed most of the existing systems on various NLP tasks by using a masked language model (MLM) pre-training method. Moreover, instead of reading the sentence in a sequential manner (left-to-right or right-to-left), BERT reads the entire sequence at once in a unidirectional manner. In addition, BERT goes deeper by expanding the base model to 12 layers while ELMo is a shallower model with only 2 LSTM layers. We use the Tensorflow[3] implementation of the BERT-base-uncased model by fine-tuning it with best parameters (BERT-1). DocumentRNN implementation of the Stacked pretrained BERT along with LSTM is done using FLAIR (BERT-2).

RoBERTa moves one step ahead of BERT by pre-training the model over larger data and with bigger batches. This approach improved previous state-of-the-art on certain tasks by choosing better training strategies and design choices. We trained a RoBERTa classifier by finding the best parameters over both original and oversampled dataset using the FLAIR framework.

---

[1]https://github.com/zalandoresearch/flair
[2]https://github.com/allenai/allennlp

[3]https://github.com/google-research/bert

We also experiment with classical algorithms such as MultinomialNB, Logistic Regression and Support Vector Classifier for comparison.

3 Results

In this section, we briefly summarize the evaluation and results of the models used for the task. The metric used for evaluation is standard F_1 score. In addition, precision (Pr) and recall (Rc) are also reported.

Table 3 represents the performance of all the models trained on the training dataset and evaluated on the development data for the SLC Task. We see that the RoBERTa model gives the best performance on the oversampled dataset for the detection of propaganda in news articles with an F_1 score of 0.60 and a recall of 0.79. The highest precision of 0.66 was recorded by SVM and BERT-1 model. The results obtained from Table 3 show that models such as Naive Bayes, Logistic Regression and SVM perform decent with respect to deep learning-based models for the classification of propaganda in sentences.

Table 3: Performance of different models on development data for SLC Task

Model	F_1	Pr	Rc
Naive Bayes (count vectorizer)	0.44	0.57	0.36
Logistic Regression (count vectorizer)	0.41	0.58	0.31
SVM (Linear Kernel) (tf-idf vectorizer)	0.40	**0.66**	0.28
BERT-1	0.57	**0.66**	0.51
BERT-2	0.55	0.45	0.73
ELMo-1	0.51	0.46	0.56
ELMo-2	0.49	0.61	0.40
RoBERTa	**0.60**	0.49	**0.79**

Further, the performance of the transformer models were also evaluated on the original training dataset to observe the effect of oversampling. Fig. 2 helps us to compare the F_1 scores of these models. We observe that oversampling the examples of the minority class i.e. propaganda in this dataset, provides a significant improvement in the classification performance.

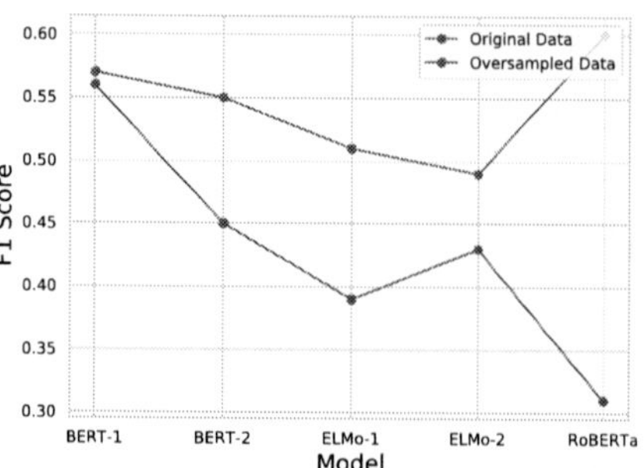

Figure 2: Effect of oversampling on the training data for different models

4 Error Analysis

In this section, we briefly highlight the error analysis of our best performing model "RoBERTa" with oversampled data. Since the labels for the development and the test set were not provided, the analysis is done on the test set synthetically created from the training dataset. 20 percent of the sentences were randomly chosen as the test set for prediction. Fig.3 shows the confusion matrix for the test data. In general, the most incorrect predictions were made for the non-propaganda classes while the model performed pretty good on detecting the propagandistic sentences.

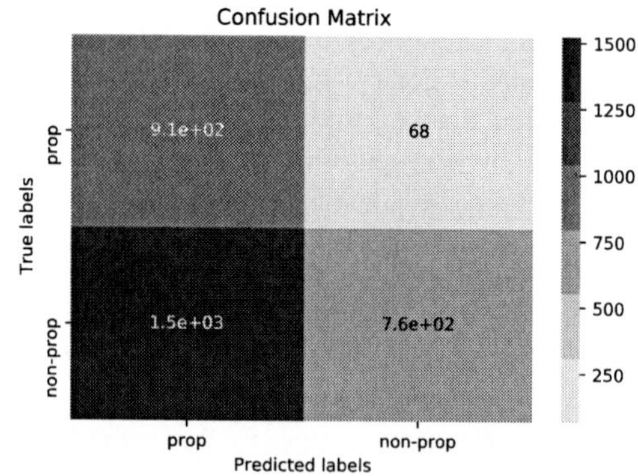

Figure 3: Confusion Matrix on 8:2 Training to Testing split

5 Conclusion and Future Work

In this work, we report our models and their respective performance in SLC task of "Second Workshop on NLP for Internet Freedom

(NLP4IF): Censorship, Disinformation, and Propaganda", EMNLP-IJCNLP 2019. We showed how transfer learning of transformer-based pretrained models perform well with the provided dataset. Our final submission on test set was made from BERT-1 weights and the team ranked 21st with an F_1 score of 0.43 in the SLC Task in the final evaluation of the test set. Hence, there is a significant room for improvement.

In the future, we would like to investigate the effectiveness of these models on the FLC Task of the workshop where the aim is to detect fine-grained propaganda techniques from 18 different classes. In particular, we intend to conduct a comprehensive analysis of the task by cleaning the annotated data and drawing out patterns specific to the given problem of propaganda detection. We would also like to experiment with other machine learning architectures like OpenAIGPT2, XLNet, etc for better performances specific to the dataset.

6 Code and Reproducibility

We provide the code for FLAIR based models on the Github Repository located at `https://github.com/Kartikaggarwal98/Propaganda_Detection-NLP4IF`. The results can be reproduced using the weights for the models provided in the github repository. The Tensorflow implementation of the BERT-1 model can be reproduced using `https://github.com/google-research/bert`. The datasets for the tasks are not provided according to the workshop guidelines.

References

Alan Akbik, Tanja Bergmann, Duncan Blythe, Kashif Rasul, Stefan Schweter, and Roland Vollgraf. 2019. Flair: An easy-to-use framework for state-of-the-art nlp. In *Proceedings of the 2019 Conference of the North American Chapter of the Association for Computational Linguistics (Demonstrations)*, pages 54–59.

Ramy Baly, Georgi Karadzhov, Dimitar Alexandrov, James Glass, and Preslav Nakov. 2018. Predicting factuality of reporting and bias of news media sources. *arXiv preprint arXiv:1810.01765*.

Alberto Barrón-Cedeño, Giovanni Da San Martino, Israa Jaradat, and Preslav Nakov. 2019. Proppy: A system to unmask propaganda in online news. In *Proceedings of the AAAI Conference on Artificial Intelligence*, volume 33, pages 9847–9848.

Giovanni Da San Martino, Alberto Barron-Cedeno, and Preslav Nakov. 2019a. Findings of the nlp4if-2019 shared task on fine-grained propaganda detection. In *Proceedings of the 2nd Workshop on NLP for Internet Freedom (NLP4IF): Censorship, Disinformation, and Propaganda*, NLP4IFEMNLP '19, Hong Kong, China.

Giovanni Da San Martino, Seunghak Yu, Alberto Barron-Cedeno, Rostislav Petrov, and Preslav Nakov. 2019b. Fine-grained analysis of propaganda in news articles. In *Proceedings of the 2019 Conference on Empirical Methods in Natural Language Processing*, EMNLP '19, Hong Kong, China.

Jacob Devlin, Ming-Wei Chang, Kenton Lee, and Kristina Toutanova. 2018. Bert: Pre-training of deep bidirectional transformers for language understanding. *arXiv preprint arXiv:1810.04805*.

Matt Gardner, Joel Grus, Mark Neumann, Oyvind Tafjord, Pradeep Dasigi, Nelson Liu, Matthew Peters, Michael Schmitz, and Luke Zettlemoyer. 2018. Allennlp: A deep semantic natural language processing platform. *arXiv preprint arXiv:1803.07640*.

Aditi Gupta and Ponnurangam Kumaraguru. 2018. Misinformation in social networks: Analyzing twitter during crisis events. *Encyclopedia of Social Network Analysis and Mining*, pages 1329–1338.

Stephan Lewandowsky, Ullrich KH Ecker, and John Cook. 2017. Beyond misinformation: Understanding and coping with the "post-truth" era. *Journal of Applied Research in Memory and Cognition*, 6(4):353–369.

Yinhan Liu, Myle Ott, Naman Goyal, Jingfei Du, Mandar Joshi, Danqi Chen, Omer Levy, Mike Lewis, Luke Zettlemoyer, and Veselin Stoyanov. 2019. Roberta: A robustly optimized bert pretraining approach. *arXiv preprint arXiv:1907.11692*.

Matthew E Peters, Mark Neumann, Mohit Iyyer, Matt Gardner, Christopher Clark, Kenton Lee, and Luke Zettlemoyer. 2018. Deep contextualized word representations. *arXiv preprint arXiv:1802.05365*.

Hannah Rashkin, Eunsol Choi, Jin Yea Jang, Svitlana Volkova, and Yejin Choi. 2017. Truth of varying shades: Analyzing language in fake news and political fact-checking. In *Proceedings of the 2017 Conference on Empirical Methods in Natural Language Processing*, pages 2931–2937.

Svitlana Volkova, Kyle Shaffer, Jin Yea Jang, and Nathan Hodas. 2017. Separating facts from fiction: Linguistic models to classify suspicious and trusted news posts on twitter. In *Proceedings of the 55th Annual Meeting of the Association for Computational Linguistics (Volume 2: Short Papers)*, pages 647–653.

Gap in pagination due to formatting issues.

Pages 148-149

Sentence-Level Propaganda Detection in News Articles with Transfer Learning and BERT-BiLSTM-Capsule Model

George-Alexandru Vlad, Mircea-Adrian Tanase, Cristian Onose and
Dumitru-Clementin Cercel
Computer Science Department, Faculty of Automatic Control and Computers
University Politehnica of Bucharest, Romania
{georgealexandruvlad, mirceatanase1994, onose.cristian, clementin.cercel}@gmail.com

Abstract

In recent years, the need for communication increased in online social media. Propaganda is a mechanism which was used throughout history to influence public opinion and it is gaining a new dimension with the rising interest of online social media. This paper presents our submission to NLP4IF-2019 Shared Task SLC: Sentence-level Propaganda Detection in news articles. The challenge of this task is to build a robust binary classifier able to provide corresponding propaganda labels, propaganda or non-propaganda. Our model relies on a unified neural network, which consists of several deep leaning modules, namely BERT, BiLSTM and Capsule, to solve the sentence-level propaganda classification problem. In addition, we take a pre-training approach on a somewhat similar task (i.e., emotion classification) improving results against the cold-start model. Among the 26 participant teams in the NLP4IF-2019 Task SLC, our solution ranked 12th with an F_1-score 0.5868 on the official test data. Our proposed solution indicates promising results since our system significantly exceeds the baseline approach of the task organizers by 0.1521 and is slightly lower than the winning system by 0.0454.

1 Introduction

The most widely agreed upon definition of propaganda was formulated by the Institute for Propaganda Analysis (1937) and describes the phenomenon as actions exercised by individuals or groups with the purpose of influencing the opinions of target individuals. This phenomenon was present in the news industry throughout history. However, the concern over the presence of propaganda techniques in news articles has grown exponentially since the rise of social media platforms, especially after the massive impact it had in recent political events, such as the US 2016 elections or Brexit (Barrón-Cedeño et al., 2019a).

Automating the detection of propaganda in news articles is considered very difficult since propaganda uses various techniques (Da San Martino et al., 2019) that, in order to achieve the pursued effect, should not be discovered by the target individuals. The Shared Task of Fine-grained Propaganda Detection of NLP4IF workshop (Da San Martino et al., 2019) consists in two tasks: FLC (Fragment-level Classification) and SLC (Sentence-level Classification). We participated in the SLC task which implied sentence-level classification for the presence of propaganda.

Recently, a series of approaches have been studied in respect to language modeling to obtain a deeper understanding of language (Devlin et al., 2018; Peters et al., 2018; Radford et al., 2018). Thus, the latest solutions of obtaining language representations keep track of the word context to model the relationship between words. Here, we choose to use Bidirectional Encoder Representations from Transformers (BERT) embeddings as it showed performance improvements on a series of Natural Language Processing (NLP) tasks, such as the SQuAD v1.1 and SWAG datasets (Devlin et al., 2018). Moreover, we aim to study the newly developed architecture of Capsule Networks (Sabour et al., 2017) which were first applied in the field of computer vision (Xi et al., 2017). Between the word embeddings generated by BERT and the Capsule layer, we integrate a Bidirectional Long Short-Term Memory (BiLSTM) (Schuster and Paliwal, 1997) layer to capture the semantic features of the human language by cumulating prior and future knowledge for every input token.

In our paper, we analyze the impact of different architectures based on the main components previously mentioned in order to validate our final unified model, namely BERT-BiLSTM-Capsule. Moreover, we study the relationship be-

Proceedings of the 2nd Workshop on NLP for Internet Freedom: Censorship, Disinformation, and Propaganda, pages 148–154
Hong Kong, China, November 4, 2019 ©2019 Association for Computational Linguistics

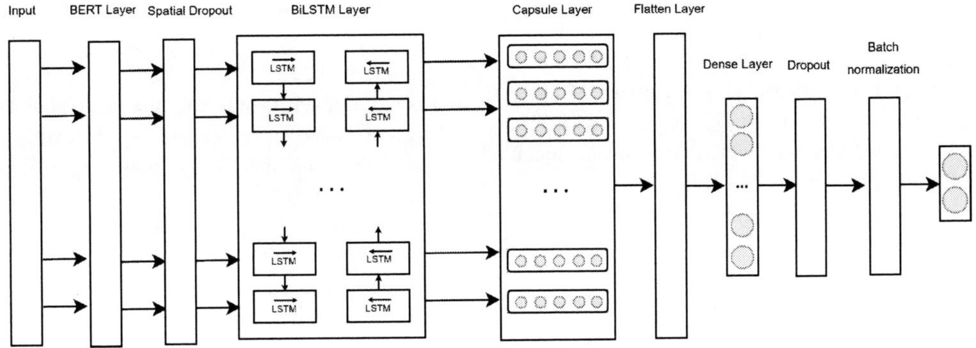

Figure 1: BERT-BiLSTM-Capsule model architecture.

tween emotions and the presence of propaganda by pretraining the BERT-BiLSTM-Capsule model on an emotion labeled dataset. We therefore use the learned weights as a starting point for training on the propaganda dataset.

The remainder of the paper is structured as follows: in Section 2, we present an analysis of the literature on the topic of propaganda detection, in Section 3 we offer an in-depth description of our system and in the Section 4 we present the experimental setup and the results obtained in the SLC challenge. Finally, we present the conclusions of this work.

2   Related work

At first, the task of automated propaganda detection was approached as a subtask of the broader problem imposed by fake news detection (Traylor et al., 2019). The automated detection of fake news has gained a massive interest in the research community with the rise of machine learning algorithms that enabled the development of powerful NLP techniques. One of the consecrated fake news dataset was created by (Shu et al., 2018) and the authors also presented an overview of the data mining based techniques employed for this task and their results in (Shu et al., 2017).

In recent research, propaganda detection in news articles was approached as a standalone problem (Da San Martino et al., 2019). The first part of the task consists of creating a correctly labeled dataset. Some of the earlier works (Rashkin et al., 2017) attempted labeling news outlets as trustworthy or not and considering all the articles published by an outlet as having the same label. This method was proved inaccurate, as propagan-

distic news outlets also publish objective articles in order to gain readers' trust. Barrón-Cedeño et al. (2019a); Barrón-Cedeno et al. (2019b) designed Proppy, a real time propaganda detection system designed to monitor news sources, which computes a propaganda index using a maximum entropy classifier based on a variety of features including n-grams, readability scores and lexicon features. Baisa et al. (2017) introduced a corpus of more than 5,000 Czech newspaper articles annotated for propaganda use, with a large set of features extracted for each one.

Most recently, Da San Martino et al. (2019) proposed a different annotation level, where not only the articles are labeled individually in a binary way (propagandistic or non-propagandistic), but also each fragment of a sentence containing one of eighteen identified propaganda techniques is labeled accordingly. The authors also test several state-of-the-art NLP models such as BERT, obtaining promising results in both binary classification and identifying individual propagandistic fragments.

3   Methodology

3.1   BERT-BiLSTM-Capsule Model

In this subsection, a detailed description of the BERT-BiLSTM-Capsule model is presented. A high-level overview of our model is illustrated in Figure 1.

BERT Layer. In order to obtain word encodings from the raw sentence, we use BERT (Devlin et al., 2018). The BERT model is based on the Transformer architecture (Vaswani et al., 2017) which follows an encoder-decoder design commonly used in neural machine translation.

BERT model stacks multiple Transformer layers to obtain a deeper representation of the input and applies a masking procedure on the token sequence named Masking Language Model. In contrast to the masking procedure used in Transformer architecture, which performs a sequential masking of the words by replacing the words to be predicted with a mask token, BERT masks a percentage of words at random, determining the bidirectional characteristic of the model. This procedure enables BERT to attain information surrounding the masked word in both directions and also enables a human-like approach in determining a missing word within a context.

BERT model comes in two sizes: BERT-Base (L=12, H=768, A=12, # of parameters=110M) and BERT-Large (L=24, H=1024, A=16, # of parameters=340M), where L means layer, H means hidden, and A means attention heads. In our implementation, we used the BERT-Large model with pretrained weights[1].

The BERT model could take as input a sentence or a pair of sentences depending on the task in hand. The input sentence is represented by a vector of indices, a mapping of the raw sentence words into integer values accordingly to a dictionary based on the BERT vocabulary.

In our model, we use a single sentence as input to the BERT model. We extract the last encoder layer as the output of the BERT layer, which will be further used as input layer to the BiLSTM layer. To decrease the chance of overfitting, we add a spatial dropout layer (Srivastava et al., 2014) after the BERT layer.

BiLSTM Layer. The BiLSTM layer (Schuster and Paliwal, 1997) takes as input the output of the BERT model which returns a sequence $V \in \mathbb{R}^{t \times d}$ where t is the number of encoded tokens returned by the last BERT layer, matching the number of tokens provided as input to the BERT model, and d the dimension of the token encoding. The BiLSTM layer consists of two LSTM layers which processes the input from both left to right and vice versa. Each LSTM produces a sequence of hidden states h which encodes the current token and the prior knowledge of the processed tokens. The resulting hidden states of each LSTM cell for both directions $\overrightarrow{h_l}$ and $\overleftarrow{h_l}$ are concatenated together for each time step $i = 1 \ldots t$ with t the number of input tokens. The resulted sequence of t hidden

states $h_i = \overrightarrow{h_l} | \overleftarrow{h_l}$ is then passed to the next layer.

Capsule Layer. The Capsule Networks (Sabour et al., 2017; Hinton et al., 2018) proposed a new approach in selecting the most salient features extracted by precedent layers, acting as a replacement for the more common Max Pooling technique. The Max Pooling step implies dropping the knowledge gathered by activation of several neurons depending on the window of Max Pooling and passing forward only the boldest features, which might imply ignoring relevant information. Capsule Networks not only overcome this disadvantage but also propose a more intuitive approach in determining the presence of concepts by grouping information from a hierarchical standpoint, base concepts validating the existence of more complex ones.

We used a two-layer Capsule Network to determine the relationship between concepts, a primary capsule layer to capture the instantiated parameters from previous layers and a convolutional Capsule layer to determine the routing between capsules.

The primary capsule layer applies a convolutional operation over the sequence of hidden states $x \in \mathbb{R}^{t \times d}$ from the previous layer where t is the number of embedded tokens and d the dimension of the embedding. In our case, depending on the chosen architecture, the embedding sequence x comes from the recurrent layer or directly from the output token embeddings of the BERT layer. Connection between capsules is determined by a procedure called routing-by-agreement.

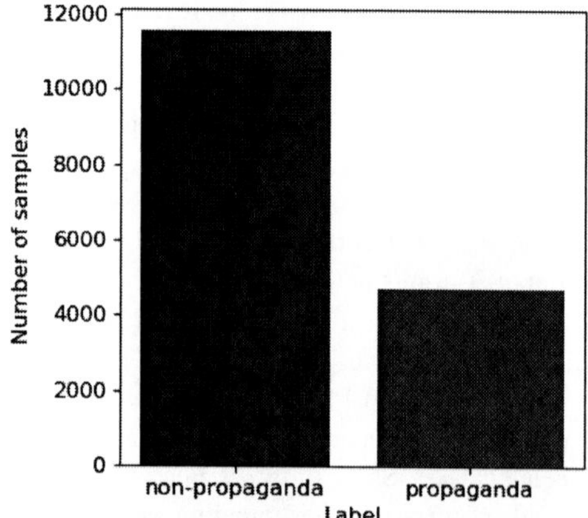

Figure 2: Class label distribution for SLC propaganda dataset.

---

[1] https://github.com/google-research/bert

Dense Layer. The results of the Capsule layer are flattened, and a dense layer is stacked on top of them. In order to make the model more robust to overfitting, we add both a batch normalization layer as well as a dropout layer. The output is then passed to a final dense layer consisting of 2 neurons, one for each class, propaganda or non-propaganda. Softmax activation is used over the output layer to generate a probability distribution over the two classes.

3.2 BERT-Emotion System

In our proposed model, we freeze the BERT transformer layers to preserve the already pretrained weights and only fine-tune the BiLSTM, Capsule and Dense layers. This procedure is applied with success in the field of computer vision, transferring and freezing the weights of top-performing models becoming a common practice in order to conserve the feature extractive layers. This drastically reduces the computational power required for training step with a slightly lower performance than fine-tuning all the BERT layers (Beltagy et al., 2019).

This procedure is applied in training of the BERT-BiLSTM-Capsule model on both datasets, i.e., propaganda and emotion. After training the BERT-BiLSTM-Capsule model on the emotion dataset, we use the learned weights to initialize the model to be trained on the propaganda task. We will further refer to it as BERT-Emotion.

4 Evaluation

4.1 Data

The SLC task provides a dataset containing 350 articles, annotated for the presence of propaganda with two labels: propaganda and non-propaganda, for the training step.

We use an additional dataset annotated for emotion and perform a transfer learning step to initialize the weights of the BERT-BiLSTM-Capsule model trained on the propaganda task. The emotion dataset is obtained by unifying a series of datasets annotated for different classes of emotions. A solution[2] of unifying multiple emotion datasets was proposed by Bostan and Klinger (2018). To this dataset, we add the Daily dialogue dataset (Li et al., 2017) that contains 11,318 transcribed dialogues manually annotated for 7 emotions: neutral, anger, disgust, fear, happiness, sad-

ness and surprise. The third dataset we use to augment the emotion dataset is the Semeval-2019 Task 3 dataset (Chatterjee et al., 2019) containing 15k records for three emotion classes (i.e., happy, sad and angry) and 15k records not belonging to any of the previously mentioned emotion classes. From the resulted dataset, only the entries annotated for the 4 basic emotions are selected, namely neutral, joy, anger and sadness.

4.2 Preprocessing

The provided dataset contains empty strings which are labeled as non-propaganda. We extract all the non-empty entries from the SLC dataset. The obtained dataset contains 16,297 sentences. The distribution between propaganda and non-propaganda classes in the resulted dataset is illustrated in Figure 2.

Because the emotion dataset suffers from severe class imbalance, we decided to restrict the number of samples of the neutral class, which has the highest presence, to 30k entries. The class distribution of the obtained emotion dataset is shown in Figure 3.

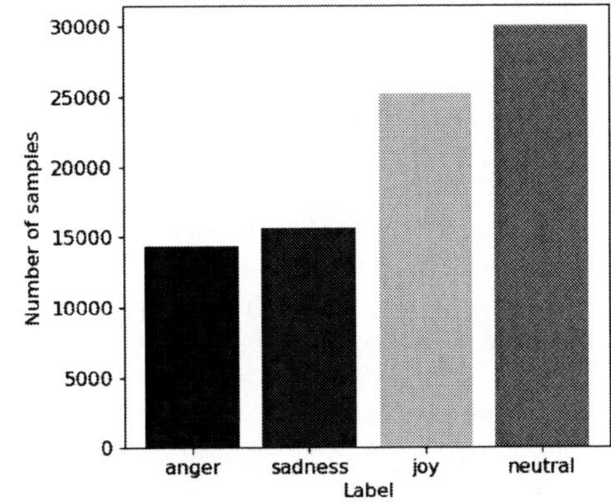

Figure 3: Class label distribution for emotion unified dataset.

We further split both the propaganda and emotion datasets in train and validation sets with the following ratio 0.9/0.1. Because the class distribution is not balanced, we preserve the initial distribution in both splits to keep the validation results relevant for the model's performance.

For the preprocessing step, we use the BERT tokenizer to transpose each word into corresponding index based on the BERT vocabulary. This vocabulary contains entries for 30,522 tokens. The resulting sentence encoding is delimited by the

---

[2]https://github.com/sarnthil/unify-emotion-datasets

[CLS] token at the start of the sentence and by the [SEP] token at the end.

4.3 Experimental Settings

During the experiments, we use the Adam optimizer (Kingma and Ba, 2014) with a learning rate of 0.001 which decreases with a factor of 0.1 after 7 epochs of no improvement until a lower bound of 10-e5. The BiLSTM hidden size is set to 200 and the second last dense layer has a size of 100. The Dropout technique is used with a probability of 0.12 on the features extracted by capsules and a spatial dropout of 0.1 on the embeddings returned by the BERT layer. For the Capsule layer, we also use 10 capsules of dimension 10. The hyperparameters for our model were chosen empirically.

After performing the stratified splitting of the propaganda dataset into training and validation sets, the class distribution remains unchanged in both splits, the propaganda and non-propaganda classes maintaining the original ratio 0.72/0.28. We use a weighted cross-entropy loss in order to increase the amount of attention paid to samples from an under-represented class. The weights associated for every class are computed as follow:

$$\frac{1}{w_n} = \frac{a_n}{\sum_{t=1}^{n} a_t} \tag{1}$$

where a_n represents the number of samples of class n in training set. A similar approach is used in training the BERT-BiLSTM-Capsule model on the emotion dataset.

4.4 Results

Effect of Various Model Parts. First, we study the impact of each component of our BERT-BiLSTM-Capsule model by removing one layer at a time and retraining the resulted model on the propaganda dataset. The ablation study on the components of our model enables to objectively choose the top performing architecture. Because the F_1 score is the official metric by which the challenge evaluation is made, we assess the performance of each architecture with respect to it.

The results are shown in Table 1. The BERT-BiLSTM-Capsule model outperforms the other architectures by over 2.1% and achieves highest precision. Based on these results, we choose to use the BERT-BiLSTM-Capsule model for the transfer learning step.

Model	Rec.	Prec.	F_1	Acc.
BERT-BiLSTM	**0.8557**	0.8292	0.5909	**0.7723**
BERT-Capsule	0.8506	0.8284	0.5870	0.7687
BERT-BiLSTM-Capsule	0.8126	**0.8508**	**0.6164**	0.7656

Table 1: Ablation study of our BERT-BiLSTM-Capsule model on the validation set. For each metric, the best result is highlighted in bold.

Comparison with our Baselines. We test our proposed solution against two baseline models to validate our BERT-Emotion system. The baseline methods are described below, and we report their results in Table 2.

Model	Rec.	Prec.	F_1	Acc.
XG-Boost	0.6737	0.4862	0.5648	0.6993
BERT-Simple	0.7797	0.8543	0.6086	0.7490
BERT-Emotion	**0.8082**	**0.8618**	**0.6338**	**0.7717**

Table 2: Comparative results against our base models on the validation set. The best results are shown in boldface.

First baseline model is represented by the simple BERT model in which we unfreeze the last dense layer and add another dense layer of size 2 with softmax activation to map the obtained features to the output propaganda classes. We will refer to it as BERT-Simple.

As a second baseline model, we used an XG-Boost classifier (Chen and Guestrin, 2016) based on the following features:

- First, the lemma of the words was extracted and the TF-IDF scores (Jones, 2004) were computed for the n-grams obtained, with n = 1, 2, 3.

- Secondly, parts of speech were tags were extracted using the NLTK Python package[3] and the TF-IDF scores were computed for the tag n-grams obtained, with n = 1, 2, 3.

- Thirdly, TF-IDF scores were computed for character n-grams, with n=1, 2, 3.

---

[3]https://www.nltk.org/

System	Rec.	Prec.	F_1
Ituorp (1nd)	0.6648	0.6028	0.6323
BERT-Emotion (12th place)	**0.5747**	**0.5995**	**0.5868**
SLC baseline	0.4941	0.3880	0.4347

Table 3: Comparative analysis against the official baseline result as well as the best performer of the SLC task. Our result is shown in boldface.

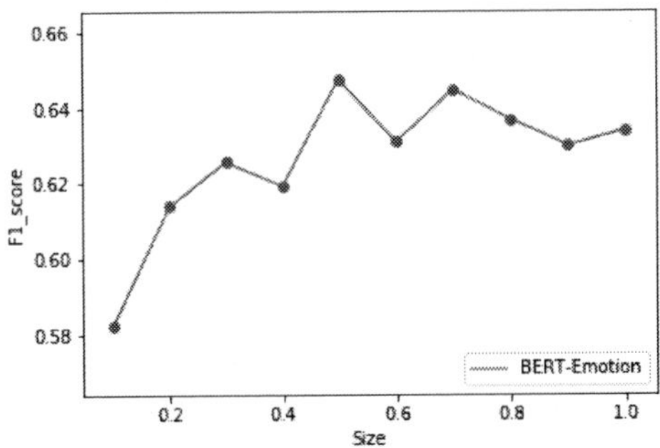

Figure 4: Learning curve on the training set.

- Sentiment analysis features were obtained using the VADER tool (Hutto et al., 2015).

- Other lexical features were added, such as number of characters, words, syllables and the Flesch-Kincaid readability score (Kincaid et al., 1975).

Leaderboard. We submitted for evaluation our BERT-Emotion system and obtained competitive results on the SLC task. In Table 3, we present our results on the test set in comparison to the SLC task baseline and the highest-ranking team.

Effect of Size of the Training Data. In order to determine the correlation between the number of samples provided in training set and the F_1 score obtained on the validation set, we choose to plot the learning curve. Thus, we study the data insufficiency issue for our model and examine the possible need of a larger training dataset in achieving a better performance. We split the training set in 10 blocks, every block employing a percent of the original training dataset between 10% and 100% with a step of 10%. In splitting the original training set, we maintain the original class distribution to keep the relevance of the results. Figure 4 plots the obtained results.

Our model's performance on the validation set is dependent on the dataset size until the 5th block containing 50% of the original dataset, after which the learning curve reaches a plateau. This implies not only that the amount of data provided for training is sufficient but also that our model has a good understanding of the data, being capable to abstract the knowledge needed for the propaganda classification task and successfully generalize the learned information on the new data.

5 Conclusions

In this paper, we described our system (BERT-Emotion) submitted to the Shared Task of Fine-grained Propaganda Detection of the NLP4IF 2019 workshop. We proposed a transfer learning approach by pretraining our BERT-BiLSTM-Capsule model on a distinct task (i.e., emotion classification), procedure which has proven to successfully increase our system's inference ability on the target task (i.e., sentence-level propaganda classification). We based our model on the BERT-Large version for getting word embeddings instead of classical pretrained embeddings and explore the promising design of Capsule Networks.

Our final system obtained substantial improvements against competition official baseline and our baseline systems as well. In the future, we intend to adopt additional contextualized embeddings such as ELMo (Peters et al., 2018) and FLAIR (Akbik et al., 2018) to test the BERT-Emotion performance.

6 Acknowledgments

The work was supported by the Operational Programme Human Capital of the Ministry of European Funds through the Financial Agreement 51675/09.07.2019, SMIS code 125125.

References

Alan Akbik, Duncan Blythe, and Roland Vollgraf. 2018. Contextual string embeddings for sequence labeling. In *Proceedings of the 27th International Conference on Computational Linguistics*, pages 1638–1649.

Vít Baisa, Ondrej Herman, and Ales Horák. 2017. Manipulative Propaganda Techniques. In *RASLAN*, pages 111–118.

Alberto Barrón-Cedeño, Giovanni Da San Martino, Israa Jaradat, and Preslav Nakov. 2019a. Proppy: A system to unmask propaganda in online news. In *Proceedings of the AAAI Conference on Artificial Intelligence*, volume 33, pages 9847–9848.

Alberto Barrón-Cedeno, Israa Jaradat, Giovanni Da San Martino, and Preslav Nakov. 2019b. Proppy: Organizing the news based on their propagandistic content. *Information Processing & Management.*

Iz Beltagy, Arman Cohan, and Kyle Lo. 2019. Scibert: Pretrained contextualized embeddings for scientific text. *arXiv preprint arXiv:1903.10676.*

Laura Ana Maria Bostan and Roman Klinger. 2018. An analysis of annotated corpora for emotion classification in text. In *Proceedings of the 27th International Conference on Computational Linguistics*, pages 2104–2119.

Ankush Chatterjee, Kedhar Nath Narahari, Meghana Joshi, and Puneet Agrawal. 2019. SemEval-2019 Task 3: EmoContext Contextual Emotion Detection in Text. In *Proceedings of the 13th International Workshop on Semantic Evaluation*, pages 39–48.

Tianqi Chen and Carlos Guestrin. 2016. XGBoost: reliable large-scale tree boosting system. arXiv. *2016a. ISSN*, pages 0146–4833.

Giovanni Da San Martino, Seunghak Yu, Alberto Barrón-Cedeño, Rostislav Petrov, and Preslav Nakov. 2019. Fine-Grained Analysis of Propaganda in News Articles. In *Proceedings of the 2019 Conference on Empirical Methods in Natural Language Processing and 9th International Joint Conference on Natural Language Processing, EMNLP-IJCNLP 2019, Hong Kong, China, November 3-7, 2019*, EMNLP-IJCNLP 2019, Hong Kong, China.

Jacob Devlin, Ming-Wei Chang, Kenton Lee, and Kristina Toutanova. 2018. Bert: Pre-training of deep bidirectional transformers for language understanding. *arXiv preprint arXiv:1810.04805.*

Geoffrey E Hinton, Sara Sabour, and Nicholas Frosst. 2018. Matrix capsules with EM routing.

C Hutto, Dennis Folds, and Darren Appling. 2015. Computationally detecting and quantifying the degree of bias in sentence-level text of news stories. In *Proceedings of Second International Conference on Human and Social Analytics.*

Institute for Propaganda Analysis. 1937. How to detect propaganda. *Propaganda Analysis*, 1(2):5–8.

Karen Spärck Jones. 2004. A statistical interpretation of term specificity and its application in retrieval. *Journal of documentation.*

JP Kincaid, RP Fishburn, R Rogers, and B Chissom. 1975. Derivation of new readability formulas for Navy enlisted personnel (Research Branch Report 8-75). *Memphis, TN: Naval Air Station, Millington, Tennessee*, page 40.

Diederik P Kingma and Jimmy Ba. 2014. Adam: A method for stochastic optimization. *arXiv preprint arXiv:1412.6980.*

Yanran Li, Hui Su, Xiaoyu Shen, Wenjie Li, Ziqiang Cao, and Shuzi Niu. 2017. Dailydialog: A manually labelled multi-turn dialogue dataset. *arXiv preprint arXiv:1710.03957.*

Matthew E Peters, Mark Neumann, Mohit Iyyer, Matt Gardner, Christopher Clark, Kenton Lee, and Luke Zettlemoyer. 2018. Deep contextualized word representations. *arXiv preprint arXiv:1802.05365.*

Alec Radford, Karthik Narasimhan, Tim Salimans, and Ilya Sutskever. 2018. Improving language understanding with unsupervised learning. Technical report, Technical report, OpenAI.

Hannah Rashkin, Eunsol Choi, Jin Yea Jang, Svitlana Volkova, and Yejin Choi. 2017. Truth of varying shades: Analyzing language in fake news and political fact-checking. In *Proceedings of the 2017 Conference on Empirical Methods in Natural Language Processing*, pages 2931–2937.

Sara Sabour, Nicholas Frosst, and Geoffrey E Hinton. 2017. Dynamic routing between capsules. In *Advances in neural information processing systems*, pages 3856–3866.

Mike Schuster and Kuldip K Paliwal. 1997. Bidirectional recurrent neural networks. *IEEE Transactions on Signal Processing*, 45(11):2673–2681.

Kai Shu, Deepak Mahudeswaran, Suhang Wang, Dongwon Lee, and Huan Liu. 2018. Fakenewsnet: A data repository with news content, social context and dynamic information for studying fake news on social media. *arXiv preprint arXiv:1809.01286.*

Kai Shu, Amy Sliva, Suhang Wang, Jiliang Tang, and Huan Liu. 2017. Fake news detection on social media: A data mining perspective. *ACM SIGKDD Explorations Newsletter*, 19(1):22–36.

Nitish Srivastava, Geoffrey Hinton, Alex Krizhevsky, Ilya Sutskever, and Ruslan Salakhutdinov. 2014. Dropout: a simple way to prevent neural networks from overfitting. *The journal of machine learning research*, 15(1):1929–1958.

Terry Traylor, Jeremy Straub, Nicholas Snell, et al. 2019. Classifying fake news articles using natural language processing to identify in-article attribution as a supervised learning estimator. In *2019 IEEE 13th International Conference on Semantic Computing (ICSC)*, pages 445–449. IEEE.

Ashish Vaswani, Noam Shazeer, Niki Parmar, Jakob Uszkoreit, Llion Jones, Aidan N Gomez, Łukasz Kaiser, and Illia Polosukhin. 2017. Attention is all you need. In *Advances in neural information processing systems*, pages 5998–6008.

Edgar Xi, Selina Bing, and Yang Jin. 2017. Capsule network performance on complex data. *arXiv preprint arXiv:1712.03480.*

Synthetic Propaganda Embeddings to Train a Linear Projection

Adam Ek   **Mehdi Ghanimifard**
Centre for Linguistic Theory and Studies in Probability
Department of Philosophy, Linguistics and Theory of Science
University of Gothenburg, Sweden
{adam.ek,mehdi.ghanimifard}@gu.se

Abstract

This paper presents a method of detecting fine-grained categories of propaganda in text. Given a sentence, our method aims to identify a span of words and predict the type of propaganda used. To detect propaganda, we explore a method for extracting features of propaganda from contextualized embeddings without fine-tuning the large parameters of the base model. We show that by generating synthetic embeddings we can train a linear function with ReLU activation to extract useful labeled embeddings from an embedding space generated by a general-purpose language model. We also introduce an inference technique to detect continuous spans in sequences of propaganda tokens in sentences. A result of the ensemble model is submitted to the first shared task in fine-grained propaganda detection at NLP4IF as Team Stalin. In this paper, we provide additional analysis regarding our method of detecting spans of propaganda with synthetically generated representations.

1 Introduction

Automatic propaganda identification is a task which requires a full set of natural language technologies, including language understanding, discourse analysis, common-sense reasoning, fact-checking and many more. By focusing on the genre to political news articles, it is possible to some extent identify content expressing propaganda based on its stylistic features, readability level, and keyword features (Barrón-Cedeno et al., 2019).

We propose a simple method for extracting and curating features of propaganda by utilizing contextualized token representations obtained from pre-trained language models. Contextualized token representations have been used successfully in several natural language understanding tasks, such as question answering, natural language inference and more (Devlin et al., 2019; Peters et al., 2018a; Wang et al., 2018). A contextualized token embeddning represent a token in-context, i.e. the same word in different contexts will have different contextualized embeddnings. The embeddnings in this paper is used for the task of identifying fine-grained propaganda. The task of fine-grained propaganda detection is defined as finding which spans of tokens in a text express some type of propaganda.

The standard procedure for using pre-trained models is to *train* a language model on unlabeled data, then *fine-tune* its learned feature representations as contextual embeddings on specific tasks. Often, the fine-tuning of pre-trained language models require a large annotated dataset to be able to extract invariant and discriminatory features for the task. While fine-grained propaganda detection potentially can benefit from the these model designs, the available annotated data for fine-grained propaganda techniques is relatively small. This pose a problem, as the distribution of propaganda classes is imbalanced, in addition to the dataset being small.

In this paper, we explore a data augmentation procedure aimed at balancing the dataset by generating synthetic contextualized embeddings of propaganda techniques based on expert annotations. This address the problem of fine-tuning the model for our task, as we both balance the class distributions and increase the size of the dataset.

The remainder of the paper is organized as follow: Section 2 gives a brief introduction to the task, Section 3 presents a detailed description of our system, and in Section 4 an evaluation of our system is performed and discussed.

---

* Authors sorted alphabetically.

Proceedings of the 2nd Workshop on NLP for Internet Freedom: Censorship, Disinformation, and Propaganda, pages 155–161
Hong Kong, China, November 4, 2019 ©2019 Association for Computational Linguistics

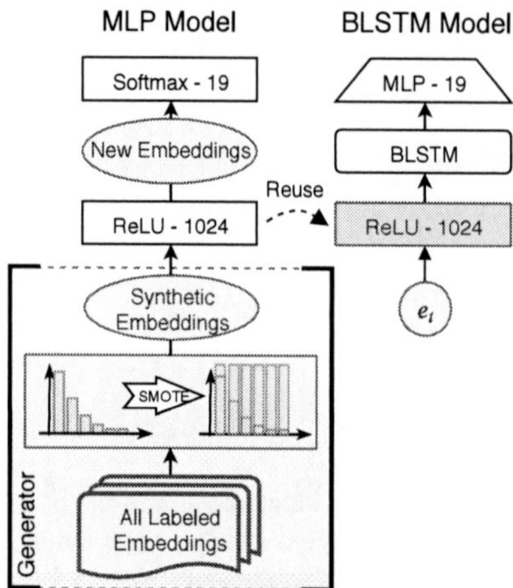

Figure 1: The STALin system architecture

2 Task overview

The task our system is trying to solve is the following: given a text, identify all spans of text (can be multiple tokens) that contain propaganda. Propaganda is categorized into 18 different classes, spanning single tokens in some cases and longer phrases in other. Thus, a successful system must identify both short and long spans of text that include propaganda. While some classes appear simple such as *name_calling*, *labeling* and *exaggeration/minimization*, other classes such as *straw man* require both world and context knowledge to solve. The propaganda classes and the task is further described in Da San Martino et al. (2019).

3 STALin Procedure

STALin is our proposed procedure to generate **S**ynthetic propaganda embeddings to **T**rain **A Lin**ear projection for contextual embeddings.[1] The neural network model we use is designed to be minimal and simple. The architecture is displayed as a schema in Figure 1. The general idea is that we use pre-trained contextual embeddings as feature representation of each token, then sample synthetic embeddnings from the representations. Then a neural classifier is trained for token level fine-grained propaganda prediction in two steps, first we use a MLP layer followed by a bidirectional LSTM layer.

Since the annotated data is small (350 articles) and the number of token instances for each of the 19 classes are not balanced, we propose a simple method to project contextual embeddings into a more balanced embedding space with synthetic samples. To create a balanced embedding space, we use synthetic minority over-sampling (SMOTE) (Chawla et al., 2002) to generated token embeddnings for the minority classes in the dataset. With the balanced training data we train the classifier described previously to predict labels for tokens representations on the propaganda identification task. After training using the balanced embedding space, we use the learned representation in an additional bidirectional LSTM. The contextual embeddings represent each token in its context, in other words, these representations not just encode the knowledge about each token they also encodes features about the current context.

Contextual embeddings In this report, we compare the performance of 3 different models of pre-trained contextual embeddings. We use an implementation with 1024 dimensions:

- ELMo (Peters et al., 2018a) is a weighted sum of multiple layers of BLSTM trained on a large sequence of text corpora as a word predicting language model.[2]
- BERT (Devlin et al., 2019) is a bidirectional transformer encoder trained on large corpora of documents for two tasks of language modeling (1) token predictions (2) next sentence prediction.[3]
- GROVER (Zellers et al., 2019) is a generative language model a transformer-based encoder similar to GPT-2 language model (Radford et al., 2019), which specifically is trained to generate news articles conditioned with metadata about title, authors, source and date of publication. We use the hidden state of the model as embeddings for propaganda identification task.[4]

The tokenization scheme in ELMo is based on white-space as token boundaries. We used the

---

[1] Our implementation is available at: `https://github.com/GU-CLASP/nlp4if19-stalin`

[2] We use version 2 implementation trained on 1 billion words at `https://tfhub.dev/google/elmo/2`

[3] We use *BERT-large cased* at `https://storage.googleapis.com/bert_models/2018_10_18/cased_L-24_H-1024_A-16.zip`

[4] We use the hidden states in *GROVER-large* trained on *realnews* corpus.

same tokenization for BERT according to the *bert-as-service* implementation. However, GROVER is using subwords vocabularies with *byte pair encoding* (Sennrich et al., 2016).

SMOTE oversampling As it was discussed earlier, contextual embeddings for each token represent token-in-context. Having tokens annotated by their propaganda techniques, we can over-sample on the contextualized embeddnings of the minority classes using SMOTE. The SMOTE algorithm, generates nearest neighbor vectors for all categories of token-context vectors then it balances the number of instances on each category by oversampling from minority class. The generated synthetic samples are not representative of any specific token-in-context but they are in proximal interpolations of the known token-in-context embeddings.

In our model, for a class k we generate new synthetic samples based on the 20 nearest neighbours within that class. We use a one vs all strategy during the sampling. For each class C_k we generate N synthetic samples where $N = |C| - |C_k|$, i.e. we pairwise generate new synthetic samples for the class based on the number of samples in the other propaganda classes. We use off-the-shelf implementation of the SMOTE algorithm in (Lemaître et al., 2017).

MLP Model The MLP model consists of two dense layers trained with categorical cross-entropy loss and Adam optimization:

1. Dense layer of size 1536 projecting embeddings on to a 1024 space with ReLU activation and a dropout rate of 0.5

2. Dense layer with softmax activation to predict one of the 19 possible labels: the 18 classes of propaganda and a non-propaganda label.

After training the plain model, we use the first dense layer as a fixed projection function to transform any new contextualized embeddings into the new embedding space.

BLSTM Model We use the projected of embeddings from the first layer of the MLP model as the input for a one layer of bidirectional LSTM with 1024 units. The BLSTM layer use a dropout rate of 0.5. We then use a copy of the MLP model described above to predict which class a token belong to. For the BLSTM model we also use categorical cross-entropy loss and Adam optimization.

3.1 Training

We use contextualized embeddings as inputs to the model, and do not update the language model parameters. First, the MLP model is trained with a batch size of 1024 for 20 epochs. The input to this model is the synthetically generated token as described previously. Secondly, we freeze updates on the parameters in the first layer of MLP model, and we use it as inputs to the BLSTM model. The BLSTM model is trained for 10 epochs with same batch size. When training the BLSTM for GROVER, we used a batch of 256 due to the GPU memory limitations.

3.2 Inference

Despite using softmax activation to fit the model with one of the 19 classes during training, it is needed to infer concurrent classes. To select the most probable classes for each token, we apply a threshold to the softmax output. We experimented with several different techniques for generating a threshold but found that using the proportion of non-propaganda tokens to propaganda tokens in the training data gave the best results. Thus, all classes whose probabilities for a token is higher than the proportion of propaganda to non-propaganda in the training data is selected as a possible label for the current token.

After assigning possible propaganda labels for each token, we run two post-processing step on the predicted labels. First, we fill the gap between two labeled tokens: for each sub-sequence of three tokens, if the head and tail tokens have any propaganda labels, the intersection of their labels is going to be assigned to the middle token. Second, instead of reporting all token labels, we collapse continuous propaganda tokens into one label, representing one span. The final label for a multi-token span is determined by the label which has the highest estimated likelihood of all the labels assigned the span of tokens.

To summarize, we use one model to both detect relevant spans of text and to label them with the classes.

3.3 Ensemble model

For our final predictions on the test set we created a mapping from models to labels as we noted that some models performed better on certain classes of propaganda than other in our validation data. Thus, our ensemble model is a mapping between labels and models.

We selected the model-label mapping based on the F1-score of the models over our randomly selected sentences in the validation set split[5]. On our validation set, BERT did not perform well, thus it was not used in our final model. In our final submission, we used GROVER for: *Slogans, Doubt, Repetition, Name-calling,Labeling, Loaded_Language, Whataboutism* and *Obfuscation* and ELMo for the remaining classes.

4 Evaluation

4.1 Ablation study

Hypothesis Generating balanced data with SMOTE and using BLSTM to extract features of propaganda from language model embeddings improve the models ability to detect propaganda.

Method We perform an ablation study on ELMo, BERT and GROVER by including/excluding SMOTE and/or the BLSTM model. The results are obtained from the development set and are shown in Table 1.

	SMOTE	BLSTM	F_1-score	Precision	Recall
ELMo	-	-	0.041	0.022	0.278
	+	-	0.010	0.013	0.008
	-	+	0.069	0.039	**0.289**
	+	+	**0.141**	**0.137**	0.146
BERT	-	-	0.048	0.026	0.276
	+	-	0.098	0.089	0.111
	-	+	0.037	0.019	**0.279**
	+	+	**0.116**	**0.155**	0.093
GROVER	-	-	0.148	0.141	**0.156**
	+	-	0.076	0.067	0.089
	-	+	**0.153**	0.157	0.149
	+	+	0.125	**0.233**	0.085

Table 1: Effect of using SMOTE and BLSTM fine-tuning on the pre-trained language model using macro-averaged F1-score.

Results and discussions The results of our ablation study show mixed results for both SMOTE and BLSTM. Using SMOTE appear to lower the recall on all models, while also lowering the precision in ELMo and GROVER. However, for BERT the precision is increased when using SMOTE. This seems to indicate that synthetic sampling works better for BERT than for ELMo and GROVER.

One of the key differences between BERT and ELMo/GROVER is that BERT is trained by using masking, where words in a sentence are removed and then predicted by the model. SMOTE may work better for BERT since it generates a synthetic sample by sampling from contextual embeddings, i.e. words in context, which can be regarded as a specific word in a specific context, which is what the training of BERT capture. Using only the BLSTM and not SMOTE increase the precision in ELMo and GROVER while lowering it for BERT.

Most interesting is that even with these fluctuations the best results are obtained by combining SMOTE and BLSTM. However, this is not the case for GROVER, where only using BLSTM provide the best results. This is perhaps not so surprising when we consider what type of data the models were trained on. Both ELMo and BERT are trained on varied types of text, while Grover is specifically trained on news articles and their metadata. Moreover, GROVER embeddings must have discriminatory meta-features encoded in the data such as author, source and date. The absence of this meta-information in the SMOTE embeddings may be the cause of the lowered performance. Including meta-features could potentially enrich the context for the tokens generated. This implies that if GROVER already has high-level encoded features to identify some classes of propaganda, using SMOTE with only local features simply introduce noise into the embedding space and discriminatory features are lost. One argument in favor of SMOTE in GROVER despite its poor performance is that GROVER achieves its highest precision of all models when SMOTE and BLSTM are combined, and high precision is a useful property for creating ensemble models.

4.2 Fine grained span predictions

Hypothesis The inference method for detecting continuous propaganda sequence can distinguish spans of different propaganda categories.

Method We report results per class for the FLC task on the development data in Table 2. The

---

[5]We used 1024 (one batch) of randomly selected sentences in the validation set.

	Total	Appeal to Authority	Appeal to fear-prejudice	Bandwagon	Black-and-White Fallacy	Causal Oversimplification	Doubt	Exaggeration, Minimisation	Flag-Waving	Loaded Language	Name Calling, Labeling	Obfuscation, Vague....	Red Herring	Reductio ad hilterum	Repetition	Slogans	Straw man	Thought-terminating Cliches	Whataboutism
ELMo	**0.14**	0.00	**0.28**	0.00	0.00	**0.04**	0.10	0.16	0.12	**0.30**	0.18	0.00	0.00	0.06	**0.08**	0.00	0.00	**0.10**	0.00
BERT	0.12	0.00	0.13	0.00	0.00	0.00	0.00	0.21	**0.36**	0.23	0.12	0.00	0.00	0.00	0.03	0.05	0.00	0.00	0.00
GROVER	0.13	**0.06**	0.16	0.00	0.00	0.00	**0.13**	**0.25**	0.27	0.28	**0.20**	0.00	0.00	**0.12**	0.01	**0.11**	0.00	0.00	0.00
Test-performance	0.14	0.00	0.14	0.00	0.00	0.00	0.16	0.10	0.35	0.25	0.25	0.00	0.00	0.35	0.10	0.07	0.00	0.07	0.03
Train	-	160	106	123	107	127	125	45	62	24	27	120	78	97	17	25	80	32	115
ELMo	-	307	22	-	10	25	29	15	31	13	16	-	6	86	10	21	-	9	35
BERT	-	93	22	-	10	23	31	15	21	12	13	-	6	65	10	13	20	25	40
GROVER	-	74	22	-	69	26	40	15	20	11	13	-	5	28	10	11	20	18	44

Table 2: (1) F1-score for classes in the FLC task. (2) Mean character length for each class in the training data, and in the labels predicted by the models on the development set.

F1-score per class is calculated to include partial matching as described in (Da San Martino et al., 2019). Of our three models with SMOTE and BLSTM, ELMo showed the overall best performance. However, for individual classes, the best model varies. We consider span length prediction as a qualitative analysis for the model, as some of the classes span whole phrases while some only span over single tokens.

Discussion Each propaganda span in training data represents a meaningful continuous sequence often as linguistic units such as phrases or sentences. Depending on the propaganda method, the span might be short such as a single adjective as *Loaded Language* span or it might be a long sentence as the span of *Doubt*.

Earlier, we described our post-processing inference to predict continues spans. Observing the results from Table 2, not all models are predicting meaningful span length on each class comparing to the average length in training data (i.e. the mean number of characters for Red Herring is 6 in our models, while in the training data this class appears to span phrases). We calculate the correlation coefficient (r) between the average predicted length of propaganda techniques and the average length in training data. If a model has not predicted propaganda technique k, it was removed from the correlation calculation. Thus, this measurement only deals with predicted spans compared to gold spans and does not penalize the model if it does not predict spans for some classes.

Model	Correlation (r)	p
ELMo	0.567	0.027
BERT	0.638	0.007
GROVER	0.766	0.000

Table 3: Pearson correlation (r) and p-value for the predicted span lengths of the models.

Results The results are shown in Table 3. The result indicate that GROVER is the best model for identifying span lengths for all classes, while ELMo has the worst performance. It is rather surprising as ELMo is the model which performed best on the development data. This indicates that while GROVER is good at identifying spans, ELMo is generally better at labeling them with their correct class.

5   Summary and future works

In this paper, we presented STALin, a transfer learning method with linear tuning of contextualized token embeddings in the fine-grained propaganda detection task. We showed that balancing the data representation with synthetic token embeddings with SMOTE algorithm improved the representations of ELMo and BERT token embeddings. Our ablation study indicates that representations obtained by GROVER are fairly good for detecting propaganda out-of-the-box. GROVER performs better than BERT and ELMo without any fine-tuning, and our fine-tuning method on GROVER improved the precision but resulted in a lower overall recall (See Table 1). One possible reason for the lower performance of the fine-tuned GROVER is that some meta-data is missing, which GROVER relies on to update its representations. This project also raises questions in transfer learning about what features are learned in the fine-tuning phase, and what techniques for fine-tuning are appropriate for what tasks and datasets.

This study has the potential to be improved in several directions:

- Pre-trained models use surface information as input and learn deeper relations between words "from scratch". A way of introducing inductive bias into the embeddnings would be to annotate the words with syntax (Peters et al., 2018b). As the task of propaganda detection require a deeper understanding of the text than surface information this is a promising avenue to explore.

- Compare and combine other methods of fine-tuning in the procedure. As some of our results are inconsistent (Table 1) additional evaluation using conventional fine-tuning methods would aid us in understanding what is learned by fine-tuning.

- The fine-grained propaganda classes often overlap in context and concepts. As such, collapsing the fine-grained classes into more coarse-grained classes would yield a smaller and more balanced feature space from which samples can be drawn.

- Additional studies and evaluation using GROVER for high-precision propaganda detection. High precision models can be used as another source of generating training data instead of over-sampling balancing.

- Our model design is quite simple and sentences surrounding the current sentence are not used. This could be improved by expanding the models to include previous sentences as additional context to the current predictions. Also in the case of GROVER, including meta-information such as source and author would benefit the model.

Acknowledgements

The research reported in this paper was supported by a grant from the Swedish Research Council (VR project 2014-39) for the establishment of the Centre for Linguistic Theory and Studies in Probability (CLASP) at the University of Gothenburg.

References

Alberto Barrón-Cedeno, Israa Jaradat, Giovanni Da San Martino, and Preslav Nakov. 2019. Proppy: Organizing the news based on their propagandistic content. *Information Processing & Management*, 56(5):1849–1864.

Nitesh V Chawla, Kevin W Bowyer, Lawrence O Hall, and W Philip Kegelmeyer. 2002. Smote: synthetic minority over-sampling technique. *Journal of artificial intelligence research*, 16:321–357.

Giovanni Da San Martino, Seunghak Yu, Alberto Barrón-Cedeño, Rostislav Petrov, and Preslav Nakov. 2019. Fine-grained analysis of propaganda in news articles. In *Proceedings of the 2019 Conference on Empirical Methods in Natural Language Processing and 9th International Joint Conference on Natural Language Processing, EMNLP-IJCNLP 2019, Hong Kong, China, November 3-7, 2019*, EMNLP-IJCNLP 2019, Hong Kong, China.

Jacob Devlin, Ming-Wei Chang, Kenton Lee, and Kristina Toutanova. 2019. BERT: Pre-training of deep bidirectional transformers for language understanding. In *Proceedings of the 2019 Conference of the North American Chapter of the Association for Computational Linguistics: Human Language Technologies, Volume 1 (Long and Short Papers)*, pages 4171–4186, Minneapolis, Minnesota. Association for Computational Linguistics.

Guillaume Lemaître, Fernando Nogueira, and Christos K. Aridas. 2017. Imbalanced-learn: A python toolbox to tackle the curse of imbalanced datasets in machine learning. *Journal of Machine Learning Research*, 18(17):1–5.

Matthew Peters, Mark Neumann, Mohit Iyyer, Matt Gardner, Christopher Clark, Kenton Lee, and Luke Zettlemoyer. 2018a. Deep contextualized word representations. In *Proceedings of the 2018 Conference of the North American Chapter of the Association for Computational Linguistics: Human Language Technologies, Volume 1 (Long Papers)*, pages 2227–2237, New Orleans, Louisiana. Association for Computational Linguistics.

Matthew E Peters, Mark Neumann, Luke Zettlemoyer, and Wen-tau Yih. 2018b. Dissecting contextual word embeddings: Architecture and representation. *arXiv preprint arXiv:1808.08949*.

Alec Radford, Jeff Wu, Rewon Child, David Luan, Dario Amodei, and Ilya Sutskever. 2019. Language models are unsupervised multitask learners.

Rico Sennrich, Barry Haddow, and Alexandra Birch. 2016. Neural machine translation of rare words with subword units. In *Proceedings of the 54th Annual Meeting of the Association for Computational Linguistics (Volume 1: Long Papers)*, pages 1715–1725, Berlin, Germany. Association for Computational Linguistics.

Alex Wang, Amanpreet Singh, Julian Michael, Felix Hill, Omer Levy, and Samuel R Bowman. 2018. Glue: A multi-task benchmark and analysis platform for natural language understanding. *arXiv preprint arXiv:1804.07461*.

Rowan Zellers, Ari Holtzman, Hannah Rashkin, Yonatan Bisk, Ali Farhadi, Franziska Roesner, and Yejin Choi. 2019. Defending against neural fake news. *arXiv preprint arXiv:1905.12616*.

Findings of the NLP4IF-2019 Shared Task
on Fine-Grained Propaganda Detection

Giovanni Da San Martino[1]   **Alberto Barrón-Cedeño**[2]   **Preslav Nakov**[1]

[1] Qatar Computing Research Institute, HBKU, Qatar
[2] Università di Bologna, Forlì, Italy

{gmartino, pnakov}@hbku.edu.qa   a.barron@unibo.it

Abstract

We present the shared task on Fine-Grained Propaganda Detection, which was organized as part of the NLP4IF workshop at EMNLP-IJCNLP 2019. There were two subtasks. FLC is a fragment-level task that asks for the identification of propagandist text fragments in a news article and also for the prediction of the specific propaganda technique used in each such fragment (18-way classification task). SLC is a sentence-level binary classification task asking to detect the sentences that contain propaganda. A total of 12 teams submitted systems for the FLC task, 25 teams did so for the SLC task, and 14 teams eventually submitted a system description paper. For both subtasks, most systems managed to beat the baseline by a sizable margin. The leaderboard and the data from the competition are available at http://propaganda.qcri.org/nlp4if-shared-task/.

1 Introduction

Propaganda aims at influencing people's mindset with the purpose of advancing a specific agenda. In the Internet era, thanks to the mechanism of sharing in social networks, propaganda campaigns have the potential of reaching very large audiences (Glowacki et al., 2018; Muller, 2018; Tardáguila et al., 2018).

Propagandist news articles use specific techniques to convey their message, such as *whataboutism, red Herring*, and *name calling*, among many others (cf. Section 3). Whereas proving intent is not easy, we can analyse the language of a claim/article and look for the use of specific propaganda techniques. Going at this fine-grained level can yield more reliable systems and it also makes it possible to explain to the user why an article was judged as propagandist by an automatic system.

With this in mind, we organised the shared task on fine-grained propaganda detection at the NLP4IF@EMNLP-IJCNLP 2019 workshop. The task is based on a corpus of news articles annotated with an inventory of 18 propagandist techniques at the fragment level. We hope that the corpus would raise interest outside of the community of researchers studying propaganda. For example, the techniques related to fallacies and the ones relying on emotions might provide a novel setting for researchers interested in Argumentation and Sentiment Analysis.

2 Related Work

Propaganda has been tackled mostly at the article level. Rashkin et al. (2017) created a corpus of news articles labelled as propaganda, trusted, hoax, or satire. Barrón-Cedeño et al. (2019) experimented with a binarized version of that corpus: propaganda vs. the other three categories. Barrón-Cedeno et al. (2019) annotated a large binary corpus of propagandist vs. non-propagandist articles and proposed a feature-based system for discriminating between them. In all these cases, the labels were obtained using distant supervision, assuming that all articles from a given news outlet share the label of that outlet, which inevitably introduces noise (Horne et al., 2018).

A related field is that of computational argumentation which, among others, deals with some logical fallacies related to propaganda. Habernal et al. (2018b) presented a corpus of Web forum discussions with instances of *ad hominem* fallacy. Habernal et al. (2017, 2018a) introduced *Argotario*, a game to educate people to recognize and create fallacies, a by-product of which is a corpus with $1.3k$ arguments annotated with five fallacies such as *ad hominem, red herring* and *irrelevant authority*, which directly relate to propaganda.

Proceedings of the 2nd Workshop on NLP for Internet Freedom: Censorship, Disinformation, and Propaganda, pages 162–170
Hong Kong, China, November 4, 2019 ©2019 Association for Computational Linguistics

Unlike (Habernal et al., 2017, 2018a,b), our corpus uses 18 techniques annotated on the same set of news articles. Moreover, our annotations aim at identifying the minimal fragments related to a technique instead of flagging entire arguments.

The most relevant related work is our own, which is published in parallel to this paper at EMNLP-IJCNLP 2019 (Da San Martino et al., 2019) and describes a corpus that is a subset of the one used for this shared task.

3 Propaganda Techniques

Propaganda uses psychological and rhetorical techniques to achieve its objective. Such techniques include the use of logical fallacies and appeal to emotions. For the shared task, we use 18 techniques that can be found in news articles and can be judged intrinsically, without the need to retrieve supporting information from external resources. We refer the reader to (Da San Martino et al., 2019) for more details on the propaganda techniques; below we report the list of techniques:

1. Loaded language. Using words/phrases with strong emotional implications (positive or negative) to influence an audience (Weston, 2018, p. 6).

2. Name calling or labeling. Labeling the object of the propaganda as something the target audience fears, hates, finds undesirable or otherwise loves or praises (Miller, 1939).

3. Repetition. Repeating the same message over and over again, so that the audience will eventually accept it (Torok, 2015; Miller, 1939).

4. Exaggeration or minimization. Either representing something in an excessive manner: making things larger, better, worse, or making something seem less important or smaller than it actually is (Jowett and O'Donnell, 2012, p. 303), e.g., saying that an insult was just a joke.

5. Doubt. Questioning the credibility of someone or something.

6. Appeal to fear/prejudice. Seeking to build support for an idea by instilling anxiety and/or panic in the population towards an alternative, possibly based on preconceived judgments.

7. Flag-waving. Playing on strong national feeling (or with respect to a group, e.g., race, gender, political preference) to justify or promote an action or idea (Hobbs and Mcgee, 2008).

8. Causal oversimplification. Assuming one cause when there are multiple causes behind an issue. We include *scapegoating* as well: the transfer of the blame to one person or group of people without investigating the complexities of an issue.

9. Slogans. A brief and striking phrase that may include labeling and stereotyping. Slogans tend to act as emotional appeals (Dan, 2015).

10. Appeal to authority. Stating that a claim is true simply because a valid authority/expert on the issue supports it, without any other supporting evidence (Goodwin, 2011). We include the special case where the reference is not an authority/expert, although it is referred to as *testimonial* in the literature (Jowett and O'Donnell, 2012, p. 237).

11. Black-and-white fallacy, dictatorship. Presenting two alternative options as the only possibilities, when in fact more possibilities exist (Torok, 2015). As an extreme case, telling the audience exactly what actions to take, eliminating any other possible choice (*dictatorship*).

12. Thought-terminating *cliché*. Words or phrases that discourage critical thought and meaningful discussion about a given topic. They are typically short and generic sentences that offer seemingly simple answers to complex questions or that distract attention away from other lines of thought (Hunter, 2015, p. 78).

13. Whataboutism. Discredit an opponent's position by charging them with hypocrisy without directly disproving their argument (Richter, 2017).

14. Reductio ad Hitlerum. Persuading an audience to disapprove an action or idea by suggesting that the idea is popular with groups hated in contempt by the target audience. It can refer to any person or concept with a negative connotation (Teninbaum, 2009).

15. Red herring. Introducing irrelevant material to the issue being discussed, so that everyone's attention is diverted away from the points made (Weston, 2018, p. 78). Those subjected to a red herring argument are led away from the issue that had been the focus of the discussion and urged to follow an observation or claim that may be associated with the original claim, but is not highly relevant to the issue in dispute (Teninbaum, 2009).

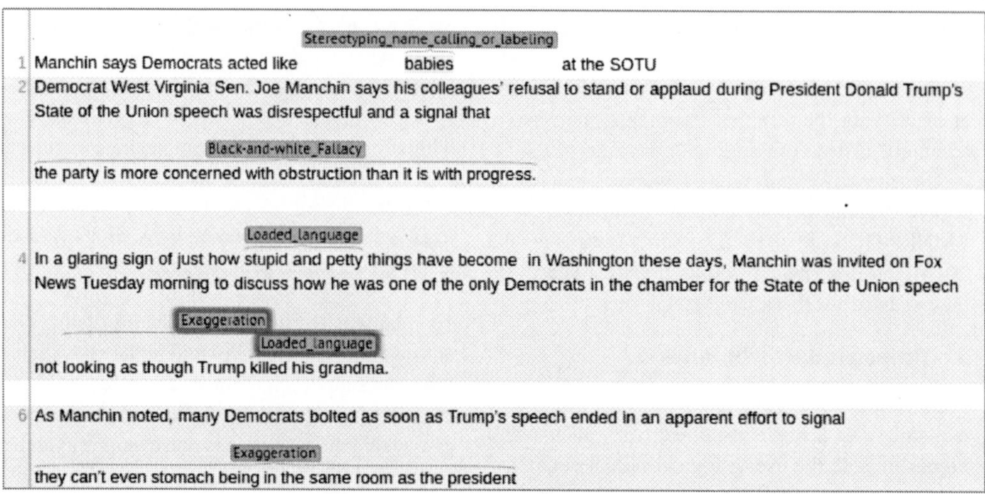

Figure 1: The beginning of an article with annotations.

16. Bandwagon. Attempting to persuade the target audience to join in and take the course of action because "everyone else is taking the same action" (Hobbs and Mcgee, 2008).

17. Obfuscation, intentional vagueness, confusion. Using deliberately unclear words, to let the audience have its own interpretation (Suprabandari, 2007; Weston, 2018, p. 8). For instance, when an unclear phrase with multiple possible meanings is used within the argument and, therefore, it does not really support the conclusion.

18. Straw man. When an opponent's proposition is substituted with a similar one which is then refuted in place of the original (Walton, 1996).

4 Tasks

The shared task features two subtasks:

Fragment-Level Classification task (FLC). Given a news article, detect all spans of the text in which a propaganda technique is used. In addition, for each span the propaganda technique applied must be identified.

Sentence-Level Classification task (SLC). A sentence is considered propagandist if it contains at least one propagandist fragment. We then define a binary classification task in which, given a sentence, the correct label, either *propaganda* or *non-propaganda*, is to be predicted.

5 Data

The input for both tasks consists of news articles in free-text format, collected from 36 propagandist and 12 non-propagandist news outlets[1] and then annotated by professional annotators. More details about the data collection and the annotation, as well as statistics about the corpus can be found in (Da San Martino et al., 2019), where an earlier version of the corpus is described, which includes 450 news articles. We further annotated 47 additional articles for the purpose of the shared task using the same protocol and the same annotators.

The training, the development, and the test partitions of the corpus used for the shared task consist of 350, 61, and 86 articles and of 16,965, 2,235, and 3,526 sentences, respectively. Figure 1 shows an annotated example, which contains several propaganda techniques. For example, the fragment *babies* on line 1 is an instance of both `Name_Calling` and `Labeling`. Note that the fragment *not looking as though Trump killed his grandma* on line 4 is an instance of `Exaggeration_or_Minimisation` and it overlaps with the fragment *killed his grandma*, which is an instance of `Loaded_Language`.

Table 1 reports the total number of instances per technique and the percentage with respect to the total number of annotations, for the training and for the development sets.

---

[1] We obtained the gold labels about whether a given news outlet was propagandistic from the Media Bias Fact Check website: http://mediabiasfactcheck.com/

Technique	Train	(%)	Dev	(%)
Appeal to Authority	116	(1.92)	50	(5.92)
Appeal to fear / prejudice	239	(3.96)	103	(12.19)
Bandwagon	13	(0.22)	3	(0.36)
Black and White Fallacy	109	(1.80)	17	(2.01)
Causal Oversimplification	201	(3.33)	22	(2.60)
Doubt	490	(8.11)	39	(4.62)
Exaggeration, Minimisation	479	(7.93)	59	(6.98)
Flag Waving	240	(3.97)	63	(7.46)
Loaded Language	2,115	(35.10)	229	(27.10)
Name Calling, Labeling	1,085	(17.96)	87	(10.30)
Obfuscation, Intentional Vagueness, Confusion	11	(0.18)	5	(0.59)
Red Herring	33	(0.55)	10	(1.18)
Reductio ad hitlerum	54	(0.89)	9	(1.07)
Repetition	571	(9.45)	101	(11.95)
Slogans	136	(2.25)	26	(3.08)
Straw Men	13	(0.22)	2	(0.24)
Thought-terminating Cliches	79	(1.31)	10	(1.18)
Whataboutism	57	(0.94)	10	(1.18)

Table 1: Statistics about the gold annotations for the training and the development sets.

6 Setup

The shared task had two phases: In the development phase, the participants were provided labeled training and development datasets; in the testing phase, testing input was further provided.

Phase 1. The participants tried to achieve the best performance on the development set. A live leaderboard kept track of the submissions.

Phase 2. The test set was released and the participants had few days to make final predictions.

In phase 2, no immediate feedback on the submissions was provided. The winner was determined based on the performance on the test set.

7 Evaluation

FLC task. FLC is a composition of two subtasks: the identification of the propagandist text fragments and the identification of the techniques used (18-way classification task). While F_1 measure is appropriate for a multi-class classification task, we modified it to account for partial matching between the spans; see (Da San Martino et al., 2019) for more details. We further computed an F_1 value for each propaganda technique (not shown below for the sake of saving space, but available on the leaderboard).

SLC task. SLC is a binary classification task with imbalanced data. Therefore, the official evaluation measure for the task is the standard F_1 measure. We further report Precision and Recall.

8 Baselines

The baseline system for the SLC task is a very simple logistic regression classifier with default parameters, where we represent the input instances with a single feature: the length of the sentence. The performance of this baseline on the SLC task is shown in Tables 4 and 5.

The baseline for the FLC task generates spans and selects one of the 18 techniques randomly. The inefficacy of such a simple random baseline is illustrated in Tables 6 and 7.

9 Participants and Approaches

A total of 90 teams registered for the shared task, and 39 of them submitted predictions for a total of 3,065 submissions. For the FLC task, 21 teams made a total of 527 submissions, and for the SLC task, 35 teams made a total of 2,538 submissions.

Below, we give an overview of the approaches as described in the participants' papers. Tables 2 and 3 offer a high-level summary.

9.1 Teams Participating in the Fragment-Level Classification Only

Team **newspeak** (Yoosuf and Yang, 2019) achieved the best results on the test set for the FLC task using 20-way word-level classification based on BERT (Devlin et al., 2019): a word could belong to one of the 18 propaganda techniques, to none of them, or to an auxiliary (token-derived) class. The team fed one sentence at a time in order to reduce the workload. In addition to experimenting with an out-of-the-box BERT, they also tried unsupervised fine-tuning both on the 1M news dataset and on Wikipedia. Their best model was based on the uncased base model of BERT, with 12 Transformer layers (Vaswani et al., 2017), and 110 million parameters. Moreover, oversampling of the least represented classes proved to be crucial for the final performance. Finally, careful analysis has shown that the model pays special attention to adjectives and adverbs.

Team **Stalin** (Ek and Ghanimifard, 2019) focused on data augmentation to address the relatively small size of the data for fine-tuning contextual embedding representations based on ELMo (Peters et al., 2018), BERT, and Grover (Zellers et al., 2019). The balancing of the embedding space was carried out by means of synthetic minority class over-sampling. Then, the learned representations were fed into an LSTM.

Team	BERT	LSTM	Word Emb.	Char. Emb.	Features	Unsup. Tuning
CUNLP		✓	✓	✓		
Stalin	✓	✓				
MIC-CIS	✓	✓			✓	
ltuorp	✓					
ProperGander	✓	✓				
newspeak	✓					✓

Table 2: Overview of the approaches for the fragment-level classification task.

Team	BERT	LSTM	logreg	USE	CNN	Embeddings	Features	Context
NSIT	✓	✓						
CUNLP	✓		✓				✓	
JUSTDeep	✓	✓				✓	✓	
Tha3aroon	✓			✓				
LIACC		✓				✓	✓	
MIC-CIS	✓		✓		✓	✓	✓	
CAUnLP	✓							✓
YMJA	✓							
jinfen	✓		✓				✓	
ProperGander	✓							

Table 3: Overview of the approaches used for the sentence-level classification task.

9.2 Teams Participating in the Sentence-Level Classification Only

Team **CAUnLP** (Hou and Chen, 2019) used two context-aware representations based on BERT. In the first representation, the target sentence is followed by the title of the article. In the second representation, the previous sentence is also added. They performed subsampling in order to deal with class imbalance, and experimented with BERT_{BASE} and BERT_{LARGE}

Team **LIACC** (Ferreira Cruz et al., 2019) used hand-crafted features and pre-trained ELMo embeddings. They also observed a boost in performance when balancing the dataset by dropping some negative examples.

Team **JUSTDeep** (Al-Omari et al., 2019) used a combination of models and features, including word embeddings based on GloVe (Pennington et al., 2014) concatenated with vectors representing affection and lexical features. These were combined in an ensemble of supervised models: bi-LSTM, XGBoost, and variations of BERT.

Team **YMJA** (Hua, 2019) also based their approach on fine-tuned BERT. Inspired by *kaggle* competitions on sentiment analysis, they created an ensemble of models via cross-validation.

Team **jinfen** (Li et al., 2019) used a logistic regression model fed with a manifold of representations, including TF.IDF and BERT vectors, as well as vocabularies and readability measures.

Team **Tha3aroon** (Fadel and Al-Ayyoub, 2019) implemented an ensemble of three classifiers: two based on BERT and one based on a universal sentence encoder (Cer et al., 2018).

Team **NSIT** (Aggarwal and Sadana, 2019) explored three of the most popular transfer learning models: various versions of ELMo, BERT, and RoBERTa (Liu et al., 2019).

Team **Mindcoders** (Vlad et al., 2019) combined BERT, Bi-LSTM and Capsule networks (Sabour et al., 2017) into a single deep neural network and pre-trained the resulting network on corpora used for related tasks, e.g., emotion classification.

Finally, team **ltuorp** (Mapes et al., 2019) used an attention transformer using BERT trained on Wikipedia and BookCorpus.

9.3 Teams Participating in Both Tasks

Team **MIC-CIS** (Gupta et al., 2019) participated in both tasks. For the sentence-level classification, they used a voting ensemble including logistic regression, convolutional neural networks, and BERT, in all cases using FastText embeddings (Bojanowski et al., 2017) and pre-trained BERT models. Beside these representations, multiple features of readability, sentiment and emotions were considered. For the fragment-level task, they used a multi-task neural sequence tagger, based on LSTM-CRF (Huang et al., 2015), in conjunction with linguistic features. Finally, they applied sentence- and fragment-level models jointly.

SLC Task: Test Set (Official Results)			
Rank Team	F_1	Precision	Recall
1 ltuorp	**0.6323**	0.6028	0.6648
2 ProperGander	0.6256	0.5649	0.7009
3 YMJA	0.6249	0.6252	0.6246
4 MIC-CIS	0.6230	0.5735	0.6818
5 CUNLP	0.6183	0.5778	0.6648
6 Tha3aroon	0.6138	0.5309	0.7274
7 JUSTDeep	0.6112	0.5792	0.6468
8 CAUnLP	0.6109	0.5180	0.7444
9 LIPN	0.5962	0.5241	0.6914
10 LIACC	0.5949	0.5090	0.7158
11 aschern	0.5923	0.6050	0.5800
12 MindCoders	0.5868	0.5995	0.5747
13 jinfen	0.5770	0.5059	0.6712
14 guanggong	0.5768	0.5039	0.6744
15 Stano	0.5619	0.6666	0.4856
16 nlpseattle	0.5610	0.6250	0.5090
17 gw2018	0.5440	0.4333	0.7306
18 SDS	0.5171	0.6268	0.4400
19 BananasInPajamas	0.5080	0.5768	0.4538
20 Baseline	0.4347	0.3880	0.4941
21 NSIT	0.4343	0.5000	0.3838
22 Stalin	0.4332	0.6696	0.3202
23 Antiganda	0.3967	0.6459	0.2863
24 Debunkers	0.2307	0.3994	0.1622
25 SBnLP	0.1831	0.2220	0.1558
26 Sberiboba	0.1167	0.5980	0.0646

Table 4: Official test results for the SLC task.

SLC Task: Development Set			
Rank Team	F_1	Precision	Recall
1 Tha3aroon	0.6883	0.6104	0.7889
2 KS	0.6799	0.5989	0.7861
3 CAUnLP	0.6794	0.5943	0.7929
4 ProperGander	0.6767	0.5774	0.8173
5 JUSTDeep	0.6745	0.6234	0.7347
6 ltuorp	0.6700	0.6351	0.7090
7 CUNLP	0.6649	0.6198	0.7171
8 aschern	0.6646	0.6104	0.7293
9 jinfen	0.6616	0.5800	0.7699
10 YMJA	0.6601	0.6338	0.6887
11 SBnLP	0.6548	0.5674	0.7740
12 guanggong	0.6510	0.5737	0.7523
13 LIPN	0.6484	0.5889	0.7212
14 Stalin	0.6377	0.5957	0.6860
15 Stano	0.6374	0.6561	0.6197
16 BananasInPajamas	0.6276	0.5204	0.7902
17 Kloop	0.6237	0.5846	0.6684
18 nlpseattle	0.6201	0.6332	0.6075
19 gw2018	0.6038	0.5158	0.7280
20 MindCoders	0.5858	0.5264	0.6603
21 NSIT	0.5794	0.6614	0.5155
22 Summer2019	0.5567	0.6724	0.4749
23 Antiganda	0.5490	0.6609	0.4695
24 Cojo	0.5472	0.6692	0.4627
25 Baseline	0.4734	0.4437	0.5074
26 gudetama	0.4734	0.4437	0.5074
27 test	0.4734	0.4437	0.5074
28 Visionators	0.4410	0.5909	0.3518
29 MaLaHITJuniors	0.3075	0.4694	0.2286

Table 5: Results for the SLC task on the development set at the end of phase 1 (see Section 6).

Team **CUNLP** (Alhindi et al., 2019) considered two approaches for the sentence-level task. The first approach was based on fine-tuning BERT. The second approach complemented the fine-tuned BERT approach by feeding its decision into a logistic regressor, together with features from the Linguistic Inquiry and Word Count (LIWC)[2] lexicon and punctuation-derived features. Similarly to Gupta et al. (2019), for the fragment-level problem they used a Bi-LSTM-CRF architecture, combining both character- and word-level embeddings.

Team **ProperGander** (Madabushi et al., 2019) also used BERT, but they paid special attention to the imbalance of the data, as well as to the differences between training and testing. They showed that augmenting the training data by oversampling yielded improvements when testing on data that is temporally far from the training (by increasing recall). In order to deal with the imbalance, they performed cost-sensitive classification, i.e., the errors on the smaller positive class were more costly. For the fragment-level classification, inspired by named entity recognition, they used a model based on BERT using Continuous Random Field stacked on top of an LSTM.

10 Evaluation Results

The results on the test set for the SLC task are shown in Table 4, while Table 5 presents the results on the development set at the end of phase 1 (cf. Section 6).[3] The general decrease of the F_1 values between the development and the test set could indicate that systems tend to overfit on the development set. Indeed, the winning team **ltuorp** chose the parameters of their system both on the development set and on a subset of the training set in order to improve the robustness of their system.

Tables 6 and 7 report the results on the test and on the development sets for the FLC task. For this task, the results tend to be more stable across the two sets. Indeed, team **newspeak** managed to almost keep the same difference in performance with respect to team **Antiganda**. Note that team **MIC-CIS** managed to reach the third position despite never having submitted a run on the development set.

[2] http://liwc.wpengine.com/

[3] Upon request from the participants, we reopened the submission system for the development set for both tasks after the end of phase 2; therefore, Tables 5 and 7 might not be up to date with respect to the online leaderboard.

FLC Task: Test Set (Official Results)			
Rank Team	F_1	Precision	Recall
1 **newspeak**	**0.2488**	0.2862	0.2200
2 Antiganda	0.2267	0.2882	0.1868
3 MIC-CIS	0.1998	0.2234	0.1808
4 Stalin	0.1453	0.1920	0.1169
5 CUNLP	0.1311	0.3234	0.0822
6 aschern	0.1090	0.0715	0.2294
7 ProperGander	0.0989	0.0651	0.2056
8 Sberiboba	0.0450	0.2974	0.0243
9 BananasInPajamas	0.0095	0.0095	0.0095
10 JUSTDeep	0.0011	0.0155	0.0006
11 Baseline	0.0000	0.0116	0.0000
12 MindCoders	0.0000	0.0000	0.0000
13 SU	0.0000	0.0000	0.0000

Table 6: Official test results for the FLC task.

FLC Task: Development Set			
Rank Team	F_1	Precision	Recall
1 newspeak	0.2422	0.2893	0.2084
2 Antiganda	0.2165	0.2266	0.2072
3 Stalin	0.1687	0.2312	0.1328
4 ProperGander	0.1453	0.1163	0.1934
5 KS	0.1369	0.2912	0.0895
6 CUNLP	0.1222	0.3651	0.0734
7 aschern	0.1010	0.0684	0.1928
8 gudetama	0.0517	0.0313	0.1479
9 AMT	0.0265	0.2046	0.0142
10 esi	0.0222	0.0308	0.0173
11 ltuorp	0.0054	0.0036	0.0107
12 Baseline	0.0015	0.0136	0.0008
13 CAUnLP	0.0015	0.0136	0.0008
14 JUSTDeep	0.0010	0.0403	0.0005

Table 7: Results for FLC tasl on the development set. The values refer to the end of phase 1 (see section 6)

11 Conclusion and Further Work

We have described the NLP4IF@EMNLP-IJCNLP 2019 shared task on fine-grained propaganda identification. We received 25 and 12 submissions on the test set for the sentence-level classification and the fragment-level classification tasks, respectively. Overall, the sentence-level task was easier and most submitted systems managed to outperform the baseline. The fragment-level task proved to be much more challenging, with lower absolute scores, but most teams still managed to outperform the baseline.

We plan to make the schema and the dataset publicly available to be used beyond NLP4IF. We hope that the corpus would raise interest outside of the community of researchers studying propaganda: the techniques related to fallacies and the ones relying on emotions might provide a novel setting for researchers interested in Argumentation and Sentiment Analysis.

As a kind of advertisement, Task 11 at SemEval 2020[4] is a follow up of this shared task. It features two complimentary tasks:

Task 1 Given a free-text article, identify the propagandist text spans.

Task 2 Given a text span already flagged as propagandist and its context, identify the specific propaganda technique it contains.

This setting would allow participants to focus their efforts on binary sequence labeling for Task 1 and on multi-class classification for Task 2.

Acknowledgments

This research is part of the Propaganda Analysis Project,[5] which is framed within the Tanbih project.[6] The Tanbih project aims to limit the effect of "fake news", propaganda, and media bias by making users aware of what they are reading, thus promoting media literacy and critical thinking, which is arguably the best way to address disinformation and "fake news." The project is developed in collaboration between the Qatar Computing Research Institute (QCRI), HBKU and the MIT Computer Science and Artificial Intelligence Laboratory (CSAIL).

The corpus for the task was annotated by A Data Pro,[7] a company that performs high-quality manual annotations.

References

Kartik Aggarwal and Anubhav Sadana. 2019. NSIT@NLP4IF-2019: Propaganda detection from news articles using transfer learning. In (Feldman et al., 2019).

Hani Al-Omari, Malak Abdullah, Ola AlTiti, and Samira Shaikh. 2019. JUSTDeep at NLP4IF 2019 Task 1: Propaganda detection using ensemble deep learning models. In (Feldman et al., 2019).

Tariq Alhindi, Jonas Pfeiffer, and Smaranda Muresan. 2019. Fine-tuned neural models for propaganda detection at the sentence and fragment levels. In (Feldman et al., 2019).

---

[4]http://propaganda.qcri.org/semeval2020-task11/

[5]http://propaganda.qcri.org
[6]http://tanbih.qcri.org
[7]http://www.aiidatapro.com

Alberto Barrón-Cedeño, Giovanni Da San Martino, Israa Jaradat, and Preslav Nakov. 2019. Proppy: A
system to unmask propaganda in online news. In
*Proceedings of the 33rd AAAI Conference on Artifi-
cial Intelligence*, AAAI '19, pages 9847–9848, Honolulu, HI, USA.

Alberto Barrón-Cedeno, Israa Jaradat, Giovanni Da
San Martino, and Preslav Nakov. 2019. Proppy:
Organizing the news based on their propagandistic
content. *Information Processing & Management*,
56(5):1849–1864.

Piotr Bojanowski, Edouard Grave, Armand Joulin, and
Tomas Mikolov. 2017. Enriching word vectors with
subword information. *Transactions of the Association for Computational Linguistics*, 5:135–146.

Daniel Cer, Yinfei Yang, Sheng-yi Kong, Nan Hua,
Nicole Limtiaco, Rhomni St. John, Noah Constant,
Mario Guajardo-Cespedes, Steve Yuan, Chris Tar,
Yun-Hsuan Sung, Brian Strope, and Ray Kurzweil.
2018. Universal sentence encoder. *CoRR*,
abs/1803.11175.

Giovanni Da San Martino, Seunghak Yu, Alberto
Barrón-Cedeño, Rostislav Petrov, and Preslav
Nakov. 2019. Fine-grained analysis of propaganda
in news articles. In *Proceedings of the 2019 Con-
ference on Empirical Methods in Natural Language
Processing and the 9th International Joint Confer-
ence on Natural Language Processing*, EMNLP-
IJCNLP 2019, Hong Kong, China.

Lavinia Dan. 2015. Techniques for the Translation of
Advertising Slogans. In *Proceedings of the International Conference Literature, Discourse and Multicultural Dialogue*, LDMD '15, pages 13–23, Mures,
Romania.

Jacob Devlin, Ming-Wei Chang, Kenton Lee, and
Kristina Toutanova. 2019. BERT: Pre-training of
deep bidirectional transformers for language understanding. In *Proceedings of the 2019 Conference of
the North American Chapter of the Association for
Computational Linguistics: Human Language Technologies*, NAACL-HLT '19, pages 4171–4186, Minneapolis, MN, USA.

Adam Ek and Mehdi Ghanimifard. 2019. Synthetic
propaganda embeddings to train a linear projection.
In (Feldman et al., 2019).

Ibrahim Fadel, Ali Tuffaha and Mahmoud Al-Ayyoub.
2019. Pretrained ensemble learning for fine-grained
propaganda detection. In (Feldman et al., 2019).

Anna Feldman, Giovanni Da San Martino, Alberto
Barrón-Cedeño, Chris Brew, Chris Leberknight, and
Preslav Nakov, editors. 2019. *Proceedings of the
2019 Workshop on Natural Language Processing for
Internet Freedom (NLP4IF): censorship, disinfor-
mation, and propaganda*. Hong Kong, China.

André Ferreira Cruz, Gil Rocha, and Henrique Lopes
Cardoso. 2019. On sentence representations for propaganda detection: From handcrafted features to
word embeddings. In (Feldman et al., 2019).

Monika Glowacki, Vidya Narayanan, Sam Maynard,
Gustavo Hirsch, Bence Kollanyi, Lisa-Maria Neud-
ert, Phil Howard, Thomas Lederer, and Vlad Barash.
2018. News and political information consumption
in Mexico: Mapping the 2018 Mexican Presidential
election on Twitter and Facebook. Technical Report
COMPROP DATA MEMO 2018.2, Oxford University, Oxford, UK.

Jean Goodwin. 2011. Accounting for the force of the
appeal to authority. In *Proceedings of the 9th International Conference of the Ontario Society for the
Study of Argumentation*, OSSA '11, pages 1–9, Ontario, Canada.

Pankaj Gupta, Khushbu Saxena, Usama Yaseen,
Thomas Runkler, and Hinrich Schutze. 2019. Neural architectures for fine-grained propaganda detection in news. In (Feldman et al., 2019).

Ivan Habernal, Raffael Hannemann, Christian Pollak, Christopher Klamm, Patrick Pauli, and Iryna
Gurevych. 2017. Argotario: Computational argumentation meets serious games. In *Proceedings
of the Conference on Empirical Methods in Natural Language Processing*, EMNLP '17, pages 7–12,
Copenhagen, Denmark.

Ivan Habernal, Patrick Pauli, and Iryna Gurevych.
2018a. Adapting serious game for fallacious argumentation to German: pitfalls, insights, and best
practices. In *Proceedings of the Eleventh International Conference on Language Resources and Evaluation*, LREC '18, Miyazaki, Japan.

Ivan Habernal, Henning Wachsmuth, Iryna Gurevych,
and Benno Stein. 2018b. Before name-calling: Dynamics and triggers of ad hominem fallacies in web
argumentation. In *Proceedings of the 2018 Conference of the North American Chapter of the Association for Computational Linguistics: Human Language Technologies*, NAACL-HLT '18, pages 386–
396, New Orleans, LA, USA.

Renee Hobbs and Sandra Mcgee. 2008. Teaching
about propaganda: An examination of the historical
roots of media literacy. *Journal of Media Literacy
Education*, 6(62):56–67.

Benjamin D Horne, Sara Khedr, and Sibel Adali. 2018.
Sampling the news producers: A large news and
feature data set for the study of the complex media
landscape. In *Proceedings of the International AAAI
Conference on Web and Social Media*, ICWSM '18,
pages 518–527, Stanford, CA, USA.

Wenjun Hou and Ying Chen. 2019. CAUnLP
at NLP4IF 2019 shared task: Context-dependent
BERT for sentence-level propaganda detection. In
(Feldman et al., 2019).

Yiqing Hua. 2019. Understanding BERT performance in propaganda analysis. In (Feldman et al., 2019).

Zhiheng Huang, Wei Xu, and Kai Yu. 2015. Bidirectional LSTM-CRF models for sequence tagging. *CoRR*, abs/1508.01991.

John Hunter. 2015. Brainwashing in a large group awareness training? The classical conditioning hypothesis of brainwashing. Master's thesis, University of Kwazulu-Natal, Pietermaritzburg, South Africa.

Garth S. Jowett and Victoria O'Donnell. 2012. What is propaganda, and how does it differ from persuasion? In *Propaganda & Persuasion*, chapter 1, pages 1–48. Sage Publishing.

Jinfen Li, Zhihao Ye, and Lu Xiao. 2019. Detection of propaganda using logistic regression. In (Feldman et al., 2019).

Yinhan Liu, Myle Ott, Naman Goyal, Jingfei Du, Mandar Joshi, Danqi Chen, Omer Levy, Mike Lewis, Luke Zettlemoyer, and Veselin Stoyanov. 2019. RoBERTa: A robustly optimized BERT pretraining approach. *arXiv*, abs/1907.11692.

Harish Tayyar Madabushi, Elena Kochkina, and Castelle Michael. 2019. Cost-sensitive BERT for generalisable sentence classification on imbalanced data. In (Feldman et al., 2019).

Norman Mapes, Anna White, Radhika Medury, and Sumeet Dua. 2019. Divisive language and propaganda detection using multi-head attention transformers with deep learning BERT-based language models for binary classification. In (Feldman et al., 2019).

Clyde R. Miller. 1939. The Techniques of Propaganda. From "How to Detect and Analyze Propaganda," an address given at Town Hall. The Center for learning.

Robert Muller. 2018. Internet Research Agency Indictment. `http://www.justice.gov/file/1035477/download`.

Jeffrey Pennington, Richard Socher, and Christopher Manning. 2014. GloVe: Global vectors for word representation. In *Proceedings of the Conference on Empirical Methods in Natural Language Processing*, EMNLP '14, pages 1532–1543, Doha, Qatar.

Matthew Peters, Mark Neumann, Mohit Iyyer, Matt Gardner, Christopher Clark, Kenton Lee, and Luke Zettlemoyer. 2018. Deep contextualized word representations. In *Proceedings of the 2018 Conference of the North American Chapter of the Association for Computational Linguistics: Human Language Technologies*, NAACL-HLT '2018, pages 2227–2237, New Orleans, LA, USA.

Hannah Rashkin, Eunsol Choi, Jin Yea Jang, Svitlana Volkova, and Yejin Choi. 2017. Truth of varying shades: Analyzing language in fake news and political fact-checking. In *Proceedings of the 2017 Conference on Empirical Methods in Natural Language Processing*, EMNLP '17, pages 2931–2937, Copenhagen, Denmark.

Monika L Richter. 2017. The Kremlin's platform for 'useful idiots' in the West: An overview of RT's editorial strategy and evidence of impact. Technical report, Kremlin Watch.

Sara Sabour, Nicholas Frosst, and Geoffrey E. Hinton. 2017. Dynamic routing between capsules. In *Proceedings of the Annual Conference on Neural Information Processing Systems 2017*, NIPS '17, pages 3856–3866, Long Beach, CA, USA.

Francisca Niken Vitri Suprabandari. 2007. American propaganda in John Steinbeck's The Moon is Down. Master's thesis, Sanata Dharma University, Yogyakarta, Indonesia.

Cristina Tardáguila, Fabrício Benevenuto, and Pablo Ortellado. 2018. Fake news is poisoning Brazilian politics. WhatsApp can stop it. `https://www.nytimes.com/2018/10/17/opinion/brazil-election-fake-news-whatsapp.html`.

Gabriel H Teninbaum. 2009. Reductio ad Hitlerum: Trumping the judicial Nazi card. *Michigan State Law Review*, page 541.

Robyn Torok. 2015. Symbiotic radicalisation strategies: Propaganda tools and neuro linguistic programming. In *Proceedings of the Australian Security and Intelligence Conference*, pages 58–65, Perth, Australia.

Ashish Vaswani, Noam Shazeer, Niki Parmar, Jakob Uszkoreit, Llion Jones, Aidan N. Gomez, Lukasz Kaiser, and Illia Polosukhin. 2017. Attention is all you need. In *Proceedings of the Conference on Neural Information Processing Systems*, NIPS '17, pages 5998–6008, Long Beach, CA, USA.

George-Alexandru Vlad, Mircea-Adrian Tanase, Cristian Onose, and Dumitru-Clementin Cercel. 2019. Sentence-level propaganda detection in news articles with transfer learning and BERT-BiLSTM-Capsule model. In (Feldman et al., 2019).

Douglas Walton. 1996. *The straw man fallacy*. Royal Netherlands Academy of Arts and Sciences.

Anthony Weston. 2018. *A rulebook for arguments*. Hackett Publishing.

Shehel Yoosuf and Yin Yang. 2019. Fine-grained propaganda detection with fine-tuned BERT. In (Feldman et al., 2019).

Rowan Zellers, Ari Holtzman, Hannah Rashkin, Yonatan Bisk, Ali Farhadi, Franziska Roesner, and Yejin Choi. 2019. Defending against neural fake news. *CoRR*, abs/1905.12616.

Author Index

Abdullah, Malak, 113
aggarwal, Kartik, 143
Al-Ayyoub, Mahmoud, 139
Al Khatib, Khalid, 76
Al-Omari, Hani, 113
Alhindi, Tariq, 98
AlTiti, Ola, 113
Augenstein, Isabelle, 45

Barrón-Cedeño, Alberto, 162
Broniatowski, David, 31

Castelle, Michael, 125
Cercel, Dumitru-Clementin, 148
Cha, Jeong-Won, 10
Chen, Wei-Fan, 76
Chen, Ying, 83
Crandall, Jedidiah R., 1

Da San Martino, Giovanni, 162
Diab, Mona, 31
Dua, Sumeet, 103

Ek, Adam, 155

Fadel, Ali, 139
Ferreira Cruz, André, 107
Fu, King-wa, 1

Ghanimifard, Mehdi, 155
Golovchenko, Yevgeniy, 45
Gupta, Pankaj, 92

Hagen, Matthias, 76
Han, Yo-Sub, 10
Hartmann, Mareike, 45
Hosseini, Pedram, 31
Hou, Wenjun, 83
Hua, Yiqing, 135

Ko, Myung, 20
Kochkina, Elena, 125
Kovaleva, Olga, 36

Lee, Ju-Hyoung, 10
Levi, Or, 31

Li, Jinfen, 119
Li, Quanzhi, 66
Liu, Yingchi, 66
Lopes Cardoso, Henrique, 107

Mapes, Norman, 103
Medury, Radhika, 103
Muresan, Smaranda, 98

Nakov, Preslav, 162
Nasrin, Nayeema, 20
Navaki Arefi, Meisam, 1

Onose, Cristian, 148

Pandi, Rajkumar, 1
Park, ChaeHun, 56
Park, Jong, 56
Park, Jun-U, 10
Pfeiffer, Jonas, 98

Qiu Shi, Dahlia, 1

Raymond Choo, Kim-Kwang, 20
Rios, Anthony, 20
Rocha, Gil, 107
Rogers, Anna, 36
Rumshisky, Anna, 36
Runkler, Thomas, 92

Sadana, Anubhav, 143
Saxena, Khushbu, 92
Schütze, Hinrich, 92
Sha, Miao, 1
Shaikh, Samira, 113
Si, Luo, 66
Stein, Benno, 76

Tanase, Mircea-Adrian, 148
Tayyar Madabushi, Harish, 125
Tschantz, Michael Carl, 1
Tuffaha, Ibrahim, 139

Vlad, George-Alexandru, 148

Wachsmuth, Henning, 76

White, Anna, 103

Xiao, Lu, 119

Yang, Wonsuk, 56
Yang, Yin, 87
Yaseen, Usama, 92
Ye, Zhihao, 119
Yoosuf, Shehel, 87

Zhang, Qiong, 66